# Close Quarter Battle

# CQB

## CLOSE QUARTER BATTLE

## MIKE CURTIS

## BANTAM PRESS

LONDON • NEW YORK • TORONTO • SYDNEY • AUCKLAND

TRANSWORLD PUBLISHERS LTD
61–63 Uxbridge Road, London W5 5SA

TRANSWORLD PUBLISHERS (AUSTRALIA) PTY LTD
15–23 Helles Avenue, Moorebank, NSW 2170

TRANSWORLD PUBLISHERS (NZ) LTD
3 William Pickering Drive, Albany, Auckland

Published 1997 by Bantam Press
a division of Transworld Publishers Ltd
Copyright © by Mike Curtis 1997

The publishers have made every effort to trace the
owners of photographs used in this book. In cases where
they have been unsuccessful they invite copyright holders
to contact them direct.

A catalogue record for this book is
available from the British Library.
ISBN 0593 040325

Typeset in 11/13pt Palatino by Falcon Oast Graphic Art

Printed in Great Britain by Mackays of Chatham PLC, Chatham, Kent

To Steven Illingsworth DCM and the crew of '82 who
never made it home – gone but not forgotten

# ACKNOWLEDGEMENTS

TO MY PARENTS AND FAMILY, WHO HAVE ALWAYS SUPPORTED ME AND stood by me. To my friends who have kept the faith, and to the three wise men who have pointed me in the right direction at different times of my life – Les Miles, Bob Powell and Harry McCallion.

# Close Quarter Battle

# PROLOGUE

AT FIRST LIGHT, 5 PLATOON WAS STILL ONLY ABOUT HALFWAY DOWN THE valley, making our way towards the gorse line that ran down to Goose Green. Six and 4 Platoons were ahead of us on the lower ground.

Suddenly we were hit from the front. Argie positions at Boca House opened up with heavy machine-guns from a range of about 1,000 metres. The weight of fire was unbelievable. Rounds stitched into the earth around me, slicing through webbing and ricocheting off rocks. One round blew the foresight off my gimpy.

Then the enemy FOOs (forward observation officers) began spotting for artillery in Goose Green and shells began raining down upon us.

'Oh, God, this is it,' I thought. 'We're too fucking exposed here.'

Six Platoon were lower down in the gorse bank and 4 Platoon were also dashing into its cover, but 5 Platoon had nowhere to go on the featureless hill – we were fish in a bowl. Jimmy Street opened up with his 2-inch mortar to try to cover our withdrawal, but the next thing I heard was him screaming, 'Taff, Taff, my legs, my legs!'

We couldn't move; we were nailed to the ground by mortar and artillery rounds and small-arms fire, and we cowered on the open hillside for an eternity.

It was Stan the Man who managed to grab hold of Jimmy and started applying field dressings to the wounds.

Everywhere I looked artillery rounds were exploding, sending

11

mud and rock into the air. Shrapnel and small-arms rounds thudded into the ground around me. Hunching my head into my shoulders, I thought, If I'm going to get hit, make it my legs, not my head.

Lieutenant Weighell had a bullet go into his helmet, round his head and out the other side. Andy Brooke had one hit his webbing and lodge itself among his magazines.

Above the din, I heard Taff Hall scream, 'My back, my back, I can't move!'

Bob and I crawled up the hill towards him. Stevie and young Pooley were already with him and had removed the webbing.

'What's wrong, Taff?'

I looked at his back and couldn't see anything wrong with him.

'I can't move, Mike. I can't move.'

I lifted his smock again. There were two tiny, brownish-red puncture marks. The poor fucker had taken a couple of 7.62 rounds in his back. We needed a medic.

'You'll be all right, boyo,' I said, taking his weapon and throwing it to one side. The others tried to make him comfortable.

As I got to my knees, I looked across and saw Ian Aird coming to our position. It was the last thing I remembered seeing before the world turned upside down.

A huge explosion erupted and blew me backwards down the slope. Debris hit me in the face and my arm whipped across my body, flinging the gimpy away into the air.

When I came round, I found myself lying on the slope with blood pissing out of my nose. Where am I? Is that me? I could remember a blinding flash, then nothing. My head felt as if someone had caved it in with a sledgehammer.

I came back again. Where the fuck are the lads? Where's my gun?

The gimpy lay about 10 feet away. I crawled towards it, and as I grabbed hold, another artillery round came screaming in behind me, spraying me with earth. I could taste my own blood now. The overpowering smell of cordite and scorched earth was everywhere and all the time the *zip-zip-zip* of the 7.62 rounds.

I looked around. The crater was still smoking – a hole about 4 feet deep and 10 feet across. I dived into it, trying to regain my senses. I told myself, 'Fucking hell, man, as soon as I get clear of this shit, I'm out of here and out of the Army. This is just crazy.'

# 1

YOU COULDN'T GO ANY FURTHER UP THE RHONDDA VALLEY THAN THE village of Maerdy – after that there was only the pit, the mountains and a pretty view. That was why no-one visited without a reason – they either lived there or were coming to see friends or relatives. In my case, I dropped into my grandmother's front room on 16 October 1957, the first-born son of a fourth-generation miner.

My father's family were from Blaenllechau, 4 or 5 miles from Maerdy, and for as long as anyone could remember they had worked the pits – fathers and grandfathers who didn't so much have coal dust in their blood as in their lungs, and slowly it was killing them.

The pits belonged to wealthy landholders who made their fortune on the backs of miners like my grandfathers. Even in the Fifties Maerdy didn't have much time for that sort of man and still got called 'Little Moscow' because of its militancy in the 1926 general strike.

In the days before wealthy mine owners sold out to the National Coal Board, a lot of miners worked twelve-hour shifts underground in atrocious conditions. Sometimes they'd carve out coal faces only 18 inches high, lying on their side with just a pick and shovel. Accidents and deaths underground were commonplace and it wasn't surprising that socialism found so many willing disciples.

As the former owners moved out of the valleys, fearing reprisals, the fledgling National Union of Miners gave the men a voice. Finally they had the security of knowing that they wouldn't lose their jobs without just cause and their families would have food on the table each day.

Both my grandfathers were called Dai and were tremendous characters, always getting up on stage and singing at the tops of their voices. They drank at different clubs, but had known each other well before my parents met. One drank at 'the Con' – the Conservative Club, which was in fact a socialist club, and where my uncle Roy was club steward and my mother's mother, Maud, cleaned the floors – and the other drank next door at the Royal British Legion, otherwise known as the 'Maerdy Shot'.

Dai Curtis was a big robust man who played rugby and had a reputation as a village hard man. During the First World War he was in the Navy while my mother's father, Dai Thomas, was a career soldier and one of the first to be sent to fight in France. As an orphan, he'd run away from his uncle's home and joined the Army at sixteen. He went on to fight and become wounded on the Somme with the Welsh Regiment and was one of the last Old Contemptibles in the valley. As a young lad I used to sit on his knee and listen to his tales about the Germans and how one day I'd be a rugby player.

'Stop filling the boy's head with your stories,' my grandmother would scold, and then she'd slip me another piece of bread to dunk in the dripping left over from the Sunday roast.

In the Second World War, Dai Thomas and Dai Curtis had worked down the pit, mining coal for the shipping. The irony of it was that the Germans couldn't kill them but they both succumbed instead to the dust underground and died of silicosis within months of each other when I was a teenager.

Both my grannies knew the meaning of hard work and they were typical of valley housewives. As young girls they went out washing and ironing wealthier people's clothes and, later, Granny Thomas cleaned the clubs in Maerdy until she was well into her sixties. Through the early years, when my parents were growing up, money was very tight, but they still had plenty of good home-cooked food on the table. It was the same when I was a lad.

My father was a very mild-mannered, quiet and unassuming sort of chap, but he held a lot of respect and I used to wish I had a few of his qualities. Everybody loved him. He was working underground when he was only fourteen, and being too young to join up in the Second World War he toiled alongside his dad to supply coal for the war effort.

At the age of seventeen he was working at the coalface when it collapsed on top of him. His father dug him out and dragged him to safety, saving his life. My dad almost lost a leg and ever after walked with a limp; he needed special shoes to be built up by the local cobbler because one of his legs was shorter than the other.

For a long while after the accident he worked on the coal surface rather than underground, which meant earning less money, but eventually he resumed his mining career driving the roadway at the side of the coalface; a hard graft. Also called Dai, he married my mother in 1957 and they moved to live in Maerdy. A few weeks after I was born they moved again to a terraced house on the side of a mountain in Ferndale, the next village down the valley. The houses stretched along both sides of the main road, each of them identical, with coal fires and no running water, bathrooms or indoor toilets, or electricity upstairs.

My earliest recollections were of going outside on a cold winter's morning to wash at the tap in the outhouse and, later in the day, waiting for my father to come home from work while my mother boiled water in pans on the fireplace to fill the tin bath; in those days there were no showers at the pit and the men bathed when they got home. I'd wait on the doorstep until he turned the corner into our street and then sprint down the hill to welcome him. He'd be covered head to toe in coal dust. I'd carry his empty steel sandwich box for him and hold his blackened hand, the coal dust rubbing off onto mine, then I'd wash his back as he sat in the small round bath in the kitchen.

Every six weeks or so, we'd get a heap of free coal dumped on the pavement outside the house. Having spent all day shovelling coal underground, my dad would get home and have to do some more, moving it to the coal shed.

Those were the days of 'King Coal'. From the back of our house, on crisp winter mornings, you would see every chimney in the village belching out plumes of smoke. Later, gas would take over in many households, but not in ours. Even when the miners were offered money in place of free coal so they could buy gas, my father refused. 'It goes against my principles,' he said firmly.

The Rhondda Valley is split into two halves – the Rhondda Fawr and the smaller Rhondda Fach. They meet up at a place called Porth and then the road continues on to Pontypridd and further down is Cardiff. My father proudly told me that in 1913 there had been seventy-three large collieries working in the Rhondda;

forty-four pits employed over 500 men and twenty-one employed over 1,000.

As young boys, my best mate Steve Evans and I used to play in the old disused mine where my father had had his accident. It had an eerie atmosphere about it. Our voices would echo around the old workshops as sunlight filtered through the cobwebs and missing tiles.

One of the largest surface buildings was the 'washeries'. Coal had to be washed after being hauled from the earth, and the river beside the mine was a black filthy ribbon that ran through the valleys until it met the sea at Cardiff. All the rocks had turned grey and the banks were coated in a black slime. Even the sheep in Maerdy were covered in coal dust. After being washed, the coal was put into railway trucks and taken to Cardiff docks. The train line and the river ran side by side, both snaking along the valley floor.

As the sun started to set over the valley I'd wander home for a meal fit for a king. My mother was a big woman with blond hair and a true talent for cooking. She came from good hard-working stock and believed in looking after her own. To make ends meet she used to clean a rich lady's house down the street and work part time of a weekend as a nurse at the hospital in Cardiff. Money was always tight but I didn't want for anything. I was happy as long as I had a football, a pair of boots and the occasional pair of jeans.

On weekends and school holidays, I'd be out by half-past eight each morning – running around the mountains or playing rugby with Steve. My mum said we were like Siamese twins. On rainy days we'd play indoors at one or the other's house.

Everybody seemed to have sons in our street until my sister Rhian was born in 1967. While she never became part of my gang, we were always close and we did a lot together – including sitting alongside each other in matching tin tubs as we bathed in front of the fire. My parents would sometimes take us on day trips to the Brecon Beacons, my dad pointing out different landmarks and telling me the names of the various hills. Later, as a teenager, I took her there a few times myself, racing her to the top of Pen-y-Fan and other peaks.

At school on St David's Day, 1 March, all the boys would wear a leek on their jumpers and all the girls wore their Welsh costumes of red, black and white checks, with a shawl around their shoulders and a Welsh bonnet tied in a bow at the neck. The importance of our heritage was taught to us from a young age and every morning at assembly we'd belt out Welsh hymns like Calon Lan and Myfanwy.

I went to the local junior school which was next to the mine, on the floor of the valley beside the river. I had to traipse all the way down the mountain from our house every morning and up again each afternoon. There were two classes, and I got separated from most of my friends when I was put into the A class. Mrs Bateson became my teacher for the next four years, a lady who had a fondness for discipline and multiplication tables.

One afternoon, just after my ninth birthday, I was in Magritelli's Italian fish shop down the road from home, buying a bag of chips. I went to school with the Magritellis' daughter, Angela. I couldn't understand it when her mother started sobbing and shooing people out of the shop; I could only make out the word 'Aberfan', which I knew to be a village 14 miles away. As I walked home, I saw grown-ups crying on their doorsteps, hugging and shouting in the streets.

I got home to find that my father and many of the other miners had already left to go and see what they could do.

'What's wrong?' I asked my mother, never having seen her cry.

She hugged me until my ribs hurt. 'A lot of children are missing. We have to pray for them.'

That night I learned how a coal tip had come down a slope and devastated Aberfan, burying an entire school and killing 145 people, 116 of them children. The sense of desolation and loss had a profound effect on us all, then and later; for years to come, grown men still cried at the memory. The next morning, at junior school, we said prayers for the victims and I looked out the window at the coal tip that rose above our classrooms. There but for the grace of God, I thought.

Two years later, thanks to the efforts of Mrs Bateson, I passed my eleven-plus and won a place at the local grammar school. There I discovered what was to become one of the great loves of my life. John Elwyn Jones was a maths teacher and quite a famous man in the Rhondda. He was an immense 6 feet 3 inches and 16 stones but had a lovely manner. He took one look at me and, being a lot bigger than most of my friends and quite a fair runner, I was drafted straight into the rugby team at the age of eleven. I took to the game like a duck to water.

J. E. Jones was a rugby teacher first and a maths teacher second. A throwback to the 1930s, he had bushy sideburns and a big bellowing voice. Right from my first day in grammar school we hit it off.

In our very first game we played against Port County and lost 9–6. I scored both tries but came off the pitch crying my eyes out with the rest of the team because we hadn't won. We were playing for John Elwyn Jones and we'd lost. Eventually he made me captain of the team and I never cried again on a rugby field.

The school had quite a reputation for the game. John Bevan, the Welsh international and British Lion, was an old boy and occasionally he'd drop by and give us some encouragement and advice. This was the golden era of Welsh rugby. Apart from Bevan, guys like Gareth Edwards, Barry John and Mervyn Davies were in their prime. The Welsh side was virtually unbeatable and they were like gods to me.

My cousin Harry took me to the holy of holies, Cardiff Arms Park, in 1972 when I was fourteen. It was a cold February day and Wales were playing Scotland. The city was awash with red and white and the pubs were so full that drinkers spilled onto the pavements. It seemed to take an eternity to get into the ground and as we reached the terraces it was like walking into a wall of sound. Beneath me was a green island floating in a sea of red and white flags and streamers. I'd never seen grass so green or witnessed such passion in all my life. It was as if the whole country had gathered and given voice.

'Wales! Wales! Wales!'

When the crush of people threatened to carry me away, Harry – a monster of a man at 6 feet 4 inches and 17 stones – picked me up so that I could see. And with a choir of 50,000 people, I sang the hymns from morning assembly at school, Sospan Fach and Calon Lan, which no longer seemed boring or pointless.

The memory of that vast cauldron of noise and the sight of my scarlet heroes running onto the field would stay with me for ever. There they were, my idols. Then came the moment that all Wales had been waiting for: the national anthem. Every part of me tingled as the crowd rose as one and sang Hen Wlad Fynhadau.

Our local hero, John Bevan, was on the left wing. Gerald Davies scored the first try with a chip ahead and a marvellous solo effort. Scotland equalized, but then Gareth Edwards scored a magnificent three points under the posts, smashing his way through a couple of Jock forwards. Then I was to witness one of the greatest tries ever scored at the Arms Park. Wales won a scrum in their own half; Gareth Edwards picked up, going down the blind side, shoving off the Scottish back row, then chipped ahead and kicked on, the whole of Wales pursuing the ball. Then Gareth kicked ahead once

18

more, finally scoring with a touchdown in the muddy south-east corner of the ground, ahead of the Scottish defenders. He emerged from the mud a hero to a million Welshmen and the team eventually ran out convincing victors, 35–12.

That night I dreamed of wearing the scarlet jumper and running onto Cardiff Arms Park. It was a dream that would dominate my teenage years. I played rugby for the Rhondda Valley at different age levels, captained the Glamorgan and Mid-Glamorgan schoolboy teams, and made the Welsh Schools Under-17 squad when I was still only fifteen. Although I was younger than the other lads, I lost nothing in terms of size.

By the age of sixteen great things were expected of me. I was captaining my school side of a Saturday morning, then playing for the Pontypridd Youth team (Under-19s) in the afternoon. Often it meant waking up, racing through my paper round, getting to school for a Rhondda game, and then throwing on my tracksuit over muddy kit and having Dad whisk me down to Pontypridd in the Morris Minor to play a big game against teams from west or mid Wales.

Afterwards, being too young to drink with the rest of the team, I'd have to catch a bus back up the valley to Ferndale and then walk up the steep hill to my parents' house. Sometimes I had to hold on to the walls because my legs ached so much from two games of rugby in a day. The Sunday papers were always delivered a little late around Ferndale.

Pontypridd Youth were a very good side in those days and we won the Welsh Youth Cup two years out of three while I was there. My only regret was that both my grandfathers missed seeing me play. They died within a year of each other, just as I was embarking on my rugby career.

Although I wasn't very academic I loved the grammar-school system. I ended up with four O levels, but didn't need them; in those days it was dead easy to get a job. A natural progression for a rugby fanatic would have been to leave school at sixteen and join the Army, but the valley wasn't a big recruiting ground for the Welsh regiments, who mainly drew volunteers from Cardiff. And anyway, nobody in my family apart from Dai Thomas had ever chosen a military career.

My childhood mate, Steve Evans, had joined the Welsh Guards. We'd drifted apart when we went to different schools and I didn't see as much of him. He fell in with a bad crowd for a while and did a stint in remand school before joining the Guards. He came home in uniform, telling me stories about how much he loved the life, but all that shouting and marching wasn't for me; I'd find something else to do, I decided.

Most of my friends were two or three years older than me, mates like Benny, Dio and Peter Terret, and they were earning good money down the pit while I was still at school. My parents didn't want me going underground and expressed hopes that I'd go to college and maybe become a gym teacher. But at sixteen I couldn't see past the folding stuff.

'Don't be a mug,' my father said, pacing the kitchen. 'You think I'd be down the pit if I had the choice?'

'I don't want to be a teacher.'

'Fine, but if you're going to leave school, get a job somewhere else – not down the pit.'

My mother kept wringing her hands on her apron. I was still her little boy.

Eventually I compromised with my father, and rather than being a pick-and-shovel miner I applied to be an apprentice fitter for the National Coal Board. It meant working both on the surface and underground, often at the coalface. As an apprentice I carried a tool bag for a qualified fitter, and one day a week I went to Merthyr technical college to study the theory, thumbing a lift there and back to save the bus fare.

There were three shifts at Maerdy colliery – days, afternoons and nights. Afternoons were the worst because you'd start work at 1 p.m. and sometimes wouldn't finish until near midnight. On my second week, I was sitting on the double-decker bus on the way to work, surrounded by grizzled old miners who coughed and spluttered. It was a summer's afternoon and I glanced across at the grammar school, where the girls were playing rounders and my friends kicked a rugby ball. There I was going underground, aged sixteen and a half; I should be running around the playground with my friends, I thought – but that's life and I'd made my choice. I wanted money in my back pocket, and this was how you got it.

At the pit I'd get dressed in a changing bay right next to my dad and we went underground together, just as he'd done with his father. The pit-head baths were always hot because this was where our work clothes were dried in their lockers. It smelled of damp clothing and dust, but with each new shift it came alive with the sound of men shouting, laughing and taking the piss out of each other. We changed out of our civvies, grabbed a towel and put on our working kit in the opposite bay down the corridor.

At the end of each shift it was even noisier because everyone had finished work for another day and could relax and shower. It stank in the 'Dirty Bay' with the funk of old boots and sweat-stained underwear. Most people changed their dirty clothes once a week, but from the information my nose gave me some of those guys didn't change them until they fell off them.

Although I had a locker next to my dad's we never actually worked together underground. I was glad as I would have found that hard because of the general bantering amongst the men: I respected my father too much ever to swear in front of him.

Crammed into double-decker cages, we dropped deeper and deeper into the darkness. As the last chinks of sunlight dis-appeared we turned on the headlamps of our helmets that were powered by a battery pack hung from our belts.

It grew colder as the cage fell and the clean, crisp air of the surface was replaced by the reek of dampness and rotting wood. It was all-pervading, and as if in response, the laughing and joking of the locker room would stop.

Maerdy Pit had three 'horizons' or levels: yellow after 726 feet, then red at 975 feet and, right at the bottom, the blue horizon, at 1,224 feet. All these horizons were connected by 'retardeus' (walk-ways), but usually you took a locomotive that dropped off miners, fitters and electricians at the various coalfaces.

Old miners like my dad were hardened after years of working underground, with bodies full of muscles and coal dust. When I first went down the pit I was amazed that nobody wore gloves, but I soon found out why: if you lost a pair, the resulting blisters were so bad that you realized it made more sense to work bare-handed from the word go and toughen up the skin.

There was a stale, musty smell underground. Sometimes it could be claustrophobic and the mind played tricks, making the walls and roof seem to press down, squeezing air from your lungs. It wasn't too bad on the headings, but God help anyone who suffered from claustrophobia at the coalface. In some of the English collieries, especially in Yorkshire, there were 6-foot coal seams and you could walk upright through the coalfaces. But in Wales and certain parts of the north-east and Scotland the seams were only 3 or 4 feet high and very cramped. My father told me stories of working on his side in 18-inch seams, digging away with a pick and shovel.

The noise on the face was unbelievable. As the coal cutter came slowly down, the jaws ripped into the seam, tearing out huge hunks of coal that fell onto the panzer (conveyor). Men were busy pushing their part of the conveyor forward as the cutter passed them. The dust was everywhere, reaching into every pore and clinging to the sweat. It was no place for the weak or faint-hearted.

The cut coal went onto a conveyor belt which took it away from the face and loaded up trolleys or belts to carry it out of the pit. As the coalface advanced, hydraulic chocks were normally used to prop up the space behind it, otherwise the whole of bloody Glamorgan would have come down around our ears.

In the faces where I worked, they normally had three sets of slom bars against the roof, pinned in place by hydraulic props which had a handle on the side to pump up and depress. As the coalface moved forwards, the slom bars were taken from the back to the front, like playing leapfrog. It meant that an area behind you became void, with absolutely nothing holding it up. You could be working in about 4 feet of headroom and suddenly, 60 or 70 yards back, the roof would come crashing down. The ground would be shaking and your heart hammering; it was scary stuff. You'd just have to sit tight and wait for everything to settle down.

I hated it when the firemen set off explosions underground. The shout would go up, 'Blowing in the hole! Blowing in the hole!'; the people inside the face stayed put and those on the roadways moved back. The blast would shake everything and I always looked around bug-eyed, convinced that whole towns were about to come crashing down on me. Inhaling rock dust and the smell of explosives, we went back to work; more coal meant more money.

If anything went wrong in the coalface, such as the cutter breaking down, the pressure was on the fitter and his apprentice to get it going again. We had to fix it pronto because the delay was eating into everybody's earnings.

I reckoned the apprentices worked just as hard as the miners – sometimes harder. I'd be up and down the coalface all day, either freezing or sweating my bollocks off. In some places, blokes were stripped down to the waist, without a vest, just their trousers, knee pads, boots and helmets. Other places it was bloody freezing and you could see your breath when you exhaled.

The blue horizon was meant to be haunted and I'd heard all the stories. On one particular night shift the fitter sent me down there alone to strip some equipment from the bottom of the pit. Miners have a series of taps, like a code, that they use to communicate. When you've been underground on your own, you tap yourself up in the cage, and the guy bringing up the cage taps back and you confirm. Then you have to wait one full minute before the cage rises.

The blue horizon was being closed and the equipment had to be salvaged from the pit bottom. The lights had already been stripped away and I was alone in the darkness, hundreds of feet underground. I did the job as quickly as possible, trying not to think about ghosts, and was soon back in the cage, tapping myself up. All of a sudden, the hydraulic gates in front of me started going up and down and the handle turned as if someone were trying to get inside.

For a full minute I waited in the cage, shitting myself and praying to get out. When I got to the top, I was absolutely terrified and told them what had happened. Everybody started laughing. They explained that pressure built up in the hydraulics now and again and this was why the handle kept releasing itself and the gates went up and down.

When they drilled the headings, cutting through rock and coal, there was always a lot of water in the pit and some blokes, like my father, had to work up to their waists in it every day. Many of them suffered from phlebitis. Eventually the Coal Board, in its generosity and wisdom, gave them 'water money' – something like an extra pound a day. Big deal!

The conditions were bloody atrocious, but there was always great banter and camaraderie underground. We all ribbed each other and had a good laugh, otherwise we'd have gone off our heads in that environment. We took it in turns to have a break, eating our sandwiches by helmet light and shouting conversations above the roar of machinery.

Food was a means to an end. Fifteen minutes for your sandwich and drink, with your hands so filthy that you were shoving coal-smeared bread into your mouth unless you put some paper on the sandwich first. My dad had always taken a metal water bottle underground with him, while I invested in a posh flask to fill with hot tea. However, after smashing my fifth flask in as many weeks I also began using a metal bottle. Surrounded by so much dust and sweat, it's amazing how simple water suddenly tastes like nectar from the gods.

Anyone slacking was soon sorted out, especially at the coalface where the bigger money was made. Fuck up and you got a bollocking, and somehow you always managed to hear the swearing above the noise.

23

There were always arguments at the face between the men and the officials. The firemen who blew the roadways either side of the face were technically in charge and there were frequent rows, with people at each other's throats. Usually matters settled down quickly and everyone got on with their job, but it was a tense environment.

We all bore the scars of occupational hazards. If you cut yourself underground and didn't get it treated straight away, the coal would settle in the wound and it became like a tattoo. My father's back was covered in them and I soon had my fair share on my arms and face. That's how you can recognize old miners in the valley – by the coal scars.

Sadly, some injuries were even more permanent. One of my mates had a leg injured in an accident that left him with a permanent limp like my father. Another childhood friend, Benny, had a coal drill driven through his stomach, ripping apart his spleen. The bucket of a JCB-type machine had hit the drill, bending it and whipping it into Benny's abdomen. He survived and got a job on the surface but was never the same afterwards. One night his father tried to wake him for his night shift and found that Benny had died in his sleep.

'I know people can't understand it when miners go on strike,' my dad said to me as we walked home from Benny's funeral, 'but if they could see the conditions they wouldn't begrudge us more money.'

I had nothing but admiration for the men I worked alongside. They earned every penny and grew old too quickly.

With money came freedom, and at night we'd socialize in the local clubs and Maerdy Workman's Hall. You could always recognize the miners from the coal dust around their eyes and on their hands, especially those who'd been at it the longest, like my dad or his pal, Big Snowy Cavelle.

Maerdy Hall was funded by the miners at Maerdy Colliery, every man contributing a small portion of his pay to subsidize the large room with a stage and a long bar. Sunday nights were packed and there were always three or four live acts or bands. Almost all of the punters were miners, or their wives or girlfriends. The camaraderie of the pit continued up on the surface, and every time I saw Big Snowy he'd raise his glass, recite my latest match score, and say a warm, beaming 'Cheers!'

Rugby still dominated my life and I cherished only the dream of playing for Wales. When not quite eighteen, I reached the final trial for the Welsh Under-19 squad – a contest between the 'possibles' and 'probables' at Cardiff. I captained the 'possibles', the only Ponty boy to make either team, and even my worst enemy would have told you I played out of my skin.

Yet when the Welsh side to play the English schoolboys was announced, I didn't make the team. Later someone from the committee put his arm around my shoulder and said, 'Look, Mike, you're a young lad, you've got plenty of time. Your turn will come next year. We're looking at you for captain.'

'OK, another year,' I said to myself and I went back to playing for Pontypridd Youth. Later in the season, however, I moved to Treorchy to play alongside all my Rhondda mates in their youth side. When the Under-19 trials came around again, I had a great game as captain of the 'probables' and selection seemed certain.

Fate, however, had decided otherwise. Shortly before the final trial, a mate of mine suggested we go for a ride on his motor bike to Aberdare. Jeff and I had no helmets – they weren't compulsory in those days – and we were bowling along quite happily when a car shot out of a side turning and struck us a glancing blow. The last thing I saw was a lipstick in the lady-driver's hand and a look of great surprise on her face as her make-up session was rudely interrupted.

I went completely over Jeff's head and bounced along the road like a runaway hub-cap. Looking up, I could see him still trapped under the bike. I didn't feel any pain as I clambered up and pulled him free. He'd broken his collar-bone. The woman driver looked out of the car window and then put her foot down. She wasn't going to wait around to tend the wounded.

It wasn't until a small crowd had gathered that I realized my left hand had been ripped open to the bone. Jeff and I spent the next week in Churchvillage Hospital and it was the end of the Welsh dream for the remainder of the season. I played only two more games that season, including the last, when Treorchy Youth won the Welsh District Cup final.

The enforced lay-off had a consolation. It meant I could spend more time with the other great love of my life, Liz Williams, to me the prettiest girl in the Rhondda. We'd met at school when I was fifteen and she was two years younger, but she didn't want to know me then. It wasn't until I left school that we started dating, doing the normal teenage things, whilst never venturing out of the valley except for visits to the beaches of Porthcawl and Tenby.

Liz typified Welsh beauty: only 5 feet 2 inches, she had straight black hair, fair skin and wonderfully bright eyes. On our first date I took her to the pictures. She lived in Maerdy and caught the bus down to Ferndale. Afterwards, being too young to go into the pubs for a nightcap, I rode home with her, making sure she got to the door safe and sound. Later I started to meet her in the evenings, after being underground all day, and we'd go to the pubs and to dances at Maerdy Hall, and in the summer we'd hire a caravan in Porthcawl on the coast.

We had our ups and downs, breaking up and getting back together like most teenagers, but it was undeniably true love. Liz came from a big family and had two sisters and five brothers. Her father was away most of the time and her mother kept the family together and made me feel welcome. This changed when her father decided to come back home to live. He didn't like me and gave Liz a terrible time, to the point where she was desperate to get out.

Although I felt I was too young to leave home, I loved her and couldn't bear to see her unhappy. So between us, with my job as an apprentice fitter and Liz's as a shop assistant, we squeezed a mortgage out of Barclays Bank and bought a little two-bedroom house in the next village down the valley. My mother and father thought I was crazy, but they lent us some money and we bought second-hand furniture.

The Seventies were a boom time in Wales, with lots of coal coming out of the ground and the finest rugby team in the world. It was a time to celebrate, and although Liz and I didn't have much money we still managed to enjoy Sunday nights at the Maerdy Workman's Hall.

There were workmen's clubs throughout the valley and only a few pubs. Women were allowed in the lounges but banned from the bars. These male bastions were all the same – thick with smoke, with everyone sitting in their little groups and eyeballing any stranger who walked through the door. The conversation revolved around the pit, politics, rugby and women – strictly in that order.

Ted Heath had been ousted as prime minister, along with his hated Conservative government: the miners had seen to that. They'd broken the Tories with a series of strikes and paved the way for Jim Callaghan to lead the Labour Party to power. Big Joe Gormley was then president of the NUM. Everyone's favourite to take over the role, should he stand down, was a young guy called Arthur Scargill, president of the Yorkshire branch of the NUM.

The Rhondda valley was socialist to its coal-blackened core. Little Moscow even had visits from Russian and Polish mine workers who came to see the mines and then enjoy a night of Welsh hospitality at the hall. Communism played quite a big part in the talk about how the pit was run and it was always a major topic among the older guys at the drinking clubs. But from my point of view, I couldn't give a stuff about politics; I had my girlfriend, I had my rugby and I had money in my arse pocket – what else mattered?

It was round about this time, 1976, that me and a mate, Tommy Vaughan, were reading in the papers about mercenaries being recruited to go and fight in Angola. I'd been reading a book or two from the local library about the Parachute Regiment, and it seemed that a lot of the lads going over there had once worn the red beret.

Tommy and I used to train together at a local gym under a cinema in Tylorstown, along with another lad, Gibby, who was from Pontygwaith and two or three years younger than us.

'Do you fancy it?' Tommy asked one day as he heaved the weights.

Gibby laughed. He would have been too young to come with us, and in any event his heart was set on joining the British army, not a mercenary one.

'I'll think about it,' I said.

The idea wasn't so strange. A lot of miners from South Wales had fought for the communists against the fascists in the Spanish Civil War in 1936 – including thirty-three from the Rhondda who did not return. I used to see a poster at the mine every day, in the lodge where the NUM members gathered in the mornings; it showed the silhouette of a soldier and on his helmet were all the flags of the countries that had fought in the civil war, among them the dragon of Wales.

'But we aren't soldiers,' I said. 'We don't know anything about it.'

Tommy pumped the barbells and grunted, 'Neither did the lads in the Spanish Civil War – but they went. Come on, it'll be an adventure. Get us away from here and give us some extra cash.'

'I'll give it some thought,' I told him.

We read that an ex-para named John Banks ran a recruitment firm called Security Advisory Services from a pub and laundrette in Camberley. The more I thought about it, the more it appealed to me; at that age, I didn't really care too much about the

27

consequences. We actually went as far as trying to contact him, but without success.

'You two are mad,' Gibby said. 'Join the regular army, why don't you?'

'Fuck that,' Tommy said.

'Ditto,' I said, but with less than total conviction.

Years later I met up with some of the guys who fought against the communists in Angola and I thanked my lucky stars that Mr Banks didn't return our call. One of them had got hit five times by an AK47, and ended up with a Cuban doctor putting a metal plate in his leg with no anaesthetic while he was biting on a piece of wood. He spent eight years in prison, a year of that in solitary, and he was still having operations because his legs were in bits.

For the next few years, Liz and I struggled to make ends meet, while I spent up to eight hours a day underground. Some days I'd come home to our little house and find a heap of coal waiting to be carried into the coal cooch at the back. At four-thirty on a wet January afternoon in the Rhondda, after a day underground, it was the last thing I wanted to do. Sometimes I'd have to play rugby, shower, have a couple of pints of shandy and then do a night shift. It wasn't hard to see why I wanted more out of life, if only for a short while. Feeling trapped or claustrophobic wasn't the problem; I loved the warmth of the people and the close-knit community, but there was just a sameness about the existence and a realization that it hadn't changed in generations. Ironically, it was this very sense of permanence which finally gave me the confidence to leave the Rhondda: there was something comforting about the thought that if I did head off to see the world, the valley would still be waiting when I got back, just the same as always.

I can't identify the precise turning-point when I decided to leave. The idea of joining the Parachute Regiment had cropped up more and more in the back of my mind, but had never graduated to being what I'd call an ambition. Even when I decided to investigate the possibility, I took a very pragmatic approach: if I joined up at twenty, I'd be twenty-three when I finished my three-year stint; I could pick up rugby again, I thought, and perhaps even play for Wales.

That summer Peter Terret and I went on surfing expeditions down to Porthcawl and West Wales. They were good days and one afternoon, before driving home, we bought a beer and Peter asked me what I wanted to do with the rest of my life.

'How do you mean?' I said.

'Well, do you want to be underground in twenty years' time?'

'No.'

'So what do you want to do?'

'Shit, I don't know. What do you want to do?'

He didn't hesitate. 'I'm going to qualify as an under-manager and one day I'm going to manage a coal mine.'

I laughed. 'Who's going to make you manager?'

'It's possible,' he said testily. 'So what's your story? They don't pay you for playing rugby.'

'I want to be a sergeant in the SAS,' I said, surprising myself as much as him. Until then I hadn't even thought about joining the Army and had simply stumbled upon a few military books in the Ferndale Library, including *The Phantom Major*, which was about David Stirling, the founder of the Special Air Service. Yet it wasn't so much Stirling who captured my imagination as another figure, Blair 'Paddy' Mayne, a rugby international from Ireland who had taken over the helm of the SAS after Stirling's capture by the Germans.

Paddy had been an immense man who inspired all those who worked with him; hard living, hard drinking, but totally professional. His exploits in North Africa were legendary in the SAS. On one operation to blow up German aircraft at an enemy compound in the desert they ran out of explosives and Paddy started ripping out the planes' consoles with his bare hands. Although an officer, he shunned the cocktail parties and preferred to drink Guinness and lead the singing at the local pub.

The idea of following in his footsteps quite appealed to me. I'd soon exhausted the local library's stock of books about the Army, immensely enjoying the graphic descriptions in *The Red Devils* and *A Bridge Too Far* about what the Parachute Regiment had done in the Second World War, especially at Arnhem under the command of John Frost.

There was an ex-paratrooper down the pit called Charlie Swannock who'd jumped into Suez in 1957, and he told me a lot of the history of 'Para Reg' as he called it. Before long I was thinking, Yeah, this is for me, this is what I'm going to do.

I talked it over with a mate called Phil Bence, who was about ten years older than me. Because of his age, Bencey seemed to straddle the divide between the older miners and the youngsters like Dio,

Pete Terret and myself. During a food break underground, I told him I was thinking about joining the Parachute Regiment.

'Fucking right,' he said, giving me a sooty grin. 'If I was ten years younger I'd be with you, mate. What you gonna do otherwise? You can still play rugby when you come out. On the other hand, you might want to stay.'

The motion had been seconded, voted upon and carried.

The final decider, if one were needed, came a few days later as a shift was ending and men were walking out of the face, climbing the hill towards the locomotive and trucks that would take them out. These were the same trucks that took the coal from the conveyor belt, and that were lifted to the surface two at a time in the double-decker cage.

The flow of coal had stopped as the afternoon shift took over and waited for the men to leave before the coal cutter started down the face again. The morning shift trudged up the hill, a pitch so steep that many of the guys held on to a steel rope on a conveyor which helped pull them up.

Above them, the locomotive would shunt the twenty or so coal trucks backwards until the last truck struck against a metal girder attached to the roof 10 yards from the top of the pitch. On this particular day, however, the girder had been tied out of the way – something the driver didn't realize. The locomotive shoved the last truck over the top, and its weight pulled all the others with it. A hundred yards below, fifty men were slowly walking upwards, heads down in the darkness. They didn't know what hit them.

My father, Big Snowy, Phil Bence, Peter Terret and Dio were all there that day. I was working in the fitting shop or I would have been there too.

Despite the shouts from the leading men, the coal trucks hurtled downhill, now pulling the locomotive with them as well. Men were knocked left and right like bowling pins, and there were bodies everywhere, yelling and screaming in the darkness. My dad, a trained medic, tried to do all he could. 'It looked as if a bomb had dropped,' he said to me later that night. 'I think I know now what it must have been like to be in the Blitz, or on the Somme. It was horrifying, Mike – I can't find the words.'

The sirens were sounding at the top of the pit and ambulances arrived to take the injured to hospital. All my other mates had survived, but Big Snowy Cavelle was in a terrible way; he'd been pinned to the side by one of the trucks and it took a Herculean effort by the men to release him. Two weeks later he died without ever leaving intensive care.

There were too many accidents underground; the working conditions were appalling and shambolic, but still the miners sweated and toiled in the darkness. If you were born in the valley, there was very little choice other than leaving and now I decided to take that option.

Without having told either Liz or my parents, I caught the bus down to Cardiff with Bencey.

'I'm telling you,' he said, 'try the RAF office. The Paras are connected to the RAF. You gotta jump out of planes, haven't you?'

Listening to these pearls of wisdom I entered the RAF office.

'I want to join the Paras,' I said to the big sergeant behind the counter.

'Yes, we have a parachute squadron.'

'The red berets?' I asked.

'No, they're the Army, son – you're in the wrong place.'

At the Army office further down the road I tried again. The Welsh Guard at reception gave me a wry smile. 'You'll be too big for the Paras. You should join the Welsh Guards,' he said.

'But I want to be a paratrooper,' I insisted.

'There's a six-foot limit and you're six feet two inches.'

He was lying. The company sergeant-major in the office knew me quite well because I'd played rugby with his son. It turned out he was also a friend of my father's from up the valley. The bullshit about being too tall was designed to get me into the Welsh Guards, a very famous rugby-playing regiment. He even came up to the village to see my dad. 'If he's going to join the Army,' he said, 'he should at least join a Welsh regiment for the rugby.'

My dad still knew nothing about my plans and was totally stunned. Eventually, he did try to talk me round but I wouldn't have it; my heart was set on the Paras. Having filled in the forms and passed the test, I couldn't put it off any longer – I had to tell Liz. We were engaged to be married by then and I knew she pictured a future life in the valley close to her family and friends.

That evening, when Liz got home from working at the shop, I told her straight out. A look of disbelief covered her pretty face.

'Why?' she said. 'Why leave everything that we've got here? What more could there be in England than we've got here?'

'I just want to see a bit of the world. I've never been anywhere. I've only been out of the valley a handful of times.'

On the verge of tears, she said, 'But what about us?'

31

'Come with me,' I said. 'They have married quarters. It'll only be for three years, then we'll come back to the Rhondda. We can rent out this place and have somewhere to come home to. It'll change our lives, I promise.'

# 2

MY FIRST TASTE OF MILITARY LIFE WAS AT SUTTON COLDFIELD IN THE Midlands, where hundreds of would-be soldiers gather for selection procedures before going to different training camps a few months later. We were only there for a few days, but I quickly learned that prospective paratroopers had to do twenty press-ups while other recruits were doing ten. Right from the beginning, we were expected to be better than everyone else.

Liz had stayed in Wales and had started planning for the wedding. Even so, I knew the Army wouldn't provide us with married quarters unless I passed my basic training. This would take place at the Parachute Regiment Depot (Depot Para) in Aldershot, Hampshire.

Two corporals picked up a group of us from the railway station. At the gates of the depot we passed an old aircraft, its wheels embedded in concrete. I'd seen Dakotas in all the books, usually with Second World War paratroopers streaming out of the side doors, and just the sight of it made my heart beat a little bit faster.

As we drove through the camp, I noticed some lads in shiny steel helmets picking up leaves, dog-ends, even matches. They were being bollocked by a big guy in a red beret with two stripes.

'Who are they?' I asked.

The driver chuckled. 'Prisoners from the depot guardroom.'

'So what did they do?'

'Went AWOL mostly. Recruits go missing, get picked up and brought back here. Then they get all the shit jobs for six months.'

'What about the guy in the red beret?'

'The provost corporal. He's your worst fucking nightmare. That's all you need to know about him.'

There were groups of guys running all over the place – some with weapons, others heading off towards the assault course or lined up outside the gym getting a 'beasting' from the PTIs. I managed to work out that PTIs must be physical training instructors, and from the way they were gesticulating and shouting, 'beasting' must be 'bollocking'.

One group had names on their vests and white painted numbers on their trousers and helmets.

'They're on P Company,' explained the driver. 'It's an extra something you have to pass before you do parachute training.'

'Is it part of the course?' I asked.

'Oh, yeah. More like a course within a course.' He laughed and the Land Rover skidded to a halt outside my accommodation block. Each block housed platoons in different stages of training, and this was where us 'crows' lived.

Day one at Depot Para was spent being screamed at from pillar to post. We were all fucking worthless civvies, but they – the corporals – would sort us out and turn us into paratroopers. That seemed to be the gist of it, anyway.

First came the haircut – a compulsory No. 1 skinhead – then documentation, clothing allocation, more documentation, more shouting, ten minutes for scoff and then assembly outside the RHQ (Regimental Headquarters) for a briefing from the CO (commanding officer). He actually seemed like quite a nice bloke after all the screaming and shouting.

'Gentlemen, you are about to undertake one of the toughest training courses in the world,' he said. 'Not all of you are going to make it because not all of you have what it takes . . .'

I looked around at my comrades. We all had identical haircuts, uniforms and brand-new DMS boots, yet we still looked like civvies pretending to be in the Army.

I was older than most of the new recruits, some of whom were as young as seventeen and straight out of school. Surprisingly, a lot of them were little guys. I expected to see some big blokes like Charlie Swannock, but discovered there are only two sizes in the Paras – either short and squat, or tall, lean and athletic. At 16 stones and 6 feet 2 inches I didn't fit either of these and kept thinking back to what the recruiting sergeant had said about me being too big to join the Paras.

34

The brainwashing started immediately. Back in the block after PT, we had to wash our kit, dry it and neatly fold it back in the locker for inspection in the morning. Everything had to be immaculate.

At the crack of dawn, the screaming started again. Beds had to be made, with the sheets and grey army blankets stacked neatly and perfectly square on top. Then came a shower, a hurried feed and more physical training.

A few days after starting, we had our first outing on the assault course, a 400-yard circuit with about twenty obstacles. We'd pottered around a so-called assault course at Sutton Coldfield but this was the real thing, with only a few strides between each ball-breaking obstacle. We were told that to start with we had four minutes to get round in, but by the end of our time at Depot Para we'd be expected to be doing three circuits in seven and a half minutes.

Up ropes, into nets, over walls; I pounded around, legs aching and chest heaving, knowing that awaiting me was one of the scariest-looking pieces of apparatus I'd ever seen: the death slide. Without hesitating or looking down, I climbed a series of metal ladders that took me 120 feet into the air. From the top I could see all of Aldershot, and everybody down on the ground looked the size of Action Man. Legs still burning from the climb, I was handed a T-bar that fitted over a metal line which ran back down to the ground at a 45 degree angle. The PTI reminded me that the idea was to hurtle down and take the impact at the bottom with my feet and knees together. I jumped, my stomach came up to my mouth, and before I knew it I was executing a perfect landing. Or so I thought. As I crashed to the deck my back seemed to twist and immediately started to ache.

For the next couple of days I tried to shrug it off, but eventually the pain got the better of me. I was limping and in agony when I arrived at the depot medical centre. They sent me for an X-ray to the Cambridge Military Hospital in Aldershot, where the doctor took one look at the pictures and shook his head. A disc in my back had collapsed and would need to be removed.

'If I take it out, there's no way you'll be able to parachute,' he said. 'You'll have to go somewhere else in the Army.'

'You're kidding me?'

He shook his head.

'But I've only just started! There's got to be something else you can do.'

I thought of all my mates in the Rhondda. Everyone knew I wanted to be a paratrooper; there was a weight of expectation on me and I couldn't just transfer to a run-of-the-mill infantry unit. Already very fit, I'd get fit again, I told myself. I could still make it as a para.

During a three-hour operation, the disc was taken out and the vertebrae either side fused together. Under anaesthetic, I dreamed I was back in the pit; all the props had collapsed behind me and I was pinned to the ground by hundreds of tons of coal. When I woke up I couldn't move, and in the days that followed I'd never felt so helpless; I couldn't even walk to the toilet or roll over without someone helping me. I was in a lot of pain.

The doctors still gave me little chance of being a paratrooper, but it was no use feeling sorry for myself – although it would have been easy. Instead, I had to focus on getting fit again.

Then something happened which astonished and inspired the entire nation, and certainly spurred me on to new levels of determination. On 5 May 1980 Arab terrorists had taken over the Iranian Embassy in Prince's Gate, London, threatening to kill all twenty-six hostages unless their demands were met. Days later, as the siege unfolded on TV, I was glued to the screen as the SAS stormed the embassy, bursting through windows from the rooftops and dramatically freeing the hostages. After that, I knew Paddy Mayne's men could no longer remain a secret force.

I was sent to the rehabilitation centre at RAF Chessington. The doctors warned me it would take four to six months of physiotherapy and, even then, my back might never be as strong again. 'Take it slowly,' they said, but soon the physios were pleading with me to slow down. I just wanted to get back to Depot Para and into basic training.

In the hospital I met some lads who'd been blown up and badly burned in the Warrenpoint bombing in Northern Ireland. The IRA had set off a remote-controlled explosion on the coastal road as 2 Para was moving location in 4-ton lorries. Cleverly, they'd also planted another device further down the road where they predicted an incident control point might be set up after the first blast. They were right. As help came for the Paras the other bomb was detonated. Sixteen soldiers from 2 Para died on the same day that Lord Mountbatten was killed in another terrorist blast.

Of the survivors I met, one, a private, had been badly burned and had lost a leg; while another, a corporal who'd been shot on an earlier tour, had terrible head injuries. He'd once been extremely fit, but now struggled to throw a tennis ball to a nurse. Each time it simply rolled out of his hand and bounced across the floor. The sight of him tugged at the heart and it struck home to me how the IRA could destroy young lives so easily.

Given a clean bill of health, I returned to Depot Para on 15 September 1980, almost one year to the day since I'd first arrived. Another intake of skinheads was running to and fro, being beasted by corporals.

From day one I got screamed at, humiliated and belittled but, as before, the abuse was psychological rather than physical: we were all worthless shits and how dare we even consider ourselves worthy of becoming paratroopers. Where had I heard all this before?

Being 'worthless shits' we started at the bottom. The floors of the block had to be polished every day – swept first, then layered and 'bumpered' into a brilliant shine – back and forth, back and forth. It was the same with the toilets, sinks and mirrors, every morning after breakfast, so that everything reeked of antiseptic. You could have performed open-heart surgery on those floors.

Every week the block got inspected by the CO. If it wasn't up to standard the whole platoon would be up for nights after, cleaning until even the fluorescent light covers were spotless.

After every run your PT kit had to be washed, dried, then put back on your shelf, folded perfectly with your other kit, locker open. On the parades in the mornings, we stood by our beds as the platoon OC and sergeant inspected. If the slightest mistake was discovered – like a sock being out of place or a blanket not precisely boxed – it meant a 'show clean' at night, parading at 10 p.m. for the provost sergeant.

The provost sergeant is always the biggest bastard in the world; that's his job, and he does it with pride. He's Dracula in a red beret and he inspected every detail down to your fingernails and inside your ears. If he found the slightest mistake or speck of dirt, he made you parade again at 11 p.m. and, if necessary, at midnight – and so on. It might not seem like much of a punishment, but in the depot you need your sleep; it's a must or you go down.

A lot of lads dropped out in those first few weeks. Maybe they expected army life to be constantly like this; I hoped they weren't right.

Mealtimes were always chaotic, with scores of skinheads queuing for food. I soon learned the army word, 'scoff', which somehow suited a meal that you barely had time to sit and race down your neck.

The cookhouse smelled of baked beans, no matter what was on the menu. I'd never tasted food like it – it was shit. The cooks were sullen bastards and they'd tell you to fuck off if you dared to complain.

Newcomers are called 'crows' by the senior paras and that's exactly what you are until you get into the battalion and even after that, until you prove yourself. As a 'crow' you're even barred from the pubs in Aldershot, but I was so skint that I couldn't have afforded to drink anyway.

When I finished at night, I'd queue for the pay phones and ring my parents' house to check everything was OK. Liz and I couldn't afford a phone.

By this stage, I'd completely forgotten about my back. I figured there was no use worrying; if I could cope with the psychological flak, the physical demands would take care of themselves.

I thought that the first time I had to run with any kind of weight on my back would be a real test because of the operation. In fact, I found carrying a bergen that weighed about 30 pounds quite easy after working underground and years of rugby training. We were running at Long Valley where the Army tested tanks and did driver training. In summer the muddy tracks were baked hard and after rain they became a quagmire.

I stayed on the heels of the DS (directing staff) in front, who kept putting on spurts of speed, trying to shake me off. Another lad stayed with us, a big cockney lad called Hudson, whom we immediately and imaginatively christened Rocky, and we were miles ahead of everybody else.

Finally the PTI stopped and said, 'Right, you two fuckers, I'll teach you to show off.'

He was clearly pissed off because we were keeping up with him, particularly as he was getting fucked and we were breathing easy. He decided to make us do press-ups until the rest of the group caught up, and as soon as they did we had to carry on. I hardly broke into a sweat, and from that day I knew that carrying weight and moving fast over ground would not be a problem for me.

I'd also learned early that the best way to tackle forced marches was to get up front with the DS and instructors and to stay with them rather than being in the middle or at the back. Inevitably the DS will push the pace and it's far easier to stay on the arse of someone and to accelerate when he accelerates than be a long way behind and running to catch up.

In the Paras you don't march, you 'tab' (tactical advance to battle). Tabbing is an art. You've got to throw your feet forward and push all the time from your hips; you know if you're doing it correctly because your hips will ache as much as your legs, heart and lungs.

The tabs grew progressively longer, with less time to recover after each. Although I was still coughing up coal dust from the pits, I really enjoyed the physical side of things, and I loved the soldiering more than I had imagined. Of course it was tough, but I assumed it was preparing me for what was to come and tried to learn the lesson.

Firing weapons was a real crack. The first time I fired live with an SLR 7.62, the kick was absolutely amazing. When you pulled the trigger the butt would dig into your shoulder and hit you on the side of the face as you looked through the rear sight. For those first few months my shoulder and right cheek ached after every session. The same went for the gimpy (GPMG – general purpose machine-gun) which quickly became one of my favourites.

Until I fired live I hadn't realized that every weapon needed to be zeroed to the person firing it, because each person has a different build, height and reach. It was a simple enough job with the screwdriver in the rifle-cleaning kit.

In a perverse sort of way I enjoyed all the screaming and abuse. It was all part of it, and if a corporal had said, 'Jump in a barrel,' I'd have jumped in a barrel. Mentally it was turning me from a civilian into a soldier – and not just any soldier, but a member of the Parachute Regiment.

Although we called the PT staff the Gestapo, the lance-jacks (lance corporals) were the worst; they had a little bit of power and one stripe on their arm. When our corporals yelled at the top of their voices in the corridors, we'd scurry like rats from the sewers. I decided one in particular, Corporal Sheznavitch, was severely deranged. He lived in our block in the corporal's bunk and had a sadistic streak that would have had Himmler writing fan letters.

Some of the lads were terrified of him, but inside I just laughed; it was all part of the brainwashing and this guy was a fucking professional. Every night after we were stood down Corporal Sheznavitch would go out of the block with his enormous bergen on his back. Later we discovered that, instead of being crazy, he was training for a thing called 'Selection' to join the SAS.

*

It wasn't until our first exercise that I really experienced what it was like to be a soldier. It was known as 'Steel Eagle', and every paratrooper went through this week of hell in the mountains and bogs of Brecon in Wales. Apart from teaching the basics, it hammered home the important rules that I guessed I'd need to remember through my entire career. First, make sure your kit is always packed away; second, keep your feet and doss-bag dry; third, make sure your weapon is always right next to you.

These things were learned the hard way. On 'Steel Eagle' we were wet and miserable for a week, getting bollocked and pissed upon from dawn till dusk. All the things we'd trained for at Depot Para were repeated in the field, such as camouflage and conceal-ment, and digging a trench for defensive warfare.

The last of these wasn't a problem – I'd spent enough time underground – but sometimes it didn't pay to be good at things. We'd been paired off to dig trenches in the driving rain and I teamed up with 'Rocky' Hudson, a big, tall Chelsea supporter and former bank clerk from London. The two of us were swinging our entrenching tools and Sheznavitch said, 'OK, lads, as soon as this is done, you can get your heads down.'

Right, I thought, that suits me. We upped the work-rate and fin-ished in record time. Then the corporal wandered back over. 'Good lads. Now you can go and help those fucking cripples over there.'

Rocky finished up being a good mate, even though we came from vastly different backgrounds, mine blue collar, his a Persil white.

There was only one other Welsh lad among the recruits, but I made a point of holding on to my accent. I knew that the folks back in the Rhondda wouldn't appreciate me coming home for a week-end with a cockney accent and spouting lots of army jargon.

The intensive training continued for another few months and included a stint of parade-ground drill. Until you pass off the square, you can't wear the red beret at the depot, yet traditionally Paras don't drill and don't even like teaching it. Other regiments spend months doing it, but Paras prefer to be out soldiering and doing the business.

We were building up to the infamous 'P Company' and some of the lads were getting jittery. Spread over three days, it involved six different trials of courage, strength and endurance. Points were to be awarded out of ten for each event but none of us knew what the pass marks were. We simply had to give 100 per cent and hope it was enough to get through.

A few weeks beforehand, I noticed some new faces at the depot. We called them 'crap hats' because they came from the Marines, RAF and other elements of the Army. They were preparing for the 'All-Arms' P Company and a lot of them were older than us, in their late twenties and thirties.

When the big day arrived, thirty of us from the platoon assembled in three ranks outside the block. For the first event we had to wear red PT vests, shorts and trainers.

Sheznavitch stood shouting into the face of a lad we called Little Paddy. He screamed, 'Why are the PT tops red, Kernaghan?'

'I don't know, Corporal.'

'So they don't show up your fucking blood, you little Irish wanker!'

Sheznavitch had a name for all of us; Paddy was an Irish wanker, Rocky was a cockney wanker, while I was, obviously, a sheep-shagging Taff wanker. There seemed to be no end to his wit.

We were marched down to the gym and I immediately saw the All-Arms lads waiting for us. 'You're gonna fight 'em,' said Tam Coyle, a corporal we'd nicknamed the 'Iceman' because he showed so little emotion. 'And don't you dare fucking lose to those crap hats!'

I'd heard about 'milling', although the fact that it still took place wasn't exactly publicized. Basically it's one minute of mayhem where two men try to batter each other into submission or unconsciousness; to get maximum points you have to go at it hammer and tongs, showing no mercy.

Four months into the brainwashing cycle, I knew that Sheznavitch would make life unbearable for anyone who didn't deliver a victory.

We were paired off according to size and weight, with the smaller guys fighting first. Rocky and I were a similar build and, initially, I worried that we might get put in together and I'd have to knock seven bells of shit out of my best mate. Thankfully, we both got drawn to fight officers from the All-Arms crowd and neither of us minded hitting a crap hat.

Most of Depot Para had come to watch, including the colonel, and the place was packed. There were two rings set up, with all the fighters seated around the sides. You could eyeball your opponent and then, after each fracas, the line moved clockwise until you reached the corner and it was your turn.

Sheznavitch and Tam Coyle were our cornermen and gave last-minute advice as they laced on the gloves.

'OK, you little Irish wanker,' Sheznavitch told Paddy. 'You fuck up on this one and your life ain't worth living.'

Tam had his own brand of advice: 'Knock his head off, you hear? Hit! Hit! Hit!'

Paddy did well, getting stuck right in.

Then it was Rocky's turn. He caught some heavy punches early and his legs buckled, but he held on and turned the fight, hammering away at his opponent's head. It could have gone either way, but the judges gave Rocky the verdict. Sheznavitch was right about the PT vest not showing the blood.

Then it was my turn and I didn't need any motivation from the cornermen. I was so hyped up that I told myself I was fighting for the whole of the Rhondda valley – then I piled into him.

He was built like a coal truck and was about as slow. I gave him a hell of a beating and kept thinking to myself, It's only for a minute, go for it, don't hold back.

Milling sounds barbaric and several lads did turn their backs and refuse to fight. However, you had to wonder how they'd cope in a real war situation. From my point of view, I accepted it as part and parcel of P Company and being a paratrooper.

The second event was a 10-miler with 40 pounds on our backs and carrying a weapon. I stuck with the PTI, never dropping more than a few feet behind his shoulder. Those that came in with him got a maximum ten points. That night we slept out and did a confidence test first thing in the morning on the 'trainasium' – an aerial obstacle course designed to get us used to heights. It was like an assault course through the tree tops, jumping from one piece of scaffolding to the next. It could be as scary as hell because of optical illusions created by the height and your own tiredness. You began thinking that particular gaps were too wide and the doubts started affecting your judgement. There were no points; it was pass or fail – and a couple of lads did fail.

Next came the stretcher race, an event that involved teams of six carrying a stretcher made from steel scaffolding poles. You support the stretcher on your shoulders; it burns, it rubs, it aches, and all you can do is grin and bear it. The race went on for miles through the muddy tracks and all the time you got yelled and screamed at by the PTIs and DS.

My neck was breaking and my chest was aching, but I kept reminding myself that it must be easier for me than for a former bank clerk like Rocky. I drove onwards, shouting encouragement to the others. Later I learned that they were looking for leaders and I'd earned a maximum ten points.

After a scoff of airborne stew – meat and potatoes cooked in a tea urn – we assembled into teams of ten for the log race. This involved wooden telegraph poles that weighed a fucking ton, each carried by eight guys holding toggle ropes. The two spare team members would take over when somebody needed a rest.

I made a pact with Rocky. 'I'm not dropping off the log.'

'You're a mad bastard.'

'Come on. What do you say?'

'I'm up for it.'

Off we went, up and down hills, carrying the wooden pole for 6 miles. Hungry Hill was about halfway round and a real bastard. All shingle at the top, you had to dig in your toes. Rocky and I were at the front and behind us guys were dropping off. It took longer and longer for someone to take their place. My wrist was bleeding and so was Rocky's nose, but we stayed on the log.

Halfway up the shingle, I screamed at Rocky, 'Don't look up! Just keep going.'

Just below the summit, some wanker at the back dropped the log, but we drove on, rounding a tree at the top. There was just time for one quick look at Aldershot below us before the DS screamed, 'Sprint! Fucking sprint!'

We ran as fast as we could for 3 more miles and actually dragged the last two lads over the line as they hung on to the post.

'Who is number forty-four?' the DS asked.

I put up my hand. I didn't know it then, but I had already passed P Company on the second day. After four events, I had thirty-nine points out of a possible forty. The only one I'd dropped was in the milling because my opponent was considered not to have tried hard enough.

There were two events on the last day – an assault course and a steeplechase. The NCOs were taking bets on whether I could break the record of fifty-eight points for P Company, which had been set by a Corporal Matt McCourt a few years earlier.

On the assault course I came in first, picking up another ten points. Then came the steeplechase, where I needed to finish in the top five to get maximum points and break the record.

The course wasn't that long, but had a lot of ditches, some of them waist deep. I slipped half a dozen times, swallowing muddy water and spitting out muck before charging onwards. My helmet

43

strap dug into my neck, hurting like crazy, but I couldn't slacken it or it would have fallen into my eyes.

Around me, the lads kept pushing me to go faster. As I came down the final rise, my lungs were screaming for oxygen and I could barely lift my knees. I crossed the line and collapsed in a heap. I'd come fourth and broken the record.

Next day I marched onto the square to receive P Company's Best Student Award in front of the whole depot. I was chuffed and a long way from that rehabilitation bed at RAF Chessington.

Yet the biggest test for my reconstructed back was still to come – when I would hurl myself out of a plane and trust my life to a 32-foot-diameter canopy of khaki-coloured silk. Until then, parachuting hadn't entered my head; it had just been a case of taking each day at a time. Now I began to get nervous.

Those who passed P Company were sent to Brize Norton, the RAF base in Oxfordshire, for parachute training. Now we were being looked after by the RAF, with nobody shouting at us or getting us out of bed at six o'clock in the morning. Instead we got up at the civilized time of seven o'clock. There was even a night-club on the base, and girls, although the latter were out of bounds of course for betrothed chaps.

For a week we practised all the landing rolls and mock jumps. There was a piece of apparatus called the Knacker Cracker, which was a box on top of a wooden structure about 50 feet off the ground, with a static line inside. It's supposed to simulate exiting a plane. You throw yourself out and then bob along about 20 feet from the ground attached to the wire line. Unfortunately, unless you adjust your tackle correctly, it pulls your balls up to your throat – and you understand where it got its name. I could never take it seriously and used to piss myself laughing, hanging in the air like a rag doll.

On Friday the big day arrived. 'You can all go home for the weekend,' the chief instructor said, 'but first there's the little matter of a jump from a balloon.'

Four of us – me, Rocky, Paddy and Mick, a Jock lad – could just about squeeze into the cage with the instructor. As he shut the barred gate behind us, he said, 'I'll just close this to keep the air in.'

Slowly the balloon rose above Oxfordshire. On such a beautiful day, the view was incredible. It stopped at 1,000 feet and there was an eerie, groaning silence. I'd never been this high before – quite the reverse, I'd been this far underground.

We were all hooked up to a bar in the centre of the cage, includ-

44

ing the PJI (parachute jump instructor). He was hanging out of the opening, looking down at the people on the deck. A badge on his arm stated, 'Knowledge dispels fear.'

Rocky turned to me. 'Yeah, that's OK if you've got the knowledge – I'm crapping myself.'

'Talk about butterflies,' said Paddy.

'Mine are fucking kittens,' I said.

We'd been numbered off on the ground, one to four, and I was number four.

The PJI pulled the bar away from the gap in the cage and said, 'Number one to the door. Ready – arms across your chest – GO!'

Mick went out as quick as that. Looking down I could see his canopy open, close and then open again. He descended.

Paddy went next, then Rocky.

My turn. I was trying my best to look cool in front of the PJI.

'You OK?'

'Yeah.'

'Your mates have left you.'

'Yeah.'

'OK, standby – GO!'

Jesus, my stomach was in my mouth. I was looking up at the tail of the balloon, then yank! My chute opened. I felt a massive adrenalin rush. It was like nothing I'd experienced before in my life, a 200 feet drop with air rushing past me.

'Steer left, number 4!' came a yell from the ground.

Fuck off, I thought, I'm enjoying this!

Ground coming in, coming in – bang! I fell over and got up. I didn't even think about my back; it never occurred to me. I packed my chute away, picked up my reserve and made my way over to Rocky and the lads.

I went home for the weekend and told everybody about it. It was a really exciting time and I enjoyed being back in Rhondda among friends and with Liz. Everything was going to plan and it's not often you can say that in life.

On Monday, back at Brize Norton, we began a series of seven jumps in seven days. Normally these were spread over two weeks, but the weather had been bad. A Hercules waited on the tarmac with its ramp down. The whole course lined up, sixty-two jumpers, lower numbers first, and we walked up the ramp.

Inside, there were nylon seats down either side of the plane and the first thing I noticed was the stink of hydraulics. It was the same smell I remembered as a kid standing by the ice-cream vans that used to drive through Ferndale.

As the ramp closed and it grew dark, I thought to myself, This is my first time on a plane and I'm not going to be landing in it.

Our parachutes were fitted with four sets of straps that adjusted and clipped into a quick-release box on your chest. It wasn't a comfortable way to travel.

Sitting across from me, Rocky looked fairly nervous. Usually he was Mr Confident. Alongside him, Paddy was nervously cracking jokes. There was only 5 feet 3 inches of him, but he was the same in any direction and looked like a beer barrel. Yet despite his lack of height, Paddy always seemed to be close behind Rocky and me on the runs.

The other member of our little gang was Jed Bull, a West Country lad and only eighteen years old; the youngest guy in the platoon.

The Herc flew over the M4 to drop us at Weston-on-the-Green. The first jump was 'clean fatigue' (no equipment), in sticks of eight each side, port and starboard. After thirty minutes of flying, the jump doors were opened and air came rushing in. The first sticks had already hooked up at their static lines and were moving down the aircraft to the doors.

I was sweating and my mouth was dry. 'For fuck's sake, it's not even your turn yet!' I told myself.

The number ones were in the doors, the red light came on, wait for the green . . . Go! Go! Go!

The first sticks went out rapidly. I glanced across at the lads – Paddy laughing, Jed and Rocky bug-eyed. We were third sticks.

In front of me was a quiet lad called Russell from Belfast, Paddy's home town.

'You OK, Russ?' I asked.

No reply.

'Russ, you OK?'

He had a thousand-yard stare. 'I don't know, Taff,' he said.

We looked up.

'Action stations.'

'Here we go,' I said, swallowing hard. My heart felt like it was pounding right out of my skin, like in a Tom and Jerry cartoon.

My right hand, clammy and sweaty, was on the strap; my left was over my reserve parachute on my chest. Moving down the aircraft in unison, I didn't bother looking at the others. We all had our own demons to fight.

46

'Red on!'

The first guy stood in the doorway, his right hand stuck out rigid holding him upright against the door frame.

'Go!'

No thoughts, nothing. He's off.

Three guys out and I'm number six on the stick. Then Russell stops and unhooks himself. The PJI grabs him, throws him to one side, takes hold of my smock and flings me out the door. The slip-stream hits me and for a couple of seconds the whole world turns upside down.

Suddenly, a huge jolt.

I look up, checking for twists in the rigging lines. Twists mean a bad exit and you have to kick like fuck to get out of them while falling to earth. If that doesn't work you deploy the reserve chute. It's your decision – at 800 feet there's no committee meetings.

I had a good exit, probably thanks to the extra shove. I was float-ing above Oxfordshire – what a view, what a buzz.

By the time we got back to Brize Norton, Russ had gone. We never saw him again. That night we all had a beer in the RAF NAAFI, celebrating the fact that we only had a week to go before becoming fully-fledged paratroopers.

The first four training jumps were clean fatigue and the fifth with a bergen dropped in a container that dangled 20 or 30 feet below you as you fell. The sixth jump was at night and even more frightening. Going first this time, I waited for the green light with the wind howling against my para smock. I could see the lights of Oxford in the distance. On green, I kicked out as far as I could into the darkness.

No matter how many times I jumped, it still terrified me. Would it ever get any easier?

Back at Depot Para, we were allowed to stitch the coveted Para wings on our right shoulder; we weren't 'crows' any more – that honour fell to the pricks running around without any hair. At least, that's what we thought.

Depot Para isn't the place to swagger. On the first day in the gym the PT staff gave us a fearsome beasting to bring us back down to earth. We hadn't done anything wrong, of course, it was just in case any of us thought we actually deserved to be para-troopers.

There were only a few weeks left before the passing-out parade. Most of the time was spent on drill and getting our kit ready; the

Parachute Regiment might not be noted for its performances on the parade ground, but when it goes on show it looks immaculate.

One question dominated our thinking: which battalions we'd be joining. I'd always fancied going into 1 Para because that was where most of the DS were from and you tend to get heavily influenced by them. Right up to the last day I assumed I'd be passing out wearing the red lanyard of 1 Para rather than the blue of 2 Para or the green of 3 Para. Fate intervened, however.

The plan had always been to get married quarters, so Liz could leave Rhondda and join me. Unfortunately there were no houses available at 1 Para, so instead I went to 2 Para and marched onto the parade ground wearing the blue lanyard.

Rocky joined me, while Paddy went to 1 Para and Jed Bull went to 3 Para.

My parents and sister came down with Liz to watch the passing-out parade. It was an exciting day and I felt 10 feet tall marching in front of them as the massed bands of the Parachute Regiment played Wagner's 'Ride of the Valkyries', the Paras' regimental march.

Afterwards we all did a balloon jump for our families – something I'd have preferred to do without. Mam and Dad met all the corporals and the OC and RSM from the depot. For a lot of the lads who came from military backgrounds, it probably didn't mean as much, but for my folks it was an unforgettable experience.

I'd fallen in love with soldiering from almost the first day. Now I'd completed the hardest induction course in the Army, having taken 150 different flavours of shit for six months before passing out the other side.

Now that I was a fully-fledged paratrooper, it was time to fulfil another part of my bargain with my fiancée. We'd decided that we could either invite all our friends and have a big wedding, or go on honeymoon; we certainly couldn't afford both. No contest; we had a typical Rhondda wedding with all our family and friends around us – though Liz's father didn't turn up and her brother had to give her away – followed by a monumental piss-up at Maerdy Hall. We had a disco in the evening, which worked fine until Liz and I were the last ones there; the minibus didn't return so I had to bum a lift off the barman. Then Liz and I went home and I carried her over the threshold. We spent the next few days watching television and doing what newly-weds are supposed to do.

Two weeks later, Liz and I left our nice little house in the valleys and drove down to Aldershot – or 'the Shot' as it was affectionately known. As we reached the married quarters, grey, bleak and run-down, she looked out of the window and said, 'Oh, look at those horrible flats over there. Who lives in them, poor things?'

'You and me, love,' I said, and she burst into tears.

# 3

EVERY NEW BATTALION ARRIVAL HAS TO PROVE HIMSELF AND I'D HEARD the horror stories about older sweats picking on the younger crows. The ride can get rough and one chap in particular singled me out for treatment. On the first day we had to queue up for kit from the stores. When I went back to the block this guy from 6 Platoon said to me, 'I want those fucking webbing pouches off you.'

I'd managed to pick up fairly old ammunition pouches which were quite sought after because when you're tabbing they don't rub against your legs so much. He obviously had new ones.

'No fucking way,' I said.

As he went to snatch the webbing, I gripped his wrist and shoved him hard up against the door.

'I might be fucking new, but I wasn't born yesterday,' I said, making it very clear that I wasn't going to take any grief. From then on, I didn't get messed around.

Two Para, known as the Jock Regiment because it had boasted so many Scotsmen since the Second World War, had just returned from a long tour of Northern Ireland and in March 1981 was still recovering from the Warrenpoint bombing. Several other members had left to join the SAS. I went to 5 Platoon, B Company to make up the numbers.

I was a 'pad' (married guy) and had to walk into the block from the 'pads' (married quarters) each morning. The block was divided into sections and as you walked from room to room you heard different tapes playing, such as Madness, Tamla Motown or Deep Purple. Everybody had their own tastes. The lads were four to a room, and the first thing I noticed was that I couldn't smell floor polish or disinfectant.

I headed for the room my section had been assigned and found the lads I'd probably be spending the next few years with – Mouse Walker, Geordie Vale, Steve Illingsworth, a lad from Doncaster in Yorkshire, who'd passed out of the depot not long before me, and 'Cautious' Bob, a born worrier from London, who was twenty going on seventy-five.

Normally it took a few days before people started talking to you, but these two, the northerner and the cockney, were friendly straight off, especially Steve.

'Where are you from?' asked Steve.

I'd barely opened my mouth . . .

'Jesus, a bloody Taff. How was depot?'

'A nightmare.'

He laughed.

Bob came over and sat on Steve's bed. 'Don't listen to this northern twat.'

'Fuck off, you cockney wanker,' said Steve. 'So where in Wales do you come from?'

'The Rhondda valley.'

'Ah, coal country.'

'What do you know about it?' I asked.

'Well, they're not digging for fucking diamonds in Doncaster, boyo.'

It turned out that Steve was also from a mining family, although he'd never been underground, and our reasons for joining the Paras were very similar. We had a lot in common, whereas he and Bob were complete opposites; they argued over everything – music, politics, religion, football, you name it. They'd be packing their bergens and Steve would say something like, 'What are you taking that for, Bob?' referring to an extra poncho.

'Can't be too careful, mate!' Cautious Bob would say, and then Steve would call him a knobber and they'd be off arguing again. Yet on exercises they couldn't have been better oppos; deep down, I guessed, they respected each other.

Those first few weeks were vital because they could pretty much decide how the rest of your time within the battalion would pan out. It's true what they say about first impressions, and you had to get stuck right in and impose yourself, showing the company what you were made of without seeming cocky.

Once a week we all chipped in to clean the block and the OC would do a ten-minute inspection. Compared to Depot Para it was amazingly informal, with no screaming and shouting. Blokes just got on with their jobs.

I hit it off with most of the guys in B Company. Our OC, Major Johnny Crosland, was a tough little bastard. He loved rugby and was an inspirational leader. Then there was Big Scouse Connell, a wise-cracking giant of a man from Liverpool. He was 6 feet 4 inches, as hard as nails and weighed about 18 stones. Scouse looked like a bag of shit but could soldier everybody else into the ground. He'd joined the Paras in the early 1970s and done numerous tours in Northern Ireland before going AWOL for a year and then coming back. Rumour had it that he'd joined the Rhodesians as a mercenary and for once the grapevine got it right. When he turned up at the gates in Aldershot with the world's darkest suntan, he got sent straight to the Army's prison at Colchester for a few months.

Scouse used the time in the glasshouse well and honed his skills with weapons drills, becoming very slick. Then he came back to the battalion. Everybody knew he should have been a sergeant or a colour-sergeant, but he kept getting busted and bouncing up and down the ranks – one day a corporal, the next a tom (private soldier), then back again as a lance-jack.

On our very first defence exercise, I found myself digging a trench with Scouse, who was relaxing to one side.

'Eh, Taff,' he said, 'you used to work in the pits. Tell you what, you dig and I'll tell the jokes.'

And that's exactly what happened; he knew thousands of them. Me, I laughed – and dug. I was a crow.

My section commander on the exercise, Dave Collins, was a sniper who had one of the highest kill ratios in the British army in Northern Ireland. Everyone respected him enormously and I was surprised when I learned that he'd twice failed Selection for the SAS. Jesus, I thought, they must all be supermen.

B Company had loads of characters. It amazed me how Mick Connor, a corporal from the north, managed to stay in Para Reg. He smoked, swore, never did a blind bit of physical work and off duty drank like a fish, yet was still up near the front on the toughest tabs.

There were two other corporals, Big Bish and Baby Bish – the

Bishop brothers – who were both my size. Both had blond hair, blue eyes and looked like the product of a Nazi experiment. They probably were.

Then there was Baz Bardsley, who was shaped like an Oxo cube and used to drive around in a Jag that made him look like a member of the Manchester mafia. He was a good mate of the comedian Bernard Manning and used to invite him down to Aldershot occasionally to have a few bevvies with the lads.

Of the others, a lot of people thought Ken Doyle, a lance-corporal, was several rounds short of a full magazine. A well-built Brummie, he was one of the fittest guys in the company and apparently prone to losing his rag when pissed. I got on fine with him.

The platoon sergeant was Ian Aird, an unassuming sort of chap and good guy. I also liked Jim O'Rourke and Jimmy Street, two older grunts. O'Rourke was about forty, an ex-fighter and all-round hard bastard who'd once boxed at Madison Square Gardens, taking dives for money when it would have been easier to win. Jimmy Street – nicknamed Strasse – was from Glasgow and I didn't understand a single word he said. A right old sweat, he gave a fuck for no-one and had been passed around all the platoons in the battalion, including mortar and anti-tank. He was an avid forty-a-day man; on the weekends he'd get completely off his face, come back to the block, and piss his mattress. It was constantly propped up against the radiator to dry.

Aldershot calls itself the 'home of the British army', although more fittingly it's the 'home of the Parachute Regiment'. On duty, we had to wear the red beret at all times, whereas most army units wear a hat as part of their dress uniform. That's why we called them 'crap hats'. Paras had their own unofficial civilian uniform, too. We tended to have short hair and to wear desert boots, faded jeans, a green bomber jacket and a maroon T-shirt. I thought it made me look a million dollars, but I must have looked a complete twat.

On weekends the civvies in Aldershot tended to stay indoors and the Paras came out like vampires. Most of the young toms hit the piss and went prowling for skirt, but I was obviously more subdued.

Aldershot is famous for Para groupies and one in particular was known as 'the Horse'. She was a big girl with blond hair and had Para Reg tattoos and a Para Reg T-shirt. Her sister – an almost identical version, only smaller – was called 'the Pony', and the two of them hung out at a place called the Globe Trotter in town. It was a den of iniquity, full of lads from 2 or 3 Para (1 Para were based in Edinburgh) and all the groupies. Often I'd be walking the half mile to work on a Monday morning, and on the way I'd pass a couple of girls who'd obviously spent the weekend putting the boys through their paces. They'd be sneaked inside, get passed around, and then slip home on Monday for a bit of R and R.

Parachuting with the battalion was something entirely different from Brize Norton. The first jump was a night exercise on Salisbury Plain, where we parachuted with a GPMG and 1,000 rounds of ammunition in our containers.

Before the jump we had about six hours of low-level flying, designed to avoid radar detection. The plane moved up and down over the terrain and us crows were sick all over the place until the stench of vomit mingled with the smells of sweat, fuel and oil.

I tried to sleep, imagining I was on a train somewhere, but kept waking up and thinking, Fucking hell, I've got to jump out of this thing. Being surrounded by lads who'd done lots and lots of jumps didn't make it any easier. They all looked so cool.

I was shocked by just how chaotic things were; the plane was jam packed with sixty-two guys, thirty-one down each side, and the PJIs walking all over our containers.

At P minus forty (parachute time minus forty minutes) we put our feet through the leg strap attached to the container, then attached the container's quick-release strap to our parachute harness. In the event of a dire emergency in the air, the container could then be ditched from your para harness, slowing your rate of descent slightly, but killing anyone it landed on.

At P minus ten, the PJI shouted, 'Stand up, fit equipment!'

We attached each container by hooks on to the lower D-rings of the parachute harness and the spare chute on to the top D-rings. I constantly checked the four straps, two from the shoulders and two under my arse, all locked into the box on my chest. Carrying so much weight, I resembled a Weeble doll – even if someone had tried to push me over, I'd have bounced straight back up again.

Steve was behind me, Bob in front. I turned to Steve and looked into his eyes under the helmet and he gave me a huge grin. I thought, This is one tough motherfucker.

'Tell off for equipment check!'

Everyone slapped the back of the guy in front and shouted his designated number, counting down to number one.

'Port stick OK.'

'Starboard stick OK.'

'Action stations!'

We shuffled towards the door.

The tailgate of the aircraft came down and I could see seven or eight other Hercules C130s flying in formation, quite an awesome sight. The wedge was shoved out with all the mortars and other heavy equipment, including motor bikes for the recce platoon.

'Red on!'

The number one grabbed his strap on the container.

Suddenly, the PJI screamed, 'Stop! Stop! Back! Back! Back! Dummy run!'

The approach run was aborted and we had to go through it again. The Hercules circled and came back.

'Action stations . . . Red on! . . . Green on! . . . Go!'

My heart was pounding like a drum and I was sweating so heavily some of the camouflage cream ran into my eyes and stung like fury.

Everybody in the stick started shuffling along, knackered, air-sick, and generally pissed off.

During training it had all been, 'lead leg, rear leg'; now it was a chaotic rush to the door. People in front of me were just flopping out of the door instead of thrusting because with 120-pound bergens and a parachute on top it was all they could do to move. Some of the smaller guys were just hanging on the end of the static line.

The wind at the tailgate hit me like a slap in the face and suddenly I flew into the slipstream, totally disorientated as my legs came up into the air. In the daytime you see a blur of blue-green, sky-ground, blue-green, sky-ground, but in the darkness you're totally lost.

Suddenly the rigging lines deployed all around and the chute opened. Thank God.

*Fuck, what's that!*

I'd gone out the back on the starboard side and another guy had gone out the opposite side. I was walking all over this guy's helmet. His rigging lines were attached to me and we were plummeting 800 feet above Salisbury Plain.

For those four or five seconds, I tried to remember what they'd taught me about staying cool. We pulled the rigging lines apart and pushed out. The guy started panicking and pulled his reserve chute, which flew up and collapsed his main canopy. How he managed to get down safely I'll never know, but he did.

Meanwhile, finally in free air, I had to remember there were sixty-one other guys in the sky with me – and that was just from my plane. Parachutes were all over the place and I constantly kept steering away from people.

I felt for the hooks and dropped my container so that it dangled below my feet, feeling the tug as it settled on the straps. Getting ready to land, I tucked in tight, assessed the drift and tried to decide if I was going in forwards or backwards. If you're going backwards, you have to pull on your front lift webs; if going in forwards, you pull on the back lift webs. Get it wrong and you increase the speed of your descent and the effect is a bit like jumping off a train at 30 m.p.h.

At night you can't see the ground, so you wait for the container to hit and a moment later you land with a thud. Any landing is a good landing so long as you can walk away.

The battalion jump typified the Parachute Regiment to me – the guts and the balls to actually jump out of a plane with all that kit hanging round you. A clean fatigue is easy – grannies can jump PX4s clean fatigue – but when you're loaded up at night and you're jumping simultaneously out of six or seven aircraft it's fucking scary.

We did a lot of parachuting in those first few months, travelling down to South Cerney near Swindon, just off the M4. Often we'd have to wait days for a weather window because even a wind speed on the ground of 10 knots would mean risking a lot of injuries.

Scoff at this place was shite and the queues were massive; TV was the only way to relieve the boredom. One Thursday night, I was watching *Top of the Pops* with Stevie, Bob and Geordie Vale, a squat, ugly Newcastle lad. An unknown band called Culture Club debuted their new single, 'Do You Really Want to Hurt Me'.

Geordie looked at the lead singer and said, 'Well, she can hurt me any time she likes.'

I took a closer look. 'That's not a she,' I said, 'that's a fucking he!'

Steve said, 'That's Boy George, you knobber.'

Bob shifted his chair further from Geordie and muttered, 'Can't be too careful, mate.'

Along with Taff Poole, Geordie had become another member of our little gang. He was a great friend of 'the Horse', and another one of those guys who smoked forty cigarettes a day, never trained and still managed to keep up on the tabs.

Our inaugural foreign exercise was in Denmark – my first time overseas. We parachuted in, which meant I still hadn't been in a plane for a take-off and a landing. It was a fairly bog standard NATO exercise with the usual scenario that the Russians were coming and we had to stop them.

The Danes provided the pretend Ruskies and we had to dig a series of trenches with obstacles at the front such as barbed wire and pickets, as well as interlocking arcs of fire for our support weapons – Milan missiles, GPMGs and mortars. At night we put out standing patrols (OP posts in no man's land) that would relay information back to the defensive position.

In the beginning it was hard work, followed by hours and then days of complete boredom. Early in your army career you never get to see the big picture, just your own little world – section, platoon and company. Denmark was obviously an exercise for the officers to co-ordinate themselves with their Danish counterparts. Para Reg rarely does defence exercises and is normally seen as providing shock troops who parachute in and cause mayhem – the Vikings of the sky.

It rained for three solid weeks and our tent city at Tuse turned to mud. The Vikings were pretty pissed off by this stage and we were finally given a day of R and R. A Company and B Company all went to the Carlsberg Brewery in Copenhagen. The brewery had been built on the orders of Adolf Hitler in the Second World War, when Germany invaded Denmark. The massive stone elephants at the gates still bore the swastikas. Stern warnings were delivered about behaving ourselves – the usual stuff about respecting the locals and being fine ambassadors for the regiment.

We were given a tour of the plant, but all we really wanted to do was have a drink.

One of the lads asked, 'What's the strongest beer you export, mate?'

'Carlsberg Special Brew,' said the foreman.

'And is that the strongest beer you make?'

'Ah,' he said, catching on quickly. 'I have just the thing you want.'

He showed us a bottle of Elephant Beer, which had a stopper rather than a metal cap. Of course we all got hammered on the stuff.

Geordie, Steve, Bob and I finished up in a strange bar later that night, all very bedraggled. Geordie had found himself an Eskimo lady who was probably the ugliest woman I'd ever seen in my life.

'I'm going to marry her,' he whispered in my ear.

'Why?'

'She knows 127 different words for snow.'

It wasn't until November 1981 – and my twentieth flight – that I finally landed in a plane. Two Para arrived in Kenya for six weeks of intensive exercises. I was really looking forward to the trip but disappointed about the timing. The battalion's rugby side had made the quarter-final of the Army Cup, a competition tradition-ally dominated by regiments such as the Welsh Guards. Two Para had never done this well before.

Unfortunately, three of our best players were in the advance party to Kenya, so we couldn't field our strongest side. This led to my one and only conversation with Colonel H. Jones, the com-mander of the battalion and a legendary figure in the Parachute Regiment.

As captain of the team, I went to see him in his office.

'What can I do for you, Curtis?' he asked, looking up from his desk, on which a photograph of his family had pride of place.

'Thank you for seeing me, sir. I wanted to ask if some of the rugby team, a couple of sergeants and a corporal, could be left behind to play in the quarter-final of the Army Cup.'

He said: 'Curtis, if you wanted to join a famous rugby battalion you should have joined the Welsh Guards. This is the Second Battalion of the Parachute Regiment and in the Parachute Regiment you are a soldier first and a sportsman second.'

'Yes, sir.'

'Is there anything else?'

'No, sir.'

'Well, good luck then.'

I saluted and did an about-turn out of his office. It was the only time we spoke, and I respected his decision because he loved the battalion and soldiering above everything.

Ultimately, Colonel Jones did send two sergeants and two officers to bolster the side, but we lost a close game to the Gloucesters and were knocked out of the cup.

No-one realized at the time how vital the training in Kenya would prove to be. For six weeks we were put through a tortuous series of exercises at places like Nanuki and Impala Farm. I'd never experienced heat like it before.

Bob, who was basically an albino, found it particularly hard, much to Steve's amusement. He nicknamed him the Milky Bar Kid.

You don't get many coloured people in the Rhondda valley and the ones in Kenya were just about the first I'd ever seen apart from on the TV. That was one of the big attractions of the Army, experiencing different cultures, but you can take it too far.

While I was on guard duty one night with Steve and Bob, a young Kenyan came up to the fence with his sister, who was wearing a pair of wellington boots and an overcoat. She would have been about eighteen, I suppose, and this guy wanted to sell her for a right-angled army torch. Apart from the fact that she wasn't that good looking, we weren't about to give a torch away, so the two of them disappeared into the bush for a quick confab.

'OK, forget the torch,' he said when he returned. 'You can have her for the batteries.'

Our only time off in six weeks was for a few days before the final exercise. I found myself at Mombasa beach, about as far removed from the Rhondda as you can possibly get. We were put up in a tourist hotel and had a fantastic time, swimming, sunbathing and living like kings. This was where Cautious Bob confirmed his nickname, when Steve discovered that when consorting with the local lovelies he had insisted on wearing two condoms. 'Can't be too careful, mate!'

Kenya culminated in a low-level parachute descent onto a place called Archer's Post and then a tough approach tab across the desert. It was hotter than a snake's belly and blokes were collapsing all over the place from heat exhaustion.

Each company worked through a live-firing attack at night, and then we came together for one massive light battalion attack with the mortar and machine-gun platoons firing us in, along with artillery support.

The entire battalion seemed to gel in a peak performance. Plastered with sweat and dust, we gathered in the desert to hear from 5 Brigade's CO, Brigadier Tony Wilson. Geordie had a fag in his mouth, Bob still looked as white as a ghost, and Steve danced a little jig in the dust, still taking the piss.

I admired the brigadier, who had gone through P Company at the age of forty. 'You are a fearsome fighting unit,' he said proudly, 'and you're ready for action anywhere in the world.'

I spent Christmas at home in Rhondda. Since leaving, I'd taken every chance to get back and keep in touch with friends. They still seemed pleased to see me and I made sure not to use army slang or spend too much time talking about the Paras. Even so, I was sure they sensed that a part of me had changed and I'd never be just a valley boy again.

Liz had quite taken to the life of an army wife. She'd made friends with other wives and we'd normally go into town on weekends for a drink and a laugh. Cautious Bob took us up to the East End and we had a good old knees-up with his cockney mates.

In the New Year we began building up for a six-month tour to Belize in Central America. We were due to leave in April and were given a few weeks off beforehand. I took Liz off to Majorca – our first holiday abroad and her first trip in a plane.

'What's it like to parachute?' she asked as we were taking off.

'Look down,' I said.

She peered out the window and suddenly went very quiet.

We stayed in a hotel in Magaluf and next morning came downstairs to discover that the entire breakfast buffet had been eaten. Then I looked up and saw half a dozen lads from 2 Para's mortar platoon. By pure coincidence they'd booked a holiday at the same hotel. Thankfully, after two or three days they got thrown out because they ate too much. Finally we could get some breakfast.

It was a brilliant holiday, but the day before we were due to leave a telegram arrived at the hotel, recalling me to Aldershot.

'It's another bloody exercise,' I said to Liz. We decided to enjoy our last day rather than lose money forking out on a scheduled air ticket.

Flying home twenty-four hours later, the news came over the tannoy that Argentina had invaded the Falkland Islands.

Liz looked at me. 'Where are they?'

I shrugged. 'Somewhere off Scotland, I think.'

'What would the Argentinians want with Scotland?'

I couldn't answer and didn't understand what had happened until I managed to grab a day-old British newspaper. On 2 April an Argentinian invasion force had captured a British colony in the South Atlantic. A map showed a tiny cluster of islands next to Argentina.

There were also photographs of British Marines surrendering at Port Stanley and stories of the Moody Brook barracks being blown up. The British flag had been lowered and the governor, Rex Hunt, had been expelled.

Back at Aldershot I escaped a bollocking by telling them that I hadn't been able to get an earlier flight. No-one knew exactly what was happening, but I assumed that we'd be off to Belize as planned, since the advance party had already left.

Bob came sprinting into the block the next morning. 'The Marines and 3 Para are off to the South Atlantic!'

'What do you mean?'

'They're gonna kick the dagos out of the Falklands.'

He was grinning from ear to ear. Bob was the most right-wing person I'd ever met and he thought the sun shone out of Maggie Thatcher's arse. It was about the only thing that he and Steve agreed upon.

'What about us?' I asked, suddenly worried that we'd miss any action.

He shrugged. 'Don't worry, the colonel won't let us down.'

Bob was right. Colonel H. had been on a skiing holiday at the time of the invasion; it took some fierce lobbying on the telephone from his mountain chalet, but eventually he convinced the MoD that after the exercises in Kenya and the build-up for Belize we were the right battalion at the right time. If the Argentinians failed to withdraw from the Falklands, he said, then 2 Para were ready to make them.

On 9 April I watched events unfold on television as our sister battalion, together with 40, 42 and 45 Commando, Royal Marines, set sail from Southampton on the *Canberra*, a luxury cruise liner. A few days later our advance party was recalled from Belize, and we were put on seventy-two hours' standby.

'Bloody hell,' I said to Liz, 'it looks like I might be getting two overseas holidays this year.'

# 4

A FORTNIGHT LATER WE LEFT THE SHOT FOR PORTSMOUTH WHERE THE MV *Norland* was ready to sail for the South Atlantic. Liz gave me a big hug at the front door, squeezing me hard.

'Everything's going to be fine,' I said. 'We'll probably only reach the Isle of Wight before we turn around again.'

Down in the block, the lads were packing and repacking their kit. Jimmy Street and Geordie were cramming fags into their bergens, while Steve and Bob were doing their usual double act.

'What you gonna do if the boat sinks, Cautious?' said Steve, knowing Bob couldn't swim very well.

'Use your head as a float.'

'Fancy not being able to swim, eh? No wonder you don't like taking a bath.'

'Look who's talking. The last time someone had a wash in Yorkshire they declared a state of emergency.'

The three new lads – Mick Lax, Taff Hall and Merlin – were walking around wide-eyed. They'd only passed out of depot a week earlier. Taff made me laugh; he was from Newport and as daft as a fish. Mick was probably the quietest person I'd ever met and Merlin's body was just a life-support system for a pair of big, strange, hypnotic eyes.

The coach ride to Portsmouth on 26 April was like a rowdy trip to an away game. We were all in high spirits and eager to catch up with 3 Para who'd sailed seventeen days earlier. We'd drawn the short straw; fitters had worked around the clock to turn a North

Sea ferry into a troop carrier complete with helipad, but to my eyes the MV *Norland* still looked like one of the old coal steamers that used to moor in Cardiff Docks.

The battalion band was playing 'Ride of the Valkyries' as we stepped from the coaches. Shouts of 'Good luck, lads!' rang out from the crowd of loved ones and well-wishers, among them the workers who had defied all odds to get the ferry boat ready for war. As we walked up the gangplank many of the guys paused to wave, but I didn't bother looking for familiar faces in the throng. I'd asked Mum and Dad not to go to the effort of driving all that way, and Liz hadn't been able to get the day off work. Then, to the haunting strains of 'We Are Sailing', the ship pulled away from the quay and slowly moved out into the Solent; leaning on the rail with Cautious Bob, waving aimlessly at the crowd, I couldn't believe the patriotic fervour that had gripped the nation. After all, we were going to be back here again within the week.

B Company got the bottom of the boat – and I mean right at the bottom – well below the cargo hold and sea level. A Company were at the top, then D Company and C Company. Conditions were cramped with two per cabin. Me and Stevie bunked together, as did Cautious and Geordie. Poor Taff Hall got paired with Strasse, Jimmy Street, who smoked for Scotland.

Below decks the *Norland* smelled like my old rugby kitbag.

'I suppose it'll be all right for a day or two,' I said.

'What do you mean?' Stevie asked as he slung a holdall onto his bunk.

'Until the politicians sort their shit out and this whole thing blows over.'

'Let's hope – but I don't think so. You've seen the crowds in Buenos Aires cheering for that wanker Galtieri. They want blood, Mike.'

'As long as it's theirs, not ours,' I grinned.

'I'll go along with that. Right, I've had enough of this rabbit hutch already – let's go meet the neighbours.'

We found Cautious Bob looking suitably nervous. 'We're fucked if a missile hits us down here.'

'Trust you to look on the bright side,' said Steve.

'I'm gonna waterproof my fags then,' added Geordie.

Jimmy had already made Taff Hall his gofer. He chipped in, 'Yeah, you can do mine for me and all, Taff.'

It took a while to get used to the sights and sounds of the ship, where everything seemed to smell of oil and bilge water.

Inevitably, we had to line up for scoff three times a day.

'Join the Army and see a queue,' Stevie said.

For the first few days, we sorted out the admin and then our kit. Then the training started. The Army had just developed a new compact radio called the Clansman and compared to the old A41 it was all singing, all dancing – and best of all, it was light. Each day had a set programme of lectures and drills, many of them connected with the Clansman, mixed up with fitness and weapon drills, and lighter activities such as a battalion sports day with a tug of war and race around the ship. The weather was sunny and warm, and I had a holiday snap of Stevie and me taken together against the rails with the blue sea behind. 'Do us a copy for my mum,' Steve said. 'I want her to see how ugly you are.'

We spent many happy hours listening to the medics explain that under fire it would be extremely difficult to get a needle into the casualty's arm; the solution would be to stick a hose up his arse and administer the fluids that way. 'Any volunteers for a demonstration?' one of them asked, his eye landing on Bob.

'No fucking chance,' Cautious said. 'I wouldn't know where it had been.'

We did several crazy submarine drills in case the ship came under attack, which meant lying on the bed wearing your helmet and life-jacket. No-one took any notice and waited by the door ready to run out. To be honest, if a missile had hit the ship, B Company would have gone to Davy Jones's locker, without a doubt.

The further south we sailed, the more serious the training became. We had to balance the GPMGs to make sure they were firing on the right gas setting, zero the SLRs and test fire the M79s, which involved live-firing 40mm grenades off the back of the ship. The Norland's crew would dump large bin-liners of trash over the side and we'd use them as targets. Seagulls swooped on the garbage and occasionally they, too, came under fire. Each company was allocated an hour in the day to test fire its weapons and make the necessary adjustments.

Two Para carried twice as many GPMGs as normal because of a decision made by H. Jones. While planning for Belize, he decided to put all our GPMGs in the armoury and arrange for a new load for the tour. It meant that we finished up with twice as many gimpies as everyone else. With so much extra firepower, each section of 2 Para was split into half-sections, one with a corporal and the other with a lance-jack. Ultimately, this system proved to be so effective that it was to revolutionize the infantry.

After crossing the Equator, we all did a mortar-firing course. Everybody had to know how to step in, just in case the mortar platoon went down. These guys were a bunch of broken-nosed old veterans who were a law unto themselves. I knew most of them from the holiday in Majorca and because the platoon supplied the bulk of the battalion's rugby team – with the accent on 'bulk'. Mick Cotton, the SM in charge, had once tried to convince me to join the platoon and I gave it some serious thought because they were a great bunch of guys, extremely skilful and a close team.

The MV *Norland* was run by civvy merchant seamen and we built up a good rapport with them. One of them, nicknamed Wendy, was gay and a real character; he played the bar piano and had the mickey taken out of him mercilessly, but gave as good as he got. Most of the evenings were free, which gave us plenty of time to socialize, play cards, write letters home, or sing through a few Max Bygraves numbers with Wendy. Stevie and I would often slip upstairs to see Scouse Connell, who'd been posted to A Company, and my old depot mate Rocky, now in D Company.

In the last hour or so at night, sitting on my top bunk, I scratched out letters to Liz and my folks. In the bunk below, Stevie did the same to his family. We told them everything would be OK and the politicians would sort it out, yet secretly we wanted to kick ass.

People drifted in and out of cabins for a rap or to listen to music. Only Jimmy's and Taff's room was shunned by visitors. It always looked as if someone had dropped a smoke grenade in there. Jimmy would lie on the top bunk, ashtray on his chest, relating to Taff, in thick Glaswegian, all his exploits in the battalion.

Merlin, the guy with the strange eyes, and whose mother was a professional tarot reader, had started dabbling himself. The whole platoon was having a go, but I stayed well clear. 'Don't fuck with the unknown,' that was my motto. Cautious Bob also declined, on the usual grounds.

When Jimmy had a go, Merlin looked at the tarot cards and said he was going to have an accident within a few weeks.

Jimmy growled back, 'Cut the crap and get to the money bit, Merlin.'

A few days later I was lying on my bunk writing a letter when Stevie walked in looking very pissed off.

'What's the matter?'

'Merlin did the tarot for me,' he said. 'I turned up the death card.'

'Forget all that bollocks – you don't want to know!'

But I could see it preyed on Stevie's mind over the next few hours; his usual grin and banter were replaced by a thoughtful frown. In the end I was quite pleased when Ian Aird got wind of the tarot readings and knocked them on the head. Stevie brightened up, too. 'Reckon there'll be a duty-free at Ascension Island?' he asked.

'Why's that?'

'I'm hoping they sell voodoo dolls and I can get one with big bug eyes.'

At Ascension Island we stayed on the boat. The *Canberra* was moored just across from us and 3 Para had done some live firing and platoon attacks on land while waiting for us to catch up.

We sailed almost immediately. H. Jones had now joined us and we were complete as a battalion. A few days later I went up on deck and saw ships all around us, dozens of them steaming southwards through grey seas and pissing rain. That's when I realized: We're on our way, boyos – this is going to happen.

The seas grew rougher and most of us were sick. Regular guards were placed on deck, often in the wind and driving rain, keeping watch for Argentinian aircraft. Mostly we saw Russian 'bears' (observation aircraft), which were monitoring the British fleet. The armada must have looked impressive from the air.

The windows of the ship were taped up with bin-liners as blackout curtains, and all the briefings were now centred on the Falklands and going ashore. We knew that diplomatic relations between Britain and Argentina had broken down and Lord Carrington, the Foreign Secretary, had resigned. International efforts were being made to find a solution, with various peacemakers conveying proposals back and forth between London and Buenos Aires, but from our point of view we still had to be ready for war.

Dave Collins, a steely-eyed bastard, typified the spirit. He'd broken his ankle in a night drop shortly before the invasion and had cut the plaster off his leg before the ship sailed. He was determined not to miss the trip.

Collins looked like a paratrooper should – with short cropped hair, a big black moustache and the 1000-yard stare. A man of few words, he had his shit together and I'd learned a lot from him, stashing all the lessons away in my head.

Each night, Collins would get all the section into one of the cabins and give us a briefing for the following day. On the evening of 1 May he told us that the RAF had bombed airfields at Port Stanley and a place called Goose Green. Eyebrows were lifted and I thought, Fuck, this really is happening.

Two days later the *Belgrano* was sunk by a British submarine with the loss of hundreds of lives, which made me think all the more about our precarious position at the bottom of the *Norland*. Then, on 4 May, HMS *Sheffield* was hit by an Exocet missile; many Brits were killed and the burning ship was abandoned.

'Surely there's no turning back now,' Steve said.

The impact of these losses was reinforced when our OC, Johnny Crosland, told us that a Sea King helicopter had crashed off the Falklands and eighteen SAS lads had died. A few came from G Squadron, but the majority belonged to Mountain Troop, D Squadron.

Crosland summed up the general shock by saying, 'Come on, let's get stuck into the bastards. Let's do it for the lads who died.'

The last day on board was chaotic. There were people giving orders and hundreds of last-minute tasks. The radios were squared away and stores of ration boxes and winter-warfare clothing were issued.

We had five days' supply of compo boxes, broken down so that only the essentials were left – chocolate, rolled oats and chicken supreme. They were arctic rations, freeze-dried.

Dave Collins gave me 1,200 rounds of ammunition. I put 1,000 in my bergen, plus my rations and spare clothing. I split the other 200 rounds with half on my webbing and the rest on the GPMG ready to go. The bergen was an absolute nightmare. I didn't actually weigh it on scales but it must have tipped 100 pounds.

The ammunition had been distributed in a particular way. The GPMG gunners were to carry between 800 and 1,200 rounds, a load which would normally have been split amongst the sections. Being a big strapping lad, I carried the ammunition on my own, but avoided having to take the two mortar bombs others had to carry. I slightly overlooked the fact that the others could drop their bombs at the mortar line when they got ashore, immediately lightening their loads. I wouldn't have that luxury.

On top of this, we all had grenades – L2s and white phos – and 66mm anti-tank weapons which could be used against bunkers and light-skinned vehicles.

Before leaving the cabin, our section received our orders from Dave Collins; eight guys crowded into one cabin. 'The task force will approach the Falkland Islands from the north-east, as if we're heading for Stanley, as the Argentinians will expect. But we will veer westwards and make for Falkland Sound, then into San Carlos Water. We will land at Ajax Bay.'

A Company were to land first, at 0315 Zulu time on 21 May, followed by B Company. 'That's in just eight hours' time,' Collins added, in case we hadn't noticed. We were to get ashore and then tab as quickly as possible up Sussex Mountain, taking control of the high ground before digging in. The SBS (Special Boat Squadron) would be on the beach to meet us, designated by red headbands or a red torch.

There were more briefings upstairs, including one by a Royal Marines expert on the Falklands. Then we were to have some scoff and enforced rest before reporting back upstairs at eight o'clock that night.

All our civvies had to be packed away and labelled. Grenades had to be primed, and somebody joked that it was probably the first time anyone had put a fuse into an L2 aboard a North Sea ferry. Steve and I got all our kit together and tried to put on our bergens, rolling around like upturned turtles. I'd never carried a heavier load. With a bit of help, I staggered upstairs to the ball-room area, where we gathered in stick formation ready to go ashore – A, B, C, D and the HQ companies.

It was a bizarre setting. We were all crammed together, talking in whispers, with the lights dimmed and windows blacked out. Flashes of light from the naval guns briefly illuminated the darkness, each followed by an ominous boom. Cautious Bob and Steve Illingsworth were on either side of me. Stevie was quiet – unusual for him.

Little Mouse Walker, all 5 feet 4 inches of him, was dwarfed by his bergen. How the fuck does he manage it, I thought? He was looking after Mick Lax, the new lad, while Jimmy kept an eye on Taff. Jimmy lay back on his bergen, casually puffing away as if waiting for the next train to Glasgow.

We'd been on the 'floating kitbag' for almost four weeks now and just wanted to get off and go for it. The room stank of sweat, tobacco smoke and weapon oil. There was ammunition every-where and barely enough room to sit down.

The padre, David Cooper, who'd be coming ashore with us, con-ducted a service. It was a solemn affair and we sang several hymns and listened to him say that some of us wouldn't be coming back, or would be injured. Stevie and I exchanged a glance, and my mind strayed to wondering what my grandfather Dai Thomas had been thinking on the night before he fired his first shot in anger in the First World War. I was sure he'd have been just as anxious and homesick. I also imagined Liz and my parents watching the TV news, praying that the diplomats would sort out the dispute and prevent any more bloodshed. But the time for talking had run out.

Suddenly the piano struck up and Wendy burst into song. I couldn't believe it – there I was, ready for battle, while a homosexual played the piano and sang 'Roll out the Barrel'.

He continued singing knees-up songs until the order came for us to move downstairs to the landing craft. A Company went first, followed by B, in stick formation. With our bergens on, we all linked up like elephants, trunk to tail, each grabbing hold of the guy's webbing in front of us. Bob was ahead of me, Stevie behind. Nobody talked.

Down in the hold, the smells of diesel oil, sweat and cam cream were overpowering. It was so hot that sweat ran down my back between my bergen and smock. Cam cream stung my eyes, but I kept a hand on Bob and shuffled forwards.

The big door opened at the side of the cargo hold for us to exit. There was a flash in the night sky and a dull thud, then another, then another. If fear has a smell, I knew then what it was. I was inhaling it down in the blackness and heat of the hold.

At Ascension Island we'd all practised disembarking from the ship into landing craft, but that had been in calm seas during daylight. Now, in the South Atlantic, in the early hours of the morning, the waves were horrendous.

Nearing the door I saw flashes of automatic weapons in the distance and could make out the slopes of the hills, lit intermittently by explosions. Fanning Head was being attacked by naval guns that created sharp bursts of light all around us.

Suddenly, the landing craft was about 6 feet beneath me and pitching up and down in the swell. The guy despatching us, a Marine, held on to my webbing and I handed down my bergen. The trick was to wait until the landing craft rose up on a swell and then jump. In front of me, Cautious Bob mistimed it and fell more than 10 feet.

I timed it right, but still landed with a whack. Picking up my bergen and GPMG, I scrambled into stick formation and waited as the landing craft filled up.

The explosions in the distance seemed brighter. I was hunched between Mouse and Jimmy. We were all so knackered, Jimmy crashed out immediately and started snoring. I fell asleep on top of my bergen and when I woke the *Norland* was still there. Sea spray stung my cheeks and I could taste salt in my mouth.

'What the fuck's going on?' I muttered.

Steve explained that we'd been going round in circles.

Having spent six weeks on board the ship, it was weird seeing it from a landing craft, more or less at sea level. In the darkness it looked massive, like a dark shadow on the night sky. Around us I could make out the black hulls of other ships.

Confusion reigned. It was only later that I discovered there had been some kind of accident in the battalion, a lad breaking his ankle jumping into the landing craft. After a tense confab between the commanders, the message came through: 'You go ahead.'

B Company was now going to be first ashore. H. Jones seemed to be giving everyone a bollocking; his landing craft came next to ours and he shouted to Johnny Crosland to go for it.

Drenched in spray and packed together like sardines, we watched the beach come closer and I thought, If they open up on us now, we'll all die and there's nothing we can do about it.

Then I looked up and saw the stars, thousands and thousands of them glittering in the black velvet, and occasionally a shooting star, all so bright and low that it seemed possible to reach out and touch them.

Imagine finding beauty on a night like that.

# 5

THE ADRENALIN WAS PUMPING SO HARD THAT I DIDN'T FEEL THE COLD.
Huddled together, no-one said a word until the ramp went down
and water came pouring around our feet.

'Troops out!'

Nobody moved.

'Troops out!'

I couldn't fucking believe it. We were still 10 yards from the
beach and they wanted us to wade ashore with all our kit. The
landing craft were supposed to drop us on the beach, but there was
no way these guys were going that far; they were shitting themselves and just wanted out.

'Troops out! Troops out!'

Reluctantly we moved. I jumped out and sank up to my waist in
water that was so fucking cold it took my breath away. Little
Mouse Walker almost drowned. If anyone had fallen over, the
weight of his bergen would have taken him straight under.
Equally, if the Argentinians had been on the beach with machine-
guns, they'd have wiped us all out, no sweat.

On the beach we were met by the SBS, who couldn't believe we
had landed. Kneeling in the shingle, weighed down by a building
on my back, I heard one of them tell Crosland, 'We thought you
were coming on the twenty-fourth.'

The OC just shrugged and said, 'Par for the night.'

Cautious whispered to me, 'So much for storming the beach.'

Getting into all-round defence, we threw ourselves down on our bergens and covered the arcs. I was absolutely soaked through, drenched from the waist down with salt water and from the waist up with cold sweat.

After fifteen minutes we were ordered up and began the march up Sussex Mountain. B Company had the longest journey, having to reach a point nearest an area known as Goose Green, an outpost held by the Argentinians.

D Company led the way, followed by A and then B Company. After weeks at sea, it felt good to be on land, but this was boggy, squelchy, putrid-smelling ground. Lurching forward through the muck, people kept falling over, causing the entire battalion snake to constantly stop and start.

Gradually we climbed and the footing grew firmer. I kept telling myself, 'Don't let your knees buckle, you won't get back up.'

Before dawn, we reached the mortar line where the lucky lads carrying bombs could leave them with the mortar platoon – but I still had 1,200 rounds about me. My neck and guts were killing me because of the weight and having to tense my stomach muscles.

All the briefings had talked about the freezing conditions we'd face, so we were done up in our thermals and with this exertion were now sweating our balls off. The sodden underwear felt like chain mail hanging off every limb. At the same time, our socks and boots were soaked from the landing and there was no time to change. It was a ludicrous decision to have sent us ashore with all our kit. The helicopters could have flown the bergens up the mountain underslung in a net the next day.

The stick formation soon broke down and it was each man for himself climbing the mountain. I was in a world of hurt, desperately trying to hold on. I looked back and spied Bob in agony. Further behind him someone stumbled. Was it Steve?

As the first chinks of daylight began showing, the sky was grey against the dark outline of the mountain.

I caught up with Tony Blythe, a half-caste kid from London who was one of the fittest men in the company. By now he was just a brown ball of sweat.

'I'm fucked, Mike,' was all he could say.

'C'mon, let's do it together.'

We began working as a pair. Tony would set off, I'd have a couple of minutes' breather, and then I'd catch up with him at his next stop. My legs cramped up every time.

As it grew brighter, we were three quarters of the way up the mountain, having broken the back of the tab. I looked down to see the Marines and 3 Para landing below us.

At about 5 a.m. we were nearing the top and I heard a shout. Looking down the valley, I could see a parachute open. Somebody's had a result, I thought.

Suddenly another jet, which I recognized as a Skyhawk, came screaming over us and banked so close I could see the pilot's face. The crescendo of noise cut the grunting, tabbing noises like a punch in the head from a 16-stone prop forward. Completely shocked, I simply stared and blinked. Nobody did anything. The Argentinian pilot must have been just as shocked – looking down to find a massive landing force beneath his fuselage.

Tony was quite a way in front of me and Bob behind; I was on my own. As another jet screamed in, I slipped off the safety catch and let rip with the gimpy. It was the first time I'd fired the gun without ear defenders and the noise was like a thunderous, mechanical scream, as if a pneumatic drill was ripping through sheet-metal plates.

Then total silence again; the tranquillity of the hill.

I'd fired a hundred rounds and missed the jet by a country mile. Falklands Lesson Number One – to hit anything travelling that fast you have to fire at least a football field in front of it.

Everyone looked around a bit sheepishly as we reloaded, then there was a shout from above: 'Keep going!'

At the top of the mountain, B Company were allocated our defensive positions, and then it was a case of digging in as best we could. The ground was like concrete, with white rock just a foot or so below the surface. This meant we'd have to utilize the natural defences on the hill. As I jabbed my entrenching tool at the unyielding earth I looked down the mountain at the ships anchored below us. The *Canberra*, white and stately, looked so out of place; she should have been moored against a sunny backdrop of palm trees in the Caribbean, not the bleak greyness of San Carlos Water, surrounded by warships.

Two Para was an attacking battalion rather than a defensive one, but we still had to know how to dig in. After working underground, I knew all about it and was probably the only guy to arrive in the Falklands with knee pads. Dad had got them from work; guys laughed at me but it was a damned sight easier to dig on your knees than to stand up and double over.

Bob, Stevie and I built a trench-cum-sangar (protected trench) out of the natural rock; we could erect a poncho behind it at night,

73

or have it slung low during the day with our bergens underneath.

With the GPMGs sited around the defensive position, it was time to sort out personal admin. There's an old army adage, 'First my weapon, then my body.' So I cleaned my gimpy before sorting out the other kit. The arctic clothing had to come off, but there was no chance of getting it dry.

'Will you look at these,' said Bob, peeling off his socks. His feet were wrinkled and turning blue.

'Same here,' I said, gently examining my blisters.

Dry socks were at a premium and putting a clean, dry pair on talcum-powdered feet was the absolute dog's bollocks. Of course, the effect was lost somewhat when you then had to put them into wet boots. Our standard DMS boots were like sodden cardboard that soaked up water and were constantly wet. Some lads' feet were fucked within days in the freezing conditions.

One trick was to put the wet socks down your underpants, close to the family jewels, which dried them out. The medics on board ship had also recommended using a buddy system, cuddling up and putting your feet under the other person's armpits. Stevie and I were fine with this, but Cautious Bob had a thing about homosexuals and he wouldn't let anyone near him.

'You can't be too careful, mate,' he muttered.

Sussex Mountain could well have been the Brecon Beacons, they looked so similar. It was strange being so far from home and the scenery looking the same, with gorse and heather, purples and browns.

B Company was perched high above a valley, with San Carlos Water to our left and D Company on the far side. Late that first afternoon the Argie jets screamed down the valley between our positions – blink and you'd miss them – hitting the ships in San Carlos Water, then screaming away. Being so high up, we had a grandstand view. This set the precedent for the following days.

The SAS gave us advance notice that the jets were coming. 'Air raid, warning red!' on the radio meant we had about two minutes before the Mirages, Skyhawks, Pucaras and Super Etendards came down 'Bomb Alley'. Then it was a free-for-all with everyone opening up as they thundered past.

On that first day, HMS *Ardent* and *Antrim* took direct hits; twenty sailors were killed.

Basically, we had no ground-to-air capability apart from a Blowpipe detachment who were right in front of our positions. Talk about a waste of space – these guys couldn't hit a barn door if it fell on them. Even so, I had a lot of admiration for the Argie pilots; considering how much small-arms firepower we threw at them, their success rate was quite phenomenal.

Our platoon's stag position faced towards 'virgin ground' to our front, covering an arc that linked up with 6 Platoon to our right. We had the task force behind us, increasing the importance of keeping watch for any wandering Argie patrols or attacks.

Two of us would be on stag for two hours and then one would go back to wake up the next pair for their shift. As any soldier will tell you, this is definitely the worst part of the job – being woken from a deep sleep and leaving the big, fat, warm, green maggot (doss bag) to brave the elements. Two hours of freezing rain, hailstones the size of lumps of coal and wind that howled through the valley flinging ponchos into the night; it was a fucking nightmare. By the end of the shift, the GPMG felt like a big lump of freezing metal, with the ammo link iced up as it hung outside the feed tray. And each time I got back into my fat warm maggot, the damp from my boots and trousers would make the bag wetter and wetter until after five days it was soaked right through.

One horrendous night I went back to wake up Taff Hall and Jimmy Street. It was matt black on the mountain and the stag position was about 50 metres away from their basha (shelter). In the sleet and howling wind, my teeth were chattering like a mechanical monkey bashing his fucking drum.

Some blokes react violently when they wake up – Jimmy was like that; he'd rip out of his doss bag, snarling. Taff was the opposite; he was docile as a puppy. After some violent shaking, he finally woke.

'Taff, Taff, you're on stag.'

No answer. Taff was in a coma. He just looked at me groggily, miles away, on another planet.

'Taff, you're on stag.'

'I'm on stag?'

'Yeah.'

'Me, I'm on stag?'

Losing my patience: 'No, I tell a lie; it's not you, it's Gary Glitter.'

'He can't be,' said Taff. 'He's not in this basha.'

Finally I snapped and dragged him out into the rain to wake him properly.

Jimmy and Taff did their two hours and then Taff was sent back to wake the next pair for the last stag. Although it was only 50 metres away, Taff got disorientated in the darkness and wandered past our position, getting lost on the mountain.

Meanwhile, at the stag position, Jimmy couldn't leave until Taff returned. He'd been there for over two hours and his feet were like lumps of frozen concrete.

Taff eventually turned up at our basha and woke Bob and me – the wrong pair. Cautious was on his way out of his doss bag when he looked at his watch and realized the time. He threw a track with Taff, calling him every fucking name he could think of, but that was mild compared to what Jimmy had to say when he finally got relieved.

The next day we rigged up some comms – nothing more elaborate than a piece of paracord – linking the stag position to the trenches so no-one would go missing again.

Our small cookers burned blocks of hexamine and the rations contained high sulphur matches that could light the blocks in wet and cold conditions anywhere on earth – except, it seemed, the Falklands. Entire boxes of matches were wasted in the wind and it became an art form to light the hexy blocks in three or four goes.

So that we could operate the weapons effectively most of us had cut the fingertips off our leather gloves, but now they were numb through. I held my fingers over the cooker as I warmed up some scoff.

'Ever noticed how the rain always seems to stop when Merlin's on stag,' said Stan the Man.

'Yeah. It's fucking amazing.'

'Makes you wonder, doesn't it?'

Others had also started to notice and this only enhanced the myth growing around Merlin as our wizard in the platoon.

On the Sunday, three days after landing, I looked up and saw a band of what looked like gypsies walking over the hill towards us. They were different from any soldiers I'd seen before in the British army. They had long hair, beards and no head-dress, just bobble hats. They were also older than most of us toms – in their late twenties or thirties.

As soon as they came up the hill, I guessed they were SAS. I got a good look and these guys were impressive. They had grenades and ammunition link hanging off them and looked like Che Guevara's men with their beards and long hair.

They'd come over to see Johnny Crosland for a confab. Dave Collins knew two of them as old sweats from B Company. 'Andy Kain's ex-mortar platoon,' he said, 'and Matt Loftus is ex-human race. Fearsome reputation as a hard bloke and all-round nasty bastard.'

An air-raid warning red sounded and a Pucara roared down the valley. As expected, we started firing, but the SAS guys had their own system. One of them got down on his knees and another lad put a GPMG on his back and used him as a tripod, spinning and keeping the jet in the sights.

At the same time, cool as you like, a New Zealander, 'Kiwi' Howard, nonchalantly lifted a Stinger missile launcher onto his shoulder, took aim and fired. The missile tore through the air and blew the jet clean out of the sky. The pilot ejected and drifted down to be captured. It was one of the most awe-inspiring things I'd ever seen.

Although I'd heard stories and knew guys in the battalion who were training to join the SAS, this was the first time I'd seen them up close and I realized immediately how different they were to the rest of us. They'd just shot down a Pucara and shrugged it off as if they were shelling peas.

As they disappeared over the hill again, they looked like the bandits you see in Westerns, stinking, dirty and bedraggled. Yet they had an air about them that I'd never forget. We carried the same weapons and rations, but they were men and we were boys.

Dave Collins told me they were from 16 (Air) Troop and 18 (Mobility) Troop. 'You want some of that?' he asked.

I nodded.

'Twice I tried,' he said. 'The mountains fucked me both times. You think of the hardest day you've ever had in the Army – P Company, tabbing up the mountain here – then you times that by ten and you get some idea of what it's like on Selection.'

'Are you saying I shouldn't do it?'

'Hell no. You should have a go. Let's just take one war at a time.'

Later I spoke to Stevie about it and he, too, seemed interested. Yet we couldn't get our heads around the fact that Collins had failed Selection. In our eyes he was the dog's bollocks – if he couldn't make it, what chance did we have?

By Monday 24 May, after five days on the mountain, the frustration began to show. We were wet, dishevelled and constantly cold, trying to keep our feet dry in sodden boots. Tony Blythe, Big Steve King and young Micky White had all gone down with trench foot and were shipped off to Ajax Bay in San Carlos Water for treatment. This put the platoon three down already.

HMS *Antelope* had been hit the previous day and was still burning. Bob and I were on stag in the early hours of Monday morning

– a surprisingly calm night – when a massive flash of light lit up the sea below us.

'She's gone,' he muttered as we watched the flames disappear beneath the surface.

'I can't watch much more of this,' I said, looking at the silhouettes of the fleet. 'What are we doing here? We should be pushing towards Stanley.'

'This weather's fucking us up – we're all going down here. I want to get stuck into the Argie wankers.'

All of us felt the same and the frustration mounted as the Argie jets screamed down the valley every few hours and delivered a severe pounding to the ships below. Realistically we didn't have the weaponry to stop them.

After six days, the waiting ended. New orders came through that we were to retake Goose Green from the Argentinians.

'Where's Goose Green?' asked Taff.

'Doesn't sound very important,' echoed Geordie.

Steve said, 'Who gives a shit – at least we get off this hill.'

Dave Collins brought the section together for a briefing.

'Goose Green is here,' he said, pointing to a map, 'about twenty-five clicks to the south-east of here.' It was the same direction the SAS had arrived from.

'There's an Argie garrison stationed at the town and this is a runway that the Pucara jets are using. You've seen the damage – you know the threat. We're going to attack with the battalion and take the town.'

Steve's and Bob's faces lit up.

'A battalion attack!' Stevie whispered to me.

'Yeah, let's get the fuckers!' echoed Bob.

It looked like a long march and the plan was to leave the bergens behind and tab in fighting order. 'Bullets and bombs only,' Collins emphasized.

I packed away my green maggot, now not much more than a soggy lump of feathers. It was a shame because the sun had come out and I could have done with drying the bloody thing.

Waiting to move off the hill, the lads were lying about, catching some Zs, smoking and having a laugh. The valley looked beautiful with lots of browns and greens. Although still cold, I could feel the warmth on my face. Jimmy and Geordie puffed away, Steve was still teasing Taff about his midnight walk and Cautious Bob, true to form, was repacking his kit, waterproofing his matches and checking his feet.

I'd become the 2 i/c of the section. Dave Collins, the section commander, had been told he couldn't make the tab because of the ankle he'd busted parachuting. He'd gone over on it again soon after we landed, but somehow had still managed to climb Sussex Mountain. It hadn't mended properly since then and he was gutted.

We'd already lost Tony Blythe, the 2 i/c, with trench foot. Neil Dance, a lance-jack, was promoted to corporal and transferred over as our new section commander, while I became a lance corporal in the field and his number two.

On 26 May, at last light, we were setting off for Goose Green. Just before leaving, each platoon put their bergens together to be collected and transported forward to Goose Green after the battle. Then we waited, eager and apprehensive, for the order to move out. Suddenly, Ian Aird, the papa sierra (platoon sergeant), announced the operation had been postponed for twenty-four hours.

The air turned blue.

'Ah well, at least I can dry the doss bag,' I said.

Twenty-four hours later we set off in stick formation in a regimental snake towards Goose Green. D Company had already gone ahead during the day as a forward recce unit, and B Company brought up the rear.

We travelled light with arctic rations on our beltkit – a brew kit, biscuits, chocolate and paste. The rest of our smock and webbing was crammed with L2, smoke and white phos grenades, and mini-flares. Slung over our shoulders were 66mm anti-tank rockets and link for the gimpies, draped like bandoliers.

After a week of being wet and cold, it was good to be moving and get the blood flowing again. The stars were out, thousands of them, and occasionally I could see one shooting across the sky. As the temperature fell, the grass started crunching underfoot and I could see the frosty imprints left behind.

Being at the back end of a battalion snake is a pain in the arse because when someone stops up front, everyone stops. You don't know if it's going to be for a minute, ten minutes or half an hour, but the trick is to get down and get as much rest as you can.

Each time we lay on the chilled ground, body heat evaporated quickly and the sweat on our backs soon turned to ice. We were getting cold again and starting to freeze. Just when the wind was slicing you to the bone, the message came down the line, 'Prepare to move.' This stop and start cycle went on through the night.

We were making our way more or less due south along a track to a place called Camilla Creek House, which was little more than a set of farm buildings on the outskirts of Goose Green. Ahead of us, D Company was to set up a defensive position for the rest of the battalion.

On a long tab, it's best not to think about the distance ahead. Once you start counting minutes or kilometres you begin feeling sorry for yourself and get tired quickly. Instead, I thought of Liz and my mum and dad back home in Rhondda. Summer was on its way there and I imagined all the things I'd do when I got home – going down the coast to Porthcawl, or to a beautiful spot called Caswell Bay near Swansea. Another 5 clicks disappeared.

Stevie, just in front of me, turned and grinned at me from time to time. One look would say it all: 'What the fuck are we doing here?' But to be truthful we wanted to be there. The cause was just, even if the real estate was a freezing, bog-infested shit-hole.

'What are you thinking of?' he asked during one of the un-scheduled stops.

'Home.'

'Yeah, me too. You're gonna love Donny (Doncaster). It's a magic place. You'll get on famously with the family – they've got a lot of time for miners.'

Through chattering teeth we swapped stories about Doncaster and the Rhondda, both of us fiercely proud of our heritage. Mouse Walker, beside me, had pulled his Para smock right up to his helmet and had his knees tucked up; he looked like a little garden gnome on his toadstool.

On the move again, we crossed a river that was partly frozen over and a few minutes later the message was passed up through the company: 'Last man's crossed.'

Soon afterwards we stopped again, this time for ages.

'What the fuck's up now?'

'I'll ask ahead,' said Stevie.

Taff, up ahead in our section, said to him, 'Maybe it's because of the message you just passed up.'

'What message?'

'Last man's lost.'

In the grand tradition of 'Send three and fourpence' Taff had misheard and severely fucked up. Stevie immediately passed another message forward saying the last man had now caught up. The fuck-up was kept in-house, but Taff felt the wrath of the lads in the section at every opportunity.

Just short of Camilla Creek House, I was shaken out of a sunny day on the South Wales coastline by the screeching sound of incoming artillery. A burst of five or six rounds hit the concrete-hard ground over to our left, *thud, thud, thud* . . . Everyone got down on one knee and waited. Nothing; silence. 'Prepare to move!' came the order.

Crosland walked down the line towards us and spoke to Geordie Vale.

'Do you know what that is, Geordie?' he asked, pointing to the crater that had been formed by an earlier round, the brown earth spilling out onto the white frost blanket.

'Yes, sir,' said Geordie. 'That, sir, is a fucking big hole.'

Crosland laughed. 'I can't argue with that.'

Although we were in no danger, the short attack had a sobering effect, because it confirmed that the Argentinian forces at Goose Green were supported by artillery.

At Camilla Creek House, the whole battalion managed to fit inside the main house and outbuildings, although one Argentinian bomb would probably have taken out most of us.

B Company were given one of the small outhouses, with 4 and 6 Platoons inside and 5 Platoon in the adjoining sheep pen. We were crammed in together, arms and legs entwined; if one person moved the rest of us had to do the same.

'Sardines with red berets,' said Stevie.

Jimmy Street was snoring for Glasgow; I guessed he felt at home in the pen.

Then I started giggling. 'Last man's lost!' Soon Stevie joined in. Taff glowered in the corner.

Stevie found an old fleece that had obviously been sheared and tossed aside. It was stinking and dirty but we put it over the two of us and cuddled together for warmth.

There were two-hour stags; a pair of lads from each platoon had to walk round and round the outhouses like Indians thrown out of the teepee. When it was my turn, I slung the gimpy across my back and hugged myself to keep warm. In the starlight, the frosted farm-yard looked like a scene from a Christmas card. Yet all I could think about were my feet, now in rag order, with the toes throbbing and growing numb. We'd come in fighting order, no arctic kit, no doss bags, and I was fucking freezing.

'Bullets and bombs,' I muttered to myself, listening to Jimmy's snores inside his little sty.

As dawn arrived on the 27th, we moved out into a field adjacent to Camilla Creek House. The sun came out periodically throughout the day as we waited for our orders to move towards Goose Green, now just a few miles away. In the meantime we alternated between doing stag and munching what rations we had on our beltkit. Being so close to the enemy, there was no brewing up or cooking, and instead we had to make do with biscuits, chocolate, peanuts and raisins.

I was lying between Bob and Steve and could feel their breathing as they dozed; it was a nice secure feeling. I looked up at the clouds; the sky looked beautiful. In the distance I could hear the sound of a helicopter I didn't recognize – which probably meant it wasn't one of ours.

During the morning two Harriers screamed overhead in the direction of Goose Green and seconds later we heard explosions. In the afternoon came the sound of automatic weapons, followed later by sporadic shots. Shortly afterwards the Patrols Platoon returned with several Argentinian prisoners, caught in a Land Rover when they came out to investigate reports of British troop movements. As the hooded soldiers were marched past my position on their way to interrogation by our Spanish linguist, a Royal Marine, I got my first sight of Argentinian infantrymen. Up until then, I'd only seen pilots baling out of burning jets.

'Get a load of the parkas,' said Bob, enviously.

'I'd give my right arm for one of those,' I said.

'And look at their boots.'

'Maybe he'd sell them to me,' I suggested.

'Maybe he'd swap them for those lovely knee pads.'

Later that day we heard about a BBC World Service announcement. To our horror, the broadcast had stated that a parachute battalion was poised to attack the settlement of Goose Green. None of us could believe the crass incompetence of the British government in pinpointing our presence to the enemy.

Within an hour we could hear Hueys and Chinooks over Goose Green, obviously bringing in reinforcements to the Argentinian garrison. Until then, G Squadron, SAS, who provided the OPs, had said there was only a company of Argentinians at Goose Green; now, thanks to the World Service broadcast, the estimate of enemy strength was being put at about 2,500.

Lying in the grass next to Bob, I began to feel apprehensive.

Slowly it sank in that within a few hours I would actually be going into battle for the first time.

'What happens if one of us gets shot?' I asked.

'We'll help each other out,' said Bob. 'I wouldn't leave you behind.'

'And I wouldn't leave you behind,' I said.

'It's not going to happen to us, anyway.'

'Why's that?'

'You know what they say – only the good die young. We're going to live to be a hundred.'

Neil Dance, the new section commander, was a bit of a space cadet, but nonetheless a good soldier. I still wasn't happy about losing Dave Collins, someone I trusted totally to make the right decisions in the heat of battle. Neil was only a year or so older than me, but I thought, Fuck it! In for a penny, in for a pound; we'll look after each other.

The sun had set when we came together as a platoon and then as a company. Johnny Crosland briefed us wearing his trademark black woolly hat – he never wore a helmet – and told us that we were going to be up against it.

'There's hundreds of the bastards, but you're the best there is,' he said. 'You're the Parachute Regiment, and we've been through a lot just to get here. I want to remind you of just one thing – I might have the initials J.C., but you've still got to look after yourselves . . .'

Our orders were to clear the SF (sustained fire) positions that protected Goose Green, so we knew that meant attacking machine-guns. Having taken out these positions and reached a place called Boca House, we were to remain in reserve for an attack on the schoolhouse at Goose Green.

'It's not going to be easy and that's why we were chosen,' said Crosland, 'because we're Paras and they know we're going to get stuck in. If we hit these bastards hard enough, make no mistake, they'll fold. So let's go kick their fucking arses.'

With those words echoing in our ears, we moved out onto the track and headed towards Goose Green.

# 6

IT WAS NOW COMPLETELY DARK. LIGHT RAIN BEGAN FALLING AS I TABBED
down the hill with Cautious Bob ahead of me and Stevie behind.
As the ground flattened out we approached a small river and
heard a thundering that sounded like a waterfall or flash flood.

'What the fuck is that?' said Bob.

It sounded as if the entire Argentinian army had upped sticks
and was running towards us.

Then suddenly, out of the darkness, came a herd of wild horses
that charged across the bridge in front of us. It looked surreal, the
white of the horses against the black mountainside. Something
had frightened them and sent them straight towards us. Seeing the
battalion snake, they stopped in their tracks and darted off in
the opposite direction.

'Obviously, their lead scout isn't wearing PNGs (passive night
goggles),' said Steve.

I gripped my gimpy tightly and moved forwards, stepping on
something lying on the ground. When it uttered a sound, I almost
blew its bloody head off. A support company sergeant from one of
the other platoons had fallen and twisted his ankle. No-one had a
chance to warn us he was there. My nerves frayed a little further.

We carried on, climbing a small hill. No-one was allowed to talk
except in a hushed whisper to the guy next to him and then he would
pass the message down the line. After crossing another little bridge
we climbed to where Patrols Platoon were laying out the start line. I
was breathing quite hard, through fear more than anything else.

Four platoon were down to my left, 6 Platoon to my right and 5 Platoon lay in the centre and just slightly to the rear of them, ready to flank left or right depending on the tactical situation. Meanwhile, A Company bypassed us, tasked with taking out Darwin Hill to our left.

I picked out the shape of Big Scouse Connell, now transferred to A Company. He was massive; it had to be him. I whispered to myself, 'Go get 'em, Scouse.'

As we lay down at the start line, it began to snow. I could feel the flakes brush my eyelashes and cheeks. The pitch blackness made it impossible to see what lay ahead, but I could smell wood smoke from the fires. For a fleeting second it brought back childhood memories of our little street gang burning our bonfire on 5 November, when the whole street would turn out. A smile passed my lips; that seemed a lifetime ago and a whole other world away.

Another smell assaulted me – human excreta. The Argentinian infantry obviously didn't place much store on latrines. Dirty bastards. We must be close to them now, I thought.

According to the OPs there were two sustained fire positions about 150 metres directly in front of us, and after the tip-off by the World Service the Argentinians would surely be expecting visitors.

They were. After lying there for an age I suddenly saw tracer to my left and heard the sound of automatic weapons. A Company had been spotted and the enemy had opened fire on them from about 200 metres away. Nobody said anything; perhaps we were equally spellbound by the sight of red tracer ricocheting off rocks and spiralling into orbit. Because everybody aims high at night, some of the rounds were zinging over the top of A Company and falling towards us. I thought, Shit, we're going to get killed at the start line. Then, overhead, came the whirr of rounds from our indirect fire-support ship, HMS *Arrow*, and explosions as they crashed into Goose Green and Darwin.

Long sustained bursts from the gimpies and single shots from our SLRs vibrated around the hills. My heart was beating hard against the frozen earth. I peered forward into the gloom, my tongue wetting dry lips. There was a hill to our right as the ground rose up and fell away slightly to the left. Other than that, just blackness. The snow had turned to sleet and my feet were in tatters again.

'It's our turn next,' I said to myself. 'It's probably going to be up close; you'll have to kill or be killed; there's no backing down.'

We lay for a long time listening to the battle to our left. Finally Crosland gave the order, 'C'mon, let's go.'

I looked at my watch; it was exactly 0300 hours GMT. From the start line to Boca House was about 5 clicks. Our orders were clear: 'Destroy all in the way,' Crosland said.

I couldn't feel my legs. Whether it was the cold, or fear, or a mixture of both, I didn't know, but I couldn't feel them. My fingers, too, were numb, and I found it hard to locate the safety button on the gimpy. I kept thinking, Shit, I wish I was five feet tall instead of six feet plus; they're sure to be aiming at me, because I'm the biggest fucker in B Company. That's what I'd do if I was a sniper – go for the biggest body mass.

There was an immense flash of light overhead as illuminating mortar rounds exploded, followed by a whirr of heavy ordnance and the crunch of explosions in front. I saw 4 and 6 Platoons directly in front of me, weapons in hand, helmets on and walking in an extended line – almost like a grainy First World War newsreel of soldiers advancing towards the enemy. Most of the lads had bayonets fixed on their rifles and, looking up and down the line, it was an awesome sight as they moved forward across the frozen mud and grass.

The artillery rounds screamed and screeched through the air like giant insects before crashing into the ground in front of us in massive explosions. Then, suddenly above us, more illuminating rounds erupted, turning night into day. This completely fucked everybody up because they screwed up your night vision. When the darkness descended again it appeared even blacker than before.

I was breathing hard, exhaling to calm my nerves and gritting my teeth. With eyeballs on stalks, I scanned left, right and in front of me.

Increasingly the ground began to slope up on the right. This had the effect of channelling 4, 5 and 6 Platoons slightly towards the flatter ground. To my front and left, a blaze of firepower exploded out of the darkness. Six Platoon had come under attack. We all went to ground initially and then 4 Platoon opened up on all fronts. As ordered, 5 Platoon held back, ready to support or go to either flank.

Squashed flat against the frozen ground, I could feel my heart pounding despite the incredible noise. Then, during a lull in the gunfire, I heard voices to my right. Although muffled, I could have sworn they were speaking Spanish.

I crawled slowly over to Ian Aird, the platoon sergeant.

'I can hear somebody speaking Spanish – I'm sure there's a position on our right-hand side.'

'Jesus! Are you sure?'

Having just got back from hearing the lingo in Majorca, I said, 'Pretty sure.'

We had expected to find an enemy position further up on our right, but now it appeared that we might have advanced too far. The danger lay in being hit from the side while on open ground.

Ian Aird reported my concern to Lieutenant Weighell and orders came back from Crosland for 5 Platoon to move right, tabbing onto higher ground and attacking any enemy positions.

As we swung over to the right of the hill we found a number of trenches, all of them vacated; to me they looked like graves. We continued on our axis, and at that moment the hill in front of us erupted; we all hit the deck as the lead hornets zipped above our heads. Mouth dry, palms sweating, I watched the green tracer zap so close I could have reached up and touched it.

The tell-tale muzzle flashes of the Argentinian machine-guns gave us a target and we let loose. We broke up into sections and then half sections. From the amount of enemy fire, it seemed likely that some of the nearest trenches might be unmanned, and I began to think that maybe what I'd heard was a radio left behind and a message transmitted in Spanish. Neil Dance told Cautious Bob and me to check it out.

Hunched low, we skirted 10 yards, Bob taking the left-hand side.

Behind us, 6 Platoon were still engaged in their contact and 4 Platoon were firing ahead of us. Despite the darkness and deafening noise, everyone seemed to know his place in the organized chaos. Star shells cascaded above us and the last embers of light were still burning when we reached the first trench, casting an eerie glow.

Gimpy and SLR fire was continuous. A grenade rocked the earth in front of me. Artillery rounds sucked the air out of the atmosphere as they screamed over our heads.

I swung the gimpy into the trench and found a guy sitting down, facing me. He lifted his head and looked at me as though I'd interrupted his quiet time. He had a poncho around him and didn't appear to have a weapon. The sight of him was so bizarre that Bob could have been a thousand miles away. I was totally engrossed by the man in the trench.

I didn't know what to do. For a split second I hesitated. It was snowing. I was soaking wet, a million miles from home. I was looking at him; he was looking at me.

Then, as the illuminating rounds dimmed to nothing, there came a vicious spit of flame and a deadly rattle from the back of the trench. A second Argentinian, hidden beneath a stretched poncho, had opened up with an automatic. The rounds zipped past my head to the left and I thought, Fucking hell, I've killed Bob – my delay has cost a mate his life.

Opening up with the gimpy, I put at least thirty or forty rounds down, killing the first guy and the bloke behind him, who was still firing as he fell.

Pulling that trigger was the hardest thing I'd ever done. Forget parachuting. Forget P Company. Forget anything else. That moment there, that decision, that was the hardest. And because I had hesitated in making it, one of my best mates was probably dead.

I turned, expecting the worst, but Bob hadn't been hit. He was on my left and, miraculously, the fire had gone smack between the two of us. I could have hugged him.

There would be no more hesitation.

By this time we'd started taking incomers from Argentinian positions further back and Crosland wanted 5 Platoon to take out various depth positions. He fired some tracer from his weapon to give us a guide. I didn't know what 4 and 6 Platoons were doing, but they now had to look after themselves – in this gutter-type fighting the first priority is to protect your own little gang.

Skirmishing forward, we got to within 50 yards of the depth positions – firing and moving, firing and moving – initially in section strength, until we broke down into half sections on the perimeter of a number of trenches.

The first attempts at clearing them had little impact. After we laid down some fire on each trench, Neil Dance's half section went forward and threw L2 grenades into it. These proved to be worse than useless and the Argentinians were soon firing back at us with machine-guns and FN rifles. With the weight of fire they threw up, fuck knows how none of us got killed.

Taff Hall was letting rip with his rifle to the right. I screamed across to Bob on my left, 'Throw us some link!' He was my number two on the gun and carried bandoliers across his chest.

I grabbed it and connected it to the link hanging out of my GPMG's feed tray, then I kept firing bursts at the positions ahead. The air stank of cordite and I could taste it in my mouth, mixed with

88

the bitter taste of gas and oil. My ears were ringing, but I still heard the screamed instructions from our lads. There appeared to be cohesion, but I was fucked if I knew what was happening elsewhere. The whole world appeared to be at war.

We were getting shot to shit and could barely see what we were supposed to be hitting. Behind me, Jimmy was throwing illuminating rounds down his 2-inch mortar. Each time we'd get about ten or fifteen seconds of light over our position. Ian Aird fired the M57, *boom boom boom*, at one trench – unable to hear any instructions I just followed his aim.

Meanwhile, the incomers rained down and grenade explosions hurled clods of earth into the air. Having no luck with the L2 grenades, some of the lads began throwing Willie Petes (white phos grenades) into the Argie trenches. In a blinding flash, the chemicals burned and we heard the screams.

It might not have been Geneva Convention, but at last we'd discovered an effective system of clearing the trenches. Everyone had seen; almost immediately the gimpies started laying down fire and a couple of lads scurried forward and threw more Willie Petes. As the phos grenades exploded in the confines of a 6 foot by 2 foot trench, anyone inside was going to burn. Then we put down a weight of fire against the trench and the nearest two or three guys got to the edge and fired inside.

After almost losing Cautious Bob, I knew it was either us or them, and I wanted to make sure my little gang were OK. It wasn't a case of not taking prisoners; I simply didn't see anybody with their hands up.

We were using classic infantry tactics – just like we'd practised over and over again on Salisbury Plain and at Sennybridge in Wales. But everything you do on training exercises, even in darkness, is all neat and precise; when it comes to doing it for real, it's incredibly confusing. The textbook drill of 'dash . . . down . . . crawl . . . sights . . . observe . . . and fire' goes out of the window.

As you start taking real live incomers and rounds are zipping about your helmet as you crawl along, you can find yourself firing with your head down, not always looking where the rounds are going. I knew it was bad practice but it was very hard to avoid.

In footage of the Vietnam war I'd seen the Yanks lying down in their trenches and just putting their hands and weapons above their heads and firing blind. I'd thought, Wankers, what sloppy tactics, but we were doing exactly the same thing now when we jumped into the Argentinian trenches. Equally, we weren't zigzagging when we pushed forward across open ground but were crawling, flat to the ground.

A Company had a fearsome battle over on Darwin Hill to our left and I could hear the explosions and see all the tracer coming in. When the 2-inch mortars and Schermuleys went off, night turned into day and back to night like some flickering black and white movie. There were screams and shouts barely audible over the din and chaos of weapon fire and exploding ordnance.

As I pushed forward in the mud and wet grass, the smell of burned clothing and chemicals from the phos grenades mingled with the cordite, like the effluent from some festering oil refinery. People were shouting at each other to co-ordinate the weapons, but most of the time their orders were drowned out by the noise. The best you could do was just aim where they were aiming, then switch arcs and go on to the next position.

We were all constantly looking left to right to see where the boys were manoeuvring to next. There were no feelings now of heat or cold or tiredness, just eyes wide open, observing, trying to listen with ears completely fucked by the gimpy as it blasted away.

I couldn't tell how many empty trenches we encountered as we edged forward; maybe ten or eleven. Had the Argies run or had they moved into other positions further down on our axis? Meanwhile the weight of fire seemed to increase rather than diminish; artillery and mortar rounds were landing all around us and it was a miracle that I hadn't seen any casualties.

It was only much later that I learned the reason. If the weather and terrain had been dry, the whole company would probably have been wiped out. Instead, a lot of the artillery shells and mortars were landing in peat bog and either not exploding or having the sodden earth take the sting out of the blast. Ironically, we'd been complaining constantly about the horrible tabs and our rotting feet, yet if the conditions had been any different, we'd have died within hours.

The last trench was causing problems and needed a consolidated effort from 5 Platoon. Stevie came up to me. I hadn't seen or spoken to him since we approached the start line. I was on my knees, getting more link onto the gun by the side of a smouldering Argie trench.

Stevie said to me, 'Mike, get my grenade out, get my grenade out.' He motioned to the back of his webbing. We'd been told to carry our grenades in our windproofs rather than the pouches at the back of our webbing, which could shrink in the rain and become difficult to open.

'What the fuck's it doing in your webbing?' I said.

'Come on, just get it out!'

'What the fuck's it doing there?'

'Fucking hell, Mike, just get it out!'

We were arguing in the middle of an Argentinian trench system while a dozen shades of shit came down on our heads. I got the grenade out, gave it to him and said, 'You fucking dick-head!'

He replied, 'Fuck you, too.'

And those were the last words we ever said to each other.

With a concerted effort, we took out the last trench and overran the depth positions. It had taken a long time – over an hour – and by now it was probably five in the morning. We were on the side of a hill and, to our left, A Company were still battling and having a tough time; green and red tracer criss-crossed one another as the boys forced their way up the hill.

Coming off the slope, Johnny Crosland got on the net (comms network) and began calling the company together. In one of the last trenches a wounded Argentinian was screaming his head off and the sound was horrible. Eventually, Crosland said, 'Get him out. Get him out. I want him to shut up!'

He turned to Jimmy Street. 'Strasse, get into that trench and get that fucking Argentinian out of there.'

Jimmy couldn't lift him. 'He's too heavy for me, sir.'

Crosland shouted, 'Where's Taff Curtis? Get that Argentinian out and stop him screaming.'

Heaving him onto the edge of the trench, I saw his head rocking back and forth and figured he must have taken a direct hit. My fingers were covered in blood, there was a sweet sickly smell and his breathing was hot on my hand. His eyes were closed.

I thought, Where the fuck do I start? He was in bits; one leg was missing from the hip, the other from below the knee. Blood pumped out of a huge wound in his stomach and half the side of his head had caved in.

Bob simply said, 'C'mon, let's fuck off – he's a goner.'

But he wouldn't die. He kept screaming the same word over and over, 'Madre! Madre! Madre!'

I held the back of his head, with my hand over his mouth, and I kept telling him he'd be OK.

'Shhhhh. It's OK, mate. Settle down. Shhhhh . . .'

91

He screamed again, 'Madre! Madre!' and that was the way he died; he just shook and his lungs gurgled and he lay there in my arms. It was only much, much later that I learned he'd been calling for his mother.

It must have been a merciful release. There was nothing left of him anyway. I couldn't honestly say whether or not my hand was covering his nose. Maybe I suffocated him, I don't know. He was in a hell of a state, he really was, and if I did hasten his death, I think I did him a favour. But at that moment, as I held his limp body, I knew that whether I lived for another five minutes or fifty years, I'd be haunted by the memory.

The company came together like a herd of sheep and Crosland tried to sort out the confusion. Artillery and mortars were still landing – I didn't know who was firing them.

Most of us had no fucking clue where we were at this stage because all three platoons seemed to have been fighting their own private wars. I thought, How the fuck did 6 Platoon come in from that direction and why are 4 Platoon behind us and to our right? It was remarkable we hadn't finished up shooting each other.

Each section commander did a head count and reported back to Crosland. Somehow, we were still intact; no casualties. Everyone had got stuck in, as asked, from the mature toms to the younger lads. Even in the trenches, when bayonets had to be thrust into the enemy, no-one had backed down.

'We're all here, we've all got ammunition, let's fucking carry on,' said Crosland after confirming our position.

We were all glad to have a leader who inspired such respect and loyalty. The lads would have followed an officer like him into the fires of hell and back again – no question.

Four and 6 Platoons were put forward, with 5 behind, to cross the ridge and descend towards the gorse line, and as we came over the crest of the hill the first chinks of light began pushing through the dark clouds. Daylight would be our enemy. Boca House was across the valley on the opposite ridge about 1,500 metres away. The beach was east, to our right.

At first light, 5 Platoon was still only about halfway down the valley, making our way towards the gorse line that ran down towards Goose Green. Six and 4 Platoons were ahead of us on the lower ground.

Suddenly we were hit from the front. Argie positions at Boca House opened up with heavy machine-guns from a range of about

1,000 metres. The weight of fire was unbelievable. Rounds stitched into the earth around me, slicing through webbing and ricocheting off rocks. One round blew the foresight off my gimpy.

Then the enemy FOOs (forward observation officers) began spotting for the artillery in Goose Green and shells began raining down upon us.

Oh, God, this is it, I thought. We're too fucking exposed here.

Six Platoon were lower down in the gorse bank and 4 Platoon were also dashing into its cover, but 5 Platoon had nowhere to go on the featureless hill – we were fish in a bowl. Jimmy Street opened up with his 2-inch mortar to try to cover our withdrawal, but the next thing I heard was him screaming, 'Taff, Taff, my legs, my legs!'

We couldn't move; we were nailed to the ground by mortar and artillery rounds and small-arms fire, and we cowered on the open hillside for an eternity.

It was Stan the Man who managed to grab hold of Jimmy and started applying field dressings to the wounds.

Everywhere I looked artillery rounds were exploding, sending mud and rock into the air. Shrapnel and small-arms rounds thudded into the ground around me. Hunching my head into my shoulders, I thought, If I'm going to get hit, make it my legs, not my head.

Lieutenant Weighell had a bullet go into his helmet, round his head and out the other side. Andy Brooke had one hit his webbing and lodge itself among his magazines.

Above the din, I heard Taff Hall scream, 'My back, my back, I can't move!'

Bob and I crawled up the hill towards him. Stevie and young Pooley were already with him and had removed his webbing.

'What's wrong, Taff?'

I looked at his back and couldn't see anything wrong with him.

'I can't move, Mike. I can't move!'

I lifted his smock again. There were two tiny, brownish-red puncture marks. The poor fucker had taken a couple of 7.62 rounds in his back. We needed a medic.

'You'll be all right, boyo,' I said, taking his weapon and throwing it to one side. The others tried to make him comfortable.

As I got to my knees, I looked across and saw Ian Aird coming to our position. It was the last thing I remembered seeing before the world turned upside down.

A huge explosion erupted and blew me backwards down the

slope. Debris hit me in the face and my arm whipped across my body, flinging the gimpy away into the air.

When I came round, I found myself lying on the slope with blood pissing out of my nose. Where am I? Is that me? I could remember a blinding flash, then nothing. My head felt as if someone had caved it in with a sledgehammer.

I came back again. 'Where the fuck are the lads? Where's my gun?'

The gimpy lay about 10 feet away. I crawled towards it, and as I grabbed hold another artillery round came screaming in behind me, spraying me with earth. I could taste my own blood now. The overpowering smell of cordite and scorched earth was everywhere and all the time the *zip-zip-zip* of the 7.62 rounds.

I looked around. The crater was still smoking – a hole about 4 feet deep and 10 feet across. I dived into it, trying to regain my senses. I told myself, 'Fucking hell, man, as soon as I get clear of this shit, I'm out of here and out of the Army. This is just crazy.'

Cautious Bob jumped in after me. 'You OK?'

I said, 'Yeah, I guess – where's Taff?'

'He's with Stevie and Ian Aird.'

Peering over the edge of the crater, I saw Stevie grabbing Taff's webbing, and heard him shout, 'We need the ammo!'

Resting my gimpy on the lip of the crater, I turned away and fired a full belt of link across the valley to give him cover. I turned back just in time to see him fall, not 15 feet away.

'Get up you fucker!' I screamed. 'Stevie, get up!'

But my friend lay very still.

I leaped out of the crater and reached his side. His eyes were still open but his head lolled back as I touched his face.

'Stevie? Oh my God, mate, what's the matter – where are you hit?'

He couldn't reply; he'd been shot through the neck and must have died instantly.

We had been pinned down on that exposed ridge for four hours, enough to drive anyone insane. I wasn't far off total shock and started to shake. My ears were ringing. There were only five or six in my half section, and of those Jimmy Street and Taff Hall had been shot and now Stevie was dead. People were going down all over the place.

Peter Davies, the company 2 i/c, stood up and called for us to

94

get to the top of the hill and onto dead ground. I looked up and thought, You're going to get it up there, boyo.

Seconds later a mortar round exploded next to him, hurling him sideways.

We had to leave Stevie and crawl up the hill, bringing Taff along with us as best we could. He was dragged and lifted to the top, along with Jimmy Street, who was in terrible pain. Taff was partly in shock; he kept looking around, wide-eyed, with the occasional moan. As we got him over the crest, Ian Aird started working feverishly to get a drip into his arm.

When I reached the top, I spotted 'Whisky' Will, a big fat lad from Signals Platoon, so-called because he drank so much of the stuff. He didn't look much like a paratrooper, but amidst the firestorm he said to me, 'I'm going down there,' and charged down the hill, picking up Stevie's body and running back again. It was one of the bravest things I'd ever seen. When it was all over, he got nothing, not even an MID (Mentioned in Dispatches). It was a bloody shame.

It was now a bright, clear morning. Looking around, I could see 6 Platoon below us in the gorse line, the hill peppered with artillery holes. Stan the Man had hold of Jimmy with some of the other lads.

I looked down at my fingers, which were caked in mud and blood – some of it my own and the rest from Stevie and the Argentinian who'd died in my arms. My smock was in rag order, with tears and rips from that first explosion. My right arm was killing me and my head still spun. I wondered if my ears would ever stop ringing.

By the side of us, the anti-tank platoon had set up a section of Milans and the *whoosh* of the missiles overhead sounded like an InterCity 125 flying past a platform.

A mate from the rugby team, Nick, shouted across to me, 'Oi, Mike, we're gonna get them wankers on that other ridge.'

Minutes later he was being carried away by two lads from anti-tanks. He'd been hit by an incomer.

The Milans began exploding in the enemy bunkers at Boca House, giving them a taste of their own medicine. Meanwhile, the Argentinian positions to the rear had been silenced and D Company was making its way along the beach to do a right-flanking attack.

Five Platoon got into a huddle, taking stock and counting heads. The dead and wounded were lying about 20 yards behind me, being looked after by B Company medics.

There was a guy I couldn't recognize.

'Who is it?' I asked Baz, who'd brought him into the aid post.

'It's Marty,' he said. 'He's been hit in the face.'

I looked again. Scouse Majerisson was a corporal I knew well from 6 Platoon. He'd been hit in the shoulder; the round had exited and hit him full in the face, knocking his teeth out and tearing his mouth apart.

Peter Davies I thought would surely die. He lay where he had fallen until ten o'clock that evening before being cas-evacced, his liver ripped apart. Now he looked the worst of the wounded and lay very still.

There's an old paratrooper tradition: 'When in doubt, brew kit out.' And that's what we did. It was eight or nine in the morning and we all had a brew. Tea had never tasted better. Sipping it slowly, I watched D Company across the valley. They'd taken out the depth position at Boca House, which was just as well because B Company were running short of ammunition.

A lad called Mark came up to me. 'Have you seen Stevie?' he asked, getting all worked up.

I thought it was odd that this guy was looking for Stevie because they'd never got on. Then it dawned on me that he wasn't trying to find him, he was asking me if I'd seen the body.

'Have you been down to see him?' he said.

Without warning, I grabbed him by the shoulders and shook him hard. 'He's dead, all right? I can't change that. OK?'

Immediately, I felt sorry for losing my temper. Like most of us, this lad was suffering from shock. He'd asked me the question because he couldn't bring himself to believe that Steve was dead.

Kev Doyle came up to me. 'Mike, have you heard?'

'What?'

'The colonel's dead.'

'Who told you that bollocks?'

'No, the colonel's dead and the adjutant's dead as well.'

I thought, I don't believe this; the two most powerful men in the regiment had been killed. The news hit me like a stomach punch and for the first time I considered the possibility that we might lose. A Company had taken a fearful battering up on Darwin Hill and a lot of good men had gone down. Their battle could still be heard in the distance. Major Chris Keeble, the battalion's 2 i/c, had become the acting CO.

96

Nobody felt like eating now. We made brews for the injured lads and watched the medics try to stem the flow of blood. Looking around at the faces, I guessed most of us were thinking that nothing could ever be this bad again. Having survived this far, we'd survive anything.

Bob sat beside me, sipping a brew. 'That first round was fucking close.'

'Tell me about it.'

'I saw you go backwards – I thought you were a goner.'

'The one you don't hear is the one that gets you, they say. I never heard that one, that's for sure!'

Geordie Vale came over and sat himself down. 'What a fucking night.'

I felt totally devastated and gripped by an overwhelming sense of loss. One of my best friends lay 20 yards away, his body covered with a poncho. He should have been next to us, sharing a brew and teasing Bob. Bob looked at me and put his hand on my shoulder. 'He was the best,' he said quietly.

As we sat huddled together, another brew on the boil, Mick Connor came over. 'You OK, Taff?'

Mick, thirty going on fifty, was a wise old Yorkshireman. He knew Stevie and I had been close. Lighting up a cigarette, he said, 'If you pray for rain, you've got to deal with the mud sometimes.'

It just about summed up the situation.

The reality of it was that 5 Platoon had been very lucky. We'd been pinned down on the side of the hill for several hours, like ducks in a shooting gallery. The Argentinians had thrown everything at us – machine-guns, artillery and mortars – and the only reason that more of us weren't hit was probably the wind that channelled through the valley and blew the small-arms rounds off-target.

D Company was mopping up the last enemy positions at Boca House. Supported by the Milans, they'd launched a classic right-flanking attack straight out of the manual. As they did the business, the Motor Transport Platoon came up the hill to resupply us with bandoliers of ammunition. Not before time; I was down to my last fifty or sixty rounds on the GPMG.

Traditionally in Para Reg the HQ guys were called 'remfs' (rear echelon mother-fuckers), but on this morning they were fetching and carrying shedfuls of ammo in boxes and had link for the gimpies strewn all over their bodies. They were working their bollocks off and I decided that I wouldn't be calling them 'remfs' again – at least, not until I got back to the Shot.

The Milans had stopped firing. Geordie lit up a cigarette and I watched him inhale deeply.

'Give us one,' I said.

'You don't smoke.'

'Just give us one.'

It was my first cigarette since I was fifteen years old and used to sneak a puff in the boys' toilets at school. Drawing the smoke deep into my lungs was a sensation I needed to take me away from this place.

We didn't speak any more but, silently, a resolution had been made to carry on. Stevie had done an immensely brave act; he knew we were low on ammo and had retrieved Taff's webbing for the section. We owed it to him to make sure that we pushed on to victory.

As the cigarette smoke began to make me feel light-headed, I thought of all the good times Stevie and I had had together – in Denmark, Kenya and at the Shot. I'd always remember him with a grin on his face.

Cautious Bob and I forced ourselves to eat, sharing the rations we had left as we sat feeling numb with cold, with exhaustion and shock. Breakfast consisted of broken compo biscuits and beef paste, washed down with tea.

Everyone looked fucked and there was none of the usual piss-taking or banter. Hexamine had taken over from cordite as the dominant smell. B Company brewed up over little fires that dotted the dead ground as we waited for our new orders.

The grey skies had turned to drizzle which leaked down my face, smearing mud and blood. I took the barrel of the gimpy and busied myself cleaning it with the pull-through from the cleaning kit and oiling the working parts.

At one point Geordie shouted out that Argentinian frogmen were down on the beach and a few lads began taking pot shots. Then Mick Connor looked through a pair of binoculars. 'Don't be fucking stupid,' he announced, 'they're sea lions!'

The gorse line was on fire and 4 and 6 Platoons extracted back to us. We were all together again, drinking, smoking and replacing the cam cream that had been sweated off during the night.

So much had happened in the previous fifteen hours. I'd killed people, seen my best friend die and cradled a dying enemy soldier who screamed for his mother. Camilla Creek House seemed like a lifetime ago.

It's true what they say, you don't realize how much you want to live until you're close to death. When the mortar and artillery rounds were falling and the small-arms stuff was whistling and whining past my head on that hill, all I wanted was to get through it and get home. I might have lost my fear of killing at the very first trench, but you never lose your fear of dying. And listening to Jimmy screaming about his legs, I'd thought, What happens if I end up in a wheelchair, or brain damaged? Yet even at the worst times, a part of me also wanted to finish the job, because that was why I'd become a paratrooper and spent all those months training. I wanted to do exactly what Crosland had said; I wanted to kick their fucking arses.

Smearing the brown and green cam cream on my cheeks, I put on my war face – something warriors have done for centuries; only the weapons had become more sophisticated.

Crosland called B Company together and said we were going to swing around the airfield and attack Goose Green from the southwest. It meant that we'd be effectively isolated from the rest of the battalion, but it was a chance he was willing to take. We'd been pinned down by the Boca House positions and also from the trenches giving A Company so much trouble on Darwin Hill. Effectively, we had been caught between the two positions, with a tremendous amount of ordnance still landing on top of us from the artillery at Goose Green.

We started tabbing off the hill in arrowhead formation over the open ground. Again, it was like First World War stuff, as the howitzer rounds whistled in and landed randomly around us. But the fear of the night had gone and I was far happier fighting in the day, knowing everybody's position. I also felt more secure to be moving forward as a company again, rather than just a platoon. Safety in numbers, I supposed. It was also reassuring to see JC wearing his black bobble hat, looking around nonchalantly. He had an aura of invincibility about him.

As we swung round the airfield, I could see Goose Green for the first time, a cluster of small houses with red and green roofs, with the sea coming right up to the edge of the hamlet.

Seconds later there was a small contact just to our left and we all got down and started firing towards the airfield. We put down a heavy barrage and very soon saw the white flag go up. Twenty

Argentinians stood up and started stumbling towards our location with their hands in the air.

The big question was, what to do with them? During the night we'd taken more than one Argentinian prisoner and, as far as I knew, they were handed back along the line to company HQ and through the system to the RSM. Prisoner handling is a difficult issue. In this sort of warfare you have to keep pushing forward, because once you lose your momentum, as we did on the hill that morning, you come to a grinding halt. History has shown this is true, but somehow you have to balance the necessity to push forward with the handling of prisoners, which will surely slow the advance. We now had twenty Argentinian POWs to take care of and a lot of fighting still ahead.

The decision was made to disarm them and turn them loose and we carried on with the long tab around the airfield, over wet, boggy, undulating ground.

We were approaching some Argentinian defensive positions only about 600 metres from Goose Green when there was a long-range contact from our left and about 200 yards in front. It was nothing like the night before, but we still put down a lot of fire. I'd drenched the working parts of my gimpy with oil and after a long burst the gun started smoking. Bad drill on my part: I should have wiped off the excess oil prior to firing. Fuck it, I thought – I'm hardly giving away any secrets, the Argies already know where we are.

The gimpy's foresight had been shattered by a round, so I had to look down the barrel to take aim.

'Bob, throw us some link!' I yelled.

'This is easier,' Geordie shouted back towards me, meaning the long-range stuff.

'Go right, go right!' Bob cried, and I switched arcs. He was spotting for me against the enemy positions.

A half dozen of us, including Cautious Bob and myself, went forward to take out the trenches. One of them had a tented building next to it and I lay down some covering fire while Dave Freestone threw a grenade. It bounced off the taut fabric of the tent and came back towards him, tearing chunks of flesh out of his hand as it exploded within six feet.

Using the 66s and GPMGs we cleared the four or five positions and could then clearly see the Argentinian soldiers taking off and running back towards Goose Green. This secured the top end of the airfield, but before we could launch a final assault on the settlement we still had to take out the mortar and artillery placements on the far side of the airport, nearest the town. These included the support company trenches and radio communications.

As we tabbed around the back of the airfield, the sun was starting to go down and the sky was getting greyer. All around there were explosions and firing. D Company was attacking the airfield behind us and A Company had almost captured Darwin Hill. C Company had launched an attack on the Argies in the schoolhouse area. These were the bastards who had killed a rupert from D Company when he went to collect the surrender: a white flag had gone up at the schoolhouse and he was going forward when they opened fire. They weren't going to get much change from John Geddis and the C Company lads.

We went firm in the position outside Goose Green. In the middle of the battle, Bob and I found ourselves in a small trench with a tin shelter overhead. It was only 4 feet deep and we had to keep our heads down because rounds were zinging through the galvanized tin and each one sounded like a cymbal clash. I guessed they were overshoots from D Company, who were having a fearsome battle on the other side of the airfield.

We were there for about half an hour, lying on a poncho left behind by the previous occupants. Finally Bob looked underneath and discovered we were lying on a stockpile of mortar bombs. One unlucky ricochet and we'd have been blown to kingdom come.

Explosions and tracer were whizzing through the air from so many directions it was hard to determine where the shots were coming from. Then above us, from nowhere, Argentinian Pucaras appeared. They started strafing the ground with cannon fire.

I looked up and saw one arc in the air as a missile was fired towards it. For whatever reason the jet didn't pull out of its loop; instead the screaming drone of the engine grew louder and louder as it powered towards the ground.

'Fuck meeeeee!' Bob shouted, both of us scrambling into a trench.

The noise became a deafening crescendo as the jet exploded into B Company's position. Flames and smaller explosions filled the air as I peered out of the trench. I saw lots of other heads. Unbelievably, none of us had been hit.

Then another wave of jets swooped over.

'Where the fuck are *our* planes?' I screamed at Bob.

He shrugged. 'Having their pictures taken for the six o'clock news.'

101

Two massive fireballs erupted on the other side of the airfield towards D Company's location; it was only later that we learned the pilot was dropping napalm canisters on us.

Pucaras aren't as fast as most jets, so everyone let rip, firing wildly. I knelt and fired the gimpy, teeth clenched, one long sustained burst.

One of us had a result. The explosion was tremendous and a massive ball of flames hung in the sky and then dropped earthwards.

Bob and I dived back into our trench. Aviation fuel showered over most of the company, but each of us was too busy claiming the hit to worry about it.

Then, at last, the cavalry arrived, three Harriers flying from the north-west; they headed for the point, a piece of land that jutted from the village, and dropped their payloads of cluster bombs. Now I could enjoy the noise and the fireworks, knowing they weren't aimed at me. Even where I lay, I felt the earth vibrate; to the Argies directly underneath it must have been Armageddon. I never found out why the RAF took so long to arrive. They blamed bad weather conditions, but that didn't explain how enemy jets were managing to operate all the way from mainland Argentina.

As the light was fading, I heard helicopters in the distance. I signalled to Bob. 'Reinforcements?'

'Not before fucking time.'

I thought they'd probably sent the Marines from San Carlos Water or perhaps the Welsh Guards. But as the choppers started landing about 1,000 metres to the south-east I made out the distinctive sounds of Hueys and Chinooks.

'We don't have any fucking Hueys!' I said in disbelief.

They were Argentinian and were obviously bolstering the defences at Goose Green. My heart sank; we'd been fighting for a long time and our ammunition was running low. For much of the afternoon many of the lads had been using ammo and weapons captured as we overran positions. Crosland brought down artillery onto the chopper's landing point, but it was too late; their payload – reinforcements for Goose Green – had debussed, and the six Hueys and one Chinook were now skyward.

Now on the outskirts of the settlement, we expected to launch the final attack that night. But with new Argentinian reinforcements the picture looked far bleaker. We were stuck out on a limb, exposed to the enemy, with no chance of resupps and our nearest support, D Company, about 2 clicks away. If the reinforced garrison at Goose Green decided to counter-attack during the night, it was highly unlikely that we'd have the numbers or the ammunition to prevent being overrun. Paratroopers don't run away, but in this case there would really have been no option.

It was getting dark as Crosland called his herd together. Bedraggled bodies emerged from the enemy trenches and sangars that we now occupied; we had been in battle for the best part of thirty-six hours, with hardly any food, drink or sleep.

The OC had decided to take us to a knoll just behind our position – the highest feature around Goose Green – and to form into all-round defence. As we made our way wearily up the hill, the cold breeze stiffened and I suddenly became aware of my senses again. I was fucking knackered, cold and hungry.

With no digging tools, we had to use bayonets to carve out shallow trenches in the frozen mud. Something told me it was going to be a long, hard night.

'We've done bloody well today,' he said. 'OK, we've lost some lads and we've lost the CO. Now we've really got to show our mettle. It's not over yet, we haven't got our objective. We're about a thousand metres from D Company; enemy helicopters have landed to our south and there's a considerable force at Goose Green. We're on our own and could be in a fairly sticky position.'

The whole company lay in the cold mud, covering the arcs, with Crosland in the middle. It reminded me of the Battle of Little Bighorn. I had about 200 rounds left on the gun – fuck all – and I began thinking, Shit, this is it; they're going to come up here at any moment and we've got nowhere to go.

I knew a lot of the lads were nervous and apprehensive. Like me, they felt we'd pushed too far forward and left ourselves exposed. But at the same time, it's no good taking ground and then retreating. Lying in the rain and sleet, we could only stare along gun sights into the blackness, waiting for the attack to come. My feet were in bits from the cold and damp and I'd forgotten what it was like to feel my toes. The only food left from the rations was some coffee, powdered milk, sugar and crumbs of hard tack biscuits. Bob mixed the first three ingredients into a paste and smeared it on the biscuits. It was fucking horrible but I ate it gratefully. Then we took it in shifts – an hour on, an hour off – to guard the makeshift stockade.

The wind whipped up, turning the sleet to needles. I was beginning to wish I hadn't eaten Bob's concoction of coffee paste. The last few drops of water from our canteens were long since gone.

Bob did the first stag and I lay next to him, staring up at the black sky. Sleet stung my cheeks so I turned on my side; I could smell the earthy peat. As I thought about the horrors of the previous night, I fell asleep, exhausted.

What seemed no more than a split second later, Bob was shaking me.

'Mike, Mike, it's your stag, mate.'

'Jesus, it's fucking cold,' I said, already shivering.

'It's all in the mind.'

Two minutes later, Bob was pushing out the Zs for his hour of makeshift heaven.

The butt and trigger guard of the gun were icy cold to the touch. Peering along the barrel into the blackness, it was hard to make out any shapes or forms. Things were looking pretty grim, but I consoled myself with the thought that we had each other and that was what counted the most.

Ken Doyle slid next to me – a wonderful lad, though well-known in the battalion for being a biscuit or two short of a full ration pack.

'C'mon Mike,' he whispered, 'let's go into Goose Green, get some ammunition and come back up here.'

'I don't think that's a very good idea, Ken.'

'Sure it is, we can take them by surprise.'

'Just you and me, like?'

'Yeah.'

If I'd said, 'Yes,' Ken would have gone and tried to take on the entire Argentinian garrison. That was how crazy he could be.

The night was filled with the sounds of small-arms fire, artillery and mortar rounds, putting everyone's already frayed nerves even more on edge. In the early hours of the 29th, snow and sleet began to fall heavily. Tucking myself into a foetal position I pressed my face into my smock and tried to forget about the cold and the hunger that racked my body.

Needles of light were now trying to pierce the black carpet that lay above us. Another carpet, this one white, lay on the ground. I woke Bob just before dawn.

'I can't believe we've lain out here like fucking sheep,' I said, slapping my hands around my chest.

'At least those fuckers have got sheepskin jackets,' he replied.

As I looked around our defensive perimeter, the lads were moving about trying to get some warmth back into their freezing limbs, keeping as low as possible to avoid being skylined. I lay in Bob's position beside the gun; the ground was still a little warm from his body but my feet were wet and frozen, my toes completely numb. The moisture in my smock and trousers was beginning to ice over.

As dawn broke the hamlet of Goose Green could be clearly seen, along with the grass runway, now covered with snow. The radio had been chattering away in the centre of the perimeter where Crosland and Company HQ were situated. Porky Blackburn, the fattest lad in the company, but incongruously Crosland's runner, came round with some good news.

'A surrender's been negotiated with the Argies!'

I looked at Bob dumbfounded.

'Oi, Porky, get back here,' I said. 'Tell me more.'

'That's all I know, Taff,' he said, and was gone.

I looked down at the gimpy, then at Bob, amazed but wanting to believe it. Bob, wary as ever, said, 'I just can't fucking see it, mate.'

For the next hour, we kept our positions, not knowing if we'd be thrust into battle once more or be celebrating a victory.

Again Porky came round, puffing hard and his cheeks bright red.

'They're definitely going to surrender,' he cried. 'They're going to fucking surrender!'

Minutes afterwards, Crosland confirmed the news.

None of us had known about Chris Keeble's trip into Goose Green to negotiate a surrender. The acting CO had told the Argentinians that they were surrounded and unless they threw up their hands the attack would go on, this time complemented by Harriers. It came as a shock and a huge relief because, after the enemy reinforcements had arrived, we obviously expected to fight for every metre.

'Look! Look!' someone shouted, pointing to the airfield.

A trickle of soldiers had begun appearing and we watched as it turned into a human wave, the Argentinian troops streaming onto the runway and lining up. There were hundreds of them.

I knew then that Keeble had pulled off a huge bluff. Yes, if called upon, we would have taken Goose Green that day; and yes, we would have killed many Argentinians in the process, but how many of our boys would have been lost?

It was also hard to comprehend what might have happened had the Argies decided to attack us the previous night. We would have fought to the last round, of that I was sure, but looking at how many soldiers were lined up below us, I doubted if B Company could have held out.

An overwhelming feeling of euphoria filled me to bursting point. Bob and I grabbed each other and hugged, as did everyone else. The exhaustion, cold and fucked-up feet were forgotten as we laughed and joked.

'I just can't fucking believe it,' I said.

'Neither can I,' echoed Geordie, a big smile on his face as he lit up a victory cigarette.

Ian Aird came across and told us we were moving down the knoll onto a track that would take us into the outskirts of the village. Frost and snow crunched underfoot as we moved off, but all around us smoke rose in wisps from the ground, testament to the heavy fighting of the previous day.

The sun had come out but it was still bitterly cold as we reached the artillery positions just short of the village. Rubbish lay everywhere. Looking round, I saw bits of military clothing mixed in with empty ammo boxes, shells, human excreta, food tins, Argentinian newspapers and magazines. We were to go firm here and await further orders.

I entered one of the sheds around 5 Platoon's position and found piles of abandoned technical and radio equipment. More importantly, I found scoff. Half a dozen lads followed me inside and we started opening tins – none of them labelled. They contained some kind of meat in a putrid sauce but we found a saucepan and heated up the contents with the last of our hexamine. It tasted like total shite, but our stomachs were so empty it could have been fillet steak. This was our first hot food since Sussex Mountain.

There were photographs on the walls of a family and kids. I wondered if the father was dead or alive – would his family see him again, or would they get the tragic telegram? As I pondered the uncertainties, I could hear choppers in the distance, getting closer – and at last they were ours. Our gear was being airlifted from Sussex Mountain by Chinook.

When the bergens were unloaded everyone went straight for the scoff. I got some Mars bars down my neck and made friends with my stomach.

Since leaving the *Norland*, we'd been through the full range of South Atlantic weather conditions. Now the sun was out again, turning the snow to slush. But with the warmth came the pain as my feet began to thaw out, and I had the first pangs of the problems that lay ahead.

B Company lined up on the path and began walking into Goose Green. The settlement was little more than a few houses in a peat bog, but the 120 or so locals were obviously very proud of their town and ecstatic to be liberated. Each house had a small fence encompassing a neat garden. Unfortunately, the gardens had been turned into rubbish tips by the Argies and there were mounds of smouldering garbage and debris.

None of this could diminish the feeling of euphoria and elation. We'd done what we were asked to do – we'd hit the enemy hard and yes, they had folded. Victory belonged to 2 Para.

Only one thing could temper the joy we felt and that was the extra burden we carried into Goose Green. For along with our own bergens, we shouldered those of lads like Stevie who'd been wounded and killed. They, too, were a part of the victory.

# 7

THE TOWNSFOLK CHEERED AND WAVED AS WE STROLLED INTO GOOSE Green wearing our red berets. They'd been imprisoned in the community centre since the invasion and had listened as the battle raged around them.

Looking at them, they could have come from any village in Britain; young kids ran alongside us, dancing and laughing; old folks dabbed tears from their eyes and mothers held up their toddlers to see the parade.

A pretty young girl of eighteen or nineteen waved enthusiastically.

Geordie waved back. 'I'm going to enjoy myself here.'

'Bags her, I saw her first,' said Mouse.

'She'd eat you for breakfast, you little wanker.'

'I only wish.'

The rest of us laughed.

As the battalion descended on the town, the full price of victory became clear. A Company had taken a battering up on Darwin Hill. Two good mates of mine, Ginge Shorrock and Graham Worrall, had been shot. For a few anxious hours rumour had it that a third, Big Scouse Connell, was dead. Later we learned he'd been shot, but was alive on the hospital ship. In all, 2 Para had lost fifteen dead and thirty wounded. Early estimates of the Argentine dead ranged from 200 to 250, and the same number wounded.

Amongst D Company, I spied Rocky Hudson, my old mucker from Depot Para.

'Hey, Taff, plenty of sheep here for you, mate,' he joked.

'Good to see you,' I grinned, giving him a friendly dig in the shoulder.

Dinger Black and Dave Lee, also from D Company, told me about their battles. Dinger was a back-rower in the rugby team and Dave a chirpy cockney. Both looked as filthy, dirty and ragged as I did. My windproofs were in rags, I was covered in shit, mud, oil and blood, and my boots were falling apart on my feet.

B Company hung together on one side of the village square and D Company on the other, equally bedraggled and exhausted. There was a strong sense of shared achievement. Two Para had always had a sense of brotherhood, but the battle for Goose Green had forged an even stronger bond.

We bunked down in one of the shearing sheds. The smell of sheep was overpowering and the Mortar Platoon sergeant, Pip Hall, pug-nosed and as wide as he was tall, couldn't resist a dig.

'Oi, you Welsh sheep-shagger, don't go getting a hard-on in here,' he yelled.

We had a day to relax and sort out our bodies. Stores and compo arrived and the cookers were soon working overtime, brewing up and warming scoff.

My first priority was to sort out my feet. We had been told to keep our boots on, because if we took them off our feet would swell to twice their normal size. Mine were in such rag order that I had to have a look. Gingerly peeling off my socks, I inspected the damage. Both feet were icy white; the balls of them were shrivelled up as if I'd been soaking them all day, and I had a hot stabbing sensation in my toes that wouldn't go away.

We carried morphine syrettes in a groove inside our helmets and for the first time I considered using the powerful painkiller. Quite a few lads had already been stretchered out because of their feet.

Deciding to keep the morphine in reserve, I washed, dried and powdered my feet before putting on a dry pair of socks.

That afternoon, Mouse, Bob and I had a mooch around the town. The Argentinian prisoners were being placed in a huge hangar and some were being used for work details. The British army is very meticulous and always designates a central rubbish point and latrine. The Argies had no such system and Goose Green stank of shit and half-empty tins of food that had been thrown away.

The POWs were silent and forlorn, huddled in groups. A smell of smoke went with them, clinging to their olive drab fatigues.

I respected them as fellow soldiers who had fought well, but didn't feel sorry for them. Before leaving home I'd seen the TV pictures of thousands of Argentinians in the presidential square in Buenos Aires, cheering the leaders of the military junta for having invaded the Falklands. I thought to myself, Fuck you, you brought this fight upon yourselves – you wanted it, and you got it.

That night I found myself sleeping next to Merlin. I hadn't forgotten about the tarot cards and how Stevie had drawn the death card and Jimmy had had his 'accident'. It made me wonder, but I was too tired to move.

Getting up next morning, I couldn't get my boots back on and thought, Fucking hell, I'm in serious trouble here, my feet have swollen up. Then I discovered I was trying to squeeze into Merlin's boots which were only a size nine. I was a size eleven.

We were all in high spirits and the black humour quickly surfaced. Someone put a boot with an Argentinian foot still inside into Pip Hall's bergen. At breakfast he went to get a tin of beans out, saw the appendage and didn't bat an eyelid. Instead he pulled out his rations, repacked the bergen with the boot still inside and carried on as if nothing had happened.

That day we went back over the battlegrounds looking for lost kit and Argentinian casualties. The smells of burned flesh, charred clothing and human shit would live with me for ever. It was an eerie experience watching the work-party prisoners putting their dead on a tractor trailer. It looked like a scene straight out of the Black Death. One of the lads, with gallows humour, said out of the corner of his mouth, 'Bring out your dead! Bring out your dead!'

The driver of the tractor was a Welsh farmer, who'd only landed in the Falklands a month before the invasion, planning to start a new life. He was from Caerphilly in South Wales, about 20 miles from the Rhondda valley. One of my uncles owned a pub there.

'Do you know the Angel Hotel?' I asked.

'Know it? I used to drink there!'

We had a brief yarn about various people and places we both knew, then got on with our work. Holes still smoked from mortar rounds that had spilled mud and peat. The scent of cordite still hung in the air – a firework smell that reminded me again of Guy Fawkes' Night and the bonfires I used to build with Steve Evans at Ferndale in happier days.

Looking towards the airfield, the remains of the schoolhouse still smouldered, and all around the ground had been ripped open by gimpies.

I was keen to see the Boca House position where we'd been pinned down on the hill. The whole area was strewn with Milan wires from the wire-guided missile system. These had saved B Company's arse, and 5 Platoon's in particular.

For some reason the Argentinians had kept civilian suitcases in the trenches and now their shirts, ties and family photographs were strewn amongst the mud and blasted earth. I picked up a scorched super hero comic written in Spanish; ironically, the hero wore a red beret like a British paratrooper.

As we moved through the trenches a lot of our lads were picking up souvenirs such as pistols and FNs (rifle). Some of them had two or three rifles slung over their shoulders, but I didn't take anything; I just wanted to get on with the job.

For those next three or four days we didn't know what would happen to 2 Para – whether we'd be going forward or staying at Goose Green. We were veterans now, which increased the chances of our being used again, but after what the battalion had been through we all felt enormously close and I couldn't have wished to go into battle with anybody better.

Hexamine had now become the chief smell in the shearing shed. Over copious brews we chatted about the battle, finding out how each of us had fared. The arctic rations were excellent – stacks of chocolate and everyone's favourite, rolled oats.

Early in the evening of 2 June I had a gobful and was listening to Mouse when an explosion ripped through the air, shaking the walls of the shed. Everyone hit the deck, thinking it was an incomer.

In fact it had come from the other side of the village where the work parties were collecting ammunition and a box had exploded. Nine Argentinian soldiers were badly burned and two died instantly; a third, the POW who had been moving the box, had his limbs blown off and the rest of him turned into a human torch. A medic took one look at him, drew his pistol and put him out of his misery. I'd have done exactly the same.

With the colonel dead, Chris Keeble had been put in charge – a good man who was more in touch with the blokes. In the Paras the term 'allie' is used to describe someone who looks cool, and Keeble always fitted the part in his faded smock and his OGs (olive greens), with his beret tipped rakishly to one side. Personally, I thought Johnny Crosland should have been given the job but Keeble, as second in command, deserved his chance. He should

111

have been allowed to lead the battalion right through to the end, but instead the MoD decided to appoint Lieutenant Colonel Sean Chaundler, and he parachuted in within a week.

The new CO spoke to each of the companies in turn. He told us that after all the British losses at sea the actions of 2 Para at Goose Green had given the whole nation an uplift. He told us, too, all the usual stuff about how chuffed to the bollocks all the bigwigs at the MoD were with our achievements, but what gripped me was his statement that never again under his command would 2 Para go into battle without proper and adequate fire support.

'That'll do for me, Geordie,' I said.

'Aye, put my name down and all.'

Our new orders arrived: we'd be moving forward within a day or so. Early rumours suggested that we'd be going forward to support 3 Para, who were tabbing across the Falklands with one of the Marine battalions. Some of us were a little surprised that we might be thrown straight in again, but we were all keen to get to Port Stanley. Generally, we felt that the worst was over – we'd never have to take another attack like that on Goose Green.

In the meantime, we had to patch up our bodies and come to terms with what had happened. Crosland arranged for the padre, David Cooper, to come and speak to the lads and check on our morale. He wanted to make sure that we were ready for another fight. The message came back loud and clear: ready, aye ready.

The British had just one Chinook operating in the Falklands theatre, all the rest having gone down on the *Atlantic Conveyor* when it was sunk by an Exocet. On 3 June it airlifted B Company out of Goose Green to the coastal town of Fitzroy, overlooking Bluff Cove, about 25 miles from Port Stanley. From there we tabbed into the hills above the cove and started digging in. We were now officially back with 5 Infantry Brigade, which consisted of ourselves, 2nd Battalion Scots Guards, 1st Battalion Welsh Guards, 1st/7th Gurkha Rifles, and a troop of Blues and Royals – all under the command of Brigadier Tony Wilson.

My feet were still fucked and a medical officer visiting each company's location around Fitzroy told me to report to the medical centre that had been set up in a schoolhouse in town. I hobbled down to the settlement and stayed overnight before being flown out to a hospital ship at Ajax Bay in San Carlos Water.

At one point the doctors were talking about having to amputate the little toe on my left foot.

'You're not gonna cas-evac me out now,' I told them.

'If you go back, you risk permanent damage to your feet,' one of them said.

'I'm not leaving my mates.'

He shook his head in frustration, then shrugged. After injections in both feet, I hitched a ride in a helicopter back to Fitzroy, pleased to have missed out on two days of stagging and sleeping in the open. The rain still lashed down incessantly, whipped into cold needles by a fierce wind.

We had a mail delivery and I received letters from all sorts of people I didn't expect, even from Liz's sister and a couple of my mates who I thought would never put pen to paper. The letters were a couple of weeks old and had been posted before we even landed. This meant they were full of references about taking care of myself and keeping my head down.

Rittaz, my old rugby pal wrote, 'I really wish I was with you.'

I wrote back mentally, 'Yeah, I wish I was with you, too.'

At Bluff Cove the Scots Guards had come ashore on the night of 5/6 June, looking the worse for wear after a rough last night on board. I saw quite a few of them in Fitzroy when some of us from the platoon came down off the hill to fetch supplies. The Welsh Guards were still in the bay on board the LSL *Sir Galahad*, a transport ship.

'What are the sheep-shaggers still doing out there?' asked Geordie.

'Fuck knows,' I said. 'I wouldn't want to be moored out there – they're like sitting ducks.'

Geordie nodded: 'I couldn't wait to get off the *Norland*.'

The Welsh Guards had always held a special place in my heart. My cousin Harry had been one, as had Steve Evans, my childhood mate, who'd been sent to Borstal at the age of fifteen. While I'd gone to the grammar school and had rugby to keep me on the straight and narrow, Steve had got into trouble and paid the price. But he'd joined up on his release and had made good.

Then there was Gibby from two villages down the valley from Ferndale, who used to train with me at the sweaty old gym in Tylorstown. I'd encouraged him to join the Paras, but he'd been waylaid at the recruiting office and joined the Welsh Guards.

On the morning of the 8th we were surprised to see two transport ships still down in Bluff Cove, as obvious as a couple of turds on a billiard table.

'What are they playing at, Bob?'

'Fucked if I know. Glad I'm not aboard though.'

A work party was needed to fetch supplies up from Fitzroy. Normally this was a case of making yourself scarce, but this particular day it seemed a better idea than twiddling my thumbs on the mountain so I volunteered. Besides, I might get the chance to ask after my two old mates.

At about 1300 hours, as we were nearing the sheep sheds where the rations were stored, the tranquillity of the afternoon was shattered when four Argentinian Skyhawks and Mirages screamed across Bluff Cove. Everybody ducked; there had been no air-raid warning, but as the explosions echoed through the town I didn't need to wonder what the target might be.

Running to the cove, I looked across at the blazing hulks. Both transport ships had been hit; the *Sir Tristram*, nearer the jetty, had been struck on the stern deck; from the *Sir Galahad*, thick, belching smoke was spiralling upwards and helicopters already buzzed around its hull. There were now life rafts in the water, trying to pull away from the ship.

I'd never felt so helpless. I could see the boys piled into boats and hear their cries. Their accents were the same as mine and they were in distress and in pain. This, more than anything else, brought home the full horror of war.

We waded into the cold, grey sea, dragging the boats to shore. There were lads in a terrible state with their hair gone and skin peeling off in charred strips; some had lost limbs.

One lad kept saying, 'Mam, Mam!' He was crying and I felt like crying for him. We did what we could, then waded ashore and waited for the other boats.

One lad told me he was from Bargoed in Wales.

'Do you know Steve Evans?' I asked.

'Yeah.'

'Was he on board? Did he get off? Is he OK?'

He turned and asked some of the other lads. They all agreed that Steve had come ashore on the previous night with the Patrols Platoon.

'Are you sure?'

'Yes, definitely,' he insisted.

'What about Gibby from the Rhondda valley?' I asked.

They weren't so sure.

'Did any of you see him?'

They shook their heads.

I stood there dripping wet, hit by a mixture of emotions. Steve was alive – the lad who'd shared all my early years. We were a team back then – we smoked our first cigarettes together and drank our first cider in the gullies (alleys) of the Rhondda. He was part of my childhood and still with me.

But what of Gibby, I wondered, as I watched more boats come ashore. I'd encouraged him to join the Army and now I didn't know if he was among the many who surely must have perished on the *Sir Galahad*.

In truth, the troops should never have been on the ship. I was just a tom in the Paras, but even I could see they were sitting ducks moored there in Bluff Cove; why could no-one in command see the futility of having a battalion of men unprotected on the water, just waiting for the inevitable? The brigadier I had admired for getting his parachute wings late in life was in charge of 5 Infantry Brigade; was he to blame or was the guilty party further up?

Five days later, 2 Para received confirmation that the next phase of the war would see us act as reserves for 3 Para or 45 Commando during their battles for Mount Longdon and Two Sisters, in preparation for the final push against Port Stanley. That was us passed back to 3 Commando Brigade, but in reality we didn't give a fuck – we were still 2 Para and it didn't matter one jot what brigade we were fighting for.

On 11 June, forming up in stick formation, we boarded a fleet of Sea Kings for the lift towards an LUP (lying-up position) to the west of Mount Kent, where we left our bergens and began tabbing at last light in the by now familiar battalion snake towards the base of Mount Longdon. There we were to await any decision to move in support of the Marines or 3 Para. It would be good to go into battle with our sister battalion, I thought.

This time, I had brought as much scoff as I could carry in my webbing and smock, because I knew that I was going to get cold again, but I didn't want to be hungry as well. Even without our bergens we carried about 30–40 pounds of link, 66s (lightweight throw-away anti-tank rocket), extra water bottles, food, grenades and ammunition.

B Company were in front, with Crosland in the lead, and this time Dave Collins refused to be left behind. He'd rejoined us at Goose Green, bitterly disappointed to have missed the action. His leg was still in bits but he was determined not to miss out on any more. All the boys were bouncing and ready to go for it, no problem. We wanted to finish the job.

Before leaving Fitzroy the colour-sergeant had come over and presented me with a new pair of boots because mine had fallen apart.

'Look, Mike,' he grinned, 'a gift from the Scots Guards – no questions asked.'

'Brilliant!' I said.

They were big, size twelve, but had a major flaw. They were Guards' ammo boots, with leather soles, shiny metal toecaps and metal hobnails and studs on the soles. My feet might just as well have been inside a freezer. Tabbing through the rocky outcrops and over frosty ground as the snow tumbled down, I kept slipping and sliding on the metal studs and couldn't stay on my feet.

Soon we heard the artillery firing up towards Longdon above our heads. At least it was our artillery this time. About time the gunners got stuck into the Argentinians, I thought. Then we could hear the battles raging for Longdon and Two Sisters. Going by the volume of red and green tracer 3 Para and 45 Commando had a grim fight on their hands.

It had been a ball-breaking tab on a brutally cold night. Sweating buckets, we moved into an LUP at the base of Mount Kent and awaited the inevitable: we were going to freeze. I sat hunched up on the ground and shivered as I wondered what would be happening to us next. In all probability we'd be going in support of 3 Para; from what I could hear they were having a much harder task against a well-defended Mount Longdon. Meanwhile we waited – and froze.

After several hours the message finally came to move towards Mount Longdon. So be it, I thought; at least we'll be fighting alongside our sister battalion.

It wasn't long before enemy shells were pounding us. You'd hear it coming and everyone would duck for a few seconds and then just carry on.

'I don't think I'll ever get used to that fucking horrible noise,' Geordie said, matter-of-factly.

Dave Collins limped the entire way and kept passing back messages from Crosland's signaller about 3 Para being on the start line and then moving off. Soon we could actually see the battle as we tabbed around. It was a hell of a fight and gave me a better idea of what we'd faced at Goose Green. I kept muttering, 'Get stuck in, 3 Para, I don't want to go up there. Come on, boys!'

By now we'd walked to the base of Mount Longdon and were waiting to be called up. Several times during the night we were given notice: 'Get ready, you're going soon.' Each time we waited for the order but, thank God, it didn't arrive. By daybreak we learned that the lads in 3 Para had done the job on their own.

Meanwhile, the Marines had taken out Two Sisters, which meant that very little stood between us and Port Stanley apart from Wireless Ridge – and that had 2 Para's name written all over it.

The attack was scheduled for that night, but then delayed for twenty-four hours. In the meantime, we dug in at the base of Longdon and weathered the artillery rounds being fired from Stanley. Three of us were on stag that afternoon when a shell landed between us and we escaped unscathed. We looked at each other and grinned. What else can you do when you've been that lucky? I didn't hear the next shell coming. It landed fucking close – perhaps not as close as the one at Goose Green, but close enough. It erupted and I dived. Shrapnel ripped through my smock, but somehow it missed my body.

The sun came out on 12 June, and although it was still cold it was good to have its rays on your face. We used the stream running through our position to make brew after brew, and I started to feel a bit less hard done by. When I came off stag, however, I made a fatal mistake. One of the lads had gone over to one of the Scimitar tanks, taken off his boots and socks and begun to thaw out his feet on the engine. It looked a good scheme and I did exactly the same, drying my feet and socks. I might just as well have been putting my feet directly into a fire. I paid for the mistake – that night and for years afterwards. Despite the pain, I still didn't take the morphine – for all I knew, I might be needing it on Wireless Ridge.

That afternoon, Collins gave us the orders from Crosland. The following night, we were to attack Wireless Ridge, a dual spur feature running off eastwards from Mount Longdon, and after that, push on to Stanley. The ridge was dominated by the higher ground of Mount Tumbledown, so the plan was for the porridge gobblers (Scots Guards) to attack that night so as to give us a clear run at our target the next evening. So, another night out in the open without doss bags; by now my feet were feeling like blocks of ice and with no prospect of a tab to get the blood flowing.

Dave Collins got us together again in the afternoon. It was to be a noisy night attack; and, unlike at Goose Green, this time everyone was coming to our party. Three Para would be firing us in from the flank with mortars, Milans and machine-guns; there were also two batteries of 105mm guns, the light tanks – Scimitars and Scorpions – of the Blues and Royals with their 76mm guns, and naval gunfire support from HMS *Ambuscade* with her 4.5 inch gun offshore – all in all, the dog's bollocks, and a bloody big dog at that.

'The enemy on the ridge are the Seventh Infantry Regiment,' Collins said, 'along with elements of their First Parachute Regiment. But we're more than a match for the wankers.'

Phase one would involve D Company taking out new enemy positions west of the northern spur, and initially all the fire support would be for them. In phase two, A and B Company were to sweep up the main ridge in extended line and make their assault, and the fire support would switch to us. We had to convince the Argentinians that they faced a two-battalion night attack and not just two companies. Each section was to make out it was a platoon, each platoon was to make out it was a company, and each company was to make out it was a battalion. Another battle, but this time we'd have the world's supply of fire support, and that's all an infantryman wants to hear.

As we made our way to the start line the fire support opened up, a deafening roar from the artillery and mortars, all firing us in from the different hills around Wireless Ridge, lighting up the sky. Then the Scimitars and Scorpions opened up as well, and as the combined tons of ordnance rained down on the Argie positions it felt as if the whole world was shaking. We didn't know it at the time, but the mortar platoon – some of the hardest men in the Falklands – were so determined to do their job that four of them had suffered broken ankles. The ground was so boggy and sodden that the base plates for the mortar tubes wouldn't bed in properly, so the lads had chosen to stand on them instead. As the rounds were dropped into the tubes, the impact of firing shattered bones in their feet.

We lay in a gully at the base of Wireless Ridge, with water streaming down the slope and going right up the arms of our smocks. Although the ridge was lit up, we were in darkness.

Bob was lying next to me, bayonet fixed; next to him, no-one. We were the extreme right flank of the battalion night attack. I pulled my smock over my nose and mouth and blew hot air down inside. My body stank; our last shower had been weeks before on the MV *Norland*.

Heavy mortar and artillery rounds from the enemy were landing randomly around our positions and claiming casualties. One anti-tank rocket went straight through the company and into the ground just behind us. We were very, very lucky.

I didn't know how long we lay in that freezing gully waiting to move. It might have been an hour, it might have been two. The fire support became a shuddering wall of sound and vibration crashing down on the ridge above us. I felt as if I was about to walk into someone else's nightmare; the ridge was erupting before my very eyes.

In the midst of this hell I saw glimpses of beauty. Milan missiles flew majestically towards their targets. Then an amazing sight, a one-in-one stream of tracer that looked like a laser beam above our heads. Normally every fifth round is a tracer bullet, but this was one-in-one from the cannons of the Scimitars and Scorpions, creating a single, unbroken beam.

I was lying on my side, cradling the gimpy in my arms. It hadn't given me a single stoppage. It was on gas setting three – too much gas and you get a carbon build-up on the gun that causes problems; too little and you get the dreaded 'dead man's click' when the working parts stop at the vital moment. You don't need that on top of an enemy trench.

I thought again of my grandfather, Dai Thomas, at the Somme, and I wondered if he'd felt the same way as he waited for his turn to go over the top. Nothing had really changed in sixty years except for the weapons and firepower. He'd been wounded; hopefully I'd be luckier. I thought briefly about Goose Green, when I'd hunched up; all I was thinking this time was, Let's get those bastards off our mountain.

For the second time in one week we were going into battle, but I didn't feel the apprehension of Goose Green. Nothing could ever be that bad again. This time I knew what to expect and we had back-up; it seemed as if the entire British army was firing us in.

'OK, let's go,' said Dave Collins to my left.

After lying prone for so long, my body refused at first to respond. My legs, feet and arms were numb.

Almost immediately Ian Aird began shouting, 'Spread out! Stop fucking bunching! Push out on the right! Push out, Bob!'

As I looked left I saw the whole company moving in unison in the rain. The light cast long shadows behind us as we moved up the ridge in an extended line.

Mortar illumination rounds were erupting above the enemy positions and explosions ripped through the ridge. The tracer was criss-crossing, with patterns of red light hitting rocks and ricocheting into orbit. Milans were firing from our right side, roaring towards the bunkers. The Scimitars and Scorpions were putting down an unbelievable rate of fire, hundreds and hundreds of rounds. Why the fuck couldn't we have had those beasts at Goose Green?

The summit was being bombarded with such force I figured maybe the tactic was to raze it rather than have to run up it.

About 200 yards short of the summit, we came under fire.

'Push right! Push right!' came the cry, as the section commanders began pushing B Company out to the extreme right as planned. Bob and I began running now as the battalion moved; we were the hinge for the barn door.

Until then we'd mainly been advancing in darkness, with only the enemy positions on the ridge lit up by the mortars. Now the illumination rounds became a double-edged weapon.

The rounds were stopped and everything plunged into blackness.

'Anyone got ten pence for the meter?' Bob shouted.

Rounds hammered into the earth around us.

'Stop, stop, Taff! Give it some on the gun!' he shouted.

We got down and I aimed at a position next to a pile of boulders that I'd committed to memory before the darkness fell. I fired the gimpy, a tracer hit the target and bounced off in all directions. Then I let loose with a full belt.

'Link! Bob, link!' I screamed.

The Argies beside the boulders were still firing back at us with their green tracer. I gave them another 200 rounds and their position fell silent.

B Company were now static as A Company were pivoting on our hinge. Then it was our turn to move and we began pepper-potting (firing and manoeuvring) forward. Two hundred yards became 150, and again enemy rounds whizzed around our heads. Down in the prone position, I raked the right-hand side of the ridge.

'Push right, push right! We're gonna take that position!' Dave Collins screamed.

'Move, Bob!' I shouted.

We were taking incomers and the ground erupted with small-arms fire.

Collins shouted, 'Go right! Go right!'

Suddenly, the ground disappeared from beneath me and I was up to my neck in water. I'd fallen through a frozen pond.

The water was so cold I was in instant shock. My heart seemed to stop beating. Then I came to my senses, swallowing and gagging on the filthy black bog water. Flailing around, weighed down by ammunition, for a split second I thought I was going to drown.

'Bob!' I cried. 'Fuck! Help me, mate!'

The cold felt as if I'd walked in front of a train. I couldn't breathe.

Collins was screaming, 'Taff, Taff, get the fucking gun going!'

'OK, OK,' I yelled, 'when I get out of this fucking pool!'

Bob reached me, grabbed a fistful of smock and dragged me out. 'C'mon, Mike, we're off!'

I was frozen to the bone and taking sharp intakes of air. I couldn't feel my fingers.

Dave Collins was still screaming for me to take out the position on the right.

The gimpy was slung around my neck. Unable to find the trigger, I tore my gloves off and tried again, cursing my useless fingers.

The Argie bunker was only about 100 metres in front of me, on the right of the ridge. I was a gibbering wreck.

Where's the fucking trigger?

Found it!

'Fuck you!' I screamed and fired the gimpy from the hip, ripping rounds into the bunker located between two rocks. My brain and limbs were again functioning together.

Mick Connor screamed across at me, 'Mike, stop fucking firing! We're all going up!'

Firing and manoeuvring towards the top of the ridge, we were actually walking through the middle of a minefield, although we didn't know it at the time; it was only the next day that Crosland found out and told us the ground had been so cold that the anti-personnel mines had frozen solid and didn't explode.

Now less than 100 metres away, the Argies started running in front of us, deserting their positions. They'd jacked it in and were fleeing towards Port Stanley.

Reaching the summit, we discovered devastation on a scale that I'd never seen before. Smoke and cordite filled the lungs and the entire ridge was a mass of torn and incinerated earth. Bunkers had taken direct hits and their smouldering remains added to the debris and chaos.

We jumped into the trenches and continued firing at the fleeing

Argentinians, taking advantage of finally having the higher ground.

Then the first incomers arrived from Stanley. I heard them flying through the sky, a low whistle at first, turning into a screeching manic noise as it reached our positions. A huge explosion rocked the ground, sending out familiar shock waves. Fuck, it was close. The Argies had obviously DF'd (direction find) the ridge in case they had to pull out. The artillery in Stanley had all the co-ordinates to pound us into the smoking earth.

'We're going firm and digging in,' screamed Ian Aird. 'So take fucking cover – it's going to be a long night.'

Almost before he'd finished, three more incomers exploded randomly on our new positions.

Collins started putting us into enemy bunkers then thought better of it. A peat bank, about 8 feet tall, provided better cover and B Company began digging in. It was a good decision as one of the bunkers was hit during the night, blowing rocks and wood into oblivion.

I was fucking freezing and dug like a man possessed. My clothes were soaked and the wind cut right through me.

Collins took one look at me and said, 'You've got no fucking chance at all. We've got to get you out of here.'

'No-no-no fu-fu-fucking way,' I replied through chattering teeth.

'You're fucking mad – get your Welsh arse on the ship and get warmed up by the nurses.'

'That would be g-g-good,' I said, trying to smile. 'How about a f-f-fag instead.'

'I thought you didn't smoke.'

'It's a ha-habit I'm picking up.'

Pete Richens the company sergeant major came up to me. 'There's a helicopter coming, you need to be on it.'

'Exc-cuse me-me, sir, bu-bu-but I'm staying.'

'Right, well get a fucking change of clothing.'

I could hear the familiar *wop-wop-wop* of the chopper blades. Our wounded were being cas-evacced, among them another lad from 6 Platoon who'd also fallen into a frozen pond. But wild horses couldn't have dragged me away; I'd come this far and had my eyes on the ultimate prize – Port Stanley.

The lads had a whip-round of kit and put together a change of clothes.

For the rest of the night, from half-past two in the morning until daybreak, we maintained our defensive positions under the bombardment. Dave Collins kept giving me cigarettes and I smoked them furiously. I needed another sensation to take me away from the cold.

He talked to me, keeping me awake, because he feared I was going down with hypothermia. The change of clothing slowly worked; only my feet still hurt as the stabbing sensation returned with a vengeance.

'You still thinking of doing Selection, Taff?' he asked.

'Ha, if my feet ever thaw out.'

'Give it a couple of years, get some experience, then go for it.'

'Maybe, maybe.'

In truth, I was still thinking of the promise I'd made myself at Goose Green: that if I got out alive, I'd quit the Army altogether.

Throughout the night, the guns in Stanley kept up the bombardment, and soon we could judge from the incoming sound whether that particular round was meant for us. Then we'd hug the ground as it exploded near our position.

'Too much of this would send a bloke around the twist,' said Geordie.

'So you've had more than your fair share, then,' remarked Bob.

Relief on a black night.

Just before first light, the Argentinians counter-attacked up the ridge. D Company, which was now in front of us, beat them back down to Moody Brook barracks with the loss of another three lads dead and eleven wounded. Although we didn't realize it then, these were the last shots fired in the Falklands War.

It had snowed during the night, covering the ground in a clean, crisp layer. The sun was trying to peek through – I was willing it out – and along the ridge heads were popping up. We merged on Crosland as a company to get the latest.

General Jeremy Moore from the Royal Marines, who was in charge of land-based forces, had requested 2 Para to go firm and stay on the ridge. When the message was passed down to Crosland, he told his signaller via his runner Porky Blackburn, 'Tell him his transmission is unworkable to us,' meaning his voice had broken up on the net.

JC didn't wait for a reply because he knew the Marines were angling to be the first troops into Port Stanley. We'd already got word that white flags had been seen in the town.

'Come on, let's get there before the Marines,' said Crosland. 'We deserve it.'

As we moved through D Company's position, they looked as knackered as we did, hardly recognizable behind the stubble on their chins and thick cam cream, with only their eyes peering out beneath their para helmets. They were lying about, smoking, winking, nodding and grinning. Their DPM trousers and smocks all seemed to be a deep brown in colour and everyone had bandoliers slung around them.

Then, from the top of the ridge, I got my first glimpse of Stanley – the prize. It looked disarmingly pretty, with red and green rooftops, like a larger version of Goose Green. The sea was a calm blue-grey and seemed to frame the colonial-style buildings and green hills. Some of the buildings reminded me of those I'd seen in travel brochures for Barbados, but without the sun and the palm trees.

Although white flags had apparently been sighted, none of us had forgotten the death of the officer in D Company when they were taking a 'surrender' at Goose Green.

Bob didn't have to say a word.

'I know, mate,' I said. 'You can't be too careful.'

It was an amazing sight as we walked off the ridge – A and B Companies first, with D Company just behind. The ground looked like a moonscape, with craters everywhere; scattered amongst the debris were the remains of enemy soldiers. Before coming to the Falkland Islands I'd never seen a dead person; now I'd been through two battles and seen enough of twisted, battered and broken bodies to last me a lifetime.

We made our way off the west ridge heights down towards Moody Brook, where it had all started just a few weeks ago on 2 April, when the Argentinians had attacked the Marines' barracks. We cleared the bridge over the Murrell River, then made our way carefully to the high ground by the side of the road, eyes skinned for mines and booby traps.

Suddenly there were jubilant shouts all around from the signallers: 'Ceasefire!'

I looked at Cautious and laughed. 'We did it, buddy.'

All around us looks of apprehension were replaced by smiles. I joined the others in replacing my helmet with my red beret, and it was the proudest thing I'd ever done.

Collins, Mouse, Geordie, Merlin and Bob had huge grins. In a surprising display of emotion, Bob actually hugged me.

'Fuck me, Bob,' said Geordie, 'what's happening – you come out?'

He got a hug, too.

The road into Stanley was a mess, having turned into muddy slush from the snow and heavy troop movements. To the left was the sea and to our right rows of bungalows that lined the shoreline.

Rifles, pistols, clothing, helmets, webbing, compo tins, boxes, boots, newspapers, magazines, blood, mud – all of it strewn about in a panic or chaos. There had obviously been a major pull-out of troops, many of them injured, going by the evidence of bloody field dressings that littered the ground. It became clear that there would be no more fighting. The Argentinians had fled towards the airport and would remain there until the surrender had been sorted.

A and B Companies were the first friendly troops into Stanley, and we celebrated by punching each other on the shoulders, back-slapping and grinning broadly. Behind us came the other companies of 2 Para and 3 Para.

We continued walking towards the racecourse until Crosland stopped us at a row of neat bungalows.

'This'll do us!' he said, sending the platoon sergeant around the back to let us in.

Along the street the various platoons followed his lead. Inside it was just like Christmas, with pantries stocked full of food, and lovely warm kitchens. I even found fresh towels that had obviously been left by the Argentine naval officer who'd been using the house since the real owner had been imprisoned.

We found potatoes and chip fat, so a fry-up became the first priority, and at the same time we polished off a hoard of chocolate bars. Meanwhile, Mick Connor took off his smock and put it on a set of bathroom scales. Even without the webbing, it weighed 20 pounds with all the grenades, spare magazines and sheer water saturation.

After a couple of hours of kicking back and getting warm, we watched the Marines arrive and, of course, they took a lot of stick from us as they walked down the road. I was struck by how physically large they were compared with typical Paras – more my size.

While they moved further into Stanley, we were content to stay in our warm houses and try to fathom what we'd achieved. I sat down and wrote some letters to Liz and my parents, but couldn't explain how I really felt. Instead I talked about the weather.

Later we were allowed to send one telegram home from the Port

Stanley post office. Mine said, 'I'm OK, Mam and Dad. See you soon. Love Mike.' I learned later that my mother framed it and hung it in the house in Ferndale.

After all the nights of freezing our bollocks off, it was heaven to sleep inside a warm bungalow and sit on a proper toilet. When the owner came back a couple of days later, having been released from Argentinian captivity, he was more than happy to have us in his house – especially when he saw we took our boots off before entering. The locals, of course, were extremely grateful to us and thoroughly pissed off with the Argies. Most of them had had their houses wrecked and looted, but were thankful to be alive.

Our section got the front room. We cooked in the kitchen and dossed on the floors. The chip pan was on overdrive and so were our stomachs. Compo is a means to an end – initially it tastes OK, although everyone adds curry powder to almost everything – but after a few weeks you might as well be eating cardboard because it tastes so bland and boring.

Gradually my toes and fingers started to get the blood flowing through them again, but my feet were still giving me a lot of pain. The toenails were black and numb to the touch. At least six of us in the platoon had feet like Fred Flintstone, and most of the others were wincing and limping like old men. Mick Connor had looked rough before the conflict even started, but now he could have been old man Steptoe.

It wasn't long before the colour man (colour-sergeant) was organizing fresh rations from the ships as well as copies of the *Sun* and *Mirror* newspapers. Now we could read what they were saying about us back home. It was a fantastic feeling because when the crisis started, the media had been banging on about how the Marines were going to do this and the Marines were going to do that. Now the stories were dominated by the Parachute Regiment and I felt it was nice to be getting the recognition we deserved. I'd wander through the bungalow without any boots, with a mega brew in one hand and a copy of the *Sun* in the other. Fucking marvellous!

On the second day, I wandered down to where 3 Para were staying in their bungalows. I wanted to catch up with a guy from Tylorstown, John Hedges; I'd worked down the pit with his dad. John had joined Junior Para at the age of sixteen and I didn't know him very well. For some reason he was an 'Aldershot orphan', and never really came back much to the Rhondda.

We had a few brews together and he told me about 3 Para's

126

monster tab from San Carlos and the severe hammering they took on Mount Longdon. Quite a few of them had been killed or wounded. Sadly, I learned that one of them was Jed Bull, my pal from Depot Para. He was a lovely West Country lad and an excellent football player. He couldn't have been much more than twenty years old.

This added to the feeling of pain and sadness because I was still mourning the loss of Stevie. I felt devastated that he wasn't with us to share in the victory, yet I forced myself to be philosophical about it; the death toll could have been far worse and as Mick Connor said, 'If you pray for rain, you've got to deal with the mud.'

In total we lost eighteen men from the battalion, with a further forty-two wounded. The Argentinians weren't so lucky. I went to the hospital in Stanley, which looked like an abattoir and wasn't far short of one. The smell of death hung in the air and everywhere I could see the brown stains of old blood. There were piles of amputated arms and legs just lying in a corner, waiting to be taken for incineration.

In the operating theatre I came across an Argentinian doctor who spoke perfect English, with an American accent. He'd studied medicine in the States and then found himself drafted into the war as a medic. He took us through the hospital, explaining how horrendous the casualties had been.

Geordie, Bob and I managed to get ourselves some boots from the stockpile of discarded clothing left by the Argentinian casualties. Clothes and shoes had been tossed out of the window, forming a rubbish tip.

The Argentinian boots were far better than the ammo boots I'd been wearing or anything the Parachute Regiment issued. Come to that, a lot of their kit was better than ours.

'If I'd had boots as good as this, my feet wouldn't be in this fucking state,' I said, tossing my old pair away.

'Don't you want to keep them as a reminder?' Geordie asked.

'What the fuck for?' I said.

He couldn't think of a reason.

Along with a few towels monogrammed with the crest of the Argentine Navy, the pair of enemy boots were the only souvenirs I took home from the Falklands.

I ventured into the town just once with Geordie and Bob after our hospital visit. It was like a gigantic rubbish tip, with debris strewn everywhere in the gardens and the streets. The reek of human shit and rotting food clogged up the nostrils. In one of the gardens, I saw an old woman weeping by the side of her white painted wooden fence. 'It will take me the rest of my days to clear up this mess,' she cried. She spoke in the kind of West Country accent that the locals seemed to have.

We made our way towards the harbour, where we came across about fifty dejected-looking Argentinians sitting against a fence, guarded by Marines. Geordie went over to talk to a group of them and started offering around cigarettes. Bob and I went off to one side and were chatting to some guys from D Company when Geordie called us over.

'Ask my mate what you just asked me,' he said to one of the two pale-skinned Argies standing with him.

In perfect English, the Argie said, 'I was just asking, are any of you guys Welsh?'

No wonder Geordie had been taken aback.

'Yes, I am,' I said.

'Me too,' he said. 'And my friend here can't speak English, but he speaks fluent Welsh.'

I was stunned. I had heard of the community out in Patagonia, fervent Welsh-speaking descendants of immigrant forefathers, with bloodlines that could be traced directly back to Cardiff, Merthyr and Swansea.

'I was up on Wireless Ridge,' he went on, his voice edged with sadness. 'I've lost contact with my brother – he was at Goose Green.'

For a moment or two I was lost for words. Then I said, 'I was there. I hope you find him. There were a lot of prisoners.'

With that they were all told by their officer to stand up and march towards the ship. I shook his hand and he grabbed my shoulder.

'Good luck,' I said.

'You too.'

I shook his friend's hand, too; I couldn't believe it, three Welshmen, all fighting for our countries. It had been one of the strangest encounters of my life, and as I watched the group disappear down towards the harbour I thought, That fucking twat Galtieri has a lot to answer for. The Argentinian junta had pushed for a war, then brought in people like the Patagonians to fight it for them. I vowed there and then that one day I'd go to Patagonia and visit the Welsh community. I only hoped that this lad's brother had marched onto the airfield at the end and had not died a horrible death in a trench or in a para's arms, screaming for his *madre*.

On 15 June we formed up in three ranks and marched to the pretty stone church in the town, somehow managing to cram the whole battalion of 600 men inside. I remembered the church from the TV footage that I'd seen of the Argentinian invasion; they'd marched down the same road just ten weeks earlier.

The BBC had set up its cameras and filmed as the chaplain, David Cooper, reminded us of what he'd said the night before we landed, when we were gathered upstairs aboard the MV *Norland*. He'd said that not all of us would be coming back. 'What did you think about when you thought you were going to die?' he said. 'Was it your wife, your girlfriend, your parents, or even your dog?'

There was laughter, then silence; you could almost hear the lads thinking. I had prayed to God when we were pinned down for four hours on the hill opposite Boca House and I was certain I was about to die, but I hadn't spoken to him since.

Now it was time to pray for those who'd lost their lives. Most paras aren't overly religious or sentimental souls, but the fallen occupy a place in our hearts that ensures they will never be forgotten.

# 8

ON FRIDAY 25 JUNE, OUR LAST MORNING IN THE FALKLANDS, I CHOPPERED back to Goose Green to represent Stevie Illingsworth at a service at Darwin, one final act of remembrance for our boys.

It was a miserable, grey day, the wind and rain lashing at us as we waited to board our Chinook. Moments before taking off, I watched, horrified, as a fierce gust picked up one of the small Gazelles parked nearby and flipped it down the hill, shearing off the rotor blades. I hoped it wasn't an omen.

We flew low over Wireless Ridge to Bluff Cove and Fitzroy, all the ground we had struggled so hard to tab over, finally landing at the bottom of Darwin Hill.

It was pissing down and we stood shivering in the freezing cold as David Cooper spoke of the bravery and sacrifice of guys like Stevie. Was it already a month ago? It seemed like yesterday. We stood in a sombre semicircle, the COs of 2 and 3 Para, the captain of the *Norland*, Major Keeble, and representatives, like me, of our fallen from the companies. We were on a hill overlooking the township, where the locals had erected a simple cross of black steel atop a stone monument on a small hill, strategically positioned so it could be viewed from both communities, Darwin and Goose Green. The gesture meant a lot to us.

While Cooper was talking I looked around me. I could clearly see the spot on Darwin Hill where our leader, H. Jones, had died, and across to the right the remains of the schoolhouse.

After the service the settlers bade us farewell, and as the twin

130

rotors on the Chinook began thumping the air I took a last look back at Goose Green; I thought about the lads that had died there to secure the freedom of this community, and especially about Steve. Startlingly, as I looked at the gorse line, I saw that it was still smouldering, a month later.

I met up with the rest of B Company on the pier as we waited to board the MV *Norland* for the voyage home. The RMPs (Regimental Military Police) were trying to organize the commotion and were generally being ignored. They weren't popular at the best of times.

Three Para were sailing with us – that should be a laugh, I thought. There'd always been a good-natured rivalry between the Para battalions and, having fought together, the camaraderie was even stronger. I felt sorry for 1 Para, who'd missed the action and spent the war on tour in Northern Ireland. It was a shame because all three Marine battalions had been included in the task force.

Cautious Bob and I got a room together, and Stan the Man Standish was there to greet us. It was good to see Stan again. His feet had jacked on him after Goose Green and he'd been cas-evacced to one of the hospital ships, the *Uganda*, missing out on the battle for Wireless Ridge.

'Stan, you wanker!' went up the cry when we spied him.

He told us how, after the hospital ship, he'd been given the task of escorting Argie POWs down to Chile on the ships.

'Fuck that for a laugh!' said Bob.

'Where were they sleeping?' asked Geordie.

'Right in these bunks,' said Stan.

'The bastards!' said Geordie, none too happy that some smelly Argie had been festering in his bed space.

Smoke filled the corridors from all the puffers and the platoon beat box was on full blast, thumping out the sounds of the Jam and Madness. UB40 had a track called 'Present Arms' which was all about joining the military and fighting on foreign shores. A guy from C Company in the next cabin played it all the time, and it never failed to give me goose bumps.

I had the same cabin as before, and as I lay on my bunk, looking at the door, I still half expected to see Stevie walk through and tell Bob to stop being a cockney wanker and get on his own bed.

That first night, 2 and 3 Para gathered in the ship's lounge and were addressed by General Moore from the Royal Marines, who'd been in charge of the land-based task force. Taking off his green

131

beret, he said, 'From a Marine, I'd like to thank the Parachute Regiment for all you've done.' Then he saluted and added, 'Men, you are the finest fighting unit I have ever seen.'

Coming from a Marine that was truly something.

Every year in Aldershot the Parachute Regiment celebrates Airborne Forces Day. The resident battalion gets dressed up in their No. 2s and their medals and marches down to the square with all the other battalions and their families watching. It's a very emotional day and after the parade we have a monumental piss-up.

In 1982, Airborne Forces Day fell while we were on the *Norland* heading for Ascension Island. There had obviously been no drinking on the journey down to the South Atlantic, so the crates of beer had been stockpiled for the trip home. That time had come.

We set about letting off steam and relieving some of the tremendous pressure of the previous months. Drink flowed freely and at some point during the night the wrong thing was said to the wrong person and fists flew.

This turned out to be 2 Para's third battle. As in the bar-room brawls you see in old cowboy films, everyone seemed to be drawn into the fighting. Our little group in 5 Platoon were watching through our drunken haze until Geordie took a belter from some twat in C Company. I sorted him out and Bob gave him a few just to make sure.

'Can't be too careful, mate,' he laughed.

Although the two battalions got on well, there were still a few personal scores to settle and a certain amount of inter-unit friction among some of the lads.

The sergeants and officers were in the officers' mess upstairs and when they came down to quell the fighting it wasn't long before they, too, got involved. Soon it didn't matter whether you were 2 Para or 3 Para, everyone fought each other. Eventually it calmed down and we were all sent to bed like naughty boys.

Next morning in the scoff queues there were guys with black eyes and split lips, but no hard feelings. We all agreed there'd never be another Airborne Forces Day like that one.

The MoD had made sure that 2 Para were the first unit out of the Falklands, and when we reached Ascension Island we were transferred to Hercules transport planes for the flight home to Brize Norton. Although I appreciated the gesture, in many ways I would have liked to sail home on the MV *Norland* so as to have completed the full circle.

The Marines and other infantry stayed on board their ships and arrived back to a heroes' welcome at Portsmouth – yet some of our lads who had borne the brunt of the fighting flew back to Britain in the dead of night with very few people to greet them. Sadly, C Company and Support Company arrived in the early hours of the morning and it was almost as if they had sneaked back into the country.

We arrived mid-morning and Prince Charles took the salute on the tarmac at Brize Norton. All our families were there and so were some of the wounded, like Peter Davies, the 2 i/c of B Company, who had taken shrapnel in his liver at Goose Green. Propped up by two nurses, he looked like a Belsen survivor, but had managed to sign himself out of hospital to welcome us home.

As I hobbled down the steps of the Herc, I scanned the sea of faces, eagerly looking for Liz. Being so tiny, she could easily disappear in a crowd. I had my red beret on and a clean smock and, although my feet were in bits, I felt like a million dollars.

Then I spied her near the front and limped across the tarmac towards her, and as I lifted her up she threw her arms around my neck and wouldn't let go. We were in another world on the coach trip to Aldershot, like newly-weds on our wedding day all over again.

That night, however, Liz burst into tears and was inconsolable. I discovered that a strong rumour had swept through the Rhondda that a local boy had been killed. People were coming up to my mother in the post office, saying things like, 'We're really sorry about Mike.'

This went on for days until all my friends thought I was dead and my parents were simply waiting for the phone call from the MoD to confirm the worst. Liz had heard the same stories, and although she told herself that it couldn't be true or she would have heard officially, a part of her broke inside and she wasn't going to be truly convinced until she had her arms around me.

As Liz told me the story, I suddenly flashed back to Bluff Cove, standing helplessly on the shore watching the *Sir Galahad* burn.

'Gibby?' I whispered.

She nodded her head.

I had a sickening feeling. I'd encouraged him to join the Army and now he was dead. If only he'd joined the Paras, I thought, but I knew from Stevie's fate that there were no guarantees.

I felt empty inside; a part of me wanted to rail against the futile waste of it all. But I couldn't forget that I was a soldier and my job was to protect my country; liberating the Falkland Islands had been a just cause.

Gibby's father took it badly, as did most of the community in Pontygwaith. It's easy to forget how much pressure families and wives endure during wartime. One of Liz's workmates in Aldershot, whose husband had died at Goose Green, cracked under the strain and cut all her hair off when she heard the news.

That night I talked to my parents on the phone and Dad kept asking when I'd be home.

'On Wednesday.'

'What time?'

'I don't know. Probably late afternoon or evening.'

'Can't it be during the day?'

'Why? Does it matter?'

'No. No. Of course not . . . it's just . . .'

Liz explained that some of the kids from the infant school in my street wanted to see a soldier who'd fought in the Falklands. 'They're really excited about the victory.'

To be honest, I didn't fancy being gawked at by schoolkids, I thought it would be too embarrassing, but to please my parents I drove down during the day, and throughout Wales I could see bunting out and Union Jacks. When I got to my street there were streamers, balloons, home-made confetti and a sign saying, 'Welcome Home, Mike'. Everybody came out to see me and that night there was a street party.

I didn't go, I just stayed inside the house and had a couple of cans with my father, Dio and Rittaz. I don't go a great deal on fanfares or parties; I'm not that sort of bloke.

After two or three days in Wales I returned to my other home in Aldershot to be amongst the lads who had done the fighting with me. That was where I really wanted to be because I couldn't explain to my parents or my Rhondda mates what I'd just been through. There was no way anybody could understand unless they'd been in the battle and shared the experience. I knew then that I'd have difficulty ever settling back into the valley or going down the pit again. It was nice and the people cared for me, but my other 'family' was in the Shot.

The whole battalion marched to and from the football stadium to receive the freedom of the town, and afterwards there was another monumental piss-up. Stan the Man had nicked the Argentinian flag at Goose Green and it was placed on the wall of the Queens, our local. All of us signed it and I signed for Stevie.

My parents had always hated Margaret Thatcher and loathed her even more after the Falklands war. However, I had a lot of respect for her as prime minister. She had the balls to stand up for the rights of the Falkland Islanders and not let international opinion sway her.

At the memorial service at St Paul's Cathedral on 26 July 1982, she got quite annoyed with the Archbishop of Canterbury, who gave a sermon that was rather anti-war and contrary to the sentiments of an occasion for mourning our war dead. Even so, it was a very moving service and I felt honoured to be chosen to represent Stevie. A dozen of us from 2 Para and the same number from 3 Para were invited. Dressed in our No. 2s and red berets, we arrived at the cathedral to be met by hundreds of well-wishers. As we walked through the crowd, a big coloured woman reached out and started hugging and kissing me. Feeling like a pop star, I clung to my red beret and gave her a kiss back.

Afterwards, the Paras were invited back to the Houses of Parliament for cocktails with the top brass and a host of politicians in a marquee overlooking the Thames. I got talking to Enoch Powell, who proved to know a lot about what had happened.

'Would you have preferred Keeble to be in charge of the battalion rather than Chaundler?' he asked.

Surprised, I replied, 'Yes, that was the general feeling on the ground.'

He nodded and began asking about Goose Green, wanting to know all the finer points. I should have expected as much from a man who, I found out later, was the youngest brigadier the British army had ever had.

When Mrs Thatcher arrived, I didn't get a chance to speak. She's not the sort of woman you can interrupt mid-sentence, so I chatted to her husband Denis and made sure both our glasses were never empty.

It had been a great day and we'd been drinking all afternoon. I finished up with Tom Harley, a corporal in D Company, and neither of us fancied catching the coach back to Aldershot. We decided to make ourselves scarce and miss the bus, encouraged by one of the MPs, who promised to take us out drinking all night.

Unfortunately the RSM found us and, although quite angry, he admitted, 'How can I give you boys a bollocking after what you've just achieved?'

Boarding the coach, we rejoined the rest of the paras back at the base. In the sergeants' mess Crosland came up to me and said, 'I want you to meet someone.'

He led me across the room and introduced me to Stevie's mother and sisters. Mrs Illingsworth started to cry and I put my arms around her, but soon I was crying as well. They'd come all the way from Doncaster for the memorial service and she wanted to know about Stevie's final moments.

'He died a hero,' I told her, glossing over the details of the fatal shot. 'He went to retrieve ammunition from one of the wounded because he knew we were running low. He wanted to get it back up the front to the lads who were fighting. That's how he got killed.'

She smiled through her tears. 'He always spoke very highly of you.'

Not surprisingly, we did a lot of drinking after the Falklands at places like the Globe Trotter, the Queens and the Trafalgar in Aldershot. The bars were full and paratroopers were popular with the local girls and landlords.

Of course, we continued doing exercises, but it's hard to get motivated by something like a blank firing drill when you've experienced the heat of battle first-hand. I'd made up my mind that I was going to stay in the Army, even though I'd been scared shitless and sworn that I'd get out at the first opportunity. I'd been to war and not many twenty-two-year-old lads could say that. Being a soldier was exciting and I was enjoying it. I knew that I couldn't go back down the pit. Four years underground is enough for anyone. Instead, I remembered the band of 'gypsies' I'd seen on Sussex Mountain. That's what I wanted to do – join the SAS.

When I explained this to Liz, she knew that I'd never be happy back in the valley as a miner. At the same time, she enjoyed her lifestyle in Aldershot and had a huge circle of friends. If I made it into the SAS, we'd have to move to Hereford near the Welsh border.

'It'll be closer to home,' I told her. 'And the money's better; and the lifestyle.'

'But I like it here,' she said.

'Kev Doyle's going for Selection.'

'Yes, but he's single.'

She didn't say anything more about it for weeks and then one day asked, 'When would it be?'

'Not for a couple of years yet – I want more experience.'

It was Liz's way of saying yes.

Dave Collins and my old platoon sergeant from the depot, Bob Powell, had both advised me to get a couple more years under my belt before applying for Selection. Bob had always wanted to do it himself, but had been promoted pretty quickly and his wife had been against the idea.

I needed more experience because, at that time, unless you were at least a corporal or a senior corporal, the SAS wouldn't look at you. They wanted older recruits who had the maturity and wisdom to think for themselves and make decisions under pressure.

One of the first things I did after the Falklands was to get my promotion courses out of the way. 'Drill and Duties' they call it in the Paras – four weeks of learning how to instruct drill movements and then six weeks of infantry tactics. After that I got made up to lance corporal.

I came back in time for another sad duty. At their families' request, the bodies of several of the guys who'd died in the Falklands were exhumed from San Carlos Water and flown home for burial in Aldershot. Cautious, Geordie, Merlin and I spent a week practising the slow-drill movements we'd be using to carry Steve Illingsworth to his final resting place. The coffins, each draped in the Union Jack, had been placed in the gymnasium on wooden plinths; the bodies had been treated with chemicals which gave the gym a sweet sickly smell that I dreaded.

The funerals were held on 26 November, nearly six months to the day since the first burials. It was a fittingly cold day, and as I stood over Steve's coffin at the cemetery in Aldershot the memories came flooding back. I looked across at Bob and realized how lucky we had been. If soldiering has a downside, I said to myself, then this is it: devastated families standing around graves as a twenty-one-gun salute shatters the air.

In February 1983, 2 Para finally made it to Central America, having missed our first posting because of the war. The Royal Anglians had been sent to Belize in our place and two of their battalions had done six-month tours before we arrived at Holdfast Camp near the village of San Ignacio. Someone had left us a message in one of the observation posts: 'Bad luck, Paras, the only thing to kill here is time!'

The tour was six months long – quite a long haul, but good

experience because most of us had never done a jungle tour. This was a whole different world for me, a steamy, rotten, damp, slimy, bug-infested shit-hole where the mozzies buzzing in your eyes and ears could drive you insane.

Most of the old crew were still together – Mick Connor, Merlin, Geordie, Bob, Stan the Man, Baz, Mouse. Dave Collins didn't come and Stan had taken over as the section corporal and I was his lance-jack. Our CSM (company sergeant-major) was Bob Powell, who'd become my mentor within the regiment since my days at Depot Para. We'd kept in touch with each other after each major battle in the Falklands, making sure that we were OK.

The further south you went in Belize, the thicker the jungle, and B Company did well to get stationed at Holdfast Camp, on a main road in the north. D Company was at the Airport Camp next to Belize City, C Company was further south at Punta Gorda by the sea, and A Company drew the short straw and got Salamanca Camp in the middle of fucking nowhere.

Holdfast wasn't bad and even had a swimming-pool. All the tin huts had fans, although most of the time we were training away from camp and carrying out a campaign of 'hearts and minds' in the area. Belize, formerly British Honduras, had gained its independence in 1981. However, it had an agreement with the UK that we could train there, and in return we would supply a reaction force consisting of an infantry battalion and supporting elements, including two Harriers. Neighbouring Guatemala had been threatening to invade for years, claiming that a part of the country belonged to them. Guatemala was ruled by a ruthless military regime and had a very good army for a third-world country. Without British support, Belize would be no match for them. Both countries gained from the arrangement – safety for the Belizians and invaluable jungle training in Central America for the Brits.

Between Holdfast Camp and the nearest large village, San Ignacio, was a place called Esperanza, a lawless outpost full of *bandidos* which was strictly out of bounds – for our own safety. A British soldier had been macheted to death there a few years earlier.

Esperanza was little more than a series of huts and brick buildings that sprawled from the edge of Holdfast, but it had its own marijuana field and the *bandidos* would trade in drugs, weapons and anything else they could turn a profit on. There were hutloads of half-naked kids running around with no shoes, mongrel dogs picking through rubbish heaps and a curious smell of smoking logs and red beans and rice – the staple diet.

San Ignacio, 3 miles away, was a thriving metropolis in comparison. It had plenty of bars, some of them makeshift and others official, as well as one hotel with a disco, where every other track seemed to be Michael Jackson. If we weren't on exercise or on duty at Holdfast, we'd get down to San Ignacio for a night out, probably about once a fortnight.

We'd been at Holdfast for a couple of months when Airborne Forces Day gave us a good reason to party. While we celebrated down at the river, the locals challenged us to a tug-of-war contest using the rope that normally pulled a raft across the wide stretch of water. They took up the rope on one bank and we were on the other side – all pretty pissed after drinking in the sun. The wager was for a crate of beer and when the referee screamed, 'Pull!' We gave it everything for Britain and the regiment.

'Come on, pull you weak bastards!' I cried, anchoring our challenge, but no matter how hard we tried, we couldn't even budge the villagers on the far side. We lost four pulls in a row before someone sussed what was happening: they'd tied their end of the rope to a tree. Rule number 1,054 since joining the Paras: never underestimate the intelligence of the locals.

Of course, I ended up lying in bed with a monster hangover, trying to motivate myself to get up and drive to San Ignacio. One of my duties as a lance-jack was to go and ferry the cleaners from the village to the camp and home again at night.

A friend of mine, Andy, had gone easy on the beer and he offered to pick them up for me.

'Cheers, mate,' I groaned. 'I'll owe you one.'

The road to San Ignacio went straight through Esperanza and, unfortunately, Andy ran over and killed a local who was sleeping it off on the side of the road. Instead of turning around and coming back to camp, he carried on and picked up the cleaning women. By the time he drove back through Esperanza, a big crowd had gathered at the accident scene and were ready to string Andy up from the nearest tree.

We had to square it with the locals and after delicate negotiations an uneasy peace was struck.

A few weeks later, we had reports in camp from the Field Intelligence NCOs that the local Mennonite community had complained of being attacked and robbed by *bandidos* on their way to market in Belize City. The Mennonites were an Amish-like group

139

of settlers of Dutch–German origin, who had arrived as missionaries years earlier. They dressed like the Amish, with the men in wide-brimmed hats and the women wearing hoods.

They were nice people and we used to refer to them as the 'mechanized' and 'non-mechanized battalions' because one group of Mennonites had farm machinery and four-wheel drives and the other still used horses to plough the fields and take their produce to market in horse-drawn carts.

I didn't know how successful they were in converting the South Americans but they were certainly very clean, and when we visited them to pick up milk for the camp I was impressed by the white painted fences and pristine buildings.

For the non-mechanized Mennonite battalion, the journey to market took two days and, having sold their wares, they were being robbed at gunpoint on the return journey. In one case a woman had been raped. Normally it would be a local police matter, but the officer in charge at Holdfast Camp decided we should put out patrols to help investigate.

I was with my platoon commander when we went to interview the victims.

'When did it happen?' the officer asked.

'Four moons ago,' said an elderly spokesman.

'How many of them were there?'

'A dozen, perhaps more. Wouldst thou care for some refreshments?'

'Did any of you fight back?' I asked.

'Thou must understand, we do not believe in violence.'

'Not even when your women are being raped?'

He shook his head.

We were taken to the jungle clearing where the robbery had occurred and the local policemen from San Ignacio looked decidedly nervous about entering *bandido* country.

Two patrols had been sent out, 5 Platoon and 6 Platoon, and from the clearing we went off in different directions into the jungle, looking for a trail. In charge of 6 Platoon was Manny Eismann, an interesting character whose father had been a German paratrooper in the Second World War. He'd been a part of 6 Platoon in the Falklands, soldiering alongside Marty Majerisson, the Scouse corporal who'd been shot in the face.

Each platoon took it in turns to push further into the jungle. Minutes after 6 Platoon had taken over from us, we heard the sound of gunshots. They'd emerged into a village clearing and come across a group of no-gooders armed with two shotguns. One of them was the head honcho, who was easily recognizable because he only had one leg and looked like Long John Silver.

Unfortunately this guy made the mistake of swinging around and raising his gun towards Manny – something you don't do when four paratroopers with Armalites are lined up against you. The lads opened up, killed the leader and wounded two others. The rest scarpered into the jungle.

It turned out that we'd stumbled upon the illegal runway being used by the Esperanza bandits. A search of the village uncovered hashish, cocaine and bundles of hundred-dollar bills, along with maps that plotted where the Mennonites had been attacked.

The dead guy was chopped out in a body bag and the incident made the local Belize newspapers. We got the English version and posted if off to the Anglians with the message, 'Only killing time?'

Unfortunately the British army wasn't so pleased with our efforts, particularly when Manny had to go to court to face a possible murder charge. Army solicitors defended him and several lads were called to give evidence confirming that the *bandido* had raised his shotgun as if about to fire.

He won the case, but feelings in Esperanza were running high; many locals were unhappy that the *paracadistas* had now killed two of their fraternity, including a village leader.

The Army decided to punish us and took the Armalites away, replacing them with SLRs, which is quite a blow when you're on the jungle tour because they're a lot heavier and harder to maintain in the wet.

Towards the end of our stint in Belize we set out to forge a route through the jungle from one side of Belize to the other, crossing the Great Divide, a feat that had never been done before. Four of us from 5 Platoon were choppered in for the fourth leg, flying over an impenetrable canopy. The jungle was so thick a person could turn around and get lost within a few yards.

We landed and took over from John Geddis's patrol, which consisted of Mouse, Merlin and Geordie. John had been with Patrols Platoon in the Falklands and had joined us from C Company. A South African, via Newcastle, he was a hard bastard and we hit it off straight away. After the Belize tour he was planning to tackle Selection.

Our patrol consisted of myself, Stan the Man, Cautious Bob and Mark, a tough little Brummie who'd joined the platoon just before

Belize. We carried on the tab and basha'd up for the night quite a distance from the main river.

I'd never experienced jungle rain before and there was a massive downpour that night. Raindrops were hitting my poncho like a big brass drum, bending it inwards as it collected the torrent. I shoved the water off and seconds later it had filled up again. Thunder crashed overhead.

Eventually these same sounds lulled me to sleep. I dreamed of splashing through the surf at Porthcawl and when I woke my legs were flapping away underneath me. It was pitch-black.

'Bob, fucking get up!' I screamed.

We were up to our waists in the river, which was rising all the time.

In the darkness we collected what we could – weapons and bergens were the priority. Luckily dawn was approaching and come daylight we found ourselves on an island in the middle of a monster river. The night before it had been barely 25 metres wide; now it was huge and the colour of milk chocolate.

We did a map appreciation and decided that the best course was to go downstream, travelling along the river bank until we hit a particular junction. Then we could tab over the top of a ridge to where our part of the journey finished.

'Are we all agreed?' asked Stan.

'Yeah,' we chorused, although Cautious Bob sounded less enthusiastic. 'We'll stay near the riverbank?' he asked.

'Of course,' Stan said. 'But what's wrong with getting a bit wet?'

Bob pulled a face. 'I can't swim,' he said.

'Uncle Mike'll look after you,' I said.

Wrapping our ponchos round our bergens, making bundles that could float, we attached them to us by paracord and waded into the fast-flowing water. But the current was too strong and no sooner were we up to our waists than the water whipped us away, sweeping us downstream at a rapid rate of knots as we clung to our floating bundles. As the jungle flashed by us, including our junction in the river, there was nothing we could do. We might as well have been four children riding a water slide.

As the current slowed slightly I desperately tried to get back to the bank. Trying to cling on to his bundle, Bob began to struggle as a Y-junction in the river came up fast.

Stan cried out, 'He's lost his bergen!'

Bob had a shotgun tied to his wrist and I could see this was also flailing about.

'Mike? Mike?' he shouted.

'Hold on! I'm coming!'

I manoeuvred towards him. Bob was going under and thrashing around; his bergen had already gone, along with the radio. Ahead there was a large log midstream. Bob grabbed hold of a branch and clung on; I managed to grab hold of the log and pull myself to him. Meanwhile Mark and Stan were swept on downstream.

'The bergen was dragging me down – I panicked,' said Bob, clearly upset.

'We can't stay here. We can't lose the others.'

Bob looked worried.

'Come on, just hold on to me,' I said.

He attached himself like a limpet and off we went, being carried along by the torrent deeper and deeper into the jungle. Our plan had failed and now it was a case of survival.

By the time we struggled ashore, we were miles further downstream than planned, well past the junction and definitely 'tactically misplaced' – the Army term for lost.

Bob was gutted. The radio had gone, but nobody blamed him.

'Stevie would have given you some shit, though, if he'd been here,' I said.

Rejoining the others, we sorted ourselves out and basha'd up on the riverbank, trying to consolidate our meagre stores and rations. We had no comms, but on the plus side Stan had managed to keep hold of the TACBE (radio/distress beacon) in his beltkit, plus some smoke grenades for signalling. He also had maps, but they weren't much good to us unless we could find some landmark or navigational feature that we could connect to the map.

All our scoff had been washed away and we were left with just the emergency rations on our beltkit. These consisted of a couple of packets of broken hard tack biscuits, glucose sweets and chocolate.

Bob looked at the maps. On our leg of the tab there were no villages or settlements. The map consisted of unbroken green, with the river snaking like a python through the centre. Only now it was a giant python, with dozens of other pythons joining it.

'Where the fuck are we?' exclaimed Bob.

'We're fucking lost,' said Stan. 'No doubt about it. Which means we stay here till they find us – or until we figure out where we are.'

Mark said, 'How long do you reckon before they'll start looking?'

'The way I see it,' I said, 'either we stay here and wait for help or we get a brew on now and then start tabbing out of here.'

'Where to?' Bob said.

Stan shrugged. 'There's nothing we can aim for.'

'Well I don't fancy fucking waiting here,' I said.

'Me neither,' said Mark.

'It could fuck us up even more to move,' Stan said. 'I reckon two days at the most and they'll find us.'

'Stan's right,' Mark said. 'We'll sit it out and wait for help. We'll make matters worse if we stumble on out there.'

'OK,' I nodded. 'We'll still get a brew on though!'

Although we knew basic survival techniques, we were just raw kids when it came to living in the jungle.

Our Zippo lighters had to be dried out, fire being a priority, then shelter. At least the rain had stopped. We cut a small clearing in the jungle and switched on the TACBE. The smoke canister wasn't to be used until we heard a search aircraft.

We set up two little bashas in the clearing, Bob and I sharing one. Then we got a fire going and our kit began to dry out gradually. However, hexamine was in short supply, as was brew kit, so we decided to ration ourselves to one brew in the morning and one in the evening.

Next day we explored to different points of the compass, trying to connect some recognizable feature with the map and pinpoint our location. Apart from this, we tried to conserve energy and not walk around much. The sun burned down into our clearing, drying out the jungle and creating a smell of steaming, rotting vegetation.

Now and again a plane could be heard high up in the sky and we tuned the TACBE to Channel 1, sending out the international distress tone that an aircraft should pick up. There was no response.

Surely they were out looking for us, but what was taking them so long?

We rationed ourselves to two biscuits of hard tack per day, but these ran out after two and a half days, and by now we were sharing a brew between four of us. The navigation exercises had proved futile and so were our attempts at hunting for iguanas and monkeys to eat. We weren't jungle experts, and had no knowledge of how to build traps or navigate through a green wall.

Day four arrived and so did the headaches. Bob, in particular, was getting dizzy spells whenever he stood up. We kept reassuring each other that help was coming soon.

'I can't fucking stand this,' I grimaced. 'I want to be doing something.'

'Yeah, but how long would we last out there?' Bob said, glancing at the jungle. The vegetation was so dense, any attempt to move would be futile. We simply had to rely on the others to find us and get us out.

No matter how hard I tried, I couldn't stop thinking about my granny's bread and dripping and Mum's Sunday roast and Liz's spaghetti Bolognese. And it didn't matter what we talked about, the conversation always came back to scoff.

'I fucking hate those fly biscuits (the garibaldis in the ration packs), but I'd walk a mile over red coals for a packet right now,' said Bob, sat propped against a tree.

'Do you realize,' I said, 'that in the few years since we've known one another it's been one fucking nightmare after another.'

'Yeah, the sooner you fuck off to Hereford the better, mate.'

'You might go as well.'

'How do you reckon that?'

'I might end up eating you here.'

The river still hadn't gone down. Every day the rains came for two to three hours, feeding the flood and keeping the current racing along. When the sun came out, the mozzies returned with a vengeance. We gathered the rainwater and poured it into our water bottles after Steritabbing it. This gave the water a chemical taste that, after so long without food, began making us retch.

The other major worry was the TACBE. It didn't have an exceptionally long battery life and we'd been putting it on only periodically during the day.

On the fifth morning I tried to stand and felt dizzy. My mind began playing tricks and I swore I could hear the distant sound of chopper blades. The night before had seen our last brew; now we only had our Steritabbed water left. Mark had been retching, unable to vomit, and Bob was feeling pretty weak.

'Geordie's probably tucking into red beans and rice back at camp,' I said.

'Yeah, fuck him. I hope he chokes.'

The morning downpour was stronger than before, ripping through our little clearing. We collected the water in the spare poncho.

Stan and I were the strongest of the patrol and I began wondering whether one or both of us should leave and seek help. But the ground seemed to rise all around us, apart from the river, and the vegetation was so dense that I doubted if we'd ever find the patrol again.

Around about midday, I heard it, this time for real. *Wop-wop-wop-wop*.

Mark and Bob were under the bashas. Stan and I were in the clearing, discussing the different possibilities.

'Did you hear that?'

Stan cocked his head and listened. I thought maybe I was imagining it again.

*Wop-wop-wop*.

'Fuck me!' said Stan.

The TACBE was already turned on to the emergency channel. The sound of chopper blades grew louder. Stan turned to channel two and began speaking. 'Hello, heli, this is Bravo two–two, over.'

The pilot responded in a thick Spanish accent: 'Bravo two–two, this is Yankee two–zero. Have you got smoke?'

Setting off the smoke grenade in the clearing, we watched as the chopper homed in on us and lowered a winch.

Bob went up first, then Mark, me and Stan.

Ian Aird was on board to greet us; he looked at us and laughed – no sympathy here. Shouting to be heard above the blades, he grinned, 'That was a bad location to stop in, lads – didn't you notice, it's pretty wet down there.'

Looking down we saw that the chocolate python had seeped into the jungle around our position, which was surrounded by hills. There was no way we could have tabbed out of there alone. The decision to stay together had been a good one.

Mark was the worse for wear and I thought he'd go straight back to camp.

'Do you lads want to carry on?' Ian Aird asked.

Stan and I were shoving Mars bars from the compo boxes down our necks. We looked at each other. 'Why the fuck not?'

'Yeah, I'm OK – put my name down,' said Bob.

After ten minutes of flying, the chopper set us down again into the jungle. We'd have a tab of maybe a day and a half in front of us, out of the bog-infested jungle into sparser vegetation.

Remarkably, Mark decided he wasn't jacking either. We basha'd up that night and made a communal curry-from-hell, laughing about what had happened. Stan got the blame from all of us because he was the section commander. Yet deep inside, where you store the things you don't speak about, we all probably knew how close we'd come to perishing. It had been a baptism of fire in the jungle and a taste of what I could expect if I wanted to join the SAS. I'd already heard that the jungle was regarded as the toughest part of Selection.

After finishing the tour, I flew to America and met up with Liz in Miami for ten days. Having spent nearly six months apart, we didn't leave the hotel room for the first four days, but then managed to see Disneyland and Daytona Beach. Never having been Stateside, I walked around gobsmacked by the sights and sounds and smells. I fell in love with America – and the Americans.

Ironically, less than twelve months later, I was back across the Atlantic when 2 Para was sent to Fort Lewis in Washington State for joint exercises with the elite Rangers, our Yank counterparts. It gave me an insight into how the American military work, and in general we held them in high esteem, particularly the Marines and their Special Forces, who had come to the fore in Vietnam.

Fort Lewis was huge, with more helicopters on one base than the whole British army possessed. Stan and I went running every morning in the mist, bombing past various American platoons shuffling along singing their songs and barely breaking into a sweat. They all seemed so big compared to our lads.

The camp had several different bars. One of them was where all the coloured soldiers drank, listening to Tamla Motown and soul. Stan and I went in there one night and copped a lot of stares and shuffling about. We were the only whites. After a while, one or two lads came over and got chatting. They said that white guys never socialized with them.

'Why's that?' I asked.

They looked at each other.

'Must be because they're wankers,' I suggested.

I doubted they knew what a 'wanker' meant, but they roared with laughter anyway. We had a great night.

Another night we ended up in a country-and-western bar full of soldiers from the Midwest. They were decked out in checked shirts, cowboy boots and stetsons, and were doing a sort of line dance.

Ray, a short squat Jock from Glasgow, started to dance along. It looked more like the Highland fling than a line dance. A big Texan took exception to this and shoved Ray around. He looked twice Ray's size – surely no contest – but as he bent down, Ray gave him a Glasgow kiss square on the forehead.

The Yank screamed, 'Oh my God, he's hit me with his face!'

The dancing stopped and Ray came back to the bar grinning from ear to ear. Which all goes to prove, it's not the dog in the fight, it's the fight in the dog.

The purpose of the trip was to put the battalion, company by company, through the American version of our 'Brecon'. The exercise consisted of a monster tab over four days in a training area called Yakama – Native American territory.

Beforehand we were given lessons by Ranger instructors on how to survive in a harsh winter environment, where to find food and how to build shelters.

Wearing snowshoes, we tabbed high up in the snowline area in Yakama, using maps and co-ordinates to locate rations that had been left for us. If you didn't find the food, you went hungry.

The Rangers became downhearted when Bob and I found most of the scoff for them, and because of our fitness we tabbed them into the deck, despite the altitude. As a whole, the Paras were simply much fitter and hardier, and I got the impression that the Americans had grown accustomed to their creature comforts and become a little soft.

The difference could be summed up by an incident in which Bob Powell dished out instant justice to two of our lads who disobeyed orders not to drink before the parachute jump which ended the exercise. They turned up late for the parade, smelling of alcohol, and after we'd jumped Bob called them into his office.

'I'm going to give you lads a choice. Would you prefer a fine or instant punishment?'

They thought about this. A fine would normally mean two weeks' pay.

'Instant punishment,' they chorused.

Bob stood up, walked around from behind his desk, and punched them so hard he knocked both of them out and broke one man's jaw.

After all the hard work we had some R and R, and a few of us went to a port called Tacoma, 35 miles south of Seattle. It had an Indian reservation on the outskirts of a town called, remarkably, Ferndale.

As I was jumping in a taxi at Fort Lewis with Baz Bardsley, Baby Bish and Syd Baldwyn from the Mortar Platoon – all big lads and rugby players – the driver asked, 'Where do you want to go?'

'Where's all the life?' asked Baz.

'That'll be downtown, but I'd give it a miss if I were you – it's full of Indians.'

'No problem, just drop us off there.'

Rocking into the first bar, a seedy joint that smelled of whisky and chewing tobacco, we ordered beers and began shooting pool. This place was as rough as they come, with no doors on the toilets; you could actually see guys jabbing needles in their arms and shooting up.

As we enjoyed ourselves, a Native American with long hair and a stove-pipe hat wandered over to us.

'Are you guys sailors?'

'No, no, we're British soldiers,' I said.

'Wanna buy some drugs?'

'No, no, we're shooting pool, we don't need any drugs.'

This guy obviously made his living by supplying visitors with anything they wanted – and I mean anything.

'Want some women?'

'No, we don't need any women.'

'Young boys?'

Drinking up, we moved on to the next dive and behind the bar found a bloke from Whitchurch in Cardiff. We got talking and he put some old rugby footage on the video screen for us to watch. There were two other bartenders, and during the evening one of them started arguing with an Indian in a sharp suit who looked like a pimp. The commotion grew louder and louder until the customer pulled a knife and stuck it in the barman's shoulder before running out.

With our medical training, we obviously offered to help, but the Welsh guy warned us off. He said that Americans were so litigious that if the wounded barman died after we'd given assistance his family could sue us.

'The best thing you can do is get the hell out of here,' he said, as he mopped up the blood with a towel.

Outside on the pavement we took a vote on whether to carry on drinking and were all pissed enough to say, 'Yeah.'

Heading into the bar next door, who should we find having a quiet beer but the Indian in a flash suit – together with several of his mates. Thinking better of it, we decided to make our way up town.

Being so close to Vancouver, the whole area had quite a Canadian influence and an overspill of rugby supporters. We finished up in a rugby bar chatting to an American who seemed decent enough, although a bit of a spiv. Later that night he took Baz and me back downtown where the booze was cheaper and the bars never shut. Syd and Baby Bish headed back to the camp.

Inside a new bar, I volunteered to get the drinks in and stopped off at the toilet on my way. Inside, I was immediately surrounded by six or seven guys, most of them Indians. A set-up, I thought – they're going to rob me.

A door leading outside was open and I contemplated rushing them. It wouldn't have mattered because half a dozen of their mates were waiting in the courtyard outside. Suddenly I was blinded by lights coming from every direction. Trying to shield my eyes, I realized that I was in the centre of a scrapyard, surrounded by cars – some of them rusting wrecks that were still wired up to batteries so their headlights functioned.

A 20-foot high chain-link fence completed the arena, which was filled with people, all wearing baseball caps, cowboy boots and checked shirts.

I was shoved forward onto a patch of bare, rock-hard earth about 10 feet by 10 feet.

'D'ya know how to fight, boy?' asked a grizzled white guy.

'I'm not fighting anyone.'

'Are you a pussy, boy? Where you from – Pussyland?'

The crowd were laughing and a couple of Indians began jabbing me in the ribs.

Then I spied the guy I was supposed to fight, an Indian who was about 6 feet 5 and built like a barrel. He was drinking a beer and looking at me from under his hat.

The crowd were hurling abuse and the white guy leaned closer. 'I think it might be a good idea if you took this guy on.'

The message was clear – I had no choice.

There were no rules, of course. It was a bare-knuckle, boots-and-all fight with the winner getting twenty bucks. My grandfather, Dai Curtis, was quite a mountain fighter in the days when miners used to square up on a mountain top above the village after a session in the pub on Sunday mornings. Now I had to carry on the Curtis family tradition by beating this Indian who had a huge tattooed beer belly.

The best option, I decided, was to get straight in and hit him hard and early. A problem arose when he shrugged off these blows as if he'd collided with a feather. He didn't feel a thing and might have been on drugs. For about a minute he threw me around while the crowd screamed encouragement until finally I landed a punch deep into his guts and felt him crumple. I gave him a quick left and a right as he went down, and stepped back as he lay on the ground fighting for breath.

The crowd wanted me to kick him when he was down, but I refused and turned away. The old white guy gave me twenty dollars and said, 'Good fight, Limey. Now get outta here.'

I ran down an alleyway to the main street, expecting to get jumped at any moment, and doubled back to the bar. I found Baz at the counter, ordering drinks. When I'd told him what had happened he looked at me and said, 'Fuck you, Taff, some people will do anything to avoid buying a round.'

The bastard American had disappeared, having no doubt got his cut from the fight promoter. I dragged Baz out, realizing, for all our exploits in battle, that we were babes when it came to the streets of Tacoma.

Back at the camp my hands were in a pretty bad state from the fight, but I managed to keep it a secret, especially from Bob Powell. I just put it down to experience and vowed it wouldn't happen again.

At home Liz was pregnant, with the baby due in late October. The date became an important issue because 2 Para had a six-month tour of Northern Ireland beginning in early November.

Liz asked, 'What if you're away when the baby is born?'

I said, 'No problem, love, I'm sure they'll send me back,' knowing full well there wasn't a snowball's chance in hell. You don't come back from an operational tour unless it's an emergency, and the Army doesn't consider first-born children to fall into this category.

With great timing, Rachel arrived on 17 October, and I managed to have ten days with her before leaving. She'd be six months old when I next saw her. That's the Army for you.

Liz had been scheduled to have a Caesarian at 0930 hours; I'd taken her to the hospital the previous afternoon, and that night B Company were having a big do. However, the plan went to shit when Liz's waters broke during the night, by which time I was well under the influence, fast asleep in bed with two alarm clocks to wake me up at 0800.

The ward sister rang me at 0300 for about thirty minutes, but to no avail. When I arrived at the hospital the next day, she gave me a hearty bollocking for not being there – but did I care? I was elated; Liz was in bits, but there was Rachel right next to her, sucking her thumb. She was the most wonderful thing I had ever seen in my life; I picked her up and couldn't put her down.

Six weeks later I lodged my application form to join the SAS and learned that Selection would begin in August 1985. Every spare moment during the tour of Northern Ireland was spent in the gym and running round the helipad.

At the age of twenty-six I had the experience and the navigation skills and was the fittest I'd ever been, but was it enough to pass the toughest selection procedure of any army unit anywhere in the world?

# 9

ON A LAZY SUNDAY AFTERNOON IN HEREFORD, WITH HARDLY ANYONE ON the roads, I got lost trying to find Stirling Lines, the headquarters of 22 SAS Regiment. Eventually I pulled up at a garage to ask the attendant. A teenaged girl looked up from a magazine and said, 'You're the seventy-first person to ask me that today.'

'Sorry.'

'I suppose you're down for Selection?'

'Yeah.'

She smiled knowingly. 'Good luck – you're going to need it.'

Finding the camp, I booked in with the MoD lodge at the main gate. There was a list of names on a blackboard giving details of room allocations and mealtimes. All courses were to report to the gym at 1900 hours.

The camp was quieter than I'd expected, and smaller. The training wing accommodation was sited away from the Sabre Squadrons' barracks and right next to the cookhouse.

'That's handy,' I said to another trainee, hoping to break the ice.

'Yeah,' he said, looking away, cutting the conversation dead.

Then it dawned on me that I wasn't the only nervous one. Most of us were on edge and sizing each other up, wondering who would still be there at the end of the six-month ordeal.

There were lads from all the different regiments trying to get in and I was pleased to find Scouse McVey and Davey Lee, both paras, in my room. I knew we'd have a good laugh. Scouse was as skinny as old man Steptoe, but a tough motherfucker, and it didn't matter how much weight you put on his back, he'd still tab most other people into the ground. His brother Mick, who was also on Selection, was exactly the same.

Scouse and Davey cold-shouldered everyone, calling them 'crap hats', but I wanted to keep an open mind and be more laid back. It didn't last long. The guy in the bunk opposite had a complete chemist's shop inside his locker, every vitamin known to mankind and an assortment of creams and lotions. We christened him 'the Chemist'. Another guy kept packing and unpacking his bergen.

'Fucking hat!' Scouse decided.

At seven o'clock we assembled in the gym. There were 160 lads from all corners of the Army, wearing their different head dress. We paras bunched together and looked like an open box of matches in our red berets.

As I looked around the vast hall I noticed parachute harnesses suspended from the roof and a helicopter mock-up high in the rafters with an abseiling rope dangling from its open door. As I was taking this in a Para officer I knew well from the Falklands strolled in, wearing his red beret at a jaunty angle on his head, old jungle boots and jungle denims. I'd already been told he was the officer in charge of the training wing.

'Just an informal brief, gentlemen,' he said. 'Basically to say there will only be about a third of you left here after the first month. You are all volunteers for this course. It won't be easy, but I guarantee you the rewards at the end will be worth all the pain and suffering. I wish you luck.'

One of the DS, an ex-Scots Guardsman, stepped forward and said he was going to show us the basics of packing a bergen. Tom Williams couldn't have been more than 5 feet 6 inches tall; he was certainly the shortest ex-Guardsman I'd ever seen.

'It's important to balance the weight inside the bergen,' he said, showing us what essentials to carry – warm kit, a poncho, talcum powder, spare socks. 'Put them in a plastic bag,' Tom said, 'and then put that plastic bag inside another plastic bag.'

After the briefing, Davey looked around our room at the lads feverishly practising packing their bergens and said, 'Fuck this, let's go for a pint.'

'Good idea. I'm going fucking nuts in here,' said Scouse.

The three of us went down town for what was to become a nightly ritual of two pints of Guinness and a fish-and-chip supper, eating them as we walked back to the camp.

*

Selection is basically split into three parts. The first is fitness and navigation, which involves a month spent in the Brecon Beacons; the second is jungle training in the rainforests of Brunei and the third is combat survival.

On the first morning, the 4-tonners arrived and we piled on board with our bergens and were taken into the mountains. We spent all day tabbing round the hills, the main aim being to stay with the DS and not fall behind.

The 4-tonners carted us home, too exhausted to speak. I cleaned my FN 7.62, got in the queue for the armoury and then raced across the block for a bath. A shower was no good – it had to be boiling hot bathwater with Radox. The welts on my shoulders stung like fuck, but I was luckier than some lads who had fearsome blisters on their heels and toes.

The block smelled like a rugby changing-room; the medicinal odours of Algipan and liniment hung heavy in the air as the lads applied handfuls of the stuff to various sore parts of their bodies.

'C'mon, Taff,' said Davey, 'I can hear the Guinness calling me.'

'Foooooood, glorious fooooood!' sang Scouse.

Before going into town we had a quick look at the daily detail on a blackboard at the end of the corridor, which gave timings and weights for the next day.

'B/FAST 0530. ARMOURY 0600. RTM 0615. WEIGHT 40 lbs.'

Davey shook his head. 'And my travel agent recommended this place.'

We packed our bergens and weighed them on a set of scales in the corridor.

Scouse said, 'Forty pounds – spot on. Let's go.'

Downtown, we drank at the first pub we came to, sitting outside and enjoying the long twilight. The walk back helped stretch away the aches and pains.

Although it was only ten o'clock when we got back the room was in total blackness with everyone tucked up in bed – fucking hats! The following day, one guy actually went out for a run after we got back from the hills. I just stared at him in disbelief as he put his running kit on. It was 'the Chemist' and needless to say he came off the next day, failing Selection because he couldn't finish the tab. Dickhead!

On the fourth morning we gathered in the gymnasium. The OC sat at a table and each of the DS had a chair. The scene struck me as familiar and I suddenly remembered my first day of P Company.

One of the first bouts, and probably the best, was Scouse McVey and his brother Mick. Talk about sibling rivalry. I doubted if any of the other lads realized they were brothers as they waded into each other like mortal enemies, neither giving an inch. The fight ended in a draw and the officer announced from his throne, 'That's what we want to see here this morning.'

There were a lot of nervous faces but the Para Reg lads had been through this before – a minute of mayhem and all-out aggression. As at Depot Para, the bouts were arranged by weight and I was among the last to fight.

I'd been paired up with an officer and knew the DS were watching for any sign of weakness or fear. I waded into this big guy and put him down four or five times within forty-five seconds. He left Selection that day. As I sat down in the corner, there was another uneven fight and the OC seemed disappointed.

'Right, put the winner in with Big Taff again,' he said.

This time I had to fight a big Welsh officer and after about thirty seconds he began to waver. I pressed home the advantage and he went down towards the end. My heart and lungs were burning.

The first week culminated on Friday with the 'Fan Dance' – a punishing tab carrying bergens that started up the old railway line in Torpanto. The DS, Bob Shepherd, started like a runaway express train and we were all strung out after only a few hundred metres. I managed to stay with him over the Fan (Pen-y-Fan) and down the other side, where I expected that we'd stop for a five-minute breather. Not a chance, Shep just turned round and came straight back. This set the standard for the coming weeks and a lot of blokes failed before Selection had barely begun.

We had the weekend off and I took Liz and Rachel down to the seaside at Porthcawl, staying in a caravan and eating fish and chips on the pier. I'd booked the caravan for a month, planning to work hard all week on the hills and reunite with them both at the weekends to relax in the sunshine.

'How is it going?' asked Liz, grimacing when she saw the welts on my shoulders and bruises on my face.

'Not bad. I'll live,' I said.

Over the previous few months, she'd seen me training and knew how badly I wanted to pass. Normally we never talked about my work, although we did discuss the future. I'd promised her a better way of life if I passed the course, with more money and better accommodation, maybe even our own house. The Rhondda would be only an hour's drive away. These were like carrots dangled in front of her, because she found it hard to think of leaving all her friends in the Shot.

Rachel and I went splashing about in the sea on a beautiful day and the salt water stung the blisters that had started forming at the base of my back during the Fan Dance.

On Sunday night I reported back to Hereford and we spent the next five days carrying progressively heavier weights in the Radnor Forest area, navigating in groups of four and then down to groups of two.

Finally we did a night tab in pairs and I partnered an MP (military policeman) who clung to my coat-tails through the hills and forests, ending up as a great big ball of sweat. I don't think he got his map out once – he just followed my lead. He probably didn't learn a thing on the night tab and I wasn't going to lose precious time by showing him how to navigate. That's the thing about doing the hills in Selection. It's a selfish effort because you need to get through quickly and then get yourself sorted out for the next day. This guy was clearly out of his depth and I never saw him again.

Week three was the hardest. After travelling in the 4-tonners to the Elan valley every day, we had to navigate and tab between certain grid references on the map. Although it wasn't a hard place in which to navigate and we had good tabbing weather, dry and cool, everything else about the place was a fucking nightmare. The terrain was covered in huge tufts of grass – we called them 'babies' heads' – which made it impossible to get up any speed or momentum. To make matters worse, the ground was normally so boggy that it sucked at your boots every step of the way.

After fighting my way through this shit for about 20 kilometres, I finally reached the DS at the designated co-ordinates.

'OK, where are you?' he shouted.

I pointed at the map with a blade of grass. 'Here, Staff.'

'OK, next grid 456789, where is it?'

'Here, Staff.'

'OK, off you go then.'

Then he sat back, pulled out his paperback and took a big swig of his brew while I charged off again, stumbling across the babies' heads.

I passed one guy who'd obviously fallen for the last time. He was so pissed off he was biting into a big tuft of grass with his teeth and pulling it out with his hands, screaming, 'I hate you fucking bastards!' He was another guy I never saw again.

That night Scouse and Dave both left Stirling Lines; they'd succumbed to injuries in the Elan valley. Our gang of three was now down to one.

'I'm gonna be back,' said Scouse, mega pissed off. I believed him.

Dave was much more relaxed, and I knew that he'd be just as happy back in his beloved Para Reg.

There was no letting up on those who remained. After one nightmare march, Joe Bailey, the sergeant major, announced, 'OK, lads, there's a 4-tonner coming in now. Those of you who want to go back for a hot meal and a shower, get on board and you'll be back in Hereford in approximately one and a half hours. The other lads can assemble to the side there and you'll be getting your maps and going out on a night tab.'

About five or six people actually fell for the trap and headed for a hot shower and scoff. Bailey took down their names and they were off the course. The rest of us then boarded the 4-tonners back to Hereford.

One particular bloke, Sean from 3 Para, had shown amazing stamina to get this far. A good soldier and a fit lad, he had one major weakness: women. Sean was a mad shagger and took every available opportunity to slip away and spend the night with one of the local girls. Before leaving each evening he'd pack his bergen and leave it by his bed; I'd make sure it was out at the wagons for him each morning. Then, at the last minute, he'd come screaming into camp after his night of horizontal tabbing and jump on board the 4-tonner.

Sean managed to keep this up for three and a half weeks until Test Week finally sorted him out. If only he'd kept his dick in his pants, he'd have made it to the jungle, no problems. But he was tabbing on two hours' kip a night and couldn't sustain the pace.

As those who'd failed packed their kit to go back to their units, the room was getting quieter. I'd ask them for their Radox as they were packing and always got the same reply, 'May as well, I don't fucking need it now!'

Test Week was indeed a bastard. We had to race against the clock in the Elan valley, tabbing all day, having our scoff and then tabbing all night. Each task was more punishing, involving greater distance and increased weight. Soon there were only three lads left in my room.

The culmination was an ordeal known simply as 'Endurance'.

The blackboard at the end of the corridor said it all:

'B/FAST 0001 FRIDAY. ARMOURY 0030. RTM 0045. WEIGHT 55 lbs. FOOD AND WATER NOT INCLUDED.'

At 1.00 a.m. the 4-tonners set off for Brecon and the tab from hell. All us racing snakes, the lads who had performed the quickest tabs over the last week, were aboard the first vehicle. I got chatting with Peter Davies, my Company 2 i/c in the Falklands who'd been badly wounded at Goose Green only yards from me. I'd thought he was dead, but he'd welcomed us back at Brize Norton, unsteady on crutches with two nurses supporting him. I remembered him looking like a Belsen survivor, having lost all his hair and with his skin pulled tight across his face. Now, three years later, he was about to undertake one of the hardest forced marches any army anywhere in the world can throw at you.

It's often not easy for an officer and a lower rank to get on, but we'd been through a lot together. Arriving at the drop-off point in the chilly early hours, Peter and I jumped off the tailgate at Talybont reservoir.

'How you feeling, Boss?' I asked.

'Fucked, and I don't fancy that monster either, Mike.'

Both of us looked up at the towering mountain before us; a big black feature against the night sky. The two lines between the ridge and the sky could just be made out.

'D'you know, I didn't think I'd get through the first week.'

'That's 'cos you're a crap runner,' I told him, and he knew it was the truth. The first week, there had been a lot of runs up and down hills in the local area, without weight. Peter was always last or thereabouts; it wasn't until they put a bergen on his back that he showed what he could really do.

The OC spied us and began smirking. 'What are you fuckers scheming about?'

'Just planning a set of tennis later,' said Peter.

Don Wilson called the first four together; a quick brief and off they went. I watched them dissolve into the hill, four figures struggling under the weight.

Eventually it was my turn. Don gave us our first grid, at the Storey Arms, about 20 clicks away, and off we went. It was a chilly night and I only had a vest on under my Para smock, but within a few hundred metres I was a sweaty mess. The bergen cut into my shoulders and the obligatory FN 7.62 'walking stick' was in my hands – no slings allowed.

Tabbing uphill at night is twice as hard because you can't make out the best routes, so I chose to go more or less in a straight line. I'd also made the decision to go it alone rather than spend hours chatting about the price of bread in Aberdeen with the other three.

Above me in the blackness I heard only grunting and swearing; below me the same. The first hill was ball-breaking. Stopping at the top, I looked down behind me at Talybont reservoir which glittered in the moonlight. The moon disappeared behind clouds again and I carried on.

Dawn was coming in fast as I jogged down the Fan, racing against the clock to make a decent time. Then it was hill after hill, hour after hour.

Several times throughout the day the bergen dug in so tightly that both my hands had pins and needles. Every muscle and joint was screaming and I tried to keep my mind off the pain by thinking about the weekend I'd planned down in Porthcawl with Liz and Rachel.

Towards the turnaround point at the Cray reservoir, I was in a world of hurt. This was where my parents used to bring me as a kid and my Dad would point out different landmarks and tell me the names of the various hills.

The DS weighed my bergen and I set off again. The OC called out to me, 'I've got a tenner on you, Taff!'

'Cheers, boss – but I don't need any extra weight.'

By the time I climbed the last hill overlooking Talybont again, it had taken me twelve and a half hours. Now it was downhill all the way, jogging through the woods and firebreaks. Thankfully I would finish in daylight, but behind me there were guys who'd be hitting these woods in the approaching darkness and they'd be in the hurt locker by then, stumbling on the edge of total exhaustion.

I'd gone off in the fourth quartet and had caught and passed everyone except Peter Davies. All day he'd been above me in the hills, but slowly I was running him down.

Eventually I came through in thirteen hours and fifteen minutes, with Peter about five or ten minutes ahead of me. He obviously had a rocket up his arse that day and was uncatchable.

We finished in daylight and had a brew together.

'A couple of clicks more and I'd have had you,' I told him and we both laughed.

Afterwards I put talc on my feet, new socks and a tracksuit, before slipping into the green maggot and crashing. When I woke seven hours later there were still lads coming over the finish line.

Ten days later, the forty-four Brecon survivors flew from Heathrow to Hong Kong and then on to Brunei. Although pleased to be still in the game, all of us knew that far harder tests lay ahead in the jungle.

Sitang Camp, which was base camp for the jungle part of Selection, was a two-hour drive from the capital, Bandar Seri Begawan, and slap bang on the South China Sea. Unfortunately there was no time to enjoy the beach, just enough to pack and repack our bergens before trying to get some sleep. As always, some flapping dickhead kept us awake sharpening his machete.

Next morning the scaleys (signallers) set up the mast for the radio and sorted out stores. At around midday we moved to the LS near the camp, where a number of American Huey helicopters with pilots from the Brunei Forces were waiting to fly us by patrols hundreds of miles into the green stuff.

It was raining hard as we disembarked onto Taff Evans's LS deep in the jungle; the majority of the DS and the RSM were already there waiting for us.

'Welcome to Hell,' said Gaz, an old sweat who was the DS of my patrol. The rain pissed down and leaked into every crease and hollow. 'I don't care what you've done before and how tough you think you are,' he said, 'because this place is going to break you unless you give it some respect. You've got to learn to live in the jungle; to become one with the jungle. You can't fight it. If you fight the jungle, you'll lose.

'Let me tell you what it's like. It rains, and when you think it's stopped raining, it'll rain some more. You won't wash and you won't shave for five weeks. You'll be wet, tired and hungry, but you'll look after your weapons and equipment before you look after yourself.

'You've got to keep on top of things in the jungle. If you're constantly eating out of a dirty mess tin because you can't be arsed to clean it, then you're going to go down with something. If you don't look after your feet then they're going to rot. Understand?'

We soon found out Gaz was right – it was hell. We marched into the jungle and each patrol of four men was assigned a small basha area. We erected four A-frames using cut poles or small trees, with cross-beams to support a green plastic Lilo sheet slipped through poles, and a poncho stretched over the whole lot to create shelter. It might not have been the Ritz, but done properly it was a snugger abode than any red-brick housing estate. This was our home away from home for the next month.

The commander of my patrol was a very tall Gurkha officer called Illingston-Price, who at 6 feet 7 inches must have terrified the poor short-arsed Gurkhas. As if to compensate, he was very softly spoken and gentle in his ways. This infuriated Gaz, a hardened para, who liked his men to shit grenades and spit bullets.

Then there was Bob Arnott, a Jock engineer, who attracted insects like a fucking leech magnet, and Barney, a guy from the RCT (Royal Corps of Transport). Everyone in the patrol had to work together as a team, which isn't always easy when different personalities are involved and you're under pressure.

Since the tour of Belize I hadn't been back to the green hell, but at least I had some experience of what to expect. The first thing I noticed was the lack of mosquitoes, a mega advantage, but on the downside, the jungle crawled with leeches. There were tiny ones and big fat bull leeches – all fucking voracious blood-suckers. I'd zap them with mozzie repellent, but poor old Bob Arnott always had two or three sucking away at his skinny frame. They obviously preferred Jock blood to Welsh.

Brunei also had stacks of peanut ants, which are fucking massive and look like they're carrying a roasted KP around on their backs; hundreds of them on their own Endurance route. My personal favourite was the basha-up beetle, which had a nightly mating call that sounded like it was being delivered with a megaphone. These guys were boasting, 'I'm gonna score tonight, but you fuckers are sleeping alone.' It would start off quietly at about 5.15 p.m. and then build up to a crescendo; it was hard to imagine anything that small making so much noise.

The learning curve was steep as daily we were taught the basics of jungle soldiering and the SOPs (standard operating procedures) of the Regiment.

The different patrols were dotted over a wide area in the jungle and each morning we woke before dawn and dressed in total darkness and silence, putting on kit which was still soaking wet and covered in leeches from the day. Then we packed up everything, leaving nothing behind, and went to a stand-to position about 10 metres from the bashas.

Gaz would be lurking out there in the jungle, waiting for us to make a mistake. That was when the phantom mess-tin kicker always surfaced and each member of the patrol cursed and blamed another.

Just before dawn, Gaz usually walked towards our positions and expected to be challenged with a pass number. If the password was based on the number nine, for example, he might say, 'Five' when challenged and the stag would have to give back 'Four'.

Gaz had given us some leeway in the first week or so, but one morning decided to make his presence felt. Having stood down at first light, we were watching for his approach, but suddenly discovered that he'd been sitting in the middle of us all the time.

'Did you see him?' I asked Bob.

'Shit, no.'

'How about you?'

'No way.'

'Fucking hell, he's cool. The guy can see and hear everything.'

After standing down we had thirty minutes to get back to the A-frames, clean our SLRs and shovel scoff down our necks with oil-covered hands. Then we quickly packed everything away again.

'Gaz's on the fucking warpath today,' said Illingston-Price.

'Yeah,' echoed Bob. 'Let's not give him any excuses. Not a pubic hair out of place, lads.'

Having done the business, we screamed up to the schoolhouse on the next ridge, near the stores basha and the LS.

Meanwhile, Gaz did his morning inspection. Within seconds he'd found an empty wrapper from a pack of hard tack biscuits and some mozzie rep.

'Congratulations, gentlemen,' he said, holding them aloft like precious rocks. 'Now you can dig a fresh shit pit. And if you fuck up again tomorrow, you'll be digging another one.'

The morning lessons in the schoolhouse, sitting on logs under a massive tarpaulin, were on navigation, demolitions, OPs, LUPs, river crossings and contact drills. Initially the jungle was a world of green to us, and most of us couldn't navigate through it. Having been lost in Belize, I knew how difficult this was. Slowly they began teaching us how to look through the green wall, so that you can make out ridges and the shapes of hills that could be applied to the brown contour lines on our maps. The jungle began opening up for me.

There were three stages of navigation training. The first, lasting several days, involved a tab further and further into the jungle and the return journey. In the Brecon Beacons there were only a limited number of routes and it was possible, if you were fit enough and knew somebody who was tackling the same route, to catch up and follow them. In the jungle this was impossible.

'OK, Taff, where are we?' asked Gaz. We'd been slogging through greenery for five hours.

'Here, Staff,' I said, pointing to the map with a corner of my Silva compass. Sweat dripped from my forehead onto the page.

'Right, I want you to go there,' he said, pointing to a new location.

There were no trails or worn pathways, we had to make our own, and after my brush with starvation in Belize, I carried plenty of emergency rations on my beltkit.

Despite the lessons, we constantly managed to get lost. Gaz, bringing up the rear, watched us get further and further off our route, until he finally intervened.

'OK, you fucking Girl Guides, what's going on?'

Nav 2 and Nav 3 were progressively longer, lasting up to four days. We stayed with Gaz for the first three weeks, then the DS changed for the final exercise, to avoid any personality clash that could affect the way we were being judged.

After navigation came the ranges and CQB (close quarter battle). This set out to test our ability to make split-second decisions under pressure in a combat situation. 'There's no room for headless chickens in the SAS,' Gaz said, 'especially in the jungle.'

We started off on a one-man contact drill, following a track through the jungle, knowing that pull-targets were likely to pop up at any time.

With my eyeballs on stalks, I crept along the jungle lane, Gaz in my shadow. I was roasting hot and sweat ran into my eyes, making them sting. I wiped it away, but the mud and gun oil on my hands just made it worse.

Where were the fucking targets?

There!

*Bang! Bang!* I fired two instinctive shots using the barrel of the SLR as the aiming marker.

I dived left, got to a kneeling position and squeezed off one good aimed shot. Nailed it!

Forward again. I could almost hear Gaz breathing.

'Stop! Safety catch!' he shouted.

I'd walked right past a target.

'How does it feel to be dead?' he said, pointing it out.

The two-man drills came next. Being lead scout was a nightmare because you worried that the guy behind you might see the target before you did. Apart from being embarrassing, it was unnerving to hear the rounds zip past your head.

Meanwhile, the other lads in the patrol were kicking back and getting a brew on while they waited for their turn. In the closed environment of the jungle, hexamine could be smelled for miles. This was training, so we were allowed to use it; on 'hard routine' we'd have to survive on warm water from our bottles.

Eventually we graduated onto four-man drills – the bread and butter of the SAS – and these had to be practised constantly until they became second nature.

In the standard exercise, the patrol had to put down a weight of fire as the lead scout was extracted back, using a technique known as fire and manoeuvre. After scores of dry runs we went live.

On my turn as lead scout, I spotted the pull-target and began firing. Suddenly, there were SLR rounds zipping around my ears from the lads behind me. I turned back, picked my lane, and tear-arsed back towards them, zigzagging like crazy and hoping to fuck they didn't shoot me.

In the confines of a thick jungle, the SLR 7.62s made an immense din, cutting down the small trees and splintering the larger ones. Roots clawed at my feet and ahead of me were vines and 'bastard trees' – so called because when you touch them by mistake you get a handful of thorns and say, 'Agh, bastard!'

The DS was in line with the third guy, Bob, watching that everyone's firing arc was away from me as I crashed through the undergrowth.

'Spot the Number Two,' I kept telling myself. Whatever you do don't cross in front of him or you're a human colander.

Vines were clinging to my arms and legs, pulling me back. Carbon and smoke were everywhere. I could hear the others screaming. Past the Number Two, I stopped, turned and fired – *bang-bang-bang-bang* – four quick shots.

'Move!' I screamed and the Number Two turned and started zig-zagging back towards the Number Three.

You don't ever do it the other way round – shout 'Move!' and then start firing. If you do this and the weapon jams or has a stoppage, it's too late; the Number Two is up and you can't cover him.

We fire-and-manoeuvred until all four of us were together at a base line. Then two moved and two fired, until we'd extracted ourselves completely away from the contact site.

At a rally point, we got into all-round defence, facing out. Speaking in whispers, we checked everyone was OK and that no vital equipment had been lost, such as the codes for the radio. We all changed magazines, one pair at a time, then we moved off in a different direction.

A four-man SAS team will never go forward from a contact because they don't know if the guy they're engaging is the lead scout of a patrol or an entire battalion. Instead they go back and regroup to assess the situation. With only four men, it's always better to run and live to fight another day.

Finishing the drill, sweat pissed out of me and I looked at my hands; they were bleeding freely where thorns had sliced through the skin. I could taste cordite and hear my heart thumping. Strangely, the jungle was completely silent. There were no birds, monkeys or even insects making a sound. The SLRs have a way of making things quiet.

This was what we practised over and over again until it was second nature. The drill is exactly the same whether contact is from the front, left, right or rear. It differs only when a member of the patrol has been shot – more often than not it's the lead scout.

'You have to get him out of there. He's your buddy, you don't fucking leave him,' Gaz drummed into us time after time.

It's knackering, carrying or dragging someone in the jungle, but there's no other way. The SAS don't leave men behind, no matter how fucked they are.

At times during the drill, the DS would shout, 'Stop! Close in for a debrief!' From our kneeling position, we rose as a patrol and formed a huddle to listen to him dismantle our performance piece by piece.

By now all the little cuts and scratches were starting to fester and pus oozed out of them. My hands were a mess, covered in scars and full of bastard tree needles. The skin between my legs was red raw and blisters were forming, my jungle trousers were filthy and laden with mud, oil, blood and salt from my sweat. They were either damp from the constant rain or drying from the heat below the canopy, which felt like the inside of a pressure cooker.

Covered in sores and rashes, I couldn't stop myself scratching at night, breaking the skin with my filthy fingernails and creating twice as many problems.

Personal admin is a priority in the jungle. A dirty mess tin will spell disaster – you'll get the shits bad and spend your nights on the pole over the shit pit. Next day on patrol you can't just take time off to dig yourself a hole in the jungle, so you crap your pants – which did happen to a couple of the guys.

The water from the rivers might appear to be clean but it's teeming with thousands of parasites. All our drinking water had to be treated with Steritabs – one tablet per litre – but on the longer nav exes, when the water sources could be shitty and off-colour, I always added a second. It tasted like I was drinking a chemical cocktail.

After two or three weeks, everyone looked gaunt under their beards and stubble. Dirty cam cream had become so ingrained that our faces were a permanent shade of brown and green. When we gathered together in the schoolhouse, the smell was nauseating – body odour mixed with the damp festering scent of rotting vegetation. At 0730 hours, with a full day of training ahead, everyone already looked bug-eyed and completely fucked. Yet there was no letting up. Day after day we practised different drills, such as river crossings and how to cache our food and then swap cache reports with other patrols so that we could find each other's supplies.

Eventually Gaz showed us the techniques he used to sneak up on us so effectively.

'You have to glide through the jungle like a fucking ghost,' he said and I thought of the *Phantom* comics I read as a kid – 'the ghost who walks'. But it's not easy being quiet when you're my size.

In theory, we had to place our heel first, then the ball of the foot, using the toe to push away any dead twigs that might crunch underfoot. The only sound you should hear is the sound of your own breath.

As the patrol moved through the jungle, each of us alternated our weapons to cover each of the arcs. Looking forward, the lead scout checked the track for enemy 'sign' and for booby traps.

'You sound like a fucking herd of elephants,' Gaz screamed.

Illingston-Price had hit his head on a low branch, I got my boot caught in a tree root and the lead scout totally missed the pull-up target.

'The enemy would have heard you wankers coming since last Sunday. The whole point of this exercise is silence and stealth.'

So he made us practise, and when we finished practising, we practised some more. And after a while a strange thing happened;

the stench of our bodies seemed to disappear and the sores and rashes didn't send the same signals of pain to the brain. We became like animals who blended in with our own surroundings and became as one with the jungle.

My ribs were showing and I guessed my face was like everyone else's – a skull. We'd been living on rolled oats for breakfast, hard tack and paste during the day and two small tins of meat at night – hardly the stuff to put on weight. Yet I didn't feel weak or hungry – I didn't have the time.

At night, back at the camp, we couldn't relax because weapons had to be cleaned, food consumed and reports written up for the next day. These included a 'going' report (patrol report) on what we'd seen, giving details of any water, animal life, possible winch points, cave systems, native sightings and so on. Then we'd be up at five the next morning to start again.

The most ordinary things in life take on a whole new meaning in the jungle; things you take for granted, like sitting on a toilet, using soft toilet paper, turning on a light, getting into a nice warm bed, having a hot shower and putting on dry clothes, filling up the kettle and getting milk from the fridge. Spend a month under pressure without them, in a steaming, fetid, wretched jungle, and you start dreaming about them.

One day a week was called Fresh Day, when we received steak, eggs, cooking oil, bread – enough to have a big old fry-up. We'd even get the afternoon off to organize the scoff. On one of these days, three weeks into the course, I almost sacrificed my place when I argued over fresh rations with Barney, the RCT guy.

I'd been chatting with a friend from another patrol and noticed he was eating a cheese sandwich. We'd been taking it in turns to pick up the fresh food and Barney had gone up from 10 Patrol. When I saw him I asked, 'Was there cheese today then?'

'Yeah.'

'Well, where is it?'

'There wasn't a lot, so I ate it.'

It wasn't the first example of his selfish attitude, so I decked him. Unfortunately Gaz turned up just as Barney landed on the jungle floor and I thought, Oh shit, I've blown everything. He pulled me aside and gave me an earful, before saying, 'All right, we'll just call it one of those things and forget it this time.'

Ultimately the cheese-stealer got his comeuppance. It happened on our final exercise in the jungle – when everything is supposed to come together. Our mission was to locate and attack an 'enemy' encampment using all the skills we'd been taught over the previous weeks. Operating on 'hard routine', we lived on water and cold rations with no naked flames allowed for cooking. We had to shit into plastic bags and take the whole lot with us, leaving no trace of our existence behind.

We weren't allowed to build A-frames and had to use hammocks slung in the trees. Before dawn, all kit had to be packed away in darkness before we went into a stand-to position about 10 metres away. We waited in all-round defence in case of possible attack, then, just before first light, we moved off in total silence, leaving the LUP area in a different direction from the one we'd entered by. We then tabbed for about fifteen minutes, 'looped the track', got into an ambush position, got the radio out and sent the sched on the radio. Only then, when we were sure that no-one was following us and the radio admin was done, did we eat our biscuits and paste and drink water, then move off on our correct bearing.

Cammed up and moving quietly, we blended in with the jungle. My senses were working overtime and the only sound I could hear was that of my own breathing. My eyes constantly scanned the whole periphery of my vision – left, centre, right. Sweat poured out of me, my concentration intense, gliding forward like a ghost. I might have looked like a bag of dirty washing, but I knew that I was at the height of my soldiering prowess.

A noise to the left. Move with the eyes first, then slowly the weapon follows. Any sudden movement of the whole body risks giving away your position.

Having become so attuned to the jungle, I could pick up unusual smells like excreta, smoke or food. That was why the rule about no cooking or smoking was so important because it protected the patrol from being compromised. Barney was a puffer and one day he couldn't resist having a fag. Gaz smelled the smoke and the shit hit the fan. Barney tried to blame someone else, but he was on a sticky wicket, seeing as the three of us didn't smoke. Within hours he was lifted out by chopper and I never saw him again.

We navigated as a patrol, coming together in a huddle to check the map and agreeing where we should carry on, all in total silence. The DS travelled behind the last member of the patrol, never uttering a sound for days on end.

We tabbed for eight days through the jungle, never talking or relaxing. Using our comms skills with Morse code, we sent back sit reps (situation reports) to base at Sitang Camp. Having reached the general area of the camp, all the patrols met up and we began going out on recces to locate any enemy 'sign' – footprints, debris, broken twigs, any indications at all of human presence.

'The jungle is neutral,' Gaz had told us, and he was right; it could be used to our advantage as well as the enemy's.

Tracking is a hard skill to master and took more than a few weeks to learn. Gaz had spent months at a time in the jungles of Fiji and Malaya, learning the black art. He'd taught us to look for a start point – the scene of a contact for example. Then, by looking at the ground, we could determine the numbers, direction of travel and speed at which they were moving. An abundance of sign indicated they were in a rush or not expecting follow-up. We would then put in a search of the general area to locate their routes to and from their location.

Having picked up their scent, we put in a CTR (close target recce) to locate the enemy camp; this had to be a 360-degree CTR of the whole encampment, telling us how many the enemy were, their routine, the number of sentries, stand-to positions, types of weapons and the locations of their huts or bashas.

Three of the CTR patrol stayed *in situ*, while two others returned to the LUP area. After studying detailed models and a blown-up version of the camp, more orders were given and these had to be of a very high standard. They had to cover not only the attack, but also an ambush down river for any enemy escaping in that direction and the evacuation afterwards, towards the LS (landing site), of the whole party.

From the LUP site, two lads from the CTR party led us towards the enemy encampment; everything had to be done with stealth and secrecy. Three of the patrols were to supply the ambush party while the rest of us attacked the camp, which the DS had by now vacated.

We were then given the enemy direction and lay down on the ground while the three cut-off patrols were taken to their positions downstream. When all patrols were in position, the attacking patrols stood up and we quietly made our way towards the encampment.

As we were almost on top of it, a large burst of automatic fire over our heads from behind signalled that we had been compromised. Everyone knew where to go and what huts to take out. There were twenty-eight guys on the attack, with five weeks of built-up tension and aggravation inside them, and now this was the release. The buildings were obliterated by the 7.62 rounds as patrols fire-and-manoeuvred towards our targets. Twenty-eight SLRs make a hell of a racket, but our screams and shouts just about topped it. We attacked right through the camp until the river line.

'Stop, stop, stop!' the DS screamed, a shout that signalled the end of the attack and the end of the living hell of jungle Selection.

The sense of elation was enormous. Lads began hurling themselves into the river, trying to wash off the stink of the previous four weeks. As I put my SLR and webbing on the riverbank, it hit me that for the first time in a month the weapon would be more than an arm's length from me.

Similarly it was bizarre stepping into open space and bright sunlight after having spent so long trying to blend into the jungle like a human chameleon. I waded into the river, still wearing most of my kit, and felt the cool water against my skin. Ducking under, drowning the bugs and termites in my hair, I held my breath and stayed beneath the surface for as long as possible before bursting up into the sunlight.

It was like waking from a horrific nightmare. Around me I saw the first smiles I'd witnessed on these gaunt, filthy faces since we arrived in the jungle.

I took off my shirt; my skin was covered in sores and scabs. Unbuttoning my trousers, I pulled them down to my ankles, along with my shreddies, and squatted down. Cool water swirled around my nappy rash. Sheer heaven. I could have stayed there for ever, dangling my tackle in that river.

As I dragged myself away, Peter Davies was taking a piss on the bank. He looked like a child's drawing of a matchstick man.

'Oi, skinny twat!' he called.

My ribs were sticking out of my chest.

'And look at you, Arnold Schwarzenegger.'

Choppers took us back to camp and we spent the next week lying on the beach at Sitang, clearing up the cuts, sores and exotic parasites picked up in the jungle. I wrote letters to Liz and my parents, even though I knew I'd beat the post home.

I felt an enormous sense of achievement, but also nervousness, because none of us knew if we'd passed or failed the jungle phase of Selection. The results wouldn't be announced for another two weeks.

'What are you going to do if you miss out?' Bob Arnott asked as we lay on the beach, sipping long cold glasses of chemical-free water.

'Stay in the Paras, I suppose.'

# 10

THREE DAYS AFTER RETURNING TO HEREFORD, WE ASSEMBLED IN THE lecture hall of the training wing.

The SSM announced, 'The following people are to queue up outside the OC's office for an interview. The rest will fall out.'

We looked at each other. What did he mean? Did those who got interviewed pass or did they fail?

He began reading out names, starting with 1 Patrol. When he got to 5 Patrol, he called out the names of two lads I didn't think were particularly good. The same was true of other patrols. These guys must have failed, I thought. When he got to 10 Patrol, my heart was fluttering. Then he moved to 11 Patrol without mentioning my name – I'd made it!

Of the forty-four lads who had started jungle Selection, only thirteen of us remained. We could now regard ourselves pretty much as being in the SAS, because Combat Survival, the last stage, was often seen as being the easiest and virtually a formality. This certainly seemed to be the case when they issued me with a house in Hereford and Liz began packing – everything was going to plan.

Combat Survival would last a month, with the first three weeks given over to lectures. We were joined on the course by soldiers from other branches of the services, such as RAF and Navy pilots, as well as Italian and French regulars.

Some of the lessons were on interrogation techniques and what to expect if we were ever captured by the enemy. Guest speakers who'd fought in the Second World War and Vietnam told horrific stories about what had happened to them and how they kept going. One old officer who had helped build the infamous Burma railway for the Japanese had tears in his eyes as he told of watching dozens of his mates perish from starvation, disease and torture. A Vietnam vet told how he'd spent nearly three years imprisoned in a small cage by the Viet Cong, and an old lady described how the Japanese had tortured her after the fall of Singapore.

I felt incredibly humble, and could only admire the resilience, courage and faith in God that had kept them going. Each of them had found something to hang on to in their bleakest hour.

'What would I cling to?' I asked myself. Rachel, I decided; I'd hang on to the thought of seeing her again.

Between lectures, we prepared for the final challenge of Selection – a survival exercise in the middle of nowhere, with no food, precious little equipment and a relentless 'enemy' hunting us down.

On the Sunday evening, we gathered in the lecture hall for the final briefing. The OC told us that we were about to enter the first part of the Escape and Evasion process. 'If any of you are caught cheating you'll immediately be off the course and RTU'd. Bad enough for the tri-service and foreigners, but catastrophic for any SAS recruits.'

We were divided into patrols of five men, with two SAS guys in each. I teamed up with Ray Garnett, a Scouse signaller, as well as two RAF pilots and an Italian. We were each strip-searched, including an anal examination to make sure we weren't carrying any concealed goodies. Each of us then received a greatcoat and old Second-World-War fatigues.

We climbed into the back of a 4-tonner, which was then battened down to make sure we couldn't see out, and we bounced and rocked over back roads and tracks for what seemed like hours. I could feel the night-time temperature beginning to plummet.

'Patrol Six,' the DS called out when the truck stopped. We piled out; the others stayed aboard, no doubt to be dropped at different locations.

'Gentlemen, you are now OTR (on the run),' said the DS. 'You have your basic survival kit and a sketch map. Your initial mission is to avoid capture and to contact your agent at the designated location by 2200 hours tomorrow night. Good luck – you're going to need it.'

Our basic survival kit consisted of a button compass, a tobacco tin containing a needle and thread and a few other bits and pieces:

174

four ten-pence pieces in case someone got hopelessly lost, condoms to carry water, some Oxo cubes, the sketch map, snares, a small saw, and a keyring torch with about thirty seconds of battery life.

'All the comforts of home,' said Ray, grinning wryly as the 4-tonner rumbled away.

'Except bog paper,' commented a pilot.

Ray said, 'I didn't think you RAF ruperts shat.'

'Oh, we do. All over your sort.'

'Cut the chatter and let's get down to business.' I called the meeting to order. A hunter force of Gurkhas with helicopters and dog teams would soon be on our trail. Our best chance of avoiding capture, I said, was to hide from them during the day and travel at night.

From that point, Ray and I took over, the rest of the lads following our instructions and bimbling along behind, as was the case with all the other patrols with SAS recruits. It wasn't a matter of arrogance, just simple practicality: the sketch map had only limited details such as river crossings and a road junction, with no indication of scale, and after our time on Endurance and in the jungle Ray and I were 6-foot Silva compasses.

Tabbing into the darkness, I was soon pissing sweat.

'It's gonna fucking rain,' said Ray.

'Yeah, I know.'

That's the problem with doing summer Selection – you finish up doing Combat Survival in November when it's cold and wet. With January Selection, you get the dry season in the jungle and are OTR in the mountains in July. Lovely.

At first light we lay up, but it's hard to sleep when you're soaked through and freezing your bollocks off.

One of the pilots already wanted to jack it in. He told me on the quiet that he'd swallowed a twenty-pound note in a Durex.

'It was going to be my escape fund,' he said.

'Well it's no fucking good to you now. You have to shit it out.'

I wouldn't let him leave and dragged him onwards.

The agent contact points were normally near a prominent feature on our sketch map such as a bridge going over a stream or a bend in the road – but of course that meant that they would be prominent to the hunter force, too. On the second night we rendezvoused at a bridge over a river. The DS had explained the previous night where the agent contact would be; code words would be 'black' and 'blue'.

175

Ray and I decided that we would do the agent contact drills so that we had the info correct. We hid the other lads well away from the bridge, an old stone structure over a fast-flowing river in the middle of rural mid-Wales – picturesque under any other circumstances, but now a danger area. Ray dropped off short and I went in for the contact, feeling slightly ridiculous.

The agent said, 'It's a very black sky.' He wore glasses and a big anorak and was fat. Must be green slime (Intelligence Corps), I thought.

I replied, 'No, I think it's blue.'

Then he pointed to the sketch map and indicated where we'd meet the following night at the same time – a set of ruins by the side of a prominent bend in the road, along a woodline many Ks to the south.

'The colours for tomorrow are green and yellow.'

'OK,' I committed them to memory.

'How many are in your party?'

'Five.'

He handed me five pieces of cheese and five pieces of bread.

'Is that it?'

'If you'd been lucky I might have given you an onion,' he said sarcastically. 'Guess you weren't very lucky. Happy eating.'

What an asshole, I thought.

The bread and cheese was all we had unless we could find our own food. This meant setting the snares and catching rabbits. The snares were a simple loop of picture wire; we set them up at first light near some possible rabbit runs and then tried to get some kip.

That evening, Ray slipped away to check our luck.

'Me Great White Hunter,' he declared on his return, holding a squirming bunny aloft.

'Well, fuck me! Look what Daddy's brought home.'

'I catch 'em, you kill 'em,' said Ray, handing me the rabbit.

Now the trick with a rabbit is not to kill it when it's frightened because it tenses up and the meat is tough. Instead you stroke it gently until it relaxes, and then club it on the neck. I hated having to do it, but we were starving and needed the food. Skinned and cooked with the Oxo cubes, that bunny tasted better than fillet steak.

On the third night, the pilot finally passed the twenty-pound note and I left him at the next agent contact site. I kept the money for the patrol – it might come in handy to buy farm produce from the 'Welsh resistance' or 'Taffia', as the locals were known.

Some of the patrols were quite open in seeking help. They simply went up to local farmers and asked for a loaf of bread; others were caught sleeping in barns and outhouses. I didn't blame them; when you're on the run and hungry, you take every break you can get. In our case, I used the twenty pounds to buy some eggs. I reasoned that if we were lucky enough to smuggle money out, why not use it. But I wouldn't even consider seeking shelter indoors – the risk of capture was too great. Instead we slept in the mud and rain, during one of the coldest Novembers for years.

Periodically through the day I could hear choppers buzzing overhead, dropping off Gurkha patrols with dogs. How many lads had already been caught? I wondered.

It had started snowing and I couldn't sleep. Ray Garnett snored beside me, next to an RAF rupert, our last remaining outsider. The Italian had also come off.

Huddled in my greatcoat, I thought about being home for Christmas in the Rhondda. Passing Selection was going to make it extra special. I'd catch some rugby games and go for a drink with Bencey and Dio at Maerdy Hall. Then home for Mum's Christmas turkey with stuffing, gravy and peas. Fucking hell, I was starving!

The only good thing about a winter Combat Survival is that the dark comes early – at around 4.30 p.m. – and we could finally stop huddling together in a freezing heap.

At the last checkpoint we were briefed by Don Wilson, the sergeant major, and immediately the blindfolds were replaced on our heads. I knew what was happening; we'd reached the final test – the interrogation.

It had worried me for days because I knew that I'd never ex-perienced anything that could come close to preparing me for this. Up until then, everything I had done on Selection – the hills, jungle, navigation, contact drills and weapons training – had been familiar to me because I'd been trained as an infantry soldier. Now I would be tested on my reaction to being captured.

I was cold, tired and hungry. Herded into a wagon, we began a bumpy journey to an unknown destination, although it was a fair assumption that it was back to Stirling Lines. Upon arrival, I was bundled into a building where I lay on the freezing floor for what seemed like hours before being hauled away for what I assumed was going to be the initial interrogation.

Although blindfolded, I could tell from the number of stairs and other clues that I was in a building I'd heard referred to as 'the embassy' – a training area for anti-terrorist drills.

Dragged upstairs, I was forced to sit cross-legged on the concrete floor with my hands on my head and my head pulled back so that I looked up at the ceiling, still blindfolded. I could hear the moans of others around me and smell something I couldn't recognize; only much later did I find out that it was the chemical smell of flashbangs.

Suddenly I was yanked upwards. Two guys holding my arms practically ran me down a corridor. They stopped abruptly and removed my blindfold.

An old grey-haired guy sat in front of me in a uniform. 'I am a doctor. Have you any injuries?'

'I cannot answer that question,' I said.

He asked again and I gave the same reply.

During the lectures they'd drummed into us the 'Big Four' – name, rank, number and date of birth.

We'd been told how the Vietnamese had taped American prisoners saying 'yes' to the offer of a cigarette and then dubbed the answer onto another taped question asking him if they'd bombed innocent Vietnamese.

We could only say the 'Big Four' and nothing else except 'I cannot answer that question.'

All the time a strong flashlight was shining in my eyes. After so long with a blindfold, it made me blink as if I was having a fit.

From what I could see of it the room was stark, with just the odd table and chair. There were slats on the windows. One of the interrogators was sipping on a steaming mug of coffee.

'Come on, lad, I'm just trying to make you comfortable. Would you like a coffee?'

'I cannot answer that question.'

I kept this up, obviously doing the right thing, because the guy began getting pissed off.

As each interrogation session ended, I was dragged to a new room and put into a stress position – either cross-legged as before, or standing with my hands high against the wall, looking up, with my feet pushed back and legs apart. After about ten minutes I couldn't feel my hands and then my arms gave way and I bashed my head against the wall.

The interrogators wanted to know all about me. One guy in particular stank of Brut aftershave and I always knew when he was close; there'd be a nauseating waft, then I'd hear him say ridiculous things like, 'You're going to fucking die.'

After twelve hours they dragged me outside and threw me into a wagon. Driven to another building, I guessed the interrogations were now going to begin in earnest. I heard the continuous and monotonous din of white noise. They forced me to strip naked with women interrogators in the room and then made me put on a boiler suit and a pair of black plimsolls. The suit and pumps were several sizes too small and my feet were killing me.

I sensed other prisoners in the room. A machine in the room made a continuous droning sound and I felt as if my head was inside a vacuum cleaner. As my mind began playing tricks, I tried to concentrate on other things to take me away from the noise and pain. Starting with the letter 'A' I tried to think of everyone I knew whose name began with that letter, then their address, their job, their children's names, their telephone number.

My hands were numb and my back in agony as I held myself against the wall.

Suddenly, another guy in the room screamed, 'I've had enough of this, get me out of here.' I didn't know if it was a ploy or the real thing.

Meanwhile the interrogation sessions continued. At one point one of the wankers ripped off my blindfold and started screaming abuse in my face. His breath stank of tea and cigarettes.

'You look like a fucking German,' he kept saying. 'Is your father a Nazi? *Sieg heil! Sieg heil!*'

Deep down, I thought, This is a bit of light relief, I can handle this shit. He was short with a beer gut and an anorak; it made him look like a pervy train-spotter.

In the next session, I had a real bastard in front of me, who started off quietly, building himself up to a crescendo of screaming vitriol and bile. Aged about fifty, with receding grey hair and bi-focals hanging around his neck, he wore neat grey slacks, a corduroy jacket with leather patches on the elbows and a dickie bow. He could have been a university professor or a don. Whoever he was, I felt like driving his nose right up into his brain.

My eyes were stinging and my throat was burning. I needed a brew badly. The Geneva Convention states that prisoners must be fed at least once every twenty-four hours and be allowed to sleep for at least an hour. Blindfolded, I was made to stand and given a piece of bread and a cup of water. Afterwards they let me lie on the concrete floor to rest. Soon I was yanked up into another stress position. The loud drone continued.

I didn't feel hungry or tired; I'd gone past both. Instead I had an overwhelming feeling of despair. I'd now been interrogated for

179

what I guessed was thirty-six hours; I started to think that the other lads had come off hours earlier and there was only me left.

The grilling grew more spiteful. A man and a woman screamed abuse into my ears, attacking my Welsh accent, my size, my manhood – anything that might get under my skin. I kept to the 'Big Four' – name, number, rank and date of birth.

When it all began I'd known it was a test. How hard could it be? I'd asked myself – it's not for real? But after a week on the Brecon Beacons – cold, dehydrated, exhausted and disorientated – my mind began playing tricks and reality became blurred. No matter how many times I tried to tell myself to switch off completely and not to listen, I was so hyped up that I heard what they were saying about me.

I'd guessed they'd attack my Welshness and it didn't bother me, but then this evil bastard began slagging down my mam and dad. He was shouting into my ear and I could feel his spittle and smell his foul breath.

And then he started on about Aberfan.

'The only good Taff is a dead one,' he sniggered.

I remembered my mother sobbing as she told me about the tragedy, and seeing grown men crying in the streets of Ferndale.

My jaw hardened. How much do you want this, Mike, I said to myself?

'You're probably a fucking Taff Guardsman, aren't you?' he spat. 'What about how you Taffs burned on the *Galahad*, eh? Now there's a decent bonfire, for you, boyo.'

I flinched.

He knew he was getting to me. I didn't have a problem with the other interrogators, but this guy was something else. Five or six times they hauled me back, and each time he waded into me, pressed a few more of my buttons. Spotting the Para tattoo on my arm, he started having a go at the battalion and what had happened at Warrenpoint. Then he saw Liz's name on my wrist.

'You're here and Liz's at home – getting a good seeing to from the milkman, I expect. That's right, isn't it? I might pop over and give her one as well – what do you reckon?'

They dragged me away again.

After another hour on the cold concrete I faced a new interrogator – an old guy with a handlebar moustache who stank of tobacco. Straight away he began screaming into my face, almost nose to nose, and I could see his yellowing teeth and smell his putrid breath.

I finally cracked.

'Fuck off!' I yelled, pushing him away, and in that instant I knew that I'd blown it.

When I wasn't immediately led away, however, I dared to hope that somehow I'd escaped punishment. After all, I'd lasted what I reckoned was forty odd hours and was up against the best of the interrogators.

Afterwards all the lads gathered in one room, looking and feeling like shit. I was so knackered, I could barely raise my head.

'Taff, you're wanted in here,' said Billy Higgs, one of the DS.

In an adjoining room, Don Wilson, the sergeant major, looked pensive.

'What's happening?' I asked.

'I'm sorry, Taff, I'm taking you back to Hereford.'

'Why, what's happened?'

'You failed, you're off the course.'

My world crashed around me. It was the most awful feeling and I couldn't speak. Exhaustion sapped my last energy and I just wanted to curl up and go to sleep. Maybe when I woke up I'd find it had all been a bad dream.

Only ten lads had reached this final stage of Combat Survival and three others were also to fail, each at the hands of the same interrogator who broke me.

'Come on, I'll take you back,' Wilson said, leading me to his car.

We said nothing on the journey. Six months wasted! What would I say to Liz? And to my parents?

Officially I wasn't notified of the failure until the next day when I was summoned to the OC's office in the training wing. As I walked across the parade ground, lads were coming up to me and saying things like, 'You would have gone to Mountain Troop, D Squadron, Taff.'

I thought, So fucking what. I'm not any more.

I still couldn't believe it.

When the OC broke the news, I didn't hesitate. 'Right, sir, I'll have Christmas off and then come back for the January course,' I said.

He told me, 'No, you're not mentally up to it, Taff. Come back next summer.'

I'd been battered, bruised and abused for six months, but would willingly do it all again. Having failed, it meant even more to me to succeed. I didn't realize that, ironically, Fate was busy dealing me another winning hand. Two of the lads who did pass, Bob

Arnott and Stew Wyndham, were assigned to Mountain Troop, D Squadron, and within six months both of them were dead, having fallen from Mont Blanc while roped together on a training climb.

Back at Aldershot, I first had to explain to Liz that we wouldn't be going to Hereford and she could unpack. She was quite happy about it because she didn't want to leave her friends, but she could see my disappointment and encouraged me to try again. At least we got to spend Christmas together as a family and I could open presents with Rachel on the big morning.

The commanding officer of 2 Para, Colonel Parker, was also very supportive. He took me to one side and said, 'Look, son, I know you're going to pass Selection, it's not a problem. Why don't you go to A Company for a few months – they've got a jungle tour to Jamaica and you'll be quite useful.'

My mates in 2 Para were surprised to see me back. Combat Survival was supposed to be a formality, the hills and the jungle were the real tests. Well, I'd busted up that theory. The interrogation phase had exposed a chink in my armour and it had to be sorted out. Aggression can be an advantage in a soldier, but also destructive. Equally, my fierce pride in my Welsh roots had worked against me.

It wouldn't happen again, I told myself. Next time I'd pass.

Posted to A Company, I found myself alongside big Griz Allen and Jocky Ash, who both planned to tackle August Selection. Griz still had one bullet in him courtesy of the Argies in the battle for Darwin Hill.

All of us got on like a house on fire and the next few months flew past.

After Brunei, the jungles of Jamaica seemed like a piece of piss, and I finished up giving many of the lectures and lessons. I got back with just three weeks to go before Selection.

Arriving at Hereford on the required Sunday, I had a huge feeling of *déjà vu*. The first person I met was Tom Williams, the chief DS. Most people who fail Combat Survival simply have to do this section again, but Tom told me that I had to repeat the whole course.

'You're kidding?' I said.

'No. But listen, take it easy. You've got nothing to prove. The real test for you is Combat Survival.'

'Can I go home then?' I joked.

'No, you start from day one.'

This was hard to swallow because I'd already done a good jungle and finished second on the Endurance stage. I figured it had to be a mental test – they'd moved the goalposts and wanted to see how I'd react.

To be honest, during that first month on the hills, I had a great time, because the weather was lovely and I knew all the routes from the year before. When Tom Williams said to me, 'Have a good day,' it meant he wanted me to put in a really quick day and then I could relax and drop my pace for the next couple. I still had to navigate, of course, but I had no pressure on me and I came through Endurance in second place again – beaten by another bloody officer, Marcus Estavez. At least he was from the Parachute Regiment.

A lot of great lads made it through to the jungle; guys like Greg Richards, from 264 Signals and Carl Newlands, a corporal from 1 Para. Griz and Jocky had also made it through, along with Ade Taylor. Ade Taylor had been in Recce Platoon in the Falklands; I liked these lads tremendously, both quiet and confident characters that I had seen around the battalion for years. And, as good as his word, Scouse McVey had tried again and succeeded.

After a huge piss-up during the stopover in Hong Kong, we arrived in Brunei nursing monster hangovers and were issued with umpteen maps and our kit. Well, here we go again, I thought. The other lads bombarded me with questions, knowing I'd been through it all before. I thought it was only fair not to help any of them – unless they were Para Reg.

Next morning we choppered into the jungle. I was happy to have Greg Richards alongside me in my patrol – he had excellent Morse code which would make life considerably easier. The patrol also included Paul, a former Green Jacket who had transferred to 3 Para, and Geordie Christiansen, a Norwegian who had joined the Fusiliers. I was half expecting to be in command, but many more officers had passed Endurance than normal and we were given a rupert from the Royal Hussars. This guy was about the worst soldier I'd ever seen in my life – an old Etonian with a first-class brain and two left feet. Here he was, dumped into one of the harshest environments on earth, and he'd never even eaten out of a mess tin before.

The OC pulled me aside on the first morning.

'I want you to look after him,' he said, nodding towards the man with the cravat.

'What the fuck is he doing here?' I said, watching him stare anxiously around him. 'How the fuck did he get through Endurance?'

The OC shrugged. 'He's here and we have to make sure he doesn't get his arse shot off.'

We were dropped into the jungle and began to build our A-frames together. Then it hit me. I hadn't minded running around the hills again, but being back in the jungle, knowing that I'd passed already and had to do it all over again, was a horrible experience. I just sat on my bergen for about half an hour and couldn't move.

'You're a dick-head, Curtis,' I told myself.

Forcing myself up, I set about pulling the patrol together. We had a head start on the others because of my previous experience but I still gave 110 per cent, because I didn't want to appear to be coasting.

Our very pukka officer was so useless it was hilarious. He fell over every fucking twig and could lose himself if he turned around twice. His webbing never looked right, and we had to put it on for him because he couldn't do it himself. The Royal Hussars are a cavalry regiment and as an officer he was used to having his squaddies do everything for him. He even looked a bit sheepish when he slipped away for a shit, and I always half expected to hear a cry of 'Finished!' from the jungle as he waited for someone to come and wipe his botty.

Yet he was such a nice guy I didn't really care; I was more worried about Paul, who must have thought he was on some sort of paperchase because he kept losing kit all the time. At first it was a couple of rifle magazines. He found them again, then lost a couple more. He also lost his rifle-cleaning kit, his maps and then at one point, while burying a food cache, he turned to me and said, 'Mike, I've lost my fucking gollock (machete).'

'Oh, Christ! Where did you last have it?'

'At the top of that fucking hill.'

I looked up. We'd just tabbed 250 metres down the steep, densely foliated bastard.

I couldn't tell our DS, Charlie Moss, about the lost property, so I had to find an excuse about why we had to go back onto the hill. When you bury a cache in the jungle, fine twigs are put at the bottom to soak up the water and keep the supplies dry. I told Charlie we were going to find these 'special twigs'. He looked at me as if I was fucking nuts.

We found the gollock and got back down just in time to basha up for the night. The next morning we moved up a big feature then down the other side before stopping for a brew. Normally we brewed up in pairs, one guy making his tea while the other watched his back and then swapping over. Finishing up, we tabbed for another two hours to the top of another big hill.

Paul took me aside and said, 'Fucking hell, Taff, I've lost my *aide memoire*.'

I stared at him in disbelief. The *aide memoire* is one of the most important pieces of equipment you carry. It has all the jungle SOPs of the SAS, amounting to a bible of operational techniques.

'You're fucking joking!'

'I'm sorry – I don't know what happened . . .'

'We can't keep this from Charlie, we'll have to tell him.'

Although the old Etonian was technically in charge of the patrol, I was calling the shots, so I went to the DS and explained, 'Look, we've got to go back. One of the patrol has left something behind.'

Under normal circumstances, I got on well with Charlie, who had a good sense of humour and had played some rugby, but he was having none of this. 'Well, I'm not fucking going back,' he said, sitting down on a log and shrugging off his bergen. 'You want it – you go get it.' I didn't blame him.

Paul and I retraced our steps, found the small green waterproof book and returned after a two-hour round trip. As we arrived back, Charlie stood up, stretched and said, 'Right, come on lads, we're off.'

This was our punishment for having held him back, and we didn't stop until nightfall.

Paul didn't last long after that. He started cracking up, telling me one day, 'Taff, the jungle's closing in on me; it's like this great green mass that's going to suffocate me.'

Geordie Christiansen, the Norwegian, got something stuck in his eye and also had to leave. That left the old Etonian, Greg and me, until we were joined by a member of another decimated patrol to bring us up to four-man strength again.

Unlike August 1985, this Selection didn't seem to be such a totally individual effort. I had good mates around me like Greg, Griz, Jocky and Carl. We all seemed to be pulling together and there were actually laughs in the jungle, mostly Greg and me pissing ourselves over the latest pratfall by our Royal Hussar rupert.

A few days before the final exercise, I was putting my hammock up in the dark, slicing through some paracord to cut a few lengths.

The machete slipped and went straight through my right index finger down to the bone. With no lights in the jungle, I did my best to bandage it up and had to wait till the next morning to see the extent of the damage.

It was my shooting finger and Charlie Moss didn't hesitate. 'You're getting out of here to a hospital – otherwise you'll lose the bloody thing.'

With only a week of the jungle to go, I didn't want to jeopardize my chances, so I had the medics close up the wound with butterfly strips and tape it up. But it's so manky in the jungle, nothing heals properly.

I would have happily sacrificed my finger if it meant getting into the SAS, but the RSM, Taff Evans, a Welsh Guardsman from Liverpool, had other ideas.

He came round checking our positions.

'How's your finger?'

'It's OK.'

'Show me.'

I lifted the bandage. Through the mess you could still see the white bone.

'Right, you're out of here. Go get a fucking suntan.'

As I was waiting on the helipad before leaving, the OC wandered over. 'You've got nothing to prove, Taff. You've done well. Get your hand stitched up and have a week on the beach. You want to be ready for Combat Survival.'

As the chopper lifted from the jungle floor, I looked down at the camp and thought about the lads who were about to start the final exercise. I knew my new pal Greg would be all right; he'd done well up until now.

Back at Sitang Camp, I lay in the sea for an hour every day, letting the salt water heal my cuts, scabs and wounded finger. I felt sorry for the lads who hadn't made it through the month. They'd probably figured on getting an immediate airlift back to the UK, or an extended holiday on the beach. Instead, most of them were made to stay on, and given menial duties at Sitang such as sorting out the scoff and equipment. They looked so forlorn that I felt sorry for them, but the guts of SAS Selection is all about the jungle, because it sorts out the men from the boys.

When the others arrived, Greg, Carl, Griz and Marcus had all been given a nod and a wink by their DS, confirming they'd passed the jungle phase. It meant they didn't have a fortnight of worrying and were keen to celebrate.

Unfortunately Brunei is a dry state and the nearest alcohol is at Sarawak, a few miles south down the coast, over the South China Sea.

Greg floated the idea of hiring a fishing boat to take us across.

'I'm up for it,' I said.

'Drink! Drink! Drink!' Carl started his mantra.

Greg did the negotiating and we piled onto a dilapidated old crate that smelled of rotting fish heads and bilge water. We sailed out of the harbour of Brunei's capital, Bandar Seri Begawan, and were dropped on a beach at Sarawak near a small village. Finding a grotty, seedy bar, we ordered Tiger beer, which was served by a toothless old woman with a face the colour of a betel-nut.

Our plan was to stay a couple of hours, but we polished off a whole crate and started on another. When they started lighting candles, we figured it was time to leave. Pissed out of our heads, we stumbled back on board the fishing boat.

The trip across in daylight hadn't been so bad, but now a storm kicked up the seas and tossed the boat around like a matchstick. I convinced myself that the South China Sea was teeming with Nobbys (Nobby Clarks – sharks). Greg slept all the way back, Carl sang, and I was looking out for the dorsal fins.

The skipper of the boat thought it was a great laugh and kept grinning at us as if we were children. He probably wasn't far wrong. I yawned in technicolour well before the boat reached harbour but improved immeasurably when we hit dry land.

After that boat ride, anything would be a doddle – including Combat Survival. I breezed through the lectures and the agent-contact drills until finally imprisoned for interrogation. There was no way I was going to fail this time. I'd spent a year on Selection to reach this point and the bastards weren't about to break me.

I actually found it was a relief to be carted away for interrogation each time, because the stress positions were so uncomfortable, particularly for someone my size.

'Tobacco-breath' wasn't there, but the angles were the same – attacking my Welshness, my parents and my wife. But I'd matured a great deal in the previous year and could now completely cut myself off from the abuse and vitriol. For hour after hour it was like water off a duck's back.

Finally I was dragged out for yet another interrogation. An officer in the Regiment said, 'OK, Taff, that's it now, it's over.'

I just kept saying to him, 'I can't answer that question.'

'I mean it, Taff, it's over. We've finished. Wait for your debrief.'

'I can't answer that question.'

The next thing I knew, the OC was called in. 'Right, you big Welsh twat,' he said, 'you're in now. It's over. Get your fucking debrief and come on, we're going back to Hereford.'

I'd passed, and although I didn't know it at the time, I'd also become the only member of the SAS ever to have done the whole of Selection twice from start to finish.

At the debriefing a young interrogator said to me, 'We liked your technique – where did you perfect it?'

'There's no technique,' I grinned. 'I just wanted to beat you bastards and join the Regiment.'

# 11

ALL MY MATES FROM SELECTION HAD MADE IT THROUGH – GREG, CARL, Marcus, Ade, Jocky and Griz Allen. The only question that remained was whether we'd finish up together when they assigned us to the various squadrons and troops of the SAS.

There are four operational squadrons – A, B, D and G – and each has four Troops of up to twelve men. Each Troop has a speciality in terms of an 'insertion skill'. Air Troop are experts in parachuting and get called the 'ice-cream boys' because they always seem to be training in exotic locations. The lads from Boat Troop are experts in amphibious work, on the surface and below, in all types of craft and conditions, from the tropical waters of Jamaica to 100 feet under the sea in Norway. Generally, Mountain Troop are the winter warfare specialists, experts in rock climbing, skiing and tabbing over rough terrain. Along with Boat Troop this is seen as the most physically demanding of the Troops. Finally there is Mobility Troop, who are the transport specialists, experts in vehicles, motor bikes and heavy weapons. These guys can patch together engines with wire and sticking plaster.

Of the four squadrons, D is traditionally the home of the Para Reg lads, although A and B also have their fair share. To get into A Squadron, it was almost obligatory to have a big droopy moustache and a 1,000-yard stare. All its members looked like extras from *The Sweeney* or *The Professionals*.

B Squadron attracted a lot of Kiwis, Aussies and Fijians, which was why it always had such a good rugby team. The Fijians were

189

already part of the British army, but the others were recruited from Special Forces in their own countries.

G Squadron is traditionally the home of Guardsmen, although there are men in it from other line units as well. The rest of the Regiment took the piss out of them, but all in good fun. G Squadron guys always dressed immaculately and you could spot one in his civvies because of the crease in his jeans.

Sergeant Billy Higgs, a rough diamond from Belfast, who'd been a DS on Selection, pushed me in the direction of Mountain Troop. I went to 19 Troop, D Squadron, along with Carl and Greg, joining an outfit that was thin on the ground after the heli crash in the Falklands and the recent climbing accident on Mont Blanc. Meanwhile Marcus went into Air Troop, Scouse McVey into Boat Troop and Griz to Mobility Troop – all within D Squadron.

Griz was chuffed because he didn't really like the physical side of things. He always had a fag in his mouth and never trained, even though he could tab like fuck. In 18 Troop he was surrounded by old sweats – everyone appeared to be a sergeant – and they all puffed their heads off.

Ade and Jocky ended up in G Squadron. Jocky was gutted; he'd set his heart on D. Apart from anything else it meant that during the next ten years we saw each other only a handful of times, including his wedding day, because we were always on different tours.

When I finally met D Squadron there were so many faces I recognized I might have been back in the Shot; lads like John Geddis, Matt Loftus and Andy Kain.

John Geddis was the first person to greet me in the interest room, putting on his hopeless Welsh accent. 'Hey, boyo, how's it going?'

'Oi, McVey,' Andy Kain shouted when he saw Scouse, one of his 2 Para protégés. 'The Mortar Platoon stores are that way!'

In the squadron interest room I saw pictures dating from as far back as Malaya and Aden, right up to the present day, with mementoes from the Falklands and other Special Forces units throughout the world.

The next twelve months passed in a blur of training and refreshers as we were taught the skills that keep the SAS at the leading edge of counter-terrorism and other specialized operations. It was strange being a crow again, and the first thing I needed was a skill; otherwise I'd be redundant within any four-man patrol. Signals is normally the first one to acquire; comms are vital in the SAS because the Regiment often operates deep behind enemy lines, working in small patrols. All new boys carry the radio and they're expected to get through to base every time!

In the Paras, only the corporal and his 2 i/c carried a small VHF radio. In the Regiment every individual had comms, and each patrol carried at least one set and sometimes three – HF, Sat Comm and UHF or TACBE.

The new generation of radios relied on burst transmission rather than Morse code, but the latter was still needed as a back-up and we had to get up to twelve words a minute to pass the course. Somehow I scraped through.

Another completely new skill was skiing. One Para had just finished a two-year stint in Norway, so Carl was pretty good on the NATO planks, but I didn't have a clue. G Squadron was going out to Norway for a couple of months and the hierarchy at Hereford decided I should go with them and learn how to slalom and schuss. Griz also came along, which greatly pissed him off because he had figured that in Mobility Troop all he needed to know was how to turn an ignition key.

Drawing a new HF radio from the stores, I joined the 'Guards' in their neatly ironed jeans at RAF Lyneham for the flight to Scandinavia. The plane wasn't actually going to land – we were parachuting onto a frozen lake.

This was our first jump with the Regiment and Griz and I were surprised at how laid back it all was. Everyone seemed to lounge about in doss bags. A couple of lads even put up hammocks to doze, something I wouldn't have dreamed of doing in Para Reg unless I'd wanted the world's biggest bollocking.

As we neared the DZ the tailgate opened and snow started swirling through the plane. Below was an amazing sight, a blanket of white with occasional hamlets lit up like scenes from a Christmas card.

Red light . . . green light . . . action stations – there was no rush. I pushed myself out of the door, dropped my container beneath me and felt the snow rushing into my eyes and nose. Landing was like dropping into a pile of pillows.

G Squadron worked out of a hotel in the remote far north of Norway. Seeing our room, Griz and I marvelled at the luxury.

'Fuck me! If this was Para Reg they'd have made us basha up next to the DZ for a month.'

I pinched myself. 'Clean sheets, soft pillows, hot water. Way to go!'

Reality turned up like a girlfriend at a stag night and we ended up spending most of our time basha'd up in snow holes, ice caves or igloos.

Feeling like Bambi on ice, I tried to ski for the first time and must have bounced off every tree in Norway. Griz spent so long on his back in the snow that he looked like the Abominable Snowman. Using cross-country techniques, we first skied without weight and then had to carry 80-pound bergens, with a rifle slung across our chests. Having perfected this, we went on to the contact drills – from one-man, then two-man, up to four-man exercises, just like in the jungle except on skis. It really was an art form.

Then, in a typical Arctic warfare operation, we flew to a target area and parachuted about 20 or 30 Ks away. Skiing towards the target, we selected an OP site; after we had tested the radio, three members of the patrol began digging while the others guarded their arses. The object of the exercise was to blow up a bridge over a frozen lake. The dummy charges, with an electrical receiver connected to the electrical detonator, were laid at night, and then we waited for the enemy to begin crossing before detonating the charges with an XM 122 transmitter. That's the beauty of electrical initiation, it's that precise. We didn't on this occasion, but we might have set an LTM (laser target marker) to illuminate the target one minute before a Phantom jet arrived to drop a bomb. The bomb then travels along the laser and destroys the bridge. It's a cleaner method and there's no risk of the patrol being compromised while laying charges.

From Bambi on ice I progressed until I fancied myself as a bit of a James Bond – all in the space of ten weeks. I even won the novice ski race – 10 Ks around a track at the hotel – although, as I told Jocky and Ade in the bar that night to rub salt into their wounds, it was only against G Squadron.

Next on the steep learning curve came rock climbing – another unknown. Within weeks of getting back from Norway, I found myself halfway up a wet rock face in North Wales. Our Troop sergeant, Trev Mountfield, was an excellent climber who'd done a trip to Everest. 'Rock climbing is all about technique,' he said, preaching to the unconverted. 'You place your feet first, look for handholds and climb with your legs.'

Well, so much for the theory. In practice Carl and I developed our own technique, grabbing hold of the rock and pulling our way to the top with our arms. It was effective but bloody tiring. Trev tried to break us out of the bad habit, but I was never going to be

▶ The Maerdy boys at the coalface on the red horizon.

▶ Milling – one minute of mayhem, fighting toe to toe. My opponent forgot the plot and a PTI had to haul me off.

▶ Keep low, move fast – that's me and Big Syd Baldwyn in the Kenyan bush, 1981.

2 Para leaving Portsmouth harbour.

Stevie Illingsworth, my best mate – a wiry guy with the heart of a lion.

Practising landing drills at Ascension Island - realistic training apart from the life jackets, broad daylight and flat calm sea.

D Company mopping up at Boca House. These Argentinians had caught us on the open ground in the background, pinning us down for several hours before they felt the effects of the Milan. *W. Owen*

Enemy troops streaming onto the airfield at Goose Green during the surrender. *W. Owen*

The scavenging had started. *W. Owen*

Tabbing through snow into Goose Green on the morning of 29 May, cold, wet, hungry and knackered. The lads at the rear are carrying Stevie's bergen.

The aftermath of the battle – some of the Argentinians who had fought bravely and died for their cause, now about to lose their boots. *W. Owen*

Cover from view but not from enemy fire – the gorse line that ran from Darwin to Goose Green. Weeks afterwards, it was still smouldering. *W. Owen*

B Company at Goose Green, amongst the huts and sheep pens that comprised most of the settlement.

The downside of soldiering. Cautious Bob and me standing over Stevie's coffin at the Paras' cemetery at the Shot, 26 November 1982, six months after he'd been killed in action. *Express Newspapers*

Day One of jungle Selection, moving off the jungle LS in Brunei, carrying ammo boxes and wondering what lies ahead.

Now it's my turn to be the DS. With my Gurkha patrol in Belize, 1987, passing on our knowledge of the rainforest.

Carl and Matty inspecting themselves for leeches, much to the amusement of Griz.

Supervising a tactical river crossing in Belize, with bergens linked together as a flotation aid, weapons on quick release on the top.

The black art of jungle survival. The students look on as I hypnotize a chicken, the most humane way to kill the bird.

▲ Standby, standby! The Three Musketeers – Mac Ross, Newlands and me.

◀ Twenty-seven storeys up on a high-rise option and I'm about to go over the edge.

The Troop moving into an LUP for the night. The gravel wadi is typical of the terrain.

Canada, Billy and Stu McDonald (far right) with Iraqi POW.

Russ Nelson and Mac Ross cover while I search a captured Iraqi for weapons, documents and ID. 20 Troop's Unimog mother vehicle is in the background.

I provide security while Russ Nelson gathers information using his best Arabic. Note the Scud tower in the background.

Carl Newlands feeling the benefit of cold-weather kit from the Arctic store, late February. Clearly visible are the jump leads, M203 40mm and vehicle commander's GPMG with night scope.

Lying up in early March – no cam nets needed as the whole squadron is in the wadi. A chance to dry kit soaked during the previous night's ambush – and for Billy to inspect his frost-nipped feet.

That's it, another war over, time to move south! Me posing by Pegasus on the day of the ceasefire. Note the dust cover on my Armalite muzzle and the unused bar mine.

▲
HVO with the hooded HOS sitting on the armour. Descendants of the
infamous Ustashi who collaborated with the Nazis, the fanatical right-wing
HOS were responsible for countless massacres in the Balkans. *Frank Spooner
Pictures/Emmanuel Suys*

Young Rambo lookalikes stand guard outside an HVO HQ, wearing the paramilitary patch that struck terror into the hearts of defenceless Muslim and Serb families. *Frank Spooner Pictures/ Marco Amenta*

HVO troops from Mostar operating with an Eastern block RP57 and a Nato 66mm for house-clearing. *Frank Spooner Pictures/Vander Stockt*

The remains of Gornji Vakuf, once a happy Muslim village. The HVO held the high ground, shelling and sniping at the inhabitants.

In any war it's always the kids that suffer. This little girl had built a UN snowman on the road to Prozor from Gornji Vakuf.

A whole family of Muslims had been living for months in this hut next to the OP position on the hotel roof.

Jim Smith and two Muslim fighters at Gorazde. The Muslims were much better at street fighting than the Croats or Serbs.

OP at Gorazde on the hotel roof. From the hills in the background the Chetniks trundled over to take out the town with their armour. The wooded area behind the hotel concealed the Muslim sniper positions.

▲
Serbian Special Forces Unit in the mountains above Gorazde. *Frank Spooner Pictures/Shone*

In Sniper Alley with the prime minister and Lynda Chalker, inspecting a water purification plant.
▼

a great rock climber – more a grunt and groan merchant who chinned my way up.

Climbers are a strange breed who seem to enjoy the adrenalin rush of being shit-scared. Most of them are built like stick insects and they travel half the length of the country every weekend to climb cliffs in places like Scotland and Wales. I couldn't see the attraction of clinging to a rock, 150 feet up a sheer face with rain pissing down, and looking down at a speck on the ground which is your buddy belaying you – controlling the safety line. More than once, I got a bad case of sewing-machine leg – the shakes – and grabbed hold of anything to pull myself to the top.

'Place your left foot six inches to the right,' Trev would shout.

'Fuck you, Trev, I'm not moving from here until I can grab hold of another big old jug (rock).'

Climbing in snow and ice is different, however. The shoulders and arms are more important because the ice picks are placed first and then you secure your feet, and there have to be three points of contact at all times. This sort of climbing suited me and I enjoyed it tremendously.

On one of our first training exercises in Norway, I found myself climbing a frozen waterfall, surrounded by magnificent walls of ice in different shades of blue. Climbing alone in a silent world, the only sounds were my own grunts and groans and the ice picks stabbing at the face. Every so often, I hammered my 'protection' (a piton) into the ice. Beneath me, my Number Two was belaying for me; if I fumbled and fell, his job was to grip the rope tight on his belay system and the 'protection' would hopefully hold and bring me jolting to a stop. Concentrating hard on my next move, I avoided looking down, although it did occur to me that it was pretty pointless being in Mountain Troop if I couldn't get used to heights.

Nearing the top after scaling 160 feet, I slipped and fell. As I tumbled downwards my last piece of protection ripped out of the ice and I continued falling for another 30 feet before the one below held fast and did the job. I crashed heavily against the ice wall and dangled 120 feet in space.

'You OK, Mike?' screamed Greg Richards.

'Ugh.'

'Well keep fucking climbing then.'

Having perfected these techniques without encumbrances, we then had to climb with weapons and chest webbing. Our bergens were left at the bottom, rigged up to lines so they could be hauled up later. Two lead climbers went ahead and laid fixed lines for the rest of the lads to come up. The first man to the top always carries a pistol in case of a reception committee – there's no point having a large weapon like an Armalite because you wouldn't have time to use it.

Almost all of this was done at night, which means wearing PNGs (passive night goggles) – tricky at first because the rock face appears farther away than it actually is. It's not like civilian climbing, when you get to wear shorts and T-shirts and feel the sun on your back. Instead we were weighed down by webbing and working in darkness on a wet, greasy rock face exposed to the elements. Don't try it at home, kids.

At first it was all quite exciting being in the SAS, but the pressure never let up. People were watching you constantly, and if anybody started fucking up even slightly they got put under the microscope. In the Paras we used to take care of our own, but in the SAS the onus was on the individual to keep on top of his game. It didn't take me long to realize it was a selfish society, but when the crunch comes every member of the team has to trust implicitly the men alongside him.

Liz found this change of atmosphere much harder to cope with, even though we'd moved into the married quarters at Stirling Lines – a house on 'the patch' – which was much nicer than Aldershot and really quite cosy.

About six months after arriving, I came into the kitchen and found her crying her eyes out.

'What's wrong?' I asked, putting my arms round her.

'I hate it here,' she sobbed. 'I want to go back to Aldershot.'

'Why?'

'I don't have a job and I miss my friends.'

'I can't go back, not after what I've been through. You'll just have to give it a bit longer.'

We sat down and we talked about things. Liz didn't know much about the Regiment or the mystique that surrounded it, but she knew I wouldn't go back to the Paras and it was simply a case of having to adapt to a new town and make new friends. This wasn't easy because Hereford didn't have the same family atmosphere as the Shot. There wasn't the same social scene, with people mixing after work and having a laugh.

Each squadron in the SAS rotates every six months between three roles, one of which is supplying counter-terrorist teams. I'd never forgotten the dramatic footage of the Iranian Embassy siege at Prince's Gate in London, which made the SAS motto 'Who Dares Wins' into a household phrase.

Anti-terrorist training was a six-month course and involved an astonishing degree of speed, slickness and teamwork. Traditionally the crows started out as snipers in the team, while the more experienced lads were the 'Black Knights' as we lowly snipers called them – assaulters in black kit, with respirators and Heckler & Koch MP5 sub-machine-guns.

On a typical training exercise involving a plane hijack and runway siege, Carl, Greg and I were out in the fields freezing our arses off, keeping watch on the cockpit and aircraft windows, while relaying commentary via the radio back to the six or seven four-man assault teams, who were sitting in a nice warm hangar sipping mugs of tea.

We'd also have to take pictures of the stronghold at night with zoom lenses and infrared film which would be processed and put on various briefing boards for the assaulters to have a butcher's at while they dunked another biscuit.

It was much the same when we staked out buildings or ships. Each sniper had to supply a commentary, using a special code. Each building, for example, is colour-coded. White for the front, black for the rear, green for the left and red for the right. If I spotted a terrorist at the front of the building, on the third floor, two windows in from the side, I'd call out on the radio, 'White, three, two.'

The sniper weapon, the PM, was designed by Malcolm Cooper, who won a gold medal for shooting in the 1980 Olympic Games. Normally, it had a maximum effective range of 800 metres for a head shot, but even with the suppressed version you could still get a guaranteed head shot from 200 metres.

Obviously there was a fine art to being this accurate; you had to set your sights and know how the wind speed and air temperature would affect the shot. We spent hours on the ranges each day, checking the various daylight, night and telescopic sights, making sure they were finely tuned to suit each weapon.

On top of this, crows also had to do assault-team training, just in case we were called upon as reserves at the last minute. If this happened, we'd come in from our sniper locations and go straight back out again with the Black Knights. I normally had to hold a ladder during the storming of a plane or go through a door in the number three or four position. Everybody wanted to be number one or two.

Halfway through the six-month training course, Carl and I were moved from being snipers to become fully-fledged assaulters on the anti-terrorist team. Not surprisingly, Greg was pretty pissed off at being left out.

As Black Knights we had to work within a four-man team that functioned as a single animal. The pre-training took almost a month and after the slow build-up we began practising in the CQB (close quarter battle) House every day of the week.

The purpose-built training area featured a block of flats and two other buildings. Inside, each room had thick rubber on the walls with metal plates to catch the rounds. It meant you could live-fire and practise various scenarios involving armed sieges and hostage-taking. We would fast-rope from the chopper to the roof, then body belay from the first man, who carried a spare rope. He would wrap the rope around himself and wedge his feet against the roof; we would then grab hold of the rope and fast-rope to the balcony.

In one drill, we were going to storm the 'stronghold' to free hostages. All of us had body armour, a respirator, non-slip boots, fireproof face masks, fireproof underwear, gloves, and overalls that carried a number on the arm showing our position in the team. Each of us was armed with an MP5 9mm slung across our chest, with four mags each of thirty rounds; and a Sig Saur pistol with three mags of fifteen rounds. Also flashbangs, door charges and a radio with a throat mike.

For training purposes we used old Agusta choppers seized from the Argentinians during the Falklands War and brought back to Britain. The pilots were excellent and used to throw them around while we hung out of the door waiting to fast-rope. You have to trust your pilot.

The exercise began and the chopper surged forwards, hugging the contours of the ground as it screamed towards the stronghold. Suddenly the target was beneath us.

'Rope down.'

The Number One was out the door, fast-roping towards the rooftop. Looking down, I glimpsed the other teams of assaulters attacking the target.

Fast-roping can be scary. The idea is to come down quickly, gloved hands only loosely holding the rope, and only lock your wrists at the last possible moment. I was out the door and sliding. Hitting the concrete roof, I crouched and looked for the Number One – he had the spare rope attached to himself for a body belay. I then grabbed the rope and fast-roped to the balcony.

Inside each of the rooms of the stronghold there were targets, some of them X-rays (terrorists) and others Yankees (hostages).

Number Two threw the first flashbang and Number One stormed inside the room as the flashes were exploding and spewing out either CR or CS gas. Number Three and Number Four were close behind him. The noise was deafening and there was smoke everywhere.

'X-ray in the corner' – *bang-bang-bang.*

'There's another – NO! It's a woman holding a baby.'

Firing live rounds in darkened, smoke-filled rooms takes a lot of balls and trust in your buddies. The skills have to be slick.

I was Number Three on the second team, the MOE (method of entry) man, whose job it was to get through locked and bolted doors. As well as door charges, I also carried a sledgehammer slung over my back and a shotgun that fired Hatton solid shot rounds which could blow off a hinge – and then some.

Amid the noise and chaos, I placed a door charge while the Number One and Number Two covered me. The door charges had already been made up at the stronghold; the whole team carries them, detonators already attached, as is the firing wire; it's just a case of quickly attaching the M57 firing device.

Thumbs up. *Bang!*

The shockwave shuddered through my legs. It was nothing compared to what the shock would have been inside the room. The door went flying inwards, followed by the flashbangs from Number Two. Anyone inside would have been stunned and disorientated by the violent series of flashes and sounds.

Each room had different targets. Number One went through first, followed by Number Two. I waited at the door in case either of them had a 'stoppage' (weapon failure) or injury. If this happened, I'd shadow the stranded man, so close to him my knee touched his back. I'd put my elbow on his head to signal him not to get up and would begin taking on the target.

When the stoppage was sorted out, I'd go back to my original position. Meanwhile, Number Four would be my back-up and the link man to the previous room.

Adrenalin pumped furiously and I was sweating like a pig under the fireproof Balaclava and respirator. When it was over and

I stumbled outside into the sunshine, totally knackered, it felt good to have the breeze on my face. Smoke still billowed from the windows of the building.

During the training debrief, each part of the assault was dismantled and discussed. The team commander gave his point of view and the targets were checked to make sure we hadn't 'killed' any innocent hostages.

'Well done, Newlands, you wanker – you just shot the ambassador's wife.'

'It wasn't me, it was Taff.'

'Bollocks, I was on the other side of the room. It was you, you tosser.'

'Oh well, I hated her cardigan anyway.'

These drills had to be practised over and over again until they ran like clockwork. There were remounts (training exercises) designed for every conceivable terrorist situation, including the Channel Tunnel and Heathrow Airport. Of course, each stronghold presents its own unique problems; a block of flats or an airliner would take three teams whereas a house would take only one.

Every attempt was made to make the remounts as realistic as possible and this included working with PT17, the police antiterrorist team, and police negotiators. The 'terrorists' were always played by instructors from the CRW (counter-revolutionary warfare) wing.

The police anti-terrorist guys from London were quite professional, but at the end of the day they were civvies. They didn't have the aggression or the speed of the SAS and tended to be quite a bit older – and heavier. Some of the guys looked like cousins of Giant Haystacks or Big Daddy; how they expected to climb through small windows was beyond me.

Remounts at Heathrow Airport were always big operations. Lord King, the Chairman of British Airways, let us play with his planes – 747s, 737s, Concorde, anything we wanted. He wanted to make sure that if any British plane was hijacked anywhere in the world we'd know what to do. And believe me, we would.

To the untrained eye looking at an aircraft, it might not be easy to see how it could be boarded with any kind of stealth or element of surprise. My team's drill involved coming in on the black side – the rear of the plane – using metal and rubber ladders that were designed to be placed silently against the fuselage. Two ladders would go up against the side of the jet and on a specific signal the cockpit crews, who were all schooled in the drill, would put the doors to manual.

As 'the doorman' I stood at the top of the ladder – which is higher than the average two-storey house. My job was to pull the heavy door open for the four-man team to storm inside and do the business. Then I'd jump from one ladder onto the next, enter the jet, shut the door and pull the handle for the emergency chute; it had to be shut for the chute to unfurl. Then I'd open the door again and begin throwing the first passengers down the slide. This entire sequence of events took approximately eight to nine seconds.

There were all sorts of new weapons and skills that had to be mastered. These included airlifting hostages off a rooftop in a big basket underslung from the Agustas. It could hold about six people and we'd all lock arms as the chopper picked us up and flew away, carrying us like a bag of oranges.

The situations were designed to mirror real life as closely as possible. In each case the planning had to be meticulous, particularly when hostages were involved. Split-second timing could mean the difference between success and failure. Sometimes we found ourselves practising for days for a particular assault, only to find out that the negotiators had reached a settlement with the hijackers and we had to stand down and return to Hereford.

But the quest for reality creates its own dangers and quite a few guys were injured in training. On one drill, as we hovered above a building ready to fast-rope to the rooftop, a lad accidentally pushed the pilot and the helicopter went lurching forwards and nearly crashed into the side of the building. I was flying down the rope as the pilot tried to avoid the disaster. The heli swung away, leaving me suddenly clutching at thin air about 30 feet above the ground. By rights the fall should have broken both my legs, but I was only winded.

There were quite a few guys hobbling around Stirling Lines with pins in their ankles, but accidents are part and parcel of Regiment life. Most are incurred on the team – a hand blown apart placing a door charge, a dems accident that takes an arm off, a fall from a block of flats. Dave, a sniper from B Squadron, got 70 per cent burns to his body and only survived because he was so fit. He'd been covered in tattoos and ended up looking like a patchwork quilt after the skin grafts. A tattoo from his arse finished up on his neck.

I didn't dwell on the dangers; as far as I was concerned, *che será será*. In rugby if you go into a tackle half-heartedly you get injured;

I took the same belief into soldiering – give it 100 per cent and you increase your chances of survival, especially on the anti-terrorist teams.

Once fully operational, the teams were split into two groups, with 'blue team' on half-hour standby and 'red team' on three-hour standby. The two rotated on a monthly basis. None of us was allowed to drink alcohol and we each carried a pager.

The red team got called out during the first six months for a prison riot at Peterhead gaol in Scotland, where warders had been taken hostage. I was on blue team, which stayed behind in Hereford on half-hour standby for Northern Ireland in case re-inforcements were needed for a terrorist situation.

The Scottish operation went like clockwork. They put explosive entries on the walls and went in, each team leader carrying a pistol and the rest with truncheons and plasticuffs. A few of the prisoners got the wrong side of a couple of baton blows, but the warders were all rescued safely.

The anti-terrorist teams spend a lot of time in Hereford, which meant that for six months I had most nights at home with Liz and Rachel. It was almost like having a nine-to-five job and being a proper family. Not surprisingly, the end result was another baby on the way.

When the six months were up, I was sent to Belize for six weeks to help train the resident battalion, the Gurkhas, as well as lads from the RAF, Royal Engineers and Royal Artillery. The plan was to set up camp for the first week and then take a different group into the jungle each week. Andy Kain was in charge and the team also included Carl, Griz and Matty Wilson.

The Gurkhas were taking over from 2 Para in Belize which meant I got to see some of my old muckers before they flew back to Aldershot. We went drinking at a bar called the Rose Garden one night and I was still there at closing time with Carl, a lager monster. When the management encouraged us to leave there was a harmless fracas.

Next morning, Andy Kain found us packing our kit ready for the jungle.

'Have you heard the latest?'

'What?'

'There's going to be an identity parade. Some local girl says she was accosted by two lads from the camp last night. They've had a parade among 2 Para and the engineers and ordnance and the REME guys. Now it's our turn.'

We assembled in the guard room – Griz, Carl, Matty, Dinger and a couple of signallers who'd been attached to us from 264. The girl, who looked no more than sixteen years old, walked along the line accompanied by Bob Powell, now the RSM of 2 Para.

'Him and him,' she said, pointing an accusing finger at me and Carl.

My jaw dropped.

'Fucking hell, Taff, I expected better of you,' said Powell, shaking his head in disgust. 'That's it! You're both finished in Belize.'

Staring imploringly at Carl, I almost felt like crying.

'I'm innocent, I swear. I've never seen this girl in my life.'

Carl backed me up. 'We never touched her!'

This went on for about ten minutes until Bob Powell and Andy Kain couldn't keep it up any longer and collapsed laughing. They'd set the whole thing up, briefing one of the girls who worked in the camp as a cleaner to pick us out of the identity parade.

After the hell of the jungle Selection, I enjoyed my first trip back to the 'J', the jungle. The SAS had been reborn there after being disbanded after the Second World War; the Malayan campaign brought them back to the fore and most of our SOPs stemmed from that campaign.

Working with Andy Kain, I developed an interest in demolitions. He was a master with explosives. During Selection I had done a little tree-blowing, but now I gained experience at blowing helicopter LSs (landing site) in the jungle. The secret was to pinpoint the best location from the map – normally on a prominent spur or a knoll with a good approach for the chopper. Then you went to work putting grooves in the bases of the trees that had to be blown, working upwards to the top. Explosives are packed into each groove and smaller kicking charges are used to make sure the heavier trees fall in a particular direction and formation, taking smaller trees with them. It takes a week of hard blowing and grafting to make a landing site big enough to take a Wessex helicopter.

Back in Hereford, I did a demolitions course, covering the basics right up to an attack on an oil refinery or a bridge. I found it's not as easy as saying, 'Blow up the bridge.' The bridge has to be CTR'd (close target recced), measuring the beams to determine the right amount of PE4 (plastic explosive). Then the charges have to be made up and placed in precisely the right position. It takes a lot of time, effort and skill, but the end is a real buzz. Look at that baby blow.

In a more complex attack on an installation, individual targets had to be pinpointed for destruction and this could be instantaneous, delayed or a mixture of both. Some of the timed fuses could be set to explode 100 days later.

Part of the course included making HME (home-made explosives) and I learned how to make a bomb from ingredients that could be bought in any town centre in Britain. Tragically the IRA probably has the same recipe book.

Dems is a precise art, with no room for fuck-ups. On the previous course, one lad lost an arm and another an eye while placing a mine into the ground. Dems is regarded as a Troop skill along with medics, languages and signals, whereas skiing, mountaineering and rock climbing are 'insertion skills' particular to Mountain Troop.

Liz was heavily pregnant by this time and I managed to be with her when the baby was born. I'd been convinced she was having a boy because the pregnancy had been so different from the first time. With Rachel, Liz had blossomed during pregnancy and looked radiant. This time she put on 2 stones and became a fire-breathing Welsh dragon. I figured she was having a line-out forward.

We'd only picked out boys' names – typical Welsh ones like Gareth and David; the possibility that it might be a girl didn't seem to figure in discussions.

Rachel had been bald as a coot and when the baby's head popped out, I looked down and said to myself, 'My son's got dark hair, not a problem.'

Then a bit more came out . . . and a bit more . . . and a bit more, until all was revealed and I cried, 'He's got no dick! He's got no dick!'

Then it dawned on me. I couldn't believe it – a little girl.

Liz's labour had been so long and painful that I decided I'd rather go through Endurance backwards and twice over than give birth; but what an amazing sight – I was now the proud father of two beautiful daughters.

Right from the beginning Sarah proved to be a completely different child from Rachel, who was quite shy and reserved. Sarah was more outgoing and physically active. She looked like Liz but had my personality. I loved them both to bits and never regretted for a single moment not having sons.

My only regret concerned how much time I was spending away from home. Within a few months of Sarah's birth I was off to Northern Ireland again, and only managed to see Liz and the girls for five days a month. Liz would take them down to South Wales and spend time with our parents, constantly fielding questions about my whereabouts with a shrug of the shoulders and a sad smile: 'He's away again.'

Having extended the family, it seemed like a good time to buy a house and move away from married quarters. Initially we found a nice three-bedroomed semi not far from the camp, and agreed a price with the owner. I even arranged to have the front gates sanded down and repainted while we waited for the final settlement. A week before moving in, when everything had been packed, Liz phoned me in tears. We'd been gazumped.

I wanted to throttle the bastard, but thought better of it and just went round to give him a piece of my mind. He was a skinny little twat and he looked at me with big imploring eyes – so what can you do?

Ironically, a week later he phoned me to say that his deal had fallen through and were we still interested?

'Not a chance,' I said. 'I wouldn't buy your fucking house if it was the last one left standing in Hereford.'

Eventually we found a similar-sized semi. It cost a few thousand pounds more but Mam and Dad came to the rescue – not for the first time – and lent us some of the money.

A lot of the lads regarded buying a house as a step towards a civilian life, away from the Army, but I was so bound up with soldiering and the Regiment that the thought never entered my head. I'd even chosen somewhere close to the camp, which meant I could just roll out of bed and be at the main gates within five minutes on those early morning call-outs.

# 12

IN THE SUMMER OF 1988, D SQUADRON FLEW TO AMERICA FOR A JOINT exercise with Delta Force, our American counterparts. Following the disastrous operation in 1980 to free the US hostages in Iran, Delta had been totally remodelled along SAS lines, with a lot of input from Hereford. 'Deltex' was designed to further that atmosphere of co-operation.

Arriving at Delta's home base, Fort Bragg, North Carolina, I was bowled over by the sheer size of the place and the amount of equipment on show. You could have fitted Hereford into their training area twice over. Fort Bragg was fitted out with the most amazing facilities, such as an indoor 7.62 and 5.56 shooting-range. At Stirling Lines we only had the 9mm equivalent; we had only one gym, while they had dozens of them, including jacuzzis, saunas and a massive climbing wall for their Mountain Troop. No wonder we renamed the place Fort Brass.

The sergeant in charge of liaison, Randy, came from Alaska.

'Hey, Mike, where did you get that crazy accent?' he drawled.

'I'm Welsh.'

'Welsh? That's Wales, right? Princess Di, that's a part of England, right?'

'No, we have our own country.'

'So you're Welshish, right?'

'Something like that.'

Among our lads, I was one of the biggest, but the Yanks in Delta were fucking huge, with massive upper body strength from pumping iron in the gym. As the days went by I began to get on quite well with a few of them and got invited back to their houses for dinner with their families. They were fantastically well paid compared to British soldiers. One guy, Derek Summers, had a boat, a car for himself and one for his wife and also a pick-up truck.

The Americans called us the 'crazy Brits' because we worked hard and played hard. A lot of them seemed to be God-fearing church-goers who drank four Bud Lites and then went home to bed. Nice guys, just a different breed.

The joint exercise involved the fictitious kidnapping of US Vice President George Bush and four of his top aides by a Middle Eastern terrorist group; also taken was a cargo of plutonium that could be used for making nuclear bombs. For the purpose of the exercises the hostages and plutonium were assumed to have been taken to a terrorist stronghold in Tripoli, and maps had been created that turned Alabama into a desert country on the shores of the Mediterranean.

Our Air Troop and Delta's parachuted into the swamps of Alabama to set up OPs and relay information back to base camp in Fort Bragg, where the remaining Boat, Mountain and Mobility Troops, along with our American counterparts, began preparing for the actual assault.

Reports coming in from the OPs indicated that the hostages were being held in four different camps which had previously been specially built for the exercise.

My assault patrol included Billy 'No Limits' Higgs, who could tab for Britain and was the original Forrest Gump. He'd survived the tragic helicopter crash during the Falklands; so, too, had Alvin, another member of our team. He'd been badly injured and spent most of his time in the Regiment working undercover in Northern Ireland. The fourth member was the new Troop boss, Ted, a young guy who'd just arrived, so Billy was more or less running things.

After studying satellite photographs and the OP reports, we decided that the best rescue plan was a black (anti-terrorist) option involving helicopters and a fast-rope descent onto the terrorist strongholds. Two tiny helicopters known as Little Birds would go in first and saturate the compound with lead from their fearsome mini-guns; they'd be followed in by a pair of Blackhawk helicopters, each of them carrying two four-man assault teams, one from Delta, one SAS, who would insert by fast-roping to the ground. The main priority was to recover the box of plutonium because of the potential risk it posed; the vice-president, we were told, was more expendable. This tickled Billy, who would happily have lined up every politician and shot them.

The green option, using normal infantry tactics, would remain a possibility in the event that we had to fight our way out of the camps.

With money no object, we had the very best in weaponry and technology at our disposal. We could practise the rescue operation as much as we wanted within the time frame, sharpening our skills and covering all the angles. The weather at our secluded training area in North Carolina was sunshine all the way, and best of all, instead of the customary urn of stewed tea which would have appeared during our rest breaks back in Hereford, old Delta had it well squared away: cool boxes were bussed out to the ranges containing hundreds of cans of ice-cold Coke.

On the first training run, four of us from the squadron sat on the port side of the Blackhawk, opposite a Delta patrol. Another Blackhawk came in behind us with two more teams of four on board. As the Little Birds flew in and strafed the compound, the OP guys on the ground opened up with their GPMGs. The idea was to create pandemonium in the camp and give us the chance to get down safely.

When the SAS are fast-roping, the two heaviest guys go first so they can straighten the rope for the others to follow. This job fell to me, so the dispatcher had curled one of the two giant ropes on my lap before take-off; now I sat there with my feet dangling out of the helicopter as we swept over the landscape, a pair of big abseiling gloves on top of my normal assault gloves, to be discarded as we hit the deck. When the pilot gave the 'Red On! Green On!', I threw the coil off my lap and jumped, not looking down until I'd slid the 120 feet, feet never in contact with the rope, relying on my heavily gloved hands to lock at the last moment to slow me down.

Hitting the ground, I planted the explosive charges against the hinges of the outer door, setting the top one first and running the det cord down to the bottom charge. Then it was a case of standing aside, with a quick look to see the other three, then taking the safety off the grip switch and blowing it open. Two of the team went straight through the door, going left or right depending on which way the door blew in. The third member stayed in the doorway ready to support them, while I was the link man. Going from room to room, we cleared the building and carried out our specific task of finding and securing the consignment of plutonium.

Because Mountain Troop had just come off the anti-terrorist

team we were very slick. In fact we were on the ground and had blown the first door before the Delta guys had even let go of the ropes.

During more than a week of these rehearsals, fast-roping down to the ground, hitting the door, blowing it open and then room-to-room combat, the Americans were always slower, weighed down by helmets, goggles, elbow pads, knee pads and body armour. Other than weapons and explosives, we kept it simple. The problem was that Delta were looking at a totally black option, whilst we were looking at a bigger picture and were catering for a possible green option, so we had our normal jungle boots and fatigues and chest webbing, no helmets or other paraphernalia.

They were slow on technique, too. There's a lot of trust involved in fast-roping; it's important not to worry about whether the pilot has got it wrong and is hovering too high off the ground for the rope to reach. We trusted him to do his job properly and would jump from the helicopter while the rope was still falling, straightening it out as we fell. The Delta teams, however, would throw out the line, wait for it to strike, and then – and only then – leave the aircraft. By this time, we'd be on the ground blowing the first door.

After finishing the training we flew down to the USS *Lexington*, the biggest aircraft carrier in the world, which was moored off the coast of Florida. This added to the impression that we were launching a rescue attempt from 'the Mediterranean' against a 'Libyan stronghold'. For the next five days we were isolated in a sanitized area, away from newspapers, radio or TV, and living in the lap of American luxury.

As the countdown began, eighty of us flew back to North Carolina in eight Blackhawks to meet up with the fleet of six Hercules C130s: one for the SAS and Delta patrols, one for the massive FARP (forward air refuelling point) fuel bladders, and four to carry the Little Birds, two in each Hercules with their rotor blades folded up. Because the choppers wouldn't be able to fly all the way to Alabama and back to the *Lexington* on a single fuel tank, the C130s were flying us to a desert landing strip in Georgia to set up the FARP. This had been marked out in advance by four patrols who'd parachuted into the desert.

The C130s landed in darkness, without lights, the pilots flying with PNGs. In our wake came the Blackhawks, and as the choppers touched down the USAAF boys scrambled to refuel them and we clambered on board.

Billy and I, Number One and Number Two in the patrol, sat in the doorway. The loadmaster coiled the 120 feet of green rope onto our laps; as a token gesture he then pulled nylon tape across the front of us, to stop us falling out. 'Let me guess,' I said. 'To keep the air out?'

Alvin and Ted were behind us; the four Delta lads at the other door. They'd compromised as well and binned their helmets and body armour during rehearsals. The penny had dropped about speed being a crucial factor.

We'd chosen to carry 5.56 Colt Commandos, a smaller version of our M203 Armalite. The MP5 we'd normally use for a black option is an excellent anti-terrorist weapon for room-to-room combat because it's small and packs a big punch, but it wouldn't be so good if it came to a longer range firefight. The Colt had a range of 400 metres compared with the MP5's 100. It carried a 40mm grenade launcher slung underneath and could have a high-power torch fitted to the side, as used in room combat on a black option; should our black option turn to a green one we'd have hedged our bets.

By now the other C130s had disgorged their cargoes of Little Birds and the order was given to go. The rotors on all sixteen choppers started up at once and the warm, muggy air was filled with the smell of hydraulics and aviation fuel. I was suddenly starring in *Apocalypse Now*. A storm of sand and dust billowed into the air as we lifted off from the desert. Last light was approaching and dark clouds covered the bright orange ball of sun.

As we flew over Georgia I could make out all the towns in neat little squares, the swimming pools lit up. On the ground it had been hot and sticky but at 1,000 feet it felt cold with the door open, my legs and Billy's being blown about in the slipstream.

As we entered Alabama airspace the Blackhawks and Little Birds peeled away in fours to their various targets.

The pilot gave the five-minute warning and my heart began thumping. The nylon tape was taken off and the Blackhawks and Little Birds started to bank sharply towards the port side. Billy and I stared down into blackness. The towns had long gone and I could no longer pick out landmarks in the darkness. I thought, If I do fall out, at least I'll be holding on to the rope. Alvin and Ted were holding on to us and had their feet wedged against the insides of the chopper. We began losing height fast.

Two minutes to target and I could just make out a faint glow on the black carpet beneath. Thirty seconds to go and I heard the Little Birds opening up with their mini-guns. Hundreds of little spurts of flame speckled the darkness ahead.

Then we were over it. Goggles on, I leaped out into nothing, falling 120 feet down the rope, Billy above me. Thud! I creamed into the bottom, quickly rolling out of the way. The heat of an Alabama evening hit me in the face.

As I discarded my gloves and Billy crumpled to the deck beside me there were weapons blazing all over the place from outside and inside the complex. The Blackhawks added their own tremendous din, whipping up sand and dust.

I had to make a decision; if I went the wrong way, chances were the others would follow me. Decide now! Schermuleys lit up the sky, giving the camp a flickering yellow glow.

I saw our building and sprinted towards it. Billy grabbed the door charge from the back of my ops waistcoat and placed it on the door for me. He then moved back; I took the safety catch off the grip switch and *boom!* the door blew in.

Billy, Alvin and Ted were in. They took out three terrorists in the first room; Alvin pounced on one of Bush's aides, keeping him down as the weapons blazed.

Grabbing the second door charge from Billy, I blew the next one. Billy and Ted stormed through, taking out two terrorists and finding the plutonium box in the far corner. Delta were waiting outside, ready to do their job: hostage reception.

Outside the compound the Blackhawks had landed to pick up the four OP lads. They swung back, touching down just long enough for us to clamber on board with the vice-presidential aide and the plutonium.

The whole operation, from the fast-rope until we took off again, had taken just eight minutes. It had gone like clockwork.

The Yanks were giving it 'Yeehah!' like cowboys at a rodeo, slapping their thighs and doing high fives.

I gave Billy a grin. 'Let's do it again tomorrow.'

'Nah, let's have a beer first on the *Lexington*.'

The choppers skimmed through the darkness, bound for the Gulf of Florida. Within minutes most of us were dozing, recharging our batteries after the excitement of the assault.

Suddenly, I felt the Blackhawk losing altitude fast. We couldn't be anywhere near the *Lexington* yet.

'What the fuck's going on?' Billy asked Ted as we came in to land.

The Troop boss shrugged. 'Wasn't on the agenda.'

As we piled out, looking for an explanation, I saw six guys in civvies standing off to one side. One of them stepped forward.

'Gentlemen, you may not realize this but your chopper has been hit and because of the weight factor has had to dump its load. That means you. You are now OTR behind enemy lines.

'In approximately half an hour from now the Eighty-Second Airborne are going to be crawling all over this place looking for you. They've got motor bikes, dogs and helicopters and if they catch you they're going to interrogate you.' He accentuated the word 'interrogate'.

'Your mission is to avoid capture and to reach the designated point on the sketch maps. You are to separate into two patrols, Delta and SAS, rendezvousing three nights from now for the pick-up.'

Once we reached the RV point the first patrols were to mark out a landing strip for the C130s and keep it open for two hours for all the patrols to come in; we had a cut-off time of 0001 hours in forty-eight hours' time.

'You are standing in the swamplands of Florida,' he concluded. 'To the north-west of here is the Yellow River which is impassable and full of hill-billies straight out of *Deliverance*. To the south there's a live-firing exercise. Cuts down the options, don't you think?' he laughed.

The other choppers, apparently, had already landed and left, their assault teams having been given the same briefing. We looked at each other in disbelief as sketch maps were distributed. They were huge.

'This is going to be a fucking monster tab,' I said to Alvin.

It pissed me off. Minutes earlier I'd been looking forward to some scoff on the *Lexington* and now I was in the middle of a hot, sticky, fetid swamp, getting bitten to fuck by mosquitoes.

Our Blackhawk took off, carrying Bush's aide, and the civvies nonchalantly got into their air-conditioned Lincolns and drove away. The eight of us, four Delta and four SAS, were alone. Already I could hear the live-firing artillery exercise to the south – our man hadn't been bluffing – and already I was wishing I'd put more scoff and fewer flashbangs in my kit. It was a long time to go without food, that was for sure.

We had forty-eight hours to reach the rendezvous point 100 kilometres to our east. None of us had more than emergency rations and survival kit on our ops waistcoats. With the 82nd Airborne in hot pursuit there would not be enough time to set traps to catch food; we'd simply have to keep moving.

'OK, it's 0200 hours,' said Billy, who was calling the shots. 'By this time, two days from now, we have to RV.'

'Hello again, Endurance,' I muttered.

'Yeah, and we can't afford to get caught. The Eighty-second hate Delta, but they hate us even more. They'd fucking hammer us in interrogation.'

With the 82nd approaching hard and fast from the west, the clear objective was to leg it east across country towards the RV. Using roads or tracks was out of the question because the 'enemy' was sure to be OPing them.

The Delta lads had already started tabbing.

Billy decided we'd head directly east, contouring round roads and staying off tracks. 'Taff, you're lead scout. OK, let's do it.'

In the early hours of the morning it was warm and muggy. The midges and mozzies were out in force, feeding on the fresh meat. Although relatively flat, the ground underfoot was boggy and we had to skirt round countless swamps and pockets of dense forest.

Billy pushed us at a furious pace in the oppressive heat. 'If you think it's bad now, just wait till the sun comes up,' I said to myself.

To cover the ground we'd have to tab night and day, with very little rest. Initially the pace wasn't a problem because we weren't carrying any kit and had only the small Colt Commandos. But in the darkness it was hard to see the boggy ground and my face kept getting clogged with immense spider webs.

The Florida swamplands are home to all sorts of creepy-crawlies and biting insects. As I broke through the webs, the spiders ran along my back and bit into my neck. They gave a nasty nip; I could only hope they weren't poisonous. But the really dangerous fucker we'd been warned about was the Cotton Mouth Moccasin, re-christened by us the Cotton Mouth Flip-Flop. We were told you couldn't see them coming in the dark until they opened their jaws because their bodies were jet black but their mouths were white. The venom could kill unless treated within twenty-four hours.

Several times during the night we heard motor bikes nearby; we stopped, waited for them to roar away into the darkness, and then pushed on.

As dawn broke we were still going like trains, not having stopped. With the 'enemy' so close and the RV deadline so tight, we simply had to keep moving.

Mid-morning, Alvin started spewing up. He was the patrol medic, but even my untrained eye could see he was going down. By midday, his eyes were rolling back into his head and he was nearly flaking out. As he lay on the ground, hyperventilating, I gripped his arm and squeezed. Billy tried to find a workable vein to put in a drip.

The trick is to break the skin and travel alongside the desired vein before making contact with it, then slowly enter; you'll know you've succeeded when you get a splashback of blood as the body pumps it out. You then slowly remove the metal needle as you push home its cover, the canula, into the vein. Then it's just a case of attaching the bag of fluid and controlling the drip into the body.

Two or three times Billy slid the needle under the skin, but to no avail.

'Alvin, I think you're dead, mate,' he grinned.

Finally, on the fourth attempt, the needle hit its target and the splashback of deep purple blood moved into the chamber. Billy slowly withdrew the needle as he slid the plastic canula hood into the vein.

The bag of fluid was attached to the other end and Alvin started taking it into his body.

'All jacked up now, Al,' I said.

Poor guy, he'd been away for twelve months in Northern Ireland lying in OPs, so hadn't done a lot of hard physical work – and we'd been tabbing for ten hours straight.

One litre heavier, Alvin lay with a fag in his mouth and Billy plugged in another bag. Meanwhile, we grabbed a few mouthfuls of emergency rations and water and did a navigation check.

The sounds of a jeep and about six motor bike outriders came from nowhere. Alvin hurriedly stubbed out his cigarette; beside him, Billy knelt on the fluid bag, then picked it up and squeezed it hard, trying to force the remaining liquid into Alvin as quickly as possible.

Thirty seconds later Alvin whispered, 'OK, that's enough.'

Ted kept watch from our wooded copse as the motor cycles buzzed around the area, trying to pick up our tracks. One rider got closer, stopping less than ten feet from Ted. I could smell the exhaust fumes. We couldn't move; legging it would mean leaving Alvin behind to be captured. Not an option. Sit tight.

After half a minute that felt like half an hour, the nearest rider eased off his clutch and roared away towards the others. The jeep veered off, heading east.

Alvin got to his feet. 'I'm all right – let's keep going,' he said. He certainly didn't look it.

We pushed onwards, tabbing through the hottest part of the day, sometimes wading up to our waists through shit-coloured water and marsh grasses.

After Alvin had gone down, we'd made it an SOP to halt for a ten-minute breather every hour, but each time we stopped the midges descended in hordes into our ears, eyes, and noses. I had to pull my smock over my head to escape the little fuckers.

All that day we tabbed, putting about 70 Ks between us and the DOP (drop off point). Alvin was looking a little better, but Billy's legs were in a bad way. The rubbing of his wet jungle trousers had chaffed the skin between his legs, creating sores that had him gritting his teeth.

We were drenched in sweat and Billy's legs got worse, but there was no way 'No Limits' was going to jack; he reminded me of the knight in *Monty Python's Holy Grail* who had his arms and legs chopped off but was still screaming at his foe, 'Come back you coward and fight me!'

I tabbed on as lead scout, periodically checking behind. It was getting dark, and above Billy the big orange ball was descending onto the horizon. Jaw firmly set, he hobbled onwards and grunted, 'All right, there?' in his Belfast brogue.

On one of the breathers, I started retching and brought up most of my survival rations. It happened throughout the night and next morning. The terrain became sparser and more open, with no canopy to give us any respite from the scorching sun.

During the afternoon, I went out to fill the water bottles with Billy and we were spotted by a motor cycle outrider. They gave chase and the place was soon crawling with lads from the 82nd Airborne. In a mad dash, we managed to stay together and lost them in a lightly wooded area.

That day was even more hard-core. We covered more than 50Ks with the sun beating down continually and no shade.

Our food had run out and by the second night we were all starving and exhausted. I was still retching. I was in another place; at one point I thought I was in Norway. I couldn't see straight, my eyes were burning and my head was thumping. Next thing I knew Alvin was putting a drip in me. I'd crashed.

Billy was next to me. 'You mad fucker, you were pushing your arms out like a cross-country skier.'

'How much further?' I asked.

'Ten Ks – about two and a half hours.'

I wasn't feeling good, my whole body was oozing fluid. I threw up again, all over myself. The smell caused Billy to spew.

The bag of rehydrate flooded into my body – the ultimate pick-me-up – and within minutes I was back on my feet: 'C'mon, let's go then.'

Back to the grind, I was at the front again, but we were nearly there.

Then, at long last, the RV area – and the first bloke I saw was Scouse McVey.

'Hey, big fella – how are you?' he said, grinning.

'Fucked,' was all I could say before my knees buckled and I collapsed on the ground.

Lying on my back, sucking in huge breaths, I looked up at the warm evening sky. Beside me Ted was gently snoring, Billy had crashed and Alvin puffed away furiously. Sure it had been an exercise, I thought, but no-one could say we didn't train for real.

An hour or so later, lifting my head, I could make out the drone of a distant C130. 'Hey, Scouse, can you hear that?'

McVey rolled over, 'Give me a dig when it lands.'

The TLZ (tactical landing zone) for the C130s had been marked out six hours earlier by the first patrol to arrive. We made contact with the pilot on the net and used infrared filters over our torches to give him a runway – two long lines of guys 50 metres apart. Although the naked eye couldn't pick up the torches, the pilot could see them through his PNGs. Having acknowledged the LZ, he swooped down from the darkness like a giant vulture screaming towards us. Initially we couldn't see the C130, only hear it, but soon the plane was over our heads, the noise awesome. He came in hard and fast.

It takes a lot of bottle to kneel, with a torch held aloft, as an aircraft that size scorches past you at a rate of knots, its huge propellers roaring. All you can do is trust the Special Forces pilot and hope he doesn't make a mistake.

The Hercules carried on past me and stopped at the end of the improvised runway. After two days of hard tabbing, I still summoned up the energy to run the length of the runway and scramble on board. God it felt good.

The pilot turned the aircraft and went hurtling back down the runway. There were no lights inside or out and it felt like being inside the stomach of a flying whale, everyone lying on top of each other, legs and arms entwined.

It had been a harder tab than Endurance, I decided; even harder than the ball-breaker up Sussex Mountain in the Falklands. 'Train hard, fight easy,' is how the saying goes. I'd also never forgotten what Taff Evans, the RSM on my Selection, had once told me. 'When the bell rings you've got to be there,' he said, and to me this summed up the Regiment.

Airlifted to Fort Bragg, we discovered that only two of the squadron had failed to make it back, one of them cas-evacced out with injuries, another suffering from heat exhaustion. The Yanks, however, were conspicuous by their absence. The majority of them had been captured, become lost, or simply failed to make the RV on time. The final score by our estimation was: SAS 14, Delta 2.

I had a theory which explained at least part of the difference. Although I was a great believer in upper-body strength and lifting weights, it wasn't much good if you hadn't got the heart and lungs to carry it. Some of the Americans went overboard on upper body strength, using all the latest equipment, but did very little aerobic exercise. They were massive men who could easily carry heavy bergens, but our guys could tab them into the ground.

A number of our lads never did any physical training at all, yet they always seemed able to keep up on the hard tabs. Barry Taylor was one of them – a forty-a-day man if ever there was one, yet he was always right up there at the front, carrying the same weight as the rest of us. In the jungle I'd seen him go down with de-hydration, have a drip put in his arm, then get up, smoke a couple of fags and carry on. An American would almost certainly have been cas-evacced.

At Fort Bragg we sorted out our kit and got clean. Then it was off to the debrief – Delta called it a 'hopwash'.

The American CO took the floor and went over each phase of the exercise, with our OC adding his comments. All agreed it had been a success. This had been a no-expense-spared exercise with Delta – a hostage rescue attempt, just as the abortive operation in Iran had been. All the actions we took in the build-up had been the same as in 1980; the only difference this time was the plutonium box. We had worked well with Delta and had built up a rapport with them. Everyone felt confident that should there ever be a need for a joint venture it would work out well.

Then the beers were brought in and a cheer went up.

The success of Deltex had the knock-on effect leading to further joint exercises, conducted twice annually – one in Britain and the other in America. Each time the organizers tried to make them just a little bit harder than the last, but each time the bell rang, we were there. And each time, Delta came second.

# 13

AT HOME IN HEREFORD, LIZ WAS STILL FINDING IT DIFFICULT TO ADJUST TO her new surroundings, and her mood wasn't improved by the news that my next posting was a year-long tour in Northern Ireland. Ever since Sarah had been born our marriage had gone through a rocky patch, and I knew that Liz basically wanted me out of the Regiment, or at least at home more often.

It had got to the stage where I'd come home after a month away and she'd say, 'Your dinner's in the oven. I'm off to bed.'

'What's wrong?'

'Nothing. I'm tired.'

'How are the girls?'

'Hard work.'

Even when I did get home for five days every month, there was a chance I'd be paged to go back to the Province because of a job. This didn't help the cause.

I had two wonderful daughters and a lovely wife, but soldiering had become my life and it would have been impossible to go back to a nine to five. I couldn't really blame Liz. It wasn't easy bringing up two kids virtually on her own and I was rarely home when the girls were sick or she needed support.

But at the same time, Liz knew from the beginning that the Army was going to take me away from her. She couldn't say it came as a complete surprise.

Before going to Northern Ireland I had to be investigated by the vetting board – an SOP before any operational tour with the Regiment. The vetting goes right back to schooldays, and the retired rupert who came to see me in Hereford seemed to know everything about me. He was convinced I was a communist because I'd once been a miner.

'What do you think of Mrs Thatcher?' he asked.

'I respect her for being tough and standing up for what she believes in.'

'Do you support trade unionism?'

'Yes, I do.'

'So you agreed with the miner's strike?'

I knew what he was trying to do but I wasn't about to disown my roots. Little Moscow had been the last pit to go back to work after the 1984 strike, severely beaten but not bowed by Margaret Thatcher. I was a tom in South Armagh at the time, and I could still remember the news footage of a march from Maerdy Hall, miners proudly striding out, banners unfurled at the front of the procession along with the Tylorstown brass band, the women from the village alongside their men – and I could still remember the huge lump in my throat.

I gave it to him with both barrels.

'Have you ever been underground, sir?'

He shook his head.

'Come down the pit with me for an hour or two and then tell me you think that miners don't deserve a pay rise. My grandfathers were both miners. They fought in the First World War and one of them got wounded at the Somme. Both of them died young from silicosis. My dad was left with a permanent limp after an accident underground. It's a dangerous, dusty, noisy, stinking, shitty way to earn a living – I know, I've done it – and I don't begrudge the miners one penny of what they earn.

'Now if you want to ask me whether I think Arthur Scargill was trying to overthrow the Government, then the answer is, Yes, I think he was. I didn't agree with that and I think Maggie Thatcher took exactly the right line.'

He didn't ask me many questions after that.

For the vetting, I'd had to provide the names of two people I'd worked with at the mine. Only a handful of my friends in Rhondda knew that I'd joined the Regiment – this is how it's supposed to be for security reasons. However, the guy from the vetting unit turned up in Ferndale, spouting about me being in the SAS. My mate there had the sense to stop things quickly and get on the telephone to my dad. The 'need to know' principle had been drummed into me from the moment I arrived in the Regiment, so much so that I rarely knew what other guys were doing; they could have been overseas or on a medic course in camp and I wouldn't know.

Terrorist organizations in NI would love to get hold of information about the SAS and our movements. Idle gossip is a killer. So much for a low profile when some dick-head of a retired rupert could shoot his mouth off so recklessly.

Because the Rhondda is only an hour's drive from Hereford, I went home whenever I had the time. I still had some great friends from the valley, people like Bencey, Rittaz (Steve Richards) and Dio (John Davies). My mates knew I was living in Hereford, but only Dio and his wife Pauline knew I was in the SAS. Pauline and I went way back. She'd been my closest girl friend since the age of seven at junior school; we were in the same class right up till leaving grammar school together, me to go down the mine, her to start work as a junior clerk. There was nobody happier than me when my old work buddy Dio had started courting her; they'd ended up getting married and had had two beautiful daughters who were my god-children.

No matter where I went in the world, this small band of close pals always took the time and trouble to write. Liz would simply say I was going away, and they would then write to our civilian PO box number and mail would be forwarded to me anywhere in the world.

My parents probably sensed that all was not well between Liz and me, but I appreciated how they let us try to work things out by ourselves. In the three-month build-up to NI, I tried to patch things up, at least for the sake of Rachel and Sarah. Yet I knew that once I went across the water the old problems would resurface.

Our training build-up concentrated on surveillance skills and reactive operations. I loved the month-long surveillance package, but at 16 stones and 6 feet 2 inches I was never likely to blend in with the crowd. A special type of person excels at surveillance – someone with enormous patience who doesn't warrant a second glance because he seems so nondescript and ordinary; a grey man.

The instructor wrote: 'Curtis would be an excellent candidate for 14 Int if he lost a foot in height and about 4 stones in weight.'

Another month of the build-up was devoted to reactive-type operations. For instance, 14 Int would do long-term surveillance on a car and at some point a decision was made to do a mobile intercept, which meant stopping the vehicle and arresting the occupants. We used cars with weapons and fast drivers at the wheel, one vehicle coming in from the front and another from behind. Based on information provided by helicopters and surveillance cars on the road, we would intercept at precisely the right moment and stop the car.

Before leaving Hereford, we also had the opportunity to learn an extra skill such as daytime and night-time photography, or lock-picking. I was lucky to get one of three places on a fast-driving course run by the West Mercia police. The two guys in charge, Fat Jack and Thin Bob, looked like Laurel and Hardy and must have been about the oldest PCs on the force. Yet they had nerves of steel, because day after day they'd sit there and hardly say a word as we drove like lunatics in souped-up cars.

It took me only a few days to realize how much there is to learn about driving a car fast. Apart from the basic driving techniques we had to learn things like handbrake turns, J turns, pursuit driving and quick getaways. Handbrake turns were a buzz. The idea was that if we were driving at speed and encountered a volatile situation, such as an illegal vehicle checkpoint set up by the IRA, we could use a handbrake turn to escape. You grab the handbrake and yank on it fully, keeping the button depressed. Then you rip the wheel all the way round, spinning the car through 180 degrees. Then you pull the wheel back to its original position, the handbrake comes off, you get into first gear, hit the accelerator and scream away.

In the pursuit drives, Fat Jack would head off and I had to stay on his tail as he took us through the back roads of Hereford at speed approaching 70 m.p.h. Then a helicopter would be called in and I'd be screaming along a B road towards Newport with the pilot giving instructions like, 'You've got a forty-five degree left-hand bend in two hundred yards.'

'Pass the lorry now . . . you can make it. Go! Go!'

I was overtaking cars and lorries on blind bends and the people driving had no idea I had help from above. They must have thought I had a death wish.

The three-week course was one of the best I'd ever done in the Army and I came away from it thinking it should be compulsory for every young kid driving around in his Golf GTI who thinks he knows how to drive fast. In all likelihood, he doesn't have a clue.

*

I finished the Northern Ireland tour in June 1990 but it left a legacy which would haunt me. A local policeman who worked with us on OPs had lost his Filofax and weapon, both of which had turned up in Andersontown, an IRA heartland. The gun had been used in several murders and a robbery. The address book contained the names of his police mates as well as three or four lads from D Squadron, me included.

The Home Office operatives turned up at our house in Hereford and began organizing all sorts of security measures, such as special clingfilm on the windows in case of bomb attacks, new garage doors, external lights, alarms and cameras both upstairs and downstairs. It took weeks to get it right. Added to this, we had to take our own precautions, such as double-checking under the car every morning for booby-trap bombs.

This was all too much for Liz.

'This is your bloody fault, not mine,' she said. 'We don't live in Northern Ireland. Why should I have to live like a prisoner?'

Every time she got into the car, she had to look down at a special lighting system by the footrest. If the light was green, it was safe to turn on the ignition, but if it glowed orange then someone had tampered with the car. A red light meant that an object had been stuck underneath. Personally, I didn't rely on flashing lights; I got down on my hands and knees for a good look before I so much as opened the car door.

Liz had taken a job teaching at the children's playgroup attached to the Regiment and she called me at work one morning.

'The light is red,' she said nervously. 'What should I do?'

'Stay away from the car.'

'But I'm late for work.'

'You'll just have to walk.'

The bomb disposal guys turned up and discovered it was a case of faulty wiring. Liz's mood didn't improve.

Each week brought some new security measure which impinged on her life. Little things angered her – like coming home to find our letter box had been taken away and we now needed a key to open a new box stuck to the front wall, away from the house.

Our marriage was basically falling apart and I didn't know how to hold things together. Having spent so long each doing our own thing, we were like strangers sometimes. In my time away, Sarah had learned to walk, Rachel had been quite ill, and the usual domestic highs and lows had come and gone. I'd missed them all.

A crack had formed between Liz and me. The tour of Northern

Ireland marked the beginning, but each subsequent tour drove the wedge in a little deeper, prising us apart.

Barely a month after Northern Ireland came a jungle trip to Malaya. Another jungle, another stone lost. Never mind the Slim Fast plan – try a month in a tropical rain forest; you'll soon get to know your ribs again.

On the journey home, on 2 August 1990, our Tri-Star landed in Bahrain to refuel.

Ray Scott from Air Troop came across to me.

'Hey, Mike, I think we've got a night on the piss in Bahrain.'

'What's up?'

He'd overheard a conversation involving the head shed (HQ). 'Iraq just invaded Kuwait.'

I knew the geography of the Middle East, but still couldn't see how this move by Saddam Hussein affected us. Ray said a British Airways 747 had been stranded in Kuwait by the invasion. There were British citizens on board and the Foreign Office wanted them out of there pronto. The RAF were asking to commandeer the Tri-Star for a flight to Kuwait.

'Maybe they'll need us?' suggested 'Kiwi' Dawson, who'd been snoozing under a hat. 'I'm up for it.'

Ray, a barrel-chested Yorkshireman, seemed less sure. He was due to get married as soon as we got back.

'C'mon,' said Kiwi, 'we can hold your stag night out here. It'll give you a chance to get some sun on your zits.'

As his nickname suggested, Kiwi had spent a lot of his life in Kiwiland before leaving home intending to join the Foreign Legion. *En route* he'd changed his mind and joined the Paras.

While the hierarchy argued over the Tri-Star, we picked up more details on the invasion. I'd never had much time for Iraq, or Iran for that matter. Iran was run by mad mullahs involved in state-funded terrorism and Iraq had used chemical weapons in the long-running war between the two countries.

Like many people, I saw Iraq as the lesser of two evils, but I wasn't impressed with such a powerful nation taking advantage of a much weaker one like Kuwait. I guessed the impact of this in terms of oil supplies and production was going to worry a lot of important people.

Somewhere back in London, however, the decision was made and the RAF didn't get the Tri-Star. We flew onwards and arrived back in the UK just eight hours late.

221

Unfortunately, poor old Ray had to cancel his wedding. As we touched down, all local and overseas leave was cancelled and the squadrons were immediately put on standby. Like a lot of the lads in D Squadron, I'd booked a holiday, expecting a month's leave. Instead we trooped to the travel agents and got our deposits back.

The camp was buzzing about the possibility that we'd be called up, but no-one was any clearer on the subject. Even so, we had to cover all the options. An obvious priority was to get some serious desert training and G Squadron was sent to the United Arab Emirates (UAE) to become acclimatized.

Meanwhile, D Squadron began training in the UK. Right from the outset, our head shed said that the emphasis should be on a mobile operation because of the terrain in Iraq and Kuwait. The lessons of the desert in World War Two had been remembered and it was clear that any operation behind enemy lines would have to be fast-moving, highly mobile, with good support weapons and demolition capabilities.

Ray Scott and I were shipped out to Netheravon in Wiltshire for an advanced Milan course that would normally take ten weeks, but was now condensed into a fortnight to accommodate us.

The CO turned out to be a D Squadron old boy who loved telling war stories about his time in 17 Troop. When he finally paused for long enough to get his orderly to make us a brew, Ray leaned across and whispered, 'We're gonna spend the next two weeks listening to this fucker talk.'

At one point, he showed us an old Troop photograph from Aden and named some of his mates. 'And that's the Troop sergeant, Tegus Richards,' he said.

'Do you know his son's now in D Squadron?' I said. 'Greg Richards.'

The CO was totally knocked off track. Maybe he suddenly felt very old.

We left him with his thoughts and threw ourselves into the course. Most days he'd be up on the ranges to see how 'his boys' were doing. Our instructor, a WO1 from the Welsh Guards, seemed thoroughly pissed off that we were getting the qualification in only a fortnight, but there you go.

Whilst Ray and I were swinging the light with our new mate down in Netheravon, the rest of the squadron had the support weapons up on the rugby pitch. Each weapon had an instructor and the

222

whole squadron would do a round robin on the 81mm mortar, the 51mm mortar, the GPMG in the sustained-fire mode (on a tripod, it gives a range of up to 1,800 metres), the M19 (a 40mm grenade launcher – a fearsome piece of equipment that can saturate an area with 40mm bombs) and of course the old faithful .50 calibre machine-gun, which packs enough punch to knock over an elephant.

Everybody figured G Squadron were in the box seat. They were out in the desert developing their SOPs – Johnny on the spot. We'd be left at home.

I found my niche with the anti-tank weapons, particularly the Milans. I'd never forgotten how they saved 5 Platoon's arse in the Falklands when we were pinned down near Boca House, getting shot to shit.

The French Milan is a wire-guided anti-tank missile, controlled from its launcher with an eyepiece and cross-hairs. Its effective range is 1,950 metres, well over a mile; after that the wire snaps and the missile decks. The Milan has aiming handles on its launcher; one for deflection, one for elevation. Once the missile is launched at a static target, it will hit it as long as the target remains in the cross-hairs. If it's moving you have to track the vehicle using the handles, and the launcher sends signals down the wire to the missile's brain.

Each missile costs £10,500, with the tandem version running out at £15,000 – and that's excluding VAT. Most of the latest tanks had ERA (explosive reactive armour), which meant that a single warhead would hit the armour and explode without penetrating the core of the tank. With a tandem warhead, a missile within a missile, the second detonation penetrates. Result: one unroad-worthy tank.

The squadron's next priority was an introduction at Sennybridge in Wales to the vehicles that were being sent out to the Emirates. Mobility Troop were given the lead hand in teaching the rest of us the tactics and idiosyncrasies of the 'Pink Panthers' or 'pinkies' – long-wheel-based Land Rovers that were considered the best vehicles for desert terrain.

The course also showed us the basics of vehicle maintenance, such as repairing a broken fan belt or a busted radiator. There were also particular ways to pack equipment such as jerrycans of water and petrol, along with the best weapon placements and the storage of ammunition.

Initially we were pissed off about being left at home, but as the

223

weeks passed it became increasingly likely that we'd be sent to the Emirates to do proper desert training. G Squadron were due to go on the anti-terrorist team, which meant returning to the UK; having done our support-weapons and vehicle training, we were the likeliest replacements.

Normally G Squadron might have stayed in theatre, but their OC had made a major miscalculation. He hadn't trained his troops on the pinkies because he believed that, in the event of war, they would tab across the border or be dropped by helicopter and then dig OPs in the sand – a bit crazy when you consider the long distances involved. As it turned out, the hierarchy at RHQ agreed with our squadron head shed and decided they wanted a force that was totally mobile rather than one on foot. In mid-September, the Guardsmen got recalled and we replaced them. Jocky and Ade were well pissed off.

A lot of my best mates also missed out. Greg Richards, Scouse McVey and Griz were all over in Northern Ireland because their twelve-month tour had overlapped with mine. I felt sorry that they were missing all the excitement.

Everywhere the Regiment travels we take the whole works with us – separate kit for the jungle, desert and European theatre. This means we can leave an exercise quickly and go straight to an operational job in another part of the world. Of course, it made packing a right fucking chore. Everything had to be counted, logged and stored, before being put into a container. At least all the pinkies and heavy-support weapons were already *in situ*; they were up and running from the moment we arrived.

I'd been in some hot countries around the world – Brunei, Kenya, Central America – but as we disembarked from the RAF VC10 at Dubai the heat hit me smack in the face. By the time we picked up our bergens from the shimmering tarmac, I was melting like fat in a frying pan.

'This is what I gave up my honeymoon for,' said Ray, as he threw his bergen into the truck. 'This place is hotter than hell.'

'Na, it *is* hell,' said Mad Mac Ross. 'The devil's in the local phone directory.'

Mad Mac was one of the few guys in the Regiment who was actually bigger than me. He came from a farm up in Wick, near John o'Groats, and had the quiet, unassuming nature of a big old farming boy. But he was fearless and had once narrowly failed to make it single-handed to the North Pole.

Mac did a lot of odd things. He was a bit of a hermit and his house in Hereford contained nothing but a table, some chairs and a cassette player, so he could listen to his Scottish bagpipe music. He could actually play the pipes himself and drove his neighbours to distraction by practising all the time.

Our home for the next six weeks was to be Camp Monama, a city of tents just off a dual carriageway in the middle of the desert. It had sand, sand, insects and more sand. The only proper buildings were the cookhouse, a mosque, the Arab accommodation and sheds for storage.

'Fuck, I hate camp beds,' said Mad Mac, as we stuck our heads inside the canvas.

'I wouldn't worry,' said Kiwi. 'No-one's gonna sleep in this heat.'

'I reckon Arabs don't sweat. They don't even have pores in their skin. How else could anyone live out here?'

Mad Mac found a mattress lying outside and dragged it into the tent. 'I don't know about you wankers but I'm going to sleep like a baby.'

The next morning his back and legs were a mass of bites. He'd been eaten alive.

I didn't know what was worse, the stifling heat or the incessant wailing from the mosque disco in the early hours, keeping everyone awake.

Training took on a whole new meaning in the desert. The pinkies and LSVs (light strike vehicles) were up and running, and we set about practising in the sand-dunes. Mobility Troop were the masters and we were the students.

Each pinkie carried three men and would also have to fit weapons, ammunition, fuel, water, spare parts, food and our bergens. I was to be a vehicle commander and was pleased to be teamed up with Kiwi and Billy Adams, who'd both gone through depot together and joined 2 Para. I was a corporal by then and remembered them vaguely. Later, they'd also gone through Selection together.

Kiwi was a training fanatic and very meticulous about his soldiering; we hit it off straight away. He looked like Zooney from *Fireball XL5* and had a warped sense of humour, but the girls seemed to love him. His New Zealand drawl had turned into a sort of West Country accent, but at least I could understand what he said.

Billy, a half-caste kid from Newcastle, reminded me of Geordie Vale because his accent was impossible to fathom. A tough little

225

guy, he looked as wide as he was tall, and they don't come much wider than 5 feet 9 inches. He'd come from a Territorial Army background and was an excellent medic.

For the first few days in the sand dunes we spent most of our time getting bogged up to the axles and having to dig out the pinkies using sand channels that were strapped to the side of the vehicles in readiness. We found that even though the LSVs looked the part, like elongated dune buggies with four fat tyres and an engine at the back, they were shit when it came to climbing sand mountains. They were designed to carry a Milan or other heavy weapons, scream in towards the target, strike, then fuck off sharpish – but that doesn't work if you're up to the axles in sand. Invariably we'd just get moving and then get bogged again. Kiwi looked ready to put a bullet through the radiator. Eventually we binned them, much to the annoyance of the Mad Max clones, and stuck to the pinkies.

Mobility Troop gave us the tip that if we let about 10 pounds of air pressure out of the tyres it would stop us tunnelling into the sand so much. But the real trick was to go full throttle and scream up the dunes until you flew over the top without losing revs or momentum. This took quite a lot of balls, especially at night and without lights. Sometimes the pinkie felt almost vertical and about to flip and I could sense Billy and Kiwi getting ready to jump.

'Piece of advice,' said Kiwi. 'If pinkies were meant to fly they'd have wings.'

'You're just a frustrated aviator,' chimed Billy.

'Nah, I'm just fed up with digging these fuckers out of the ground.'

'I thought you wanted to be Beau Geste,' I told him. 'You should love all this fucking sand.'

Kiwi had been only minutes away from signing up for the Legion. He was actually waiting in the recruiting office in Marseilles, ready to be interviewed, when the lad in front of him from England started telling stories about the Para Regiment. Apparently this kid had spent eighteen months with the Paras and was now AWOL. As he recited his tales, Kiwi thought, I'll have some of that, and he promptly left the office, went to England and signed up.

Our sergeant major, Stu McDonald, was living up to his fearsome reputation within the Regiment. Everybody called him 'Mad Dog' McDonald because he was so fucking tough. He looked like Oliver Reed and had the temperament and patience of a Rottweiler.

226

Each day training began at sparrow's fart – although the nearest sparrow was probably a thousand miles away. Dozens of different skills had to be learned or polished. I gave lessons on the Milan and .50 calibre machine-gun, while other lads covered mortars, GPMGs, M19s and satellite navigation with the new hand-held Magellan, which could give us a fix on the map down to the nearest metre.

When the support weapons were fixed on the pinkies we began practising on ranges set up in the desert. The Milans were too expensive to fuck around with, so I started the lads on the Milan simulator, a bit like an arcade video game. Then I got them to aim at the oil tankers and lorries on the main dual carriageway beside the camp, practising how to track a vehicle and keep it between the cross-hairs. It was like being back at a funfair in Porthcawl, zapping space invaders.

When we thought they were ready to live-fire, the squadron gave us a dozen live missiles to fire off.

Ray did the mental arithmetic. 'At fifteen thousand pounds apiece, that's like writing off a brand new Ford Escort every time we push the button.'

'Yeah, and that's not counting the damage it does when it lands.'

We chose two wadis on the training ranges and built some targets out of old vehicles and oil drums – six targets in each wadi – pulling them into position with Land Rovers. From the top of a high hill I could look down the long wadi and range-find the targets with laser binoculars that gave a read-out of the distance. The nearest target was 1,400 metres away, the farthest 1,900 metres.

The whole squadron came out to watch. *Whoosh!* – the sound never ceased to amaze me and always brought back memories of Goose Green. Five feet of missile flew serenely through the air and ripped into the distant target. All the lads did well – no misses.

Despite the expensive fireworks, Camp Monama still had the aura of another exercise, rather than preparation for war. In October 1990 the possibility still seemed distant. Even if the Allies did use force to push Saddam Hussein out of Kuwait, there were no guarantees that the SAS would be called upon. All we could do was be ready just in case.

The plan was to have four vehicles per Troop – two for attack and two for support. The attack vehicles had a GPMG mounted on the commander's (passenger) side, and a double-GPMG for the rear gunner. Each support pinkie had a gimpy at the front and mounts on the back for either the M19 grenade launcher or the .50 calibre Browning heavy machine-gun.

In addition, each driver had the option of putting a Minimi light machine-gun on his side at the front – a fabulous support weapon that fired 5.56 rounds either from a box or a belt; or an Armalite magazine could be fitted.

I decided not to mount the Milan directly onto our vehicle, so that we could take it off and fire it from the ground. This would give us more flexibility if the pinkie had a major mechanical failure or took a direct hit.

Having mastered the driving, support weapons and night navigation, we staged a classic mobility insertion exercise. Travelling at night, without lights, each Troop had to locate, survey and attack a different target. Ours was a cluster of satellite dishes in the desert.

Leaving base camp at hour-long intervals, the Troop convoys of four vehicles veered off the dual carriageway at particular points. We were the last to leave, and by the time we turned off the highway into the desert it was pitch-black. Unable to do a proper recce, we went straight into the sand dunes. Further along the road we could have gone around them, but we weren't to know. The dunes were more like giant slag heaps, and somehow we had to get over them. For most of the night we dug, pushed, pulled and swore.

'Let's forget about digging it out, just bury the fucking thing,' said Billy, who looked like a sweat-soaked spitball.

Climbing a dune at full throttle was a matter of standing up, foot flat down on the accelerator, eyeballs on stalks, and screaming up into the blackness, not knowing what lay ahead. As the front wheels crested the rise and pointed downwards, I slammed on the brakes – only to find another fucking sand dune waiting on the other side. So it went on, hour after hour, dune after dune.

Shortly before daybreak, Mountain Troop basha'd up in a harbour area under camouflage nets. The sun beat down all that day, but our recces on foot managed to find the satellite dishes, which were basically a couple of disused buildings in the desert.

The attack would be on foot. Waiting until nightfall, we left a patrol with the wagons at the harbour area, then moved towards the FRV (forward rendezvous). Newlands and I went forward to do a CTR. When we'd gathered all the information we needed, I slipped back to the FRV, where the guys were in all-round defence. I brought them back to the start line and we hit the camp with the combined firepower of 66s, gimpies and Minimis. With two lads covering us, Des Ford and I then blew up the makeshift dishes with PE4. Job done, we legged it back to the wagons.

Returning to Camp Monama after three days of little sleep and a whole lot of cajoling, pulling and pushing of the pinkies, most of us collapsed into bunks and crashed out, totally exhausted.

Mad Dog McDonald was having none of this. 'Right, you arse-holes. Who hasn't shaved?'

'We've spent three days in the desert, Stu,' said Carl Newlands, rubbing his bristled chin.

'What do you want – a fucking medal? Anyone who hasn't shaved has to put a tenner into the Troop Fund.'

The Troop Fund was a 'beer money' bank account, into which each member supplied ten pounds a month, drawn from his pay book, while away in Northern Ireland or on a training job. It was also bolstered by on-the-spot fines for doing such things as not shaving before coming back into camp after three days in the desert. Every so often, on a day off overseas or at Christmas, the fund was raided for a massive piss-up.

We could all now see the problems involved in attacking a camp in the desert surrounded by dunes. By far the best method would be to leave the wagons and tab forward on foot in case one or more of the vehicles bogged in.

After the debrief, we finally crashed out, only to be kept awake by the latest hits from the mosque next door.

Mad Mac summed it up: 'I don't mind the rag-heads praising Allah, but why should everyone else have to listen? I don't make you listen to my bagpipe tapes, do I?'

Our one day off in six tough weeks coincided with my birthday. I noticed a Milan box being brought into the cookhouse at break-fast, but thought nothing of it. Then, just as my curiosity was about to get the better of me, the lid popped open and out bounded Glen Unwin, probably the smallest man in the Regiment, holding a big birthday cake. It was a nice touch in front of all the lads.

A day off abroad is a perfect excuse to draw on the Troop Fund and organize a piss-up. Although Dubai is technically a 'dry' state, the international hotels sold alcohol and downtown Dubai was only 50 clicks from camp.

Mad Dog organized the transport and laid down the law about abiding by the local customs and staying out of trouble.

'You drink in the hotel; you come home on the coach. You don't go wandering around the town.' Then he told us the story of a

British guy who supposedly got six lashes for pissing in a door-way. This became a running gag as we set off on a 'twenty-lash piss-up'.

The city teemed with life, colour and commerce. There were stores selling everything from baby's prams to battleships, along with every electrical appliance known to man. After our custom-ary Troop scoff at a curry house we piled into the bar of the Holiday Inn and gave the cellar a scare.

The hotels were full of ex-pats and we'd come up with a cover story about being sailors.

'Oh really?' said a nurse to Big Mac. 'And what ship are you boys off?'

'A fucking big grey one, luv,' replied Mac. The nurse decided to cut the questioning and leave.

I was in charge of the Troop Fund and had taken along about a grand – most of which disappeared over the bar as the night wore on. Ironically, it was Mad Dog who came closest to getting in a fight when he began arguing with a couple of Yanks over a spilt beer.

I couldn't remember what time we got back to camp, but I did know that the mosque sparked up at 4.00 a.m. and I lay on my camp bed, head throbbing, and contemplating where I'd place the charges to blow the fucker to kingdom come.

Two hours later I was back in the cookhouse ready for the next day's training.

D Squadron had been in the desert for six weeks and RHQ at Hereford decided that we'd stay in the United Arab Emirates until further notice. This was good news; most of us were afraid that one of the other squadrons, A or B, would be sent out to replace us on rotation. Obviously the head shed were impressed by our mobility skills.

About a quarter of the lads were sent home in November for medic and dems refreshers, while the rest kept training. I had different orders. D Squadron was due in Norway for an exercise in January and four of us were being sent to do a military ski in-structor's course. By the end of it we'd be able to teach the 'goon squad', as ski novices in the squadron were called at the start of their two-week intensive course.

I argued the toss with Stu McDonald, hoping to stay, but the head shed had made up their minds.

'This whole thing could go for a bag of shit tomorrow,' said Mad Dog. 'Iraq pulls out of Kuwait and we're off home. That's why they're keeping the Norway commitment open.'

Back in Hereford, I had a weekend with Liz and the girls before withdrawing arctic kit from the stores at camp. The old boy behind the counter, an ex-D Squadron lad from the Malayan campaign, said to me, 'Ah, Taff, you're going to miss out on it, boyo – you're going skiing, not going off to the war.'

In the space of three days I went from being up to my neck in sand, sweating my nuts off, to freezing my arse off in minus temperatures. Shivering next to me were Kiwi, Mitch from Mobility Troop and Andy, an ex-Selous Scout from South Africa.

We'd flown into Vos with suntans to meet the Fusiliers, who were sponsoring us for the skiing course. Our shorts and T-shirts had been replaced by Goretex, bobble hats and gloves. By now I thought I was a competent skier, but our instructors were from the Norwegian army and in a different league. They spent ages trying to teach us the perfect telemark turn, but our minds were elsewhere. Kiwi couldn't open his mouth without flapping about missing out. Every time he saw me, he'd say, 'Mike, phone Stu McDonald tonight, OK? Get us back there!'

I was in charge of the group, but dealing with Mad Dog on a one-to-one basis was not easy. To keep Kiwi happy, I called McDonald once a week from a pay phone in Vos while the rest of the lads huddled around me. He must have had hundreds of things on his mind and could have done without us badgering him from Norway.

'I told you before, you Welsh twat,' he said, 'we're not going without you, OK? Now fuck off and pass the course.'

We took ten tests in all, with the Norwegians checking that we had the skills required to be an MSI (military ski instructor). All four of us passed and were given a day off to relax.

That night we were trying to drink the Norgies into the deck when the phone rang. It was the adjutant from Hereford, asking for me.

'Be at the airport at 0915 tomorrow morning. There'll be a C130 waiting to bring you back to Lyneham. A guy from the MT will drive you to Hereford.'

'Shit, this is it!' said Kiwi. 'It's going down!'

Arriving at Stirling Lines, still hung-over from the Norgie send-off, we went to see McDonald.

'Did you all pass?'

'Yes.'

'Good. Hand your kit in then, you won't be needing it – we're all on standby to move back to the Gulf.'

He told us to stay in Hereford waiting for word, but thought we'd probably leave immediately after Christmas.

At the stores, I handed back my arctic hood, gloves, headcovers and thick thermal socks. 'I won't be needing these again in a hurry,' I said, exchanging the kit for desert fatigues and jungle boots, ideal for the desert because of their lightness.

It was a week till Christmas and we began prepping personal kit – painting our webbing, bergens, ponchos and M203 Armalites with desert camouflage paint. There were a million things that needed doing, such as oiling the springs of the magazines, checking my operational torch with all the filters, making sure of the batteries and spares. All the heavy weapons had been left *in situ* in the Emirates.

After the personal admin, we reported back to the briefing room. D Squadron had just been issued with a new OC. It was a strange time to change the top man, during the build-up to a possible war. It effectively meant that McDonald would now fully take over the squadron, albeit not in rank, because the new OC would take a while to sort himself out.

I stayed in Hereford for Christmas Eve and Christmas Day and then went down to the Rhondda valley with Liz and the girls until the New Year to await our final orders. Every news broadcast was dominated by the news from Kuwait; it was hard to get away from it but nonetheless I enjoyed myself. At the back of my mind I knew that I'd be away soon, but I tried hard not to dwell on it; this was quality time with my family and I did my best to block out everything else.

Like all dads I got a big kick out of watching the girls open their presents. Liz cooked the dinner and I played with the kids. It was a good day. We finally got the girls to bed and started to doze in front of the television. Suddenly I saw a familiar face – Baz, my old B Company mucker, was in Saudi on a secondment to the 82nd Airborne, Para Reg's American cousin, and was giving an interview to the BBC. With a grin on my face I raised my glass and toasted him a merry Christmas.

Boxing Day came and went, and still the news bulletins were full of Kuwait and the diplomatic argy bargy. No-one mentioned the invasion until Rachel, now six, said, 'Daddy, are you going away to the desert again?'

'Just for a little while, sweetheart. But when I get home we're going to go on holiday.'

'Where? Where?'

'Where would you like to go?'

'Can I come to the desert with you?'

'Not this time.'

Traditionally, on New Year's Eve, Dio, Pauline, Liz and I all went out. My sister Rhian joined us this year and we all had a major knees-up at the Maerdy Hall.

Leaving well after midnight, Liz and I walked back to my parents' house. On a cold night there were still lots of people out celebrating in the streets – a slightly bizarre scene when set against my preparations to fight a war in another part of the world.

'Are you OK, Mike?' Liz asked.

'Yeah. Why?'

'I worry about you when you're away. I worry that something might happen to you.'

This was unusual. Liz rarely talked about my job and I guessed that alcohol had loosened her tongue.

'Everything's going to be fine,' I said.

For the past few months I'd carried on as if it was all another exercise, but now, as I climbed the hills to my parents' terrace, the realization finally began dawning that I might be fighting for real.

When I'd gone to war the first time, I'd been a raw young man, wide-eyed and innocent. Goose Green and Wireless Ridge had changed all that. In the Falklands the Paras had followed orders dictated from above and had been badly let down at Goose Green because we had no support. We were lucky to lose so few. A lot of water under the bridge since then, I thought. This time it would be different. The SAS was a far more sophisticated machine than the bared teeth and aggression of the Parachute Regiment. As part of a Special Forces unit, we dictated what happened on the ground and made the important decisions. If things went wrong, then normally we only had ourselves to blame.

As soon as we got back to Hereford, we got the warning order to move.

On Monday, 5 January, Liz gave me a kiss on the cheek. 'Goodbye then.'

I turned and picked up Rachel. 'Now you look after your mother and work hard at school.'

'I'm on holiday,' she remonstrated.

233

'Yes, I know. But you're going back next week.'

'Can't I wait till you come home?' she asked.

'No, but I'll be back before you know it.'

Sarah tugged at my arm. She was far too young to realize what was happening, but knew there were hugs being offered.

We piled into the family car and Liz drove me to the camp. The girls had been there hundreds of times and liked playing on the climbing ropes and fall mats in the gym. Kiwi and Billy chatted to Liz while I got my bag out of the boot. Sarah was busy hiding because she'd heard me talking to Liz about somebody called Mad Mac and was terrified he was some kind of nutter. She wasn't that far from the mark.

Liz and I gave each other a final hug and a strained smile. This was my job, this was what I was paid to do; having a family life is an added bonus in the Regiment.

'Take care,' she said.

'Of course.'

I watched them drive towards the clock tower before turning left out of the camp. Inscribed on the clock tower were the names of all the guys who had died on active service. Through superstition, I'd never read them, and now wasn't the time to start. I turned away and disappeared into the block.

# 14

WE FLEW INTO SAUDI AT NIGHT ON 6 JANUARY 1991. CAMP VICTOR LOOKED like something out of a James Bond film. The hangars and runway were all lit up and just about everywhere I looked I could see choppers and C130s being loaded and unloaded.

A Squadron were already settled into a hangar and D Squadron and B Squadron were given similar accommodation on camp beds, living in each other's pockets. Stu McDonald gave us a quick briefing. After that, the first priority was to get our kit inside our hangar, choose our bed space, erect camp beds and then try to crash out for a couple of hours.

That night, as I lay in bed, I couldn't get to sleep because of the clanking of the aluminium roof. It sounded like rain, but next morning someone explained to me how the metal roof contracted in the evening after the fierce heat of the day.

The vehicles had been prepped and waiting for us since Christmas.

Each of the Troops – Mountain, Air, Boat and Mobility – had been operating with four vehicles, but now a fifth Troop was created – known as 20 Troop – which became part of a mobile squadron headquarters. In the event of war, 20 Troop would travel with us across the border into Iraq.

Apart from having four more pinkies, the new arrangement meant that a mother vehicle – a 'Unimog,' a Mercedes Benz 4-tonner that had been stripped down to hold spare parts, rations, water, fuel and ammo – could be close to the action rather than hundreds of miles away.

Each Troop provided three lads to become part of the mobile squadron headquarters. It meant rehashing the vehicle crews but Kiwi, Billy and I stayed together. I thought we were a good combination – a totally 2 Para vehicle.

Early on it had been decided that Mountain, Air and Boat Troops should each include a senior member of Mobility to help with the driving skills and maintenance. We got Sergeant Jack Dennis, a talkative Jock, who was a good mate of my old Rhondda pal, John Hedges.

The Mountain Troop wagons were as follows:

VEHICLE No. 1 – GPMG at the front, double GPMG to the rear. Commander and Troop OC – Ted Butterton, a former Green Jacket; driver – Mad Mac Ross from the Artillery; and Mick, from 264 Signals, who had just passed Selection. (We called them the 'hat vehicle' because they were all non-Paras and therefore crap hats).

VEHICLE No. 2 – GPMG at the front, .50 cal to the rear. Commander and Troop 2 i/c – Jack Dennis, ex-3 Para and Mobility Troop; driver – Carl Newlands, ex-1 Para; and Barry Taylor, ex-Light Infantry. Barry was a fifty-a-day puffer from Newcastle who never trained. In every exercise he'd go down with heat exhaustion and need an IV drip; he'd take a litre of fluid then get up and continue tabbing as if nothing had happened.

VEHICLE No. 3 (all 2 Para) – GPMG at the front, double GPMG to the rear. Commander – yours truly; driver – Kiwi Dawson; gunner – Billy Adams.

VEHICLE No. 4 (all 1 Para) – GPMG at the front, M19 to the rear. Commander and staff sergeant – Kev Phillips; driver – Des Ford; and Little Jock Macintyre. Des and Little Jock were both quiet lads but very efficient soldiers. Des had a really cutting, sarcastic sense of humour and was a great mate of.Carl Newlands. The two of them were constantly winding up Mad Mac, even though he could have sorted them both out at the same time if he'd wanted to. Carl Newlands hadn't changed at all since I met him on Selection. A total extrovert, he seemed to specialize in close shaves with authority, but always managed to survive because he was an excellent soldier.

Wasting no time, we launched into training the next day and prepared to leave at 1400 hours for a small tented camp in the desert. This would be our base for a week of night-time assaults on a variety of targets.

The squadron head shed had made it an SOP to take off the vehicle roll bars to give us a lower profile against the horizon. We

236

also covered up the headlights with hessian sacks to stop any reflection and prevent the possibility of an ND (negligent discharge) which could compromise our position at night.

'Fuck it, Billy, take out the bulbs as well,' I said.

Kiwi was busy camming up the wagon with some buckshee paint.

'It's already been done,' Billy told him.

'I know, but it's cracking.' Typical of Kiwi, as meticulous as ever.

We loaded the training ammo, compo, fuel and water, finishing with an hour to spare.

'C'mon let's get some scoff,' I said.

Each squadron had been allotted its own stores hangar next to our sleeping accommodation. I took a look inside with Kiwi and Ray Scott. Instead of training ammo this was the real stuff, and it was stockpiled to the rafters – Milans, boxes of grenades, explosives, and as much ammunition as you could wave a shitty stick at.

At 1400 hours, the vehicles were lined up ready to set off. The sun was blisteringly hot and Kiwi and I sweated our nuts off in the front seats, while Billy sat crammed behind us among the boxes, getting pins and needles in his feet. Still, for guys who, unlike Boat, Air and Mobility, were used to tabbing everywhere humping our kit, the chance to ride on four wheels was luxury.

The exercise consisted of various attacks on different desert camps but also involved working with the Special Forces pilots to practise airlifting the pinkies behind enemy lines, using the technique of fast-ramping.

Fast-ramping had come to prominence during the Israeli raid on Entebbe Airport to free hostages held by terrorists. The Regiment had modified the drill to suit our own requirements. On the second afternoon we went through the loading drills at the airport.

We reversed three pinkies up the ramp of the Herc, with the driver looking straight ahead and obeying the directions of his vehicle commander. Once on board, the front and back axles were shackled down and locked into place with a quick-release mechanism.

Kiwi, Billy and I strapped ourselves in as the Herc took off and headed out over the desert.

The loadie gave us the one-minute warning and Kiwi jumped into the driver's seat. The plane banked sharply, dropping fast towards the desert runway. Billy and I frantically searched for the quick release and then pulled away the shackles. My stomach was in my mouth from the drop in altitude.

At thirty seconds, the tailgate was already half open. It's so noisy inside a C130 that you have to put your hand over the exhaust to check if the engine's running. Billy did ours and gave a thumbs up. We both jumped into the pinkie.

The Herc touched down and the pilot slammed on the reverse thrust. We were clinging to the sides of our vehicle, looking at the blackness and smelling the burning rubber.

The loadie had a headset so that he could communicate with the pilot.

Thumbs up.

'Go! Go! Go!'

Three pinkies shot from the belly of the bird as it screamed along the runway. The dust hurled up by the propellers was horrendous. I wore goggles with an Arab shemag wrapped round my head. As we veered off towards the target, the smell of oil and rubber was soon replaced by the clean heat of the desert.

The procedure for the Chinook was much the same. Two pinkies would reverse up ramps into the back so that they could drive out forwards at speed. Once inside they were tied down with chains over the axles and the same quick-release system. The choppers could get us closer to the target than the C130s and therefore didn't need Air Troop to mark out the LZ with infrared torches, but a heli infil created its own set of problems: a helicopter throws up a blinding sandstorm, and landing closer to the target meant you had to know the exact attack heading prior to insertion.

Then the shemags and goggles came into their own.

Meanwhile, Saddam Hussein continued to ignore Allied demands to withdraw his troops from Kuwait. He'd been given a deadline of 15 January and the likelihood of war grew with each passing day. Yet there were still no guarantees that the SAS would be involved. General Norman Schwarzkopf, the American commander-in-chief, had taken charge of the Allied operation and it was known that he didn't like using Special Forces, particularly after the cock-ups made by the Seals in Grenada, where the élite Navy force had made the unforgivable error of mixing up the actual time with Zulu time. As a result, the regular army attacked one hour after first light instead of one hour before first light.

Undoubtedly, the biggest headache confronting Allied Command was how to stop Iraq's Scud missiles hitting Israel and dragging it into the war, especially as many of the launchers were mobile and could be fired and moved before jets could be scrambled to destroy the launch sites. Ultimately, General Peter de la Billière, Commander British Forces, and the Director of Special Forces, Andrew Massey, went to Schwarzkopf and guaranteed that the SAS could stop the Scuds flying into Tel Aviv.

Stormin' Norman liked that, and was particularly sold on the promise that we'd be self-sufficient behind enemy lines and would do our own resupps of ammunition, food and gasoline. This proved to be the key, and suddenly we were in the game.

We were now told that 19 Troop's call sign was Delta Four-One; the code word 'Highlight' was placed in front of it so that the pilots would know that we were Brit Special Forces. 'Trade' was the code word to say that we had something for them.

Any operation behind enemy lines is high-risk. Preparation becomes even more important because there's no going back to pick up something you've left behind. Clothing wise, given the expected high temperatures, most of us decided to go with normal windproofs and flak jackets with desert DPM; no body armour. We had helmets, but everyone had got used to wearing Arab shemags, which were good for keeping out the dust.

Loading the wagon was an art in itself. Everything had a place: the Milan missiles; bar mines; boxes of explosives, including L2 and white phos grenades; 7.62 link for the gimpies; 5.56 link for the Minimis (contained in green plastic boxes, each holding 200 rounds); boxes and boxes of 5.56 cartons for the Armalites and M203 bombs; ten jerrycans of water; ten jerrycans of fuel; two weeks' supply of compo per man; boxes of hexamine; bergens; five complete sets per man of NBC (nuclear, biological and chemical) suits, including gloves, boots and associated items; and boxes of batteries and gas bottles for the spyglass and MIRA thermal imager. The MIRA was for firing the Milan at night, and could only be used when mounted on the Milan – hence our decision to take a hand-held spyglass as well.

For his sins, Carl Newlands had done the NBC instructors' course – the most boring in the Army – and he punished the squadron with daily lectures.

'Why don't we just send Newlands over the border and he can bore the Iraqis to death?' suggested Mad Mac.

Because of the threat posed by Iraqi tank battalions, the bar mines were important. At 3 feet long, 4 inches wide and 2½ inches thick, these steel bars had a 1,000-metre danger area. They could be buried beneath the surface and set to trigger on double impulse, so that the first tank in a convoy passes over while the second one gets blown to shit. It throws the convoy into total disarray. As a bonus, the mines were also ideal for destroying communications cables and towers.

'Jesus,' whistled Billy, when we finally stood back to examine the rig.

'That's one mean mother of a machine,' said Kiwi.

'Yeah, and if we take a hit we'll blow up half of fucking Iraq.'

'What are we gonna call her?' I asked.

We looked at each other.

'We're all from the Parachute Regiment, so let's call it Pegasus,' suggested Billy.

Having just seen the film *Memphis Belle* about the fly-boys in the Second World War, I liked the idea of having a mascot painted on the wagon. The best I could find was a picture of Madonna in a magazine. I cut it out, covered it with plastic and put it on the side of Pegasus to bring us good luck. She was our Mae West.

In the hangars, everyone listened to the BBC World Service and began counting down the days till the deadline for Iraqi withdrawal. As it got closer, D minus five became D minus four and then D minus three.

A Squadron had also been training on the pinkies and was ready to help spearhead the assault. B Squadron would basically be held in reserve for battle replacements, but their OC was pushing hard to get them more involved.

With three squadrons at the camp, the queue for scoff went on for miles. It improved when they gave us the anthrax jab because so many of us became sick. It was supposed to safeguard us from a chemical attack, but it made my arm go numb for days afterwards.

On D minus one, we received our orders. Ted Butterton, the 19 Troop boss, gathered us around the briefing table. He had a democratic style which suited the lads and I liked him a lot.

'The targets are all strictly confidential and on a need-to-know basis. You don't discuss them with anyone outside of the Troop,' he said.

I looked around the hangar and saw that the other troops were similarly poised over tables, gazing at maps, taking notes and asking questions.

Ted gave us the locations of the intended targets. The first was a comms centre with a triple A (anti-aircraft artillery) on each corner, and the comms structure in the middle. The second was a BMP vehicle compound on a roadside to the north of the triple A position. Both were hundreds of kilometres deep into Iraq.

'What do you think, Kiwi?'

He took a sharp intake of air. 'It's a fucking long way.'

'How did I know you were going to say that?'

'Could be worse,' laughed Billy. 'We could be tabbing there.'

'How many men on the first target, Boss?' I asked.

'We won't know until we do a CTR, but there could be about fifty to a hundred.'

'Anyone happen to know the range of their triple As in the ground role?'

'Four kilometres,' Kiwi said.

'How the fuck are we going to recce it?' said Newlands.

He had a point; it didn't seem possible to drive so far into Iraq without being compromised.

For a long while we pored over the maps. We had to break down each night and day that it would take to get there, looking at the likely trouble spots and deciding issues such as vehicle formations and contact drills.

'C'mon Mike, let's get some scoff,' said Kiwi, as I tried to get my head around the distance.

We wandered across the sandy ground towards the cookhouse.

'It's too far,' I said. 'We should fly in and fast-ramp.'

'A lot can happen in the next few days.'

Back in the hangar, we busied ourselves with personal admin. This is the stage in every campaign when you write your letters home in case you don't make it back. It's a very strange feeling to correspond in the past tense as if you're already dead.

I had two letters to write – one to Liz and one to my parents. They would be left at Camp Victor with Russ Nelson, a stand-in quartermaster for the squadron who'd been assigned to collect the letters and keep them safe. Poor Russ would also have the job of delivering them to the wives and families of those men who didn't return.

I lay on my bunk, trying to think of something to say to Liz. How can you sum up a lifetime of feelings in only a sentence or two? Impossible.

'Thank you for all the good times you gave me,' I eventually wrote. 'I hope the girls will be all right – don't let them forget me. And I hope you find another husband. You deserve only happiness.'

To my parents I wrote: 'Remember, this is what I wanted to do;

241

I wanted to join the Army and to travel the world. You gave me life and it's been very good to me. I had a wonderful childhood, married a great girl and had two beautiful daughters. I couldn't have asked for any more.'

Kiwi was across the way as I sealed the two letters. Music blasted out of the beat boxes, and for one brief moment I was back in the bowels of the *Norland*, surrounded by Stevie, Cautious Bob and all the other laughing faces of B Company. I looked at Kiwi and hoped that this war would not cost me so dear.

Another part of iso-prep (isolation preparation) was for each soldier to write down four things about himself. The four personal details were supposed to be just that – very personal. These facts were lodged with the Intelligence Corps for use as a form of verification should any of us be captured by the Iraqis. It was to guard against any attempt by the enemy to fake a prisoner's release in a bid to get him talking. Only when the person debriefing us could quote the four personal details about ourselves were we to accept that we were genuinely free.

'What did you put down?' asked Kiwi.

'Typical stuff. My first car was a Cortina my Dad bought for me; he's got one leg shorter than the other because of the mining accident and I was actually born in the village of Maerdy even though my birth certificate says Ferndale . . . that sort of thing. How about you?'

Without a flicker of emotion, he said, 'My sister fell into the washing-machine and drowned when I was a kid while I was having breakfast.'

I didn't know what to say.

He grinned and did his Michael Caine impersonation: 'Not many people know that.'

Because the head shed hadn't suggested any possible cover stories should we be captured, I assumed it would be pretty bloody obvious what we were doing and no-one was going to pretend the Iraqis were idiots.

Everybody was issued with a syringe and two syrettes of morphine – SOPs in the Regiment. The syrettes were tied around the neck with paracord, alongside our ID discs, which were taped up to stop them rattling or shining in the sunlight. Then we were issued with ten gold coins to barter our freedom should we be captured, and a silk escape map. We also had a note explaining in English and four Arabic dialects that anyone who gave us assistance if we were in trouble and helped us reach safety would receive a financial reward.

Afterwards, we busied ourselves with a thousand different tasks. I tested the XM 122 transmitter and all of the ten receivers onto which the electrical detonators would be placed, and the myriad of batteries and their back-ups for the MIRA, Magellan, spyglass and torches.

We were even given some new toys and I went out to test them with Jim Dalton from 17 Troop. Called PED100s, they were timers for electrical detonators, and could be programmed with a delay of up to 100 days. The PED100 was fitted onto a small keypad computer on which the desired date and time of your explosion could be punched in; you then detached it from the keypad computer and it was ready to be wired up to the detonator.

To test whether XM122 receivers or PED100s are working correctly, ISFEs are used instead of electrical dets. These have two wires, exactly the same as an electrical det; however, they have the minimum of explosive – less than a small firework – and can detonate safely in a classroom. I put an ISFE on the end of each receiver and detonated them; then I put a number on the PED100s, with different time delays, to detonate from five minutes to an hour. The PEDs were fine, precise to the second.

Back in the iso-prep area, Ted Butterton gave us our final orders. When the air war started we were to fly from Victor to an FOB (forward operating base) at Ar'ar in Saudi Arabia, taking the vehicles and equipment. D Squadron would then sneak across the Iraqi border and head north towards our targets. Two vehicles from Air Troop were to be dropped deeper into enemy territory by Chinooks to blow up a fibre-optic cable that was running into a Scud site. Afterwards, they would head south to meet up with the rest of Air Troop.

The various Troop briefings went on in total seclusion from the rest of the squadron and afterwards we began the final planning, sitting down on our bunks with anti-tank weapons, Stingers, GPMGs and other operational ammunition piled around us.

'You can't fucking move for hardware in this place,' complained Mad Mac.

Being a dems man I was responsible for the detonators. They had been checked, put back in their small plastic boxes and stowed in my claymore bag, a green canvas satchel which is a prized possession because it's excellent for carrying extra bottles and magazines; I had mine slung around my body at all times.

Looking at the slab charges, I thought about Paddy Mayne and the books I'd read in Ferndale Library as a teenager. The design of the slabs hadn't changed since the Second World War.

'Who'd have thought, eh, Paddy?' I muttered to myself.

'What are you talking about?' asked Kiwi, who couldn't sleep.

'Old memories. What are you thinking about?'

'Operation Certain Death.'

I laughed and got up to make us a brew, gingerly stepping over the ammo.

On the morning of the 15th it was confirmed that we would be moving up to the FOB later that day and crossing the border soon afterwards, to coincide with the start of the air war.

Each of us started replenishing our magazines, filling them up with armour-piercing and tracer ammunition. We had between eight and ten magazines each. Working under a burning sun, all the GPMGs were loaded, along with the explosives and ammunition. Respirators were tied in front of us, helmets strapped to the side and the water and gasoline secured. My own bergen had plenty of scoff, but not much in the way of clothing. The temperature had been stinking hot so none of us saw much need for warm clothing.

As an addition, we attached an escape bergen to the front of Pegasus with a bungee; it contained a sleeping-bag, a jerrycan of water and two twenty-four-hour ration packs. Should we have to leave the vehicle in a hurry, we could slash the bungee with a knife, grab the bergen and run.

As vehicle commander, I also carried a TACBE, a distress beacon and limited-range radio, which could be used to contact planes or helicopters overhead.

'What do you reckon the rag-heads will do to anyone they capture?' asked Billy. We'd all heard the horror stories from the Iraq/Iran war about prisoners being castrated.

'There's no fucking way I'm getting my balls cut off,' vowed Kiwi.

'Me neither,' echoed Billy.

'Right then, let's make it a pact,' I said. 'If we're under pressure and going down, we fight to the last man and the last bullet.'

'Fuck, yeah.'

The Regiment CO, arrived to speak to us. With his cigar in hand, he looked the part and gave an inspiring speech about how we were the best that Britain had to offer and were being asked to perform the hardest task.

'We've told General Schwarzkopf that the SAS can stop the

Scuds and destroy the Scud sites,' he said confidently. 'You lads have gone from number one to number ten on the Richter scale. I can't tell you exactly when you'll be crossing the border but it will be soon. Good luck.'

Going back outside, I gazed in awe at the pinkies of A and D Squadrons, lined up and bristling with enough guns, explosives and ammo to take on a small Third World country.

Ken Doyle from A Squadron, still as deranged as ever, came screaming up to me. He looked like something out of Mad Max with his flak jacket, goggles and shemag and his Armalite strapped around his back with bungee ropes.

'What the fuck do you look like, Ken?' I laughed.

'You OK?'

I nodded. 'I'm more worried about you.'

'Don't worry about me, boyo,' he said, mimicking my accent. 'I'm off to the desert for a rumble with Saddam.'

Ken, my lunatic pal from B Company, 2 Para, who had once suggested sneaking down to Goose Green to steal Argie ammunition, had joined the Regiment in 1984, two years before me, and still had a self-destruct button with a hair trigger. He'd had a few scrapes with various COs but always managed to survive because, at the end of the day, he was such an excellent soldier.

As he tore off, I turned to Billy. 'There goes A Squadron's secret weapon.'

Then we drove down to the airport and waited there for the rest of the afternoon, lying in the sun on a lovely day. We'd done all the training and preparation; we knew the capabilities of the pinkies and ourselves. My only real concerns were how often they'd become bogged down in sand and the noise created by freeing them at night.

The Hercs taxied into position, creating a fearsome din, and we reversed the pinkies up the ramps, shackling them down. I got out the green maggot and lay on top. Kiwi was swinging above me in his hammock. As the tailgate shut, I took one last look at Victor before crashing and getting some Zs.

We arrived at the FOB at Ar'ar in Saudi in the late afternoon, but it was nine o'clock at night before the rest of the squadron had touched down. Sitting it out until 3.00 a.m. we watched the French and Saudi jets taking off on reconnaissance flights and returning a few hours later. Then we formed a squadron snake and two dozen vehicles began driving down the motorway towards Al Jouef. For security reasons, weapons had to be taken off their mountings or covered with ponchos so as not to attract attention on the busiest road in Saudi Arabia.

The weather was freezing – far colder than any of us had expected, and I soon began wishing that I'd kept my arctic kit instead of handing it in after Norway. Eventually we had to stop on the hard shoulder to put on some warm kit. I was already wearing my windproof smock and jumper, and only had my NBC clothing left, so I pulled it on, including the big rubber boots.

'It's a fucking desert country – it's supposed to be boiling hot,' shivered Kiwi, as he pulled on three pairs of socks.

As we broke off the dual carriageway into the scrub, the guys from QM's stores were waiting with hot scoff, brews and extra fuel. Gaz, my old DS from jungle Selection, was now with the Regimental Quartermasters and I had a good laugh with him as we filled up the extra fuel tanks under the driver and passenger seats.

We got back in the squadron snake and carried on driving north towards the border. Up above it looked like *Star Wars* with scores of jets on their way towards Iraq. It was D Day, 16 January, and the air war had started.

We drove all the next day to reach the border, crossing very flat and barren terrain peopled by Bedouin. After a few hours it dawned on me that there was absolutely no sand. Instead the ground was hard and gravel-strewn, nothing at all like the conditions we'd been training for.

The route was criss-crossed by tracks and dotted with nomad encampments. Occasionally we'd drive through one and the kids would be outside playing in the dirt in front of a handful of tents and huts. Wearing our goggles to keep out the dust, we must have looked like creatures from another planet.

'Do you think they know there's a war on?' Kiwi asked.

'Fucked if I know. It doesn't look like they've changed in centuries.'

As we passed through one encampment I tossed some fly biscuits (garibaldis) and boiled sweets to the kids. A wizened old guy with a grey beard and a face like a deflated rugby ball took the biscuits off them but left them with the sweets.

'Obviously hasn't got a sweet tooth,' Billy said.

'He hasn't got any fucking teeth,' replied Kiwi.

During the night, as we came out of a wadi system towards slightly higher ground, there was a sudden *bang!* My heart skipped a beat and I threw myself off the wagon towards the noise.

There were shouts and confusion. Was it a contact? Dotted with rocky hills, the territory was ideal for an ambush, or perhaps a landmine. No, that would be louder, surely?

Two vehicles back, the leading Air Troop pinkie was engulfed in smoke. Everyone had fitted smoke dischargers on the front of their vehicles, three each side, which were designed to help us escape a contact site. They worked on an electrical impulse generated from the dashboard, but this one had short-circuited.

'Fucking dick-heads,' muttered Kiwi as he clambered back behind the wheel.

My heart was still thumping.

For two days we drove under grey skies with the sun trying to make an appearance. As we came over the top of a large wadi, the front vehicle stopped and started to come back towards us. They'd spotted a Crusader fort, which meant we were near no man's land between Iraq and Saudi. Saddam's boys were just a few clicks over the top of the ridge.

We LUP'd and put up the camouflage nets. We'd been practising that, and the three of us could put up our net with fibreglass poles in about fifteen minutes. You could walk 20 metres away from Pegasus, turn back, and swear you were looking at nothing more than rocks and sand.

Sixteen and 17 Troop were on the far side of the wadi, 20 Troop were in the centre basin and we had the eastern side amongst the rocks and boulders with 18 Troop. After scoff, we made our last brews before nightfall. Each crew had one man on stag, which meant two hours off and one hour on. After one of my shifts, I wrapped myself in my green maggot, looked up in the sky and counted at least eighty jets flying overhead towards Iraq. It was a marvellous sight.

Still the cold continued and we assumed it had to be freak weather. Surely someone would have checked the night-time temperatures in January?

For the next twenty-four hours we planned to do recces to find the best place to cross. The Int Corps boys had told us the Iraqis had a platoon every 8 to 10 kilometres along the border; 5 clicks further back there were OPs manning the gaps and these had a landline back to their companies. Even if we got past the platoons, there was a risk the OPs might spot us and relay the information back to the tanks. We'd be caught in a net.

A foot patrol from 20 Troop crossed the border the next morning, spotting Iraqi troops east of the fort. Meanwhile, they'd rendezvoused with Saudi customs officials and border guards at the fort, picking up more info. I didn't like the idea that these guys knew we were coming.

At 1630 hours Stu McDonald summoned us down into the wadi in our vehicles. It took us ten minutes to dekit and load up Pegasus.

As I jumped into the front seat I said to Kiwi, 'OK, let's go!'

He turned the ignition. Nothing happened.

'What's the story?'

'The engine's dead.'

'I don't fucking believe it!'

We were just about to go into battle and had to bump-start our ride in a wadi. Billy and I began pushing, building up a decent amount of speed, and I started wondering why Kiwi didn't release the clutch.

'Come on, turn her over, fuck you – what's happening?'

Kiwi coughed up; after all our intensive, highly specialized training, he didn't know how to bump-start a vehicle.

'You fucking wanker,' said Billy.

I couldn't stop laughing. Every car I'd owned as a youngster had needed a bump-start. They were all old bangers, but there was no shortage of hills around the Rhondda to park them on. When I took Liz to the pictures in Cardiff, I used to park on top of the multi-storey car park, even though the other floors were empty. It was the only 'hill' I could find in Cardiff city centre.

After giving him a bollocking, I showed Kiwi what to do and we took up our position on the wadi floor. Kiwi killed the engine and tried the ignition again. This time Pegasus coughed, spluttered and roared into life.

'Hopefully it's a one-off,' I said, trying not to worry.

The recce patrol had returned and the decision had been taken to cross west of the old Crusader fort. Unless compromised, we'd stay together as a squadron for the first couple of days and then break into Troops. I spied little Ben Graham, a good mate from 3 Para who'd fought alongside John Hedges in 5 Platoon, B Company on Mount Longdon. He was a tough mother, short and squat. Aside from us and a few old sweats like McDonald, none of the others had been in the Falklands.

Billy Adams huddled in his Norwegian army jumper, under his flak jacket and a shemag; only his eyes could be seen. Kiwi had his bobble hat on and his shemag wrapped around his neck.

The darkness was coming in fast. The sky still had shades of grey and blue but the wadi was dark like the inside of a drum.

Sitting in a long vehicle column I looked around and muttered, 'Well, here I am again on another start line.'

I started camming up.

'What are you doing that for?' asked Kiwi.

'I'm going into battle. You've got to have a war face on to go into battle.'

He wasn't sure if I was teasing him, but soon everybody was copying me. Most of the lads wore shemags. My helmet was slung to the side of Pegasus.

Ray Scott came up to me.

'Jesus it's cold,' he said, stamping his feet and slapping his sides.

'And me with all this factor fifteen,' I joked.

He looked at my blackened face and smiled.

'All the best, mate,' I said.

'Yeah, you too, Mike.'

Sitting around always increases the tension and everyone was relieved when the order came from Stu McDonald to move. Twenty or so vehicles slowly edged forwards, carrying more fire-power than 5 Airborne Brigade. Nothing was going to stop us getting across the border and anyone who tried was going to get the shock of their lives.

# 15

AS WE DROVE OUT OF THE RELATIVE SHELTER OF THE WADI, THE BITTER wind sliced straight through me. In front of us the terrain looked flatter than Kylie Minogue's chest. I could see the Crusader fort to the east, lit up like a Christmas tree against the gloom. It had about ten slit windows which had once held the bows of archers. Now there were lights in all of them. Was it a marker for the Allied planes, I wondered? Was it for our benefit?

Slowly we moved into no man's land, with Mobility Troop as the lead scouts because of their greater proficiency with the wagons. The cold crept under my windproof and I wrapped the shemag around my face to cut out the wind. Just short of the border we slowed down to a crawl, then turned off the engines to listen.

Around us I could just make out the greyish white clay and rocks of a dry stream bed. How the fuck did this happen? I thought. It had looked so flat. That's the problem with travelling at night; unless there's some ambient light, the horizon seems to change constantly.

The only sound was the clunk, clunk of the exhaust cooling down. I could make out about five or six vehicles in front of me; up ahead McDonald and the OC were making their decisions.

Billy was silent at the wheel and Kiwi behind us. He pulled out the spyglass – the only one in the squadron. We'd fought to get this extra piece of kit, even though it meant carrying more gas bottles and batteries. On a bleak night with no ambient light, it was invaluable.

Kneeling on his seat behind and above us, Kiwi scanned the horizon. Billy had one hand on the wheel and the other on the ignition key. I was standing up beside Pegasus.

'Oh fuck, there's a tank. A Russian T62,' cried Kiwi.

I jumped back in the wagon and Kiwi pointed towards blackness. Using the spyglass I could just make out the hull of a tank about 200 metres away, then I could see the barrel next to a building of some sort. Weird red shapes walked around it.

The boss of 18 Troop, Julian, came alongside me. 'Hey Mike, lend us the spyglass.'

'Fuck off, Boss.'

'C'mon, we need it. There's something up ahead.'

'Too fucking right! It's a tank – look.'

He legged it towards the front of the column with the spyglass. It was the last we ever saw of it; McDonald kept hold of it from then on.

A searchlight split the gloom, a giant beam sweeping towards the east. With no comms between the vehicles McDonald had to run the length of the convoy to pass on the message: 'Break up into Troops. Leg it north. Go for it! Go!'

The searchlight swung towards us. Billy flicked the switch and Pegasus roared. The next instant I heard the heavy rattle of machine-gun fire. They couldn't see us but they knew something was out there. This was it – whether we liked it or not we were OTR (on the run).

Flooring the accelerator, Billy took us screaming into Iraq. I had butterflies in my stomach that felt like bats. Each Troop headed off on a different axis.

As we came over the horizon, out of the dry stream bed, there seemed to be no distinguishing features. We were driving into nothing. Billy hit a large boulder, too late for me to tell him to swerve.

Kiwi, his back towards us, shouted, 'They're following.'

I turned and saw the lights of a Land Cruiser type vehicle.

'Come on, Billy, move this crate.'

A ball of concentration, he wrestled with the wheel, taking us down into wadis and up the other side without lights and hitting all sorts of stuff. My eyeballs were on stalks trying to pick out obstacles in the darkness.

Another spine-crunching thud was hard enough to wind me. I turned around in my seat; there had been no more firing after the initial burst, but the headlights going up and down told me somebody was still on our case.

The terrain had looked dead flat, but in fact was all over the fucking place. I apologized to Kylie Minogue and hung on as Pegasus hit another boulder. We were second in the Troop column. Ted's vehicle was up ahead.

To my left I saw what must have been 17 Troop going hell for leather on a different axis; we were now alone. Then behind us there was an explosion.

Billy shouted, 'What the fuck was that?'

We didn't stop. The headlights were still behind us.

'Don't those guys ever give up?' said Kiwi.

I hoped the rest of the squadron were all right. It was unnerving to see us breaking up so early and I wondered when I'd see my mates again. We were going from a big gang to a little gang and the loss of firepower and safety in numbers made me feel a little apprehensive.

Driving along on a rough bearing we kept hitting rocks that we couldn't see until too late; it was a case of going straight over the top of them. Each time we plunged down into a small wadi Billy's arse would leave the seat, but he clung to the wheel. I was almost thrown clear over the dashboard and then smashed back into my seat, jarring every bone. Behind us, Kiwi was holding on to the twin gimpies for dear life.

The Iraqi vehicle chased us for nearly three hours, but the pinkies coped better with the terrain and gradually we pulled clear. But they knew we'd crossed their border and by daylight could follow our tracks. Already they would have radioed ahead to alert the larger companies and tanks.

Somehow, Mountain Troop had managed to stay together. Ted called a halt and got out the Magellan to take a fix on our position.

'You guys all right?' I asked.

Kiwi and Billy nodded.

The other vehicle commanders, Jack Dennis, Kev Phillips and myself, closed in on Ted's pinkie. The other lads kept us covered.

Ted said, 'It looks like we've lost them.'

'What the fuck was that explosion?'

'It sounded like a mortar,' said Jack.

The Magellan is a brilliant piece of kit that navigates using satellites. If you can pick up anything between three and five satellites, it will give a ten figure grid reference, pinpointing your location down to a single metre. You can also programme your destination and the Magellan will basically navigate you there. As long as you've got batteries you should never get lost.

'I've got a fix, here's the grid,' said Ted, pointing to the map.

I'd been looking into the darkness at features that seemed to be no more than ten minutes away. Now I discovered they were 20 or 30 kilometres distant. It was like an optical illusion.

Ted made the decision. 'Let's keep going on this bearing, north-north-east, and basha up when we find a good location. They know we're here now, so they're going to be looking.'

Sliding back into Pegasus, Billy started the engine.

'OK, let's go.'

We began travelling in formation, with the lead vehicle being swapped every hour to take some pressure off the drivers and share the responsibility of finding a path through the darkness.

The NVGs (night viewing goggles) proved to be next to useless because they worked on ambient light and there was none because of the cloud cover. For the same reason the IWS (individual weapon sights) were little better. Now and again we stopped and used them to scan something the lead vehicle had seen. Often it was a pile of rocks that looked like a possible OP with an antenna. Moving forward to investigate we'd discover the 'antenna' was the branch of a tree or shrub sticking out of the rocks.

In the early hours of the morning we reached the outcrops of a mountain range. It stretched for miles, east to west, and we had no option but to go over it. We were the lead vehicle and started the climb. In low ratio, second gear, the Land Rovers could go up almost anything, and in places the gradient was 60 per cent. We bounced off massive rocks and leaned precariously left then right. With each heavy clunk from a rock beneath the chassis I expected Pegasus to start breaking apart.

Grinding upwards, the pinkies made an incredible racket, but at least the enemy vehicles weren't likely to follow us; nobody was that crazy.

At the top, we all stopped and looked ahead. The mountain range seemed to curve around like a giant bow towards the east. We began driving along the top, looking for a place to go down.

Having led up, we were now in fourth position. Standing at the top, I watched Carl Newlands drive the first vehicle over the edge. It took incredible balls. Jack Dennis and Barry Taylor didn't jump on until it had started downhill. Rocking back and forth, it seemed to teeter on the edge of oblivion.

Peering into the distance I could make out an open expanse and, further still, what appeared to be another vast mountain range – what lay between was anybody's guess.

'Do you want me to drive, Billy?'

'No, I'm OK, I'll do it.'

The other three pinkies had gone and we nudged Pegasus over the top. The slope was almost vertical.

'This is fucking madness,' I yelled. 'We're gonna roll.'

Kiwi couldn't look down; he kept staring out the back.

Billy had his foot slammed down hard on the brake pedal, causing the wagon to slide to one side and then the other. I could smell burning brakes. Metal groaned and shuddered, then the incline suddenly began to lessen.

'I thought Kiwis were supposed to be used to mountains,' said Billy.

'That wasn't a mountain,' scoffed Kiwi, 'I've dug deeper shit pits than that.'

RV'ing at the bottom, we plugged away for a few more hours and then looked for a place to basha up during the day. The first chinks of light began to show and the terrain became clearer. We were travelling down a dry stream bed, our fresh tyre tracks crossing old ones. We drove up the other side and headed across a barren, open expanse of ground covered in gravel with patches of sand. Light was coming in fast. We had to find a place to hide.

Shivering in the pre-dawn cold, we put the pinkies in a wadi against a rocky outcrop and chose an OP on the higher ground amongst a clump of large rocks. This was our stag position.

Leaving it so late could have proved a fatal mistake. We'd barely had time to get the cam nets over the pinkies before daylight exposed them. Similarly, we'd driven straight into an LUP with no time to do a loop and ambush our own tracks, just as in the jungle, to check nobody was following. Day one and already we were breaking SOPs.

It was about six o'clock and the sun was almost up. As the dems man, I still had to put the bar mines and claymores around our position, setting up a ring of steel defence with a predetermined escape route.

Using a shovel, I buried four bar mines with PE4 on top, attached to an electrical detonator and receiver for the XM122. The transmitter was kept in the stag position with all the code numbers for the ring of detonators. To fire, it was just a matter of keying in the corresponding numbers and pressing the button.

By now it was broad daylight and I knew I was compromising the safety of the Troop. I worked as fast as I could, putting the bar mines to 'Arm' so that if any vehicle did drive over one, the last thing the occupants would feel was their arse going through their brains.

Claymores have an internal electrical det and are easier to handle. It's just a case of putting them into the ground and using the sighting slit on the top to adjust the height for the maximum killing effect. Hundreds of ball-bearings are attached to the C4 (explosives) at the back of the claymores, designed to explode over a wide arc, messing up people's days no end. Having made the adjustments, I ran the cables back to the stag position and connected them to the four M57 (claymore clacker) firing devices, one per claymore.

It had taken me upwards of an hour. We'd really fucked up by stopping so late.

'From now on we pull up an hour before first light,' said Ted. 'We left our arses hanging out.'

The other dems guy in the troop was Des and we agreed that in future, to save time, he'd do the claymores, while I set up the bar mines.

One lad from every wagon did the first stag, while the rest of us 'last paraded' the pinkies under the cam nets, filling them with fuel and water just in case we had to leave quickly. Then we began cleaning the weapons before finally getting ourselves some scoff.

'It's unbelievable, not a single fucking puncture,' I said, tucking into a sachet of beef and onions.

'No, we've got a problem,' said Mac, peering under the chassis.

'What's wrong?' asked Kev Phillips.

'The track-rod ends are stuffed. They're getting bent by the rocks. It's a fucking miracle we didn't break one.'

Ted said, 'How many vehicles are affected?'

'Two of them so far.'

Jack Dennis looked worried. 'Unless we find a way of straightening those rods we're gonna have the devil's own job trying to steer.'

'I've got an idea,' said Mac. 'If we can take them off, we might be able to wrap PE around the track rods and light it to create some heat. Then we could bend them back into shape.'

'You ever done it before?' asked Kiwi.

'Fuck no, but there's always a first time.'

Mac had been in the REME attached to the Artillery and was arguably a better mechanic than Jack Dennis. Plastic explosive won't blow without a detonator, but burns at a furious pace. I knew lads who'd actually heated up their scoff with PE4, but it

255

gets so hot that it can burn a hole clean through your mess tin.

I gave Mac the PE4 and he wrapped it around the track rod, igniting it with a Zippo lighter. Bright yellow flames burned fiercely and the chemical smell caught in the back of my throat. Soon the metal was soft enough to be bent back into shape and replaced on the pinkies. Problem solved – at least for the moment.

On stag for an hour in every three, it was difficult to sleep. Replacing Billy, I scampered up to the OP. It was high enough to give a good early warning of anything approaching across the desert.

In every direction there seemed to be just barren wilderness, all of it grey or brown. Rocky outcrops were dotted haphazardly and the wadis were just dips in the ground that looked like moon craters or scars.

Apart from my Armalite, I had the firing devices for the mines and two 66 anti-tank rockets – pretty useless against tanks, but they could do some serious damage to soft-skinned vehicles.

Looking downwards, I was just admiring the four cam nets that were virtually invisible against the rocks when, in the distance, I heard a familiar *wocka-wocka-wocka* of rotor blades.

By the sound of it there were two helicopters, one of them going further away and the other coming closer.

Then I saw it – a Russian-built Hind. Was it looking for us? It landed about 500 metres from our position, perhaps checking our tracks, but then took off again a minute or so later. For the rest of the day, we were on full alert.

That afternoon, as I was changing stag with Des, a Jolly Green Giant (Chinook) with Yank markings flew down the wadi to the east, bristling with armaments of all sorts.

'What the fuck is that doing here?' I said, surprised to see it flying in the daytime so early in the war.

'Probably looking for downed pilots.'

It was heading towards the Saudi border and we heard later, on the net, that it had indeed picked up an aircrew.

Shortly before last light we gathered for Orders under Ted's cam net. The temperature had dropped even lower and it had begun to snow. Some of the lads had put their NBC kit under their desert fatigues in an attempt to keep out the wind.

Mick had been monitoring the HF radio throughout the day. He'd sent off the scheds to SHQ (Squadron Headquarters) letting them know our loc stat (location status) and sit rep (situation report). This had been done on burst transmission and only the base and ourselves had the code to crack it. The code changed every day and we burned the old codes as we went.

'Any word on the others?' I asked.

HQ had sent back a full report on the other troops.

'They're fine. Sixteen Troop lost a vehicle when we went OTR.'

'The explosion?'

Ted nodded.

'It was Colin Harris's vehicle with Ray Scott driving and Ginge Palmer on the back. Bust a track rod and had to blow the wagon.'

Poor old Ray, I thought – they'd barely made it across the border and would probably have to be airlifted back.

Ted Butterton unfurled a map and we crouched in the dusting of white.

'We've had some new orders,' he said. 'They want us to try and locate a sat comm centre on our way north. This is the rough grid.'

Unlike jungle maps, which tend to be all green, those we'd been given of Iraq looked a uniform yellow and gave no indication of the rock-strewn mountains we'd crossed on the previous night. To the north, the MSRs (main supply routes) to Jordan from Baghdad, MSR 1, 2 and 3, were clearly marked. Because of the international blockade of Iraq, these supply routes had taken on great significance, and Jordan remained the one gateway for supplies.

All of us knew our location; we'd done a thorough map study. Now, however, my heart sank when I realized how little distance we'd covered the previous night.

Kev Phillips leaned closer. 'I suppose they've picked it up from the satellite imagery.'

'Do we hit it?' I asked.

'No. We send the location back to base,' said Ted. 'They'll make the decision. OK, I want to cover at least eighty clicks tonight. Stay close but stay alert. I don't want us crashing into each other.'

Breaking up, we prepped the vehicles and rolled up the cam nets. Des and I began disarming all the bar mines and putting the dets back into the claymore bag I kept slung around me. Old electrical dets are prone to going off if knocked or mistreated; they can blow off fingers or take a good chunk out of a leg. I was always extra careful.

As we moved off into the darkness, a ground fog swallowed up the pinkie 20 yards in front of us.

Kiwi grumbled in the back. 'First snow, now fog – someone's taking the piss.'

Creeping along in column formation, we couldn't see a fucking

257

thing and had to rely on the post compass on the side of Pegasus to keep on the right heading. I had my Armalite across my lap and periodically grabbed hold of the pistol grip on the gimpy to re-assure myself.

As the fog lifted, the desert landscape was completely black. Heavy clouds again obscured the moon and stars, testing our night vision to the limit. In darkness, the secret is not to look directly at an object, but slightly to the left and right of it. The image will hit the retina where the black and white receptors are stored within the eye, rather than the colour receptors which are in the centre. The concentration it took was enormously draining and every hour the lead vehicle had to change to give the driver and commander a rest. Periodically we stopped and killed the engines, listening to our surroundings.

If anything, the wind chill had grown worse. Shemags were wrapped around every head, so that only our eyes peered out. Iraqi BMPs (armour on wheels) were faster than pinkies; we had to hope we spotted them first.

Three hours into the drive, the lead vehicle pulled up and we cut the engines.

Jack Dennis dismounted and walked back to us.

'There's a position right in front of us,' he whispered.

The information got passed down the line. Jack, Ted and I went forward to do a CTR.

'I can make out some tentage, I think it's a Bedouin encamp-ment,' I said as we edged forward.

'How sure are you?' asked Ted.

'I can't see anyone moving.'

'We can't risk it,' said Jack. 'Even if they're camel-jockeys, they'll have dogs.'

I peered through my IWS and cursed the rupert from 18 Troop who'd run off with the spyglass; the dick-head didn't take the kit-specific batteries and gas bottles so it wouldn't have been the slightest use to him.

I understood Jack's fears. In South Armagh, the dogs would smell us before we got within 100 metres of our target.

'I can't see any dogs,' I said.

As if on cue, the barking started. One, two, three, four – a pack of the little snarling, growling bastards. Then the camels started baying. We back-tracked towards the wagons and headed west to skirt around our dossing Bedouin, then we turned north again on to the bearing. The CTR had taken two hours.

Clearly it was going to take us far longer to cover the distance than we'd previously planned. Travelling at night created its own dangers and delays as we constantly stopped to check what lay ahead.

In the early hours we hit another field of rocks and had to man-oeuvre our way through. At one point, as I drove downhill, we came off a ridge so heavily that Kiwi was thrown overboard. He picked himself up, brushed off the dust and climbed back on. 'Fucking Sunday drivers,' he muttered.

It was now so cold that everyone volunteered to drive because it kept the blood pumping. Otherwise it was like bouncing around on top of an ice tray in a freezer compartment.

The starter motor on Pegasus began playing up. Every time we stopped to listen or recce ahead on foot, another pinkie had to give us a battery jump-start with leads. It was simply a case of connect-ing the two vehicles through the side wing connection, but it was soon happening so often that we ended up keeping the 20 feet of cable coiled around the wing mirror for easy access.

This time we found our own LUP rather than picking one off the map. It was also better timed, giving us the chance to stop, listen and wait for anything that might be following. The vehicles were covered and mines in place well before daylight. Mick got on the net and sent the scheds to SHQ.

I lay down and actually fell asleep – only to be woken by the *bang, bang, bang* of three rounds that came flying into the rocks above my head.

I leaped up, Armalite in hand, ready to deal with the attack. Ted Butterton poked his head out of the adjacent cam net looking mor-tified. He'd been cleaning one of the GPMGs and had had an ND (Negligent Discharge). Poor Ted was gutted and apologized pro-fusely, promising to put a few quid in the Troop Fund.

After only a few hours' sleep we were on the road again that night, now fighting the added dangers brought on by tiredness. Mac had tried to fix the starter motor with little success, and we ran into more delays with Bedouin who seemed to roam every-where in the desert and do their own thing. I felt sorry for them; they didn't appear to know what was happening.

If anything the terrain grew worse. We clattered and banged our way up another large feature, getting flung around like rag dolls in a dog's mouth. My kidneys were bruised from the constant battering against the seat.

On top of this feature we recce'd forward, with one guy out in front of the vehicles looking for a way off the ledge. As the moon peeped out from behind the cloud cover, I saw a landscape straight from a John Wayne movie, chimneys of rocks and mesas jutting skyward.

Coming down, the racket from the engines was horrendous. Kiwi went flying off the side of the wagon again and Billy went to pick him up. He was winded but otherwise OK. 'Next time you get to keep the match ball,' I said.

By 0200 hours we'd reached a point near Medesis Airfield, a massive Iraqi complex approximately halfway between the Saudi border and MSR1. The airfield was over to our right – the east – and was taking a beasting from the Allied air forces; explosions every few seconds lit the gloom of the desert night.

Pegasus was second in formation when suddenly the lead vehicle disappeared as if swallowed up by the ground. Carl Newlands had driven straight off a cliff, carrying Jack Dennis and Barry Taylor with him.

Although the terrain had looked flat, we'd in fact been skirting the edge of a large wadi. The wagon went over front end first. I sprinted to the edge in time to see it roll once before coming to a stop about 30 feet below on a rocky slope. Newlands was on his hands and knees, having been thrown clear.

Scrambling down the bank, I saw Jack crawl out from underneath; he was OK.

What about Barry? As the tail-end Charlie, he'd been sitting higher up than the others and the pinkie had no roll bars. He had to be dead.

'Barry? Barry?'

'Yeah. What took you so fucking long?'

He was trapped underneath the wagon.

'You OK?'

'I'm dying for a fag.'

'Well don't smoke here or we'll all go up,' said Mad Mac. Petrol poured from several ruptured jerrycans.

Barry didn't seem to be injured, but we had to get the wagon off him.

One of the pinkies provided protection as the other two fixed towing chains to the stranded wagon. After a bit of coaxing and a lot of noise, we managed to pull it back far enough for Barry to scramble clear.

'I can't tell how badly it's damaged,' said Mad Mac, looking at the rig.

'We'll pull it up onto the ridge and Mike can blow it with a delayed fuse.'

'It's going to take all fucking night to pull it out of there,' said Jack.

I looked at my watch. 'We've got three hours of darkness.'

Ted said, 'Let's give it a go.'

Initially we tried with two vehicles and then all three. After getting it to roll upright, a couple of us went over the edge and re-attached the towing bars and chains. Then we tried to pull it back up the slope. The engines roared, dust and stones sprayed over us and people were shouting instructions at one another. Saddam could probably hear us in Baghdad.

Medesis Airfield was too close for comfort. Two lads were doing a roving patrol with a pair of gimpies around our location. Barry was right as rain after a couple of fags and back in the thick of things.

Past caring about the racket, we finally hauled the pinkie onto the ridge. It had become a challenge and we weren't going to leave the fucking thing down there. Surprisingly, the damage wasn't too bad; the wings and bumpers were smashed up and the wagon was soaked in petrol, but the worst thing was that there were boxes of ammo, compo and explosives strewn all around the wadi.

The only major damage was to the mounting bracket of the .50 cal on the back. This was what had saved Barry's life, because the mount was high enough to keep the wagon from crushing him as it rolled.

'Well, here goes,' said Newlands, flicking the ignition switch. The engine roared to life. 'Isn't that the sweetest sound?'

We picked up the kit and repacked the wagon, racing against the dawn.

As the sky grew light, the ground around us looked as if a motor bike scramble had taken place. We basha'd up in a nearby wadi next to a rocky outcrop; it was broad daylight by the time we put up the cam nets and I had set the mines.

Soon it emerged that the LUP was less than 150 metres from a track. Throughout the day, while on stag, we could see Iraqi civilian and military vehicles passing our positions. They were the first Iraqis we'd seen, apart from the ones at the border.

It was a bad position. Apart from the noise we'd created the night before and the closeness of the track, the wadi had only two exits. If both of them were covered, we were fucked.

I'd placed bar mines and claymores on both exits, but didn't arm them in case we chose one or the other for an escape route. They would have to be detonated from the stag position if the Iraqis tried to drive into our wadi.

None of us got a great deal of sleep except for Billy 'the Sheets' Adams, so-called because he could fall asleep on a clothes line. Every time I tried to get some shut-eye, I'd hear Iraqi vehicles on the track.

The crash had finally convinced me that it was crazy driving at night. I doubted whether we could reach our target in the time available and how many more accidents would there be?

Although I didn't mention it to Kiwi and Billy I would have preferred to travel during the day. Yes, the Iraqis were more likely to see us, but with the firepower we had on board I was confident we could take them on. Newlands, Jack and Barry could easily have been killed in the crash and as far as I was concerned I'd rather die fighting than fall off a cliff in the night.

Tiredness was another factor. At most we were getting two or three hours' sleep a day and we were all knackered. It didn't surprise me at all when, that night, Billy drove straight into the back of the wagon in front because he'd fallen asleep at the wheel.

Soon it was happening regularly. I'd be talking to Billy or Kiwi as he was driving and get no response. Then I'd look across and see he was asleep. At other times we'd get rammed up the arse because the crew behind had nodded off. When this happened we'd just look at each other and laugh – what else could we do, we were that physically knackered.

Talk was kept to a minimum – the odd word now and then – and it was bloody hard work spending twelve hours on the move over rough terrain in sleet and snow, with the constant pressure of being deep behind enemy lines in such a small convoy.

Later that night it started sleeting and the temperature fell below freezing. Shortly before midnight we were driving across a flat gravel plain when a blinding flash stopped us in our tracks.

'Scud!' yelled Kiwi.

The rocket veered off at an angle through the sky, with a huge plume of brilliant white light trailing behind. I leaped out of my seat and raced 10 metres from Pegasus, grabbing my Silva compass to take a bearing. Other lads did the same. Silvas are old faithfuls, but can be affected by the metal in vehicles.

The Scud entered the clouds and we could still see the light flashing inside it like an airborne discotheque.

Ted used the Magellan to get an exact fix on our location.

Coupled with the bearings we'd taken of the Scud, this information would be sent back to RHQ to help pinpoint the launch site.

'I wouldn't fancy one of those fuckers landing on my head,' said Kiwi.

The Iraqis had managed to hit Israel with several Scuds. The big question was whether Saddam would arm them with chemical weapons. He had the resources and had shown during the eight-year war with Iran that he was prepared to use them.

Throughout the rest of the night, we heard bombs exploding in the distance to the east and west. Allied jets were targeting Iraqi positions. Sometimes we'd see the white flash and then count the seconds until we heard the low rumble. It gave us some idea of the distance.

We were still tasked with the recce of the sat comm site. On the fourth night we reached the rough grid, about 80 clicks to the south of MSR1. We basha'd up in a steep-sided wadi, with the stag position up above among the rocks, and at first light Mick spotted the tell-tale antennas and masts across a large open plain.

Des brought up the LTM (laser target marker) equipment. Looking through the sight, a reading flashed in the eyepiece giving a distance to target of 1,200 metres.

Mick got on the set and transmitted the info to RHQ, along with our grid. This would allow them to work out an exact location for the sat comm site. Then we tried to catch some Zs while they made up their minds what to do.

'I think it's a wonderful thing, you being a vegetarian, Mac,' I told him, as we cooked up some scoff. 'I mean, think of all those cuddly cows and little lambs you're saving. But you know what the best thing about it is?'

'What's that?' he grunted, his mouth full of food.

'Eco-friendly farts.'

Under the cam nets, the light of a burning hexamine block was safely hidden. It was so cold that I crouched low over the flame, soaking up the small amount of residual heat.

The message came back from RHQ: the jets were coming in that night and they wanted us to clear out of the area and then come back the next evening for a BDA (bomb damage assessment.)

Jack Dennis summed up our disappointment: 'Ah, Christ! We're looking pretty, but no-one's asking us to dance.'

Moving out that night, we basha'd up well before daylight and witnessed the arrival of the F16s, which dropped everything but the kitchen sink onto the target.

'Sort of takes the heart out of soldiering,' said Ted as we watched the awesome display of air power.

'Oh, I don't know about that,' said Jack. 'They'll always need us. Without us, those fly boys couldn't find their own arses to take a shit.'

The next night, the four pinkies crossed the open plain in arrowhead formation towards the comms set-up. Most of the Troop were dropped off short and then Ted, Carl, Kev and I moved forward to do a recce on foot.

Scrambling up a sandy bank, I could already smell what lay ahead. As I lay on the lip, I looked down and saw total carnage. Antenna masts had been twisted like paper-clips. Living accommodation, vehicles, generators, storage boxes and equipment lay smoking and in pieces. The whole site had been wiped out, and during the day the Iraqis had obviously spirited away their dead and wounded. Few would have survived.

We called up the rest of the vehicles and I went back with Kev Phillips to get them. Both of us were stunned by what we saw. From then on it was even clearer that we didn't have to go in with guns blazing. Instead, we had the luxury of communicating with aircraft, giving them the co-ordinates and allowing them to do the honours.

Back in the convoy, we grafted our way north again towards MSR1, planning to reach it the following night. Once we crossed the road, we'd be inside what RHQ were now calling 'the Iron Triangle' – an area marked out by MSR1 and two water-pumping stations, WPS1 and WPS2.

The next day we basha'd up in a rocky wadi and followed the normal procedure, which by now had become almost second nature. From the stag position we overlooked a road, or rather a track, that carried a lot of traffic, ranging from oil tankers to Bedouin caravans. The only way out of the wadi was onto the track, which put everyone on edge. To make matters worse the temperature dropped even further and it was pissing down sleet and snow throughout the day.

I came off stag and found the boys huddled together under a poncho attached to the side of Pegasus, trying to get warm.

'That settles it – next war I'm bringing all my fucking arctic kit and woolly vest, even if it's in the jungle,' I said.

I wasn't kidding. It pissed me off immensely that I'd left all my arctic kit behind in Hereford and had to use NBC clothes to keep warm. The Regiment prides itself on a detailed analysis of all there is to know about enemy locations, numbers, terrain and, of course, weather. Somebody should have known. It wasn't as if we couldn't carry extra clothes – we had the wagons.

As we huddled in our doss bags underneath Pegasus with hail-stones and sleet lashing the cam nets, it was clear that we didn't have the right equipment to survive the conditions. It was colder than the Falklands – much colder.

I remembered a famous Second World War photograph of Colonel David Stirling taken in the desert with the Long-Range Desert Patrol Group. He wore a duffel coat and I'd always thought, Why the fuck did he need a coat in the desert? Now I knew. Because it's the coldest place on earth – or it can be.

The weather hadn't improved by 1700 hours when we gathered under Ted Butterton's cam net for the Troop powwow.

The boss said, 'What do you think about staying here for the night?'

I couldn't stop my teeth from chattering. 'I'm all for keeping warm, but not here.' With only one exit from the wadi, the com-promise factor was too high. 'I vote we bug out.'

Ted looked around the group. Most of the lads nodded in agree-ment.

'Right then, let's get moving.'

I turned to Des. 'Let's get the dems.'

It was easier said than done. In the thick layer of snow it was almost impossible to find the bar mines and claymores. As light started to fade, I fumbled for them, scrambling around in driving sleet, trying not to stand on anything that could make a nasty mess of my boot. It took more than an hour and we arrived back in complete darkness.

The vehicles were decammed and we headed off. I didn't think it could get any colder but I was wrong. My feet were like blocks of ice no matter what I did to warm them. In the end I took to jogging alongside Pegasus to try to get my blood circulating and to keep my core temperature steady. My face and fingertips were constantly burning.

The next morning when Mick sent the sched to SHQ he had a reply about the make-up of the squadrons. We learned that an eight-man patrol from B Squadron, call-sign Bravo Two Zero, and under the command of Andy McNab, were OTR behind enemy lines to the north of us. There was a good possibility that all of them had been captured or shot.

None of us had even realized that B Squadron were across the border. We made Mick check that he hadn't made a mistake on the encryption.

The news was greeted with stunned silence.

Finally Jack said, 'I pity anyone who was on foot last night.'

'Makes you feel lucky,' said Kiwi, checking the sight on his Armalite.

'What were they doing way up there?' I asked. 'Talk about being out on a limb.'

'And where are we hanging?' shot back Des.

'We're fine,' said Ted, 'as long as Mac and Jack keep us moving.'

# 16

AFTER GRAFTING OUR WAY NORTH FOR TEN NIGHTS, WE FINALLY HIT THE
MSR at 0400 hours on 26 January. The sight of the six-lane motorway with flyovers and safety rails was totally surreal after spending so long driving over a barren moonscape.

'All it needs is a Granada services and it could be the M1,' said
Billy.

Kiwi said, 'You know, I never thought I'd say it, but I could
murder a Wendy burger just now.'

'And chips,' Billy said. 'Vinegar-soaked, artery-clogging chips.'

We'd been living on compo for too long.

The MSR was 100 metres in front of us, flanked by a 6-metre-
high camel fence. After doing a recce east and west, we decided
to use a flyover to make the crossing. Given the approaching
dawn, we'd tackle it one vehicle at a time, then push into the
desert and set up an LUP at the first wadi on the other side. Carl
Newlands and I skirted forwards and cut the camel fence with
wire-cutters.

'If we get caught doing this,' said Carl, 'do you think our cover
story should be that we're Brits on the piss, doing a spot of
vandalism?'

'Good idea. I'll spray Man United on the flyover as well,' I said.

We legged it back to the pinkies and the first three wagons
headed off in turn; Pegasus was the last in line.

Billy turned the key. Click. Click. Nothing.

'Shit!'

The starter motor hadn't missed a beat all night – what a time to fuck up.

Kiwi and I began waving like crazy but the tail-end Charlie in the third vehicle didn't see us and it just carried on.

We sat looking at each other.

'They'll have to come back sooner or later,' I said.

There hadn't been any traffic on the motorway for days, but almost instinctively we scanned the road. A light mist had rolled in on another gloomy night.

Kiwi spotted it first – something moving towards us from the east.

'Is that the blokes or what?' he asked.

Then he answered his own question. 'I think it's a fucking Iraqi convoy.'

'Oh fuck,' I said. With all our kit and ordnance we stuck out like Billy at a Klan meeting. 'How many vehicles?' I asked.

'Maybe a dozen,' said Kiwi. They were still a way off, travelling without lights.

I threw it open to the floor. 'Do we leg it?'

'I'd rather take our chances here than be out in the desert with just an Armalite,' said Billy.

Kiwi nodded. 'They're not getting my balls.'

We were going to brass it out and with an Arms Park full of luck they wouldn't see us.

Kiwi unlocked four 66 rockets ready to fire. I had the gimpy ready with 200 rounds. Billy put a bomb into his 203 and had a claymore bag full of spares.

I figured that if we did have a contact, the rest of the Troop would turn up and whack them from the other side. It sounded good in theory, but for the moment we were on our own.

The convoy was close enough for us to pick out the APCs and BMPs, some with soft skins. It started slowing down to walking pace. They'd obviously spotted us.

Billy was dark-skinned and could possibly pass as an Arab. Kiwi and I both had shemags around our heads.

I whispered, 'Brass it out. Smile and wave. Smile and wave.'

My heart pounded. I lifted my hand and waved. Billy did the same. The driver of the lead vehicle waved back and sped up a little. The rest of the convoy followed, continuing down the motorway out of sight.

I started laughing quietly and soon the three of us were rolling about. We couldn't fucking believe our luck.

Ten minutes later, one of the other wagons showed up on the far side of the motorway, looking for us. Given the all-clear, they recrossed and gave us a bump-start.

'I suppose you bastards have been having a kip,' said Jack Dennis.

'Nah. We've been waving at Iraqi convoys,' I said. 'They're really very friendly.'

Above us, I heard the loud drone.

'An A10,' said Kiwi, again right on the button.

The jet was flying along the dual carriageway, obviously chasing the Iraqi convoy.

'Let's get out of here before it picks on us,' said Billy.

The A10 is an air-to-ground attack plane that's slower than a normal jet but packs an awesome punch. It's also known as a Thunderbolt, which isn't far wrong. The cannons completely tear up the ground and very little survives.

As we drove across the flyover, I could see the tell-tale explosions and flashes; the trucks were burning a couple of clicks to the west and the gun-happy Yank was whacking anything that was moving. One dead convoy.

We went screaming into the desert and basha'd up in the first wadi on the other side. The entire squadron was now across MSR1 and the Troops were all within 50Ks of one another. During the morning a message came through that we were to be resupplied that night – 27 January. Our gasoline and fresh water were getting low and we could also do with more rations. By now D Squadron were spread all over the desert, but 20 Troop would sponsor the resupp and American helicopters were to fly in and drop off the fuel, food, water and spare parts.

Mick had radioed RHQ and arranged for a replacement for the busted .50 cal mount on Jack D's wagon, along with a new starter motor for Pegasus.

Once 20 Troop had the goods, the various Troops would navigate our way in at different times to pick up supplies. This prevented the whole squadron being in one place at the one time. Our time window was 0100 hours and we were going to be the last Troop to be resupplied.

We had to cover about 30Ks to reach the RV and arrived with plenty of time to spare; after laying up for a few hours, we moved towards 20 Troop's LUP at our designated time and the sentries met us and guided us in.

There was no cheery welcome from Mad Dog McDonald – he

wasn't that sort of bloke. He gave us a quick brief, pointed to the resupps and said, 'Good, now fuck off and get on with it.'

It was great to see some of the lads again and to catch up on the news. We worked quickly, filling the jerrycans and stocking up on rations. The so-called fresh water had been carried in drums and was brown and tasted rusty.

I saw Little Glyn, Gary and Neil Dixon, who'd all been seconded from Mountain Troop when 20 Troop was created. Glyn had all the info on what had happened to the rest of D Squadron since we split up over the border.

It had been Colin Harris's vehicle with Ray Scott driving and Ginge Palmer on the back that had been blown up on the first night. When Mad Dog had run down the convoy telling us to leg it, Ray had taken off, but the track rod snapped when he drove over a rock. It meant they couldn't turn right, only left, and they had to stop.

Thankfully, 20 Troop were just behind and had picked them up. They off-loaded everything they could from the pinkie and threw it into the big Mercedes Benz mother ship. With shots being fired and the Iraqis searching no man's land, they didn't waste any time.

Colin had opened two jerrycans of fuel and poured them over the wagon. He took the bar mine from the front and placed it underneath, cracking the safety fuse with the grip switch. The fuse gave them enough time to leg it. When the bar mine exploded it sent the pinkie soaring towards heaven in a fireball. One dead vehicle, but it was a big enough show to put off any pursuers for a while.

Colin had stayed with 16 Troop, bumping out one of the young toms, Mike 'Taff' Davies. Taff, Ray and Ginge then found themselves crammed into the big Mercedes Unimog support vehicle of 20 Troop.

The next night, 20 Troop also had a breakdown, for exactly the same reason – a broken track rod on a pinkie. Already overloaded with the kit from Ray's wagon, they tasked a British helicopter from 47 Squadron to fly in a spare part. At the same time the chopper picked up the three lads from 16 Troop and back-loaded them to Saudi Arabia.

'Poor old Ray,' I muttered. 'He and the lads must have been gutted.'

'Shit no,' said Glyn. 'They're coming back over.'

'When?'

'They're on their way.'

Good for them, I thought.

Glyn explained how Ray, Andy and Ginge had been choppered back to Saudi. The first person they saw when they scrambled on board was Simon Nichols, the SQMS of D Squadron, whose job was to make sure resupplies went smoothly. Simon was something of a legend in the SAS. Depending on how you looked at it, he was either the luckiest S.O.B. who ever pulled on a uniform or, to my way of thinking, the unluckiest. Somehow he'd managed to be involved in three separate helicopter accidents, none of which was his fault. He survived a crash on the Fortuna Glacier in the Falklands in 1982 and then watched as the chopper coming to rescue his patrol also went down. To top it off, Simon was also on board the Sea King that ditched into the icy South Atlantic a few days before the Task Force landed, killing most of 19 Troop. For obvious reasons, he was the last person I'd want to sit next to in a helicopter.

In the dark belly of the Chinook, Ray and the lads had had every right to be worried. A few minutes after lifting off, the alarm sounded in the cockpit: a ground-to-air missile had 'illuminated' them. The door gunners let rip on the gimpies, strafing the ground below them, while the pilot fired off chaff and began banking wildly in an attempt to shake off the missile. Inside, the lads were knocked around like dice in a cup.

For a desperate few seconds it seemed that the curse of Simon had struck again, but the missile slid by them and the chopper landed safely at Ar'ar.

After they had been debriefed by the colonel, the plan was to give the lads a new pinkie and fly them back into Iraq. They could take a resupply in to 17 Troop, who needed track-rod ends, and stay with them until they could rejoin 16 Troop.

That night the first attempt failed when the pilot turned back from the LS even though he'd received the correct signal from the IR torches of the guys on the ground; by his calculation the grid was too far north and he feared an ambush. Back in Ar'ar there were harsh words between RHQ and 47 Flight, but it didn't change the fact that Ray and the lads would have to wait another forty-eight hours to get back in the game.

'Fuck that,' said Ray. 'Give us a Magellan and a TACBE and we'll drive up there.'

The idea sounded crazy. The rest of us were at least travelling in Troop strength, but he was suggesting that a lone vehicle could cross the border and catch up with us.

Ray's a very persuasive fellow; the CO agreed to his plan and they were soon driving across the border. With them were two lads from R Squadron (Territorial Army) driving a Mercedes Benz Unimog, a smaller version of the one that 20 Troop had, and carrying no armaments.

They eventually hooked up with 17 Troop, the nearest Troop on their way towards 16 Troop.

To me the whole episode typified 'Who Dares Wins'.

Meanwhile, A Squadron had been toing and froing across the border. They'd crossed into Iraq on the same night as we did, but instead of punching north, their OC couldn't decide what to do. He was an SBS rupert – the first to command an SAS squadron.

Peter Rawlings, the RSM, packed his bergen and got a chopper to meet up with A Squadron. Peter was briefed to give the OC a rocket up the arse to get him going. Instead he told him that the commanding officer wanted to speak to him in Ar'ar. As soon as the OC boarded the chopper, Peter took over the squadron and headed them straight into enemy territory.

As we finished stocking up with supplies, McDonald wandered over.

'He's smiling – make a note in your diary,' whispered Billy.

The last of the jerrycans had been filled. McDonald grabbed hold of me. 'Taff, get all the crap together, including the oil drums, and dispose of it.'

We bundled all the rubbish together – the drums, ammunition boxes, batteries, gas bottles and cartons, a lot of them with UAE markings. I poured a whole jerrycan of petrol over the bonfire and then put a small charge into an old jerrycan that was three-quarters full of petrol. The small amount of PE4 was attached to det cord wrapped around the jerrycan; I put the PED100 on a two-hour delay, then connected the detonator to both the PED timer and the det cord. This created an incendiary device to burn the rubbish rather than a bomb that would blow it all over the desert.

I also attached a small combination switch, no bigger than a matchbox, to one of the oil drums on tension release. If anyone tampered with our rubbish tip, the switch would fire and set off the charge.

Saying goodbye to the lads, we piled into the pinkies. McDonald sent us on our way with the succinct words: 'Go fuck them!'

We drove off, and about an hour and three-quarters later there was a small thud and a fireball behind us on the horizon.

'It's gone early,' said Kiwi.

'No way – someone's set it off.'

For the third night in a row Scud missiles lit up the sky and we took bearings. After one of these stops, Pegasus failed to start again – the new starter motor had yet to be fitted. We were last in the convoy.

'Fuck it,' cried Billy at the wheel.

The vehicle ahead of us kept on going. Barry, the tail-end Charlie, had obviously fallen asleep. I leaped out and ran after them with my Armalite in hand, going like the clappers over rough ground.

'Get back here you bastards!' I yelled, giving Barry a fearsome bollocking. But I couldn't really blame him – I'd never been so tired in my life and it was a constant battle to keep my eyes open. Something had to be done or one of us would drive off a cliff or smack bang into an enemy stronghold.

As if to prove the point, that night we were badly compromised. Pegasus was the second wagon in the snake, and as we came over a ridge there were suddenly dogs barking. For a split second I thought it was an Iraqi position. Quickly pulling back onto the spur, we drove away, half expecting to hear the AKs open up. It turned out that we'd driven into a Bedouin camp with a ragbag collection of goats, camels, dogs and families.

These two incidents in the one night made up my mind about travelling during daylight rather than in darkness. I decided to raise the issue in the morning confab.

At about 0400 hours, we came over a rise and MSR2 was below us. On a cold, clear night, I could make out the grey lanes of the motorway. It wasn't such a shock to the system now. From our vantage point about 50 metres up on the side of a hill, I could see right down the motorway in both directions. Directly below us, there was a tunnel running beneath the road. An obvious crossing point? Or too obvious?

I went down on foot with Newlands and Kev Phillips to take a closer look. The tunnel was maybe 80 metres long.

'It's a fucking obvious place to booby trap,' whispered Newlands.

'Yeah, but there's probably loads of tunnels – would they do them all?'

Staring through the gloom, I could just about make out the other side. The tunnel stank of piss and animal shit – a good sign: it meant there probably weren't any traps.

We carefully went forward, stepping on turds and peering into the darkness. As we emerged on the far side, a cold breeze whipped across the open plain. I shivered as if someone had walked on my grave.

After a quick recce and scan with the IWS, Kev went back to bring the others through. Newlands and I stayed at the tunnel, scanning the desert. The pinkies started coming through the tunnel.

'I don't like this one fucking bit,' I said.

'Hey take a look at this, Taff.'

Through the night scope I could make out fresh tank tracks towards the east. From the number of different tracks, it was clear that we'd entered a major troop movement area. In for a penny . . .

Kiwi and I, Ted Butterton and Jack Dennis moved forward on foot, covered by the rest of the lads. We spotted a tank laager about half a click ahead and informed RHQ.

A jet was tasked towards our location, arriving a few hours later.

'Hello US Air, this is Highlight Delta Forty-one,' said Ted. 'We have some trade for you.'

'Hello Highlight Delta Four One, this is Cobra, US Air. Gimme the co-ordinates.'

We gave him the eastings and northings and a bearing from our IR strobe. Cobra picked up our strobe, but for some reason couldn't pick up what lay 800 metres ahead. He was way up, out of sight, but we could hear him driving around the block for about twenty minutes. Finally he announced he was running short on fuel and therefore dropping his load into a wadi.

Moments later there was a massive explosion about 2 clicks to the west.

'What a fucking wanker,' I said.

'Fucking Yanks,' replied Billy.

'Let's get out of here,' Ted said. 'This place is crowded.'

The next morning, I had a chat to Mac as he fitted the new starter motor to Pegasus in 'Mad Mac's garage'.

'What do you think about travelling during the day from now on?' I asked.

'We'd be compromised.'

'Yeah, but we've got the firepower to take them on. It's crazy travelling at night – it's taking too long and someone's gonna get killed. It's supposed to be a race against time to find the Scud sites . . .'

'I know I'm sick of fixing these fucking things,' he said, slapping his hand on the engine block.

I was thinking about the Long Range Desert Group in the Second World War, which had travelled in the day and attacked by night. Its success was legendary.

Mac didn't need much convincing. We put the idea to the boss, who called a council of war meeting within the Troop. I argued the pros of travelling during the day, in terms not only of speed and safety, but also of finding Scud sites – our prime objective.

Des put the case for continuing to drive at night. A vote was taken which was split down the middle at six apiece. Ted had the casting vote and ruled that the status quo applied: 'We keep going at night.'

Unfortunately the debate caused some friction within the Troop. I knew that Mac had the hump with some of the others, and Kiwi and I were disappointed with Billy, but the decision had been parleyed and put to a Chinese parliament – a process that is one of the strengths of the SAS.

Up on stag that afternoon, I looked across a barren wilderness. Across the wadi I could see the remains of an old fort that had probably been built by Alexander the Great. Suddenly, I heard the tinkling of bells.

Fucking hell, what's that?

A goat emerged from behind the rocks barely 20 feet in front of me; then another, then a whole herd of them, followed by an old leather-faced goatherder. In the darkness we'd basha'd up on top of a goat track and now the Iraqi shepherd was moving his herd. It was 1600 hours.

I could see him clearly, but he didn't show any signs of having seen me. He had to be at least eighty years old and wore tattered robes and carried a staff. By the looks of him, he'd spent his whole life in the desert and the path was like his main street. He knew we were there.

Thoughts raced through my head. If I killed him, the herd would bumble around and eventually find their way home. His family would come out looking for him, but by then we'd be long gone. If I let him live, he'd tell his family about us for sure, along with any soldiers he came across. We'd be compromised.

I scurried down and talked to Ted, Kev and Jack in Kev's basha.

'He's seen the four mounds up close,' I said, 'and there's a possibility he's sighted us.'

Kev said, 'We're compromised.'

275

'Yeah, but who's he gonna tell?' Jack said. 'We'll be out of here in a few hours.'

Ted said, 'That depends how close the enemy are.'

'We could tie him up,' I suggested.

'And what if nobody finds him?' Jack said. 'He'll die a slow death out here.'

Kev said, 'It'd be more humane to finish him off with a knife.'

We all looked at each other. None of us wanted to kill him, but we also knew that we weren't here on a 'hearts and minds' campaign. As the guy on stag, the task would fall to me.

'Let him go,' said Ted.

'You sure, Boss?' I asked.

Kev and Jack remained quiet.

Old leather-face shuffled past the four mounds and continued along the wadi until the dust kicked up by the goats had drifted and disappeared. 'Go on, old man, I hope you live another eighty years,' I said to myself as he ambled along with his precious goats.

Although morale was high in the Troop, there was growing frustration at the slowness of the Scud search. We seemed to be driving aimlessly around the desert, expecting to stumble across launch sites, but in reality, travelling at night, we could pass within a kilometre of a site and not see it. Something had to be done.

Kiwi, Billy and I formulated a plan to get more precise information. Having watched the MSR for most of the day, we could see that the traffic was quite busy and it was a fair assumption that some of the military vehicles were going to the Scud sites. If we could capture a driver, we could interrogate him and get the co-ordinates.

Billy, because of his dark skin, would play an Arab and lie on the road, pretending to be injured in an accident. We'd stop a soft-skinned vehicle rather than an APC and then Kiwi and I would jump out and capture the driver and any passengers. There was a track off to the side of our wadi where we could hide the vehicle, and we could blow it up at nightfall without attracting attention because it would appear to be just another explosion in amongst the nightly Allied air raids.

We put the idea to Ted Butterton, who seemed quite keen.

'How would we interrogate them?' he asked.

'Kev and Jack could do it. They've done basic Arabic.'

276

'Yeah, but it's really fucking basic,' said Jack. 'I doubt if we could get much out of him.'

'All you have to ask is, "Where are the missile sites?"' I said.

Ted said, 'What would we do with them afterwards?'

'Either kill 'em or take 'em with us.' I figured, what were one or two Iraqi deaths compared with hundreds of children in Tel Aviv?

Ted could see the sense of it, but Jack and Kev were against the idea.

Once more, the status quo remained. I felt a little let down.

That night as we drove off, the sky lit up with a massive flash. A Scud was going up somewhere to the west of us and shot across the sky with its tail blazing. We took a bearing – as did the rest of the squadron; all four Troops were within 50 kilometres of one another. After relaying the information back to SHQ, we were told the missile had hit Tel Aviv.

With orders to find the launch site, we made our way towards a planned RV with 18 Troop and 20 Troop. Meanwhile, the lads in 16 and 17 Troops were also going to join up and LUP in the vicinity.

The following morning, 29 January, Mick contacted all the call-signs to see where the others were located. It seemed the entire squadron had basha'd up within 12 kilometres of each other in a large wadi complex just north of MSR2.

We were now deep inside the Iron Triangle, in an area, according to satellite imagery, that was thick with Iraqi troops and Scud launch sites. The terrain was dominated by a large, very long wadi, with a number of smaller ones that shot off in different directions. None of them was very deep and we arranged the cam nets so they only just draped over the pinkies to give them a lower profile on the flat terrain.

As the sun rose, the first stag noticed a tower a couple of clicks to the east. His binos were covered with a camouflaged face veil to stop any chance of a reflection giving away our position.

The tower appeared to have a steel frame with a box-like structure at the top.

'What is it?' asked Des, as we squinted into the rising sun.

'Some sort of comms set-up, I suppose,' said Jack. 'I'd love to get a closer look.'

Ted said, 'We're not going anywhere until nightfall. They're sure to spot any movement.'

From our stag position, I could only see the top third of the tower. We presumed it was one of a series that ran through the Iron Triangle, linked by communication cables; we'd been briefed that each was guarded by at least two platoons. They had to be something to do with the Scuds, although it wasn't clear exactly what.

While the stag rotated, the rest of the Troop ate cold scoff and tried to catch some Zs. Although the sun had come out, the temperature rose very little and I was still wearing every layer I could find.

Then, shortly before 1400 hours, the calm was shattered by the rattle of a .50 cal opening up behind us in the distance. As we legged it to the pinkies the sound of explosions and automatic fire echoed off the walls of the wadi.

'This is it!' I cried.

# 17

WE DIDN'T KNOW IT AT THE TIME BUT 17 TROOP HAD CROSSED MSR2 ON the same night as we had and basha'd up about 11 clicks to the south of us in a deep-sided wadi. There they'd been joined by Ray Scott, Taff Powell and Ginge, as well as the two young lads from R Squadron in the Mercedes Unimog. It meant six vehicles in all, safely concealed under cam nets and guarded by a stag position above them.

As dawn broke, they spotted the Scud tower less than a click away. Although too close for comfort, there was nothing they could do until nightfall except sit it out.

About midway through the morning, an Iraqi Land Cruiser pulled up on the motorway and two soldiers got out and began walking along the MSR, looking towards the wadi entrance. The lads were given the 'stand to' and took up positions.

The soldiers stopped, returned to their car and drove away. It seemed like a false alarm. Two hours later, another pair of Iraqi soldiers approached, this time actually walking into the wadi and chatting away as if heading up the eighteenth fairway. One of them stopped, got down on one knee and pointed towards the cam nets. It was the last action of his life, for as he was getting to his feet a burst from a .50 cal knocked him over.

For 17 Troop, all hell broke loose. From the opposite ridge, about 150 metres away, thirty or forty Iraqi soldiers opened fire into the wadi. The lads retaliated, strafing the ridge with their support weapons.

'Where's it coming from?' screamed Kiwi when we heard the gunfire.

'East. Towards the tower,' said Des on stag.

We, of course, were unsure of what was happening. Yes, there was automatic fire and it sounded as if there was a big firefight going on, but we didn't know who or what it was, other than the fact that there was a huge volume of automatic fire and explosions. Could it be our blokes? If it was, they clearly had a battle on their hands. So did we crash out into the desert only to find the Iraqis having a blue-on-blue (friendly fire)? Until we had some solid intelligence we had to sit tight.

We got the cam nets down and packed away on the pinkies, keeping very low in our small wadi.

'I wish I knew what the fuck was going on,' said Kiwi.

'I know, I'm on fucking pins, too.'

Ted called me, Kev and Jack together. 'Unless we get some sort of indication or contact report we'd better sit tight.'

None of us could do anything unless we knew what was happening. On the net Mick talked to 20 Troop, who were as much in the dark as we were, but between us we worked out it was probably 17 Troop.

Further east, the boys continued to blaze away through the cam nets with GPMGs and .50 cals. As we found out later, the Iraqis were putting in a classic attack, with a large fire-support team on one ridge laying down a blanket of fire, while a platoon of about eighteen men attacked up the opposite ridge, trying to overrun the stag position. If that happened, the lads were fucked; the Iraqis would come down the hill and pick them off one by one like shooting fish in a bowl.

The lad on stag began screaming for support. The enemy platoon were firing and manoeuvring through the rocks and boulders towards him. Three lads went to his aid, two carrying Minimis and the other with a claymore bag full of L2 and white phos grenades.

They let rip with the light machine-guns, stopping the enemy advance in its tracks. Then came the grenades; as the ground erupted the Iraqis quickly decided that a frontal assault wouldn't work against the stag position.

By now the cam nets had disintegrated and hung in strips. Taff Powell was on the back of a wagon, firing the double gimpies towards the far ridge. Ray had the front gimpy and Ginge the 203. Taff took a round straight through the chest; he doubled over, clutching at the wound site, but continued firing with his other hand.

'Lads, I've been hit in the legs! I've been hit in the legs!' he screamed over and over. It wasn't his legs at all, but in his state of shock Taff was having flashbacks to the time in Florida, years before, when he was shot by some madman who opened fire on a crowd queuing outside a local disco.

The first rule when treating any casualty is warmth, rest and re-assurance – in that order. Because Taff was bellowing, Ray and Ginge didn't realize the severity of the wound and told him, 'Shut the fuck up and keep firing.'

On another of the wagons, Jim Dalton opened up on the far ridge with the M19 40mm grenade launcher. The effect was awe-some. He fired several bombs in quick succession and seconds later the explosions echoed down the wadi.

The Iraqis began retreating from the ridge. Jim raised the elevation, mentally calculating: 'They've run back another thirty yards now. Let's push 'em back some more.'

The impact of the M19 had won the firefight and changed the entire complexion of the battle. From being on the back foot, 17 Troop now had breathing space, but the Iraqis were certain to regroup and come back at them. The main priority for the lads was to get out of the wadi.

Taff had now collapsed, but was still holding the dual gimpy with one hand. Ginge ran across to get Tim Nixon the medic. They lifted Taff into the back of the Unimog and Tim whacked a drip into his arm while Willy applied field dressings to his chest. Apart from that, there was little they could do. Head, chest and ab-dominal injuries can't be treated with morphine because the drug slows down the respiratory system and masks the pain, at a time when the patient really needs to be awake and coherent.

The Iraqi fire-support team was beginning to reform on the ridge. The lads from the stag position retreated back to the pinkies and clambered on board. The shredded cam nets had to be untangled and tossed aside before the convoy could make a dash for the motorway.

Ray and Ginge were in the lead vehicle as they approached the entrance of the wadi. They were followed by the 17 Troop boss, Tom Ellis and Jim Dalton; the third member of their crew, Tim, was busy treating Taff in the Unimog.

By rights, there should have been bar mines across the entrance, but the lads had basha'd up too near first light, without enough time to set up a ring of steel.

Suddenly, two white Dodge jeeps carrying Iraqi soldiers drove into the wadi. Ray opened up with the gimpy, firing a full belt of 200 rounds into the pair of wagons, killing everyone inside. Jim made extra sure with the M19.

Under sporadic fire, the rest of the convoy began moving. The last pinkie failed to start. Another crew had to run over and try to push. Meanwhile, the rest of the convoy got the nod to keep going.

As Ray and Ginge cleared the wadi, they concentrated on the left ridge where the Iraqi fire-support team had been positioned. An automatic weapon opened up from the right, almost next to them. If the gunner had thought to fire single shots, he could probably have taken out both of them with one round. Instead, the burst on automatic made the AK47's barrel lift and the rounds went spiralling over their heads.

As they turned, Ray and Ginge could see a pile of bodies among the rocks, some dead, some alive but in rag order, missing arms and legs. These were from the platoon that had tried to capture the stag position and fallen down the hill. Two of the wounded were firing AK47s.

Ginge debussed from the driver's side, directly in the line of fire. He should have been whacked but somehow managed to sprint to the other side. Then he reached up, grabbed the gimpy on the commander's side and fired blindly at his attackers. The wagons behind him also opened up, killing the Iraqis in a hail of bullets.

The first five vehicles headed towards a section of the MSR that had no fence and drove up and over the other side on a gravel and mud bank. As they crested the road, an almighty explosion detonated behind them and they looked back to see an axle with two wheels flying through the air.

Their first reaction was that the lads still in the wadi had taken a direct hit from an anti-armour weapon. Looking around, they counted ten men out; that left seven still inside.

Meanwhile, the Iraqi fire-support team continued turning up the heat. From the mud bank, Ray and the lads set up in all-round defence and returned fire as they waited for the others to come out. Where the hell were they? What had happened?

The Iraqis had stopped all traffic on the MSR and a load of civilians had gathered further along the motorway next to their cars, watching the proceedings like sightseers. Somehow a vehicle skipped the roadblock and suddenly motored along a dirt track beside the MSR. It was a little white Skoda, with Dad, Mum and kids, seemingly unperturbed by the gunfire. They smiled, waved and weaved between the pinkies, continuing on their way.

Of the seven lads still inside the wadi, Taff was obviously injured, but the others were hopefully OK, unless the explosion had caused casualties. Thick black smoke billowed out of the wadi.

'Where the fuck are they?' said Tom Ellis.

One of the wagons went further down the road to where they could look into the wadi. They could see the Unimog still intact but stationary. The last pinkie was a smouldering wreck.

Outside on the MSR, a decision had to be made: did they go back into the wadi or continue waiting?

'Any sign of them?'

'None.'

'Maybe they tabbed out on foot,' suggested someone.

'We've got to blow up the Unimog with the M19. We don't want the Iraqis getting the kit.'

'No, what if the lads are still sheltering inside?'

'Shit, what are we going to do?'

'We've got to go back and get them.'

'But there's no-one around the Unimog – they must have gone out the far side on foot.'

'No, they wouldn't leave Taff. He couldn't walk.'

A decision had to be made quickly or the convoy risked getting compromised on the MSR. If a major force came down the motorway it would take them out. Equally, they risked getting shot to shit if they went back.

Inside the wadi, the bar mine had in fact been triggered by Willy, who cracked the grip switch when the last pinkie failed to start. They left all the ammunition on board and took only their weapons and grab bags (small bergens), with spare clothes and rations. Thirty seconds later, there was a massive explosion. This left all seven of them in the Unimog.

With only one vehicle to aim at, the Iraqis had no problem focusing their fire. They pumped the big armoured truck full of rounds until the engine gave out. The lads weren't going anywhere.

'We're on foot from here,' said Willy.

Taff was in a bad way, losing blood and on a drip; he clearly had to be carried.

Tim lifted him over his shoulder and began running.

'For fuck's sake, put me down,' said Taff. With his hand holding the field dressing on his chest and a drip in his arm, he started haring across the rocks and gravel towards the wadi entrance.

They ran towards the two Dodge jeeps that had been battered by the M19 and GPMG. The first vehicle had been blown to smithereens and the second was riddled with holes and contained three dead Iraqis. All seven of the lads piled inside on top of the bodies and turned the key. Miraculously, it started, and they made off in the direction the Dodge was facing – towards the opposite entrance of the wadi.

Breaking through, they turned south towards MSR2 and skirted around the hill with the Iraqi fire-support team. They shot through a tunnel underneath the motorway, well east of where the rest of the Troop were waiting, and continued south towards the Saudi border.

On the MSR, one of the lads looked over his right shoulder and saw a civvy-type vehicle speeding south with a cloud of dust in its wake. He had no idea the missing seven lads were on board.

Following SOPs, Tom Ellis made the decision to take the rest of the convoy to the rally point. Whether travelling in the jungle, the desert or the mountains, the SAS nominates ERVs (emergency rendezvous points) along the route, so that if the patrol or troop gets split up, everyone can make their way to the last ERV, which remains open for twenty-four hours after the time of contact. In this case, it was situated about 5 kilometres south of MSR2. The five vehicles arrived in the late afternoon, set up comms and sent back a contact report to SHQ.

'Deliberate enemy attack on LUP location by large enemy force. Seven men missing in action, one known casualty among them . . .'

It gave the grid reference of the firefight and the ERV location, along with their intention to remain there for twenty-four hours and wait for the seven to come in.

Sitting around our radio, we also picked up the message. I gave Mick a hand to decrypt the report and we found out that our guess had been right – it had indeed been 17 Troop.

'Seven are OTR,' I muttered, handing the note to Mad Mac.

'Makes bad reading.'

Ted summoned everybody under his cam net and broke the news. The word from A Squadron was similarly bleak. A pinkie carrying the SSM, Bobby McCann, had run into a tank ditch near Medesis Airfield. As they were trying to get out, the Iraqis had opened fire on them and Bobby was shot up pretty badly. The two lads with him tried to fend off the enemy but were massively out-gunned. Eventually Bobby told them to leave and save themselves. One of the lads offered to finish him off with a pistol, but the sergeant major declined and told them to go. They, too, were OTR.

Adding their names to the list meant that a total of twenty-two SAS personnel from A, B and D Squadrons were MIA (missing in action) behind enemy lines. Apart from the fact that the news was heartbreaking, the reputation of the Regiment was hanging by a thread.

The next day, 30 January, we were ordered to stand by and be ready to move south within twenty-four hours. We were in rag order and it wasn't surprising that the hierarchy wanted to pull us out.

Meanwhile, Baghdad radio was reporting that twenty-one Special Forces commandos had been killed by their soldiers in the wadi. Of course it was bollocks – there weren't even twenty-one lads there – but having so many blokes missing was a blow to the morale of the squadron.

Meanwhile, at the rally point, the rest of 17 Troop waited in vain for twenty-four hours. When the seven missing men failed to turn up, it was feared that they'd perished or been captured. In reality, Willy, Taff and the lads had driven the Dodge jeep into the deck and then started tabbing south towards the border.

Taff, bleeding heavily, kept up with them, refusing to be carried. It was quite ironic that he'd only driven into Iraq a few days earlier and for the second time he was heading out again.

They walked solidly day and night for forty-eight hours, with only their weapons, webbing and whatever they had on their beltkit. There were also two grab bags of extra food and water, but Taff got most of the fluids because he was dehydrating.

When it was clear that he'd die if they kept walking, they decided to hijack a vehicle, pulling up a truck on the gravel road and ordering the driver out at gunpoint. When he refused to leave the cab, he was shot in the arm. The lads dragged him out and gave him medical attention before leaving him at the side of the road.

Piling into the big Mercedes Benz, they headed off, with everyone in agreement that they'd run the gauntlet of any Iraqi roadblocks or military checkpoints. However, the rig was given such a pounding in the desert that the guts fell out of it after only a few hours and the lads were back on foot again.

Quite often they heard Allied planes going overhead, but with a broken TACBE they couldn't relay any messages. On the fourth day, with Taff deteriorating rapidly, they all lay in a big circle in the desert with their signalling mirrors reflecting the sun, trying to attract the attention of a plane. It didn't succeed.

Taff was lucky to make it through that night. Grey and incoherent, he was dying. They'd run out of food and were down to their last few swigs of water.

Coming across a Bedouin encampment, they saw a truck, and the decision was made to pool together their gold 'escape' coins and offer to buy it from the owner. A deal was struck and they drove south to the border, crossing near the familiar Crusader fort. Without stopping, they raced down the road towards the airbase at Ar'ar and screamed through the camp gates. Remarkably Taff was still conscious, but collapsed as they lifted him from the truck. Adrenalin had been the only thing keeping him going.

He was handed over to Doc Gillespie, the Regiment's medic, and later transferred to a French hospital where the doctors didn't believe that he'd been shot five days earlier – either that, or something pretty crucial was lost in the translation. Whichever, they treated the wound as very recent, inserting a chest drain to remove fluid. But Taff's liver was severely inflamed by this stage and the chest drain went straight into it; seeing no fluid come out of the drain, the doctors pulled it out and reinserted it with the same result. Miraculously, Taff survived, but his liver was irreparably damaged. It was a small price to pay.

The truck that carried him to safety became the property of 17 Troop, D Squadron. It had cost a handful of gold and become part of SAS history.

Meanwhile, back in the Iron Triangle, we later learned that 16 Troop was compromised in circumstances very similar to the attack on 17 Troop. Iraqi forces with armoured vehicles started pounding their LUP near one of the Scud towers. The Milan team in one pinkie had been overrun, and another crew successfully went in and extracted them under fire.

During the withdrawal, two of the lads jumped off with the Milan and took out one of the pursuing vehicles. They then came under intense enemy fire and were stranded. Two of the lads in a pinkie raced in, picked them up, and screamed back out: the SAS never leaves anyone behind. The four guys then all held on as the pinkie screamed up the side of the large wadi, under fire, to rejoin the rest of the Troop supplying the baseline of covering fire, exactly as we'd practised over and over at Manama.

Although this proved that we had the firepower to get ourselves out of trouble, it also showed that something had to be done about the towers. We'd taken a battering and it was about time we landed a few punches of our own.

At last light we packed up, collected the dems and moved out of our wadi, heading for an RV with 18 and 20 Troops. At the same time, 16 Troop made their way to 17 Troop's ERV north of MSR2 to link up with them in a half-squadron group.

Meanwhile, the head shed at SHQ were deciding whether to pull us out of Iraq. I knew that Mad Dog would fight against this; like the rest of us, he wanted to exact a little revenge for what had happened to the other lads.

Our half squadron (18, 19 and 20 Troops) basha'd up in another wadi and the Head Shed gathered for a powwow.

'Hey, Julian, where's my fucking spyglass?' I yelled. The boss of 18 Troop grinned.

'Don't look at me – McDonald took it off me,' he said.

'Well, that's the last I'll see of that.'

Kiwi, Billy and I shared a brew.

'They're gonna pull us out,' said Billy morosely.

'Nah. Mad Dog's gonna want to fuck them over real good,' I said.

After an hour, Ted and Kev Phillips returned from the meeting. They gathered us together.

'We're taking out the towers,' said Ted.

A broad grin spread across my face. I winked at Mac and he at me.

Ted continued, 'This afternoon, we're mounting a three-Troop assault on the southernmost tower, the one that gave 17 Troop so much trouble. The plan is to approach the tower from the south and to avoid being seen by the towers to the north-west. Then we drop off a mortar base line, start whacking the complex and attack across the desert with the pinkies in arrowhead formation.

'From what we've seen, each tower appears to have a company of forty to fifty Iraqi soldiers. They're likely to have strong defensive positions as well as APCs. The mission is to destroy the base.'

My mind was racing; this was history in the making, for not since the Second World War had pinkies been used in a squadron attack. I thought of David Stirling and Paddy Mayne, tearing out of a wadi in their Long Range Desert Group vehicles, hitting the Germans hard and then disappearing again.

Now these were our tactics. We were going to hit them hard, hurt them and move on.

# 18

AT 1600 HOURS ON 30 JANUARY, WE MOVED OFF IN ARROWHEAD formation, looking more than ever like a band of desperados. The sun was shining and a cool breeze swept away the dust thrown up by the wheels. Travelling in daylight for the first time, I could finally see the gravel plain up close and bare-arsed. It was littered with tiny boulders and criss-crossed with tracks.

Heading south-east towards the tower, we stopped short as two vehicles, including McDonald's, went forward to do a recce. They were gone for about half an hour. When Mad Dog drove back, he swung past us and said, 'It's going to be right flanking.'

Moving west until the tower became fully visible, we dropped off a mortar line about 2 kilometres from the target, along with the M19 and two .50 cal vehicles to act as the fire-support group. As we attacked from the right, they would pound the tower until we were almost on top of it, then move to the left to keep their fire ahead of us.

There was no talk of a fall-back plan – it was a foregone conclusion that we were going to pulverize these fuckers.

We moved off to the right, with McDonald at the apex of the arrowhead. My vehicle was immediately to the right. Mad Dog's driver was Ben Graham, a good man to have alongside you in a fracas.

In Pegasus, Billy sat at the wheel. With his beard and shades he looked as if he should have been in the South Bronx. A few of the lads had put on their helmets, but I stuck with the shemag and painted on a war face. I also wore Raybans to cut out the glare as we faced the setting sun.

'This is what it's all about, boys,' I said, sucking in a deep breath.

Strangely, I didn't feel the slightest bit afraid. I'd seen the enemy and believed there was no way they were going to beat us. With so much firepower, discipline and training, none of us was going to die of bad drills, just bad luck. Instead I had an overwhelming desire for revenge. Some of my best mates were MIA; I didn't know if they were dead, wounded, captured or still running. For that, these fuckers were going to pick up the tab.

On such an open battlefield, there was nowhere to hide. The Iraqis had been watching us and opened up with mortars and anti-tank weapons, but struggled to find the range.

Somebody from the fire-support team shouted across, 'Ready!'

The first mortars went in for ranging. The rounds rocketed upwards, leaving thin trails of white smoke. Several seconds later they exploded, kicking up clouds of dust, having overshot the Scud tower. As the tubes were readjusted, the .50 cals and M19s joined the fray.

'OK, let's go,' yelled McDonald.

Ben gave me a devilish grin and shouted, 'Airborne!'

Billy floored the accelerator and Pegasus shot off the flat plain into a wadi on the right. It was a good old-fashioned Lawrence of Arabia style charge, minus the camels. The arrowhead formation had 20 Troop at the apex with 18 Troop on the left and 19 Troop on the right.

The adrenalin rush was amazing as we careered over the rough ground. Iraqi fire hit the ground behind and in front of us. The feeling was almost euphoric – we were finally doing the business.

I glanced across at Mad Dog in the next Pinkie and he looked like a man with his eyes on the prize; Ben Graham was still grinning. Suddenly, their rear-gunner, Neil Dixon, went flying off the back. 'Fuck, he's been hit,' I cried.

Ben stopped, jumped off the vehicle, and ran back to him. Mad Dog slid into the driver's seat and drove on, with one hand on the wheel and the other reaching across for the gimpy. He was Captain Ahab, hell-bent on getting his great white whale.

Neil had only been winded; the mount had broken on the M19 and he'd been thrown backwards.

Bouncing all over the place in the passenger seat, I found it impossible to hit anything with the gimpy. As we dropped deeper into the wadi, we gradually lost sight of the tower to our left and stopped firing. We'd have to guess its position when the attack went in. Eighteen Troop went firm and we swung around on the axis until we were now all in extended line and driving hard up the side of the wadi.

'Let's go!' the scream went up.

We crested the wadi more or less opposite the tower. If we'd been on foot we probably would have paused, got our wind back and then launched the assault, but this time we simply kept the momentum going. As we came over the top of the hill I could make out the explosions from our mortars and M19s. Now there was nothing between us and the tower complex except 400 metres of gravel and sand. I let rip on the gimpy, firing the full belt of 200 rounds, and then threw the empty tin overboard. Kiwi gave me another, which I fitted and fired as Billy drove us closer and closer.

About 50 metres short, the line of vehicles stopped and we laid down a blanket of fire that was so fierce the Iraqis must have thought they were facing an entire battalion. Hundreds and hundreds of rounds were raking them left to right. Kiwi had the twin gimpies roaring; Billy and I jumped out, linked up with two others, and then began firing and manoeuvring forwards.

There was a trench system all around the tower which we cleared with L2 and white phos grenades. Already we could see the Iraqis fleeing from their positions and legging it towards the next tower a couple of clicks away. Those who remained threw up their arms in surrender as we ran into the complex and started a search of the communication room and living quarters.

The dems lads from 20 Troop were already attaching slab charges and bar mines to the comms room and tower. The fire-support vehicles joined us, picking up Ben and Nick on the way.

Looking to the north-west, we could see the Iraqis fleeing. One group stopped about 300 metres away and were trying to set up a firebase line to attack us. The gimpies and .50 cals persuaded them to get a life.

The sun was shining and we still had a few hours of daylight. McDonald looked across at the next tower and said, 'Let's go arrowhead.'

We set off again, screaming past the terrified Iraqis, who turned, dropped to their knees and surrendered, shouting, 'United States! United States!' They thought we were Yanks – what an insult.

Our mission was to destroy the towers, not to take prisoners, so we just sped past them and kept going. Behind us the bar mines exploded and destroyed the first tower.

We formed a new firebase line, and the .50 cals and M19s began landing on the new target as we launched another right-flanking assault. A few Iraqis chose to fight from the trenches, but many fled as we took out the depth positions. Then we fired and manoeuvred forward, clearing the communications bunker below the tower.

The Iraqis inside surrendered and we moved them outside the perimeter before setting up the charges. I was just wondering if they'd do the same if our roles were reversed when a snarling mongrel of a dog made straight for Kiwi, who was sitting in the driver's seat. It clearly wanted a chunk out of Kiwi's leg but finished up with a bullet in the head.

'What is it with you, Kiwi, don't you like animals?' I joked.

'Wouldn't your folks let you have a dog?' echoed Billy.

'I bet that's why he ran away from home to join the Foreign Legion.'

It was getting dark as Des and I fitted the charges for the tower – bar mines and boxes of slabs linked together with det cord. Everyone was waiting in the pinkies as we cracked the grip switches and ran, the safety fuse burning down. You're not supposed to run from a burning charge – always walk calmly – but we had no time to lose. The tower toppled like a Lego model as we headed north in the gathering gloom towards the third tower.

This time there was no reception committee; the Iraqis had deserted before we arrived. Setting up the dems again, we blew the tower but decided to booby-trap the comms centre because the Iraqis were bound to follow up.

The lads had gathered outside the perimeter and I could see them silhouetted against a fire that burned brightly in the descending darkness. Their scruffy beards, cam-smeared faces and bristling intent reminded me of the day on Sussex Mountain where I first saw the SAS in action.

This is what it's all about, I thought – being deep behind enemy lines and taking out three Scud towers in a single afternoon. Thank God the head shed hadn't recalled us to Saudi; now we had the opportunity of repairing some of the damage inflicted on the Regiment's reputation.

A light drizzle began falling as we moved off in single file, looking for an LUP for the night. We didn't go very far before circling the wagons and setting up a ring of steel about 10Ks north of MSR2. In the distance I could hear an A10 Thunderbolt dispensing some of its own medicine to an unfortunate Iraqi convoy.

An hour later, with all the vehicles and equipment oiled and watered, I slipped into the green maggot for two hours' kip before my next stag. As I closed my eyes I heard another large explosion. The Iraqis had found their comms centre intact, at least for a brief second.

An hour later, the heavens opened and plunged us into mud city. We had the ponchos fitted to the side of Pegasus, but these couldn't stop the deluge. Pretty soon the doss bags were soaked and we were lying in a sea of pinkish brown mud. Periodically, lightning lit up the desert and the sound of thunder competed with the explosions from the Allied air bombardment.

Early in the morning, while it was still dark, we moved off in arrowhead formation towards the north, having set our bearings on a Scud launched two nights beforehand. Although the rain had stopped, a fierce wind drove across the open ground. We were pissed through and the wind chill was unbelievable. I watched the sun emerge on the horizon and willed it to rise quickly.

My gloved hands were ripped to bits from clearing barbed wire off one of the complexes before laying the charges. Still cammed up, most of us had also taken on the pinkish brown colour of the mud.

An hour later, with the sun up and our clothes dry, spirits began to lift. We were back on Scud watch. Being able to travel in daylight was a relief, even though it posed a greater risk of discovery. At least we didn't have to worry about Iraqi air attacks; the Allied air dominance was so complete that it had destroyed, crippled or simply frightened enemy jets out of the sky.

Suddenly the convoy skidded to a halt. Ahead of us, the ground lay littered with twisted white sheets of what looked like plastic. They stood out like bulldog's bollocks against the light brown of the desert.

'What the fuck is that?' asked Kiwi.

Billy said, 'Beats me.'

'Some of the pieces are scorched around the edges,' I said, looking closer.

After a brief confab, we decided that the material must have come from a Scud, some sort of outer skin that had been shed in flight. Meanwhile 18 Troop had spotted something to our left, about 200 metres away. They did a recce and came back to us. They reported a massive U-shaped concrete bunker, partially buried, about 80 metres long and shielded on three sides by large man-made mounds. It had rails on one side and on the other a lifting device, possibly for a missile. Definitely a Scud site.

The area was deserted but not abandoned. The normal Iraqi practice was to bring each Scud into the desert on the back of a truck, mount it and then fire, before pulling back to their base camps.

McDonald called us together for a briefing. Afterwards, some of the lads took the Minimis up onto the surrounding mounds to give cover, while dems teams sneaked down and put slab charges on the bunker complex. Moving back, we blew the site and then inspected the damage: concrete and metal were broken and mangled very satisfactorily.

After a second round of charges were blown, just to make sure, we were finally satisfied with the job and headed north.

At about midday we came across more of the tell-tale white plastic sheets. Amidst the debris there also seemed to be parts of a motor with wires hanging off. Splitting up, we soon discovered another launch site, did the recce and laid the slab mines. This time there were heavy-vehicle tyre tracks leading from the complex and, after blowing the launch pad, we started following them. As we crested a rise, something could be seen on the horizon across the plain before us.

'What's that?' said Billy.

Squinting against the light, I tried to make it out. Without a doubt this was where the tracks had been heading, for very low, almost hugging the ground, I spotted antennas. Through the binos I could also see buildings. No movement, though. Had the Iraqis seen us and battened down the hatches?

All the vehicles came together in an extended line, scanning the horizon. Four vehicles went forward for a closer look and reported back: it was an enemy base, and a large one. There were almost certainly stockpiles of Scuds.

By now it was nearly last light. Mick got on the net and sent back the details to RHQ. They told us to LUP a couple of clicks to the south and get ready for an air strike.

At about 2300 hours, Ted Butterton opened up on the TACBE and gave our call sign. Above us, the American jets locked on to the target.

'Good work down there,' said the lead pilot, whose Tomcat had the typically Yank name of 'Chevrolet'. 'Keep your heads down, y'all, it's gonna be a big one.' He wasn't wrong. The jets blitzed the site throughout the night with bombs that made the ground shake under our feet. Nobody could have survived the onslaught, and it made me wonder how much more of this stuff Saddam would let his people endure before he threw in the towel.

Split into separate Troops again, we were due for another resupply two days later, sponsored by 20 Troop. Apart from the usual fuel, water and compo, we also needed link for the gimpies, .50 cals, extra bombs for the M19s, explosives, detonators, det cord and more ammo for the Minimis and Armalites. Oh, and a big bag of rice for Mad Mac, our resident veggie.

It was a clear, starry night, with a sharp wind that made it feel even colder. Stopping short of the RV, one vehicle moved forward at the designated time, between 0100 and 0200 hours, and met the sentries. Then the rest of us piled in and looted the sweetie shop.

'Will you get a load of this,' said Billy, holding up a long woollen overcoat.

I couldn't believe my eyes. Someone had finally listened to our complaints about the freezing conditions.

The overcoats were wonderfully warm and I felt like a kid getting his first racing bike on Christmas Day. There was only one size – extra large – which came down to my knees and positively swamped some of the other lads, but nobody complained.

Billy had a dark brown one, Kiwi's was grey and mine was fawn – all of them with tassels at the collars and gold braid around the cuffs. I vowed never to take it off.

Later we discovered that Ian Haslam, an old sweat who worked as a storeman in the QM's department, had taken matters into his own hands and gone shopping for the coats at a bazaar in Saudi. He bought about eighty of them and arranged to get them on the choppers for the resupp. What a hero. If I'd been handing out medals, old Ian would have been damn near top of the list. Morale soared, and the general feeling was that the tide had finally turned.

Next morning, we set off in arrowhead formation across the desert, looking even more like Arabs in our overcoats, shemags and beards. The new orders were that from now on we were going to travel during the day – not before time.

During the day we heard from RHQ about an incident involving A Squadron when one of the Troops had been compromised at an LUP. A group of Iraqi soldiers driving in old Land Cruisers had spotted something suspicious and began walking towards the cam nets. One of the lads was on the GPMG watching them and when they stopped, turned, and started running back to their wagons, he opened fire, killing all but one, whom they took prisoner. The prisoner turned out to be an artillery division officer and one of the Land Cruisers contained the artillery layout and divisional plans of the entire Iraqi army in that area.

The hierarchy were creaming themselves when they heard. They sent a chopper to airlift the prisoner back to Saudi and the success now prompted a message saying, 'Capture officer. If possible a Scud commander.'

'Oh yeah,' I said, not trying to hide my disbelief. 'It's just like picking fruit from the trees – we'll just go out and get ourselves a Scud commander.'

After a confab, it was agreed that 16 and 17 Troops would look for a prisoner by taking out another one of the towers, while the rest of us continued the Scud watch. A week or so earlier, during the drive north, 16 Troop had come across a deep-sided wadi with vehicle tracks leading in and out; now they had the opportunity to have a closer look in daylight.

Meanwhile we continued north, split again into Troops, crossing MSR3, which turned out to be no more than earth that had been packed hard. The landscape became rougher and more mountain-ous the further north we drove, and considering how much distance we'd put between ourselves and the Saudi border it was agreed that if we were compromised and had to go OTR, the best escape route was north towards Syria.

We now entered a particularly mountainous area with rocky outcrops that spiralled upwards, and the pinkies were taking a battering. We chose to break with SOPs and use a well-worn track to the summit. Occasionally we passed small stone sheep pens that had probably been built before Christ was born. There were no sheep now, only wild mountain goats that scurried away when we approached.

As we crested the summit we were treated to a spectacular view. It felt as if we were standing on the highest place on earth. Far beneath us we could see a sea of stones, criss-crossed by vehicle tracks and punctuated by various wadis – some deep, others shallow, wide or narrow. There was even a river, hugged by vegetation, which looked like a green snake slithering through the dirt.

'Hey, Mac, some fresh for you!' I laughed.

On top of the ridge there were huge rocks up to 10 feet tall jutting out of the ground like stalagmites. We basha'd up and soon I could smell the hexamine as the lads got the brews going.

'Take a look at this motherfucker,' said Mac, calling us over. He had a big smile on his face.

Looking down, off to the west, we could see a perfect circle of white sheets, not dissimilar to a corn circle. Slap bang in the middle of them was the launch site.

'Just beautiful,' said Ted, glancing at his watch. 'That sorts out our agenda for tomorrow.'

We'd spend the night in our seat among the gods and the next morning, bright-eyed and bushy-tailed, go down there and blow their Scud site to kingdom come.

At first light we duly drove down towards the Scud site, following the goat track towards the bottom, and swung around the feature towards the vegetation and the circle of white sheets. It was good to see some grass again after so long in this arid grey setting; such a pity that we now had to turn it into mulch. We debussed and blew the site; all very straightforward, all just part of the daily routine.

The other half of the squadron were further south, following the dozens of vehicle tracks it had seen going into the deep wadi. Moving in arrowhead, the front vehicle stopped suddenly and pulled back.

'What's the matter?' Don Matthews, the Troop boss, asked.

'There's a cam net over there,' he said. 'I don't remember seeing it before.'

'Nor did I,' echoed his mate.

'Just fucking get on with it,' said Don. 'It probably belongs to some wizened old Bedouin.'

Just as he finished the sentence, a burst of gunfire rattled out from underneath the net and they went diving for cover.

'Hey, Don,' yelled one of the lads. 'That wizened old Bedouin's carrying an AK47.'

With that, they let rip with the gimpies and a few rounds from an M19, just to be extra friendly. They'd stumbled on an Iraqi convoy that carried at least four Scuds on lorries that were hidden under cam nets.

Ginge Collins, the staff sergeant with 17 Troop, got on the net and called in an air strike.

'Fuck!' he said. 'They can't get here for at least an hour.'

'What are we supposed to do in the meantime?' asked the lads.

'Keep them here.'

'What do you fucking mean, keep them here?'

So began a bizarre game of cowboys and indians, with 16 and 17 Troops trying to prevent the convoy escaping from the wadi until the cavalry arrived. Each of the Troops took turns to draw up to the side of the wadi and hit the Iraqis.

It was a perfect opportunity to break out the Milan and the team didn't waste time. There's something quite mesmerizing about watching a wire-guided missile screaming through the air: people tend to stop and look, which is exactly what the Iraqis did until it hit them. One of the mobile Scud launchers erupted and burned fiercely.

The jets arrived in darkness and had an excellent lock-on provided by the flaming vehicle. The Iraqis were still desperately trying to get out of the wadi, but now it was too late. As 16 and 17 Troops pulled back, the American F16s set about removing the location from the map.

On 11 February, a message came through from RHQ: 'Move to Squadron RV at Wadi Tubal 12–17 February.'

A massive resupp had been planned a couple of hundred clicks to the south, with A and D Squadrons coming together for the first time since training at Camp Victor.

As we navigated south, the desert terrain looked quite flat until we came to a wadi that looked like a crack caused by an earthquake. Sentries from A Squadron escorted us in single file along the edge and down a winding track to the wadi floor. We were now hidden from the desert as if the ground had swallowed us up.

Each Troop was given an LUP and positioned a stag on the craggy rocks above the wadi at ground level. Then it was time to relax, chill out, light up the hexy and get some rest. A large re-supply was on its way and there was no time frame for our next move.

It was nice to rinse the bollocks with a drop or two of water, talcum the feet and catch up with some old faces from A Squadron. Their SSM, Bobby McCann, had been captured near Medesis Airfield and the RSM, Peter Rawlings, was now running the show. He was a real character and people tended to love him or hate him but nothing in between. An ex-Para and Mountain Troop sergeant, he tabbed around the wadi and dropped in on the various groups of lads to say hello.

When he arrived at our basha, I foolishly asked him if he wanted a brew. Peter was famous for having a sweet tooth, and I should have guessed he'd say, 'Yeah, I'll have a hot chocolate.'

Hot chocolate is a jealously guarded commodity in the ration packs – not something you give away – but I could hardly ignore the RSM, so I made him a brew.

'You brown-noser, Mike, I suppose you're going to give him your last Rolo and all!' said Kiwi.

Peter sat with us and told us about the contacts that A Squadron had got into. At one stage they'd had a prisoner tied up in the back of one of the pinkies; he had a hood on his head and the lads were feeding him biscuits and treating him well.

'Bet they were fucking garibaldis though,' I said.

'Bet they weren't washed down with hot chocolate, either,' said Kiwi.

When I saw Ken Doyle, the Lone Rider, I told him I was sorry to hear about Vince, who'd been seconded from A Squadron and was OTR with the Bravo Two Zero mission. The two of them were big buddies and had the same droopy moustaches that were straight out of *The Sweeney*.

'Heard anything, Ken?' I asked.

'Nothing.'

'There's a chance,' I said. 'Look at the lads from 17 Troop, they managed to tab out.'

'Yeah.'

I could tell he was gutted. I knew Ken. People took him at face value and usually gave him a wide berth, but we went way back; I understood him and I knew he was missing Vince.

Mad Mac made a chequerboard using Dextrose tablets as draughts, with the orange and lemon flavours representing each side. We gambled with our gold escape coins and I lost all ten of mine to Mac, although I never actually paid him. Instead I promised him a bottle of whisky.

Mac had grown a reddish-brown beard and wore a peaked DPM hat everywhere he went. As he set up another game, he said, 'I'm going to walk to the North Pole when we finish here.'

'Yes, that's a good idea, Mac. Sorry if I don't join you, but I was thinking more of Torremolinos for my hols.'

He truly was fucking mad, I thought, but knowing Mac he'd probably enjoy being on his own up there in the wilderness – just him and a few hungry polar bears. Ultimately, he did make the attempt, and only narrowly failed because of an injury to his spine. Otherwise he would have been the first person to walk single and unsupported to the North Pole.

As he beat me for the umpteenth time, Billy shouted, 'Come

298

and look what's round the corner, Mike.'

The cavalry had arrived – a remarkable convoy consisting of ten 4-ton trucks, pinkies and motor cycle outriders. They carried our fresh supplies, and it seemed as if the whole of the Regiment had descended on the wadi.

There were lads from the REME who'd come to work on the vehicles, technicians from 264 Signals to sort out the radios, and B Squadron, acting as protection, who guarded the convoy and took over our stag positions to give us a complete rest. Some of them would also be staying with us to bring the various Troops up to strength.

For the first time in a month I didn't have to worry about dragging myself up onto higher ground to go on watch every few hours. I could totally relax, put my head down and sleep, knowing that someone else was watching over me.

Over the next few glorious days, we plundered the fresh rations, scoffing boxes of fruit, rice, potatoes and onions – some of which we saved to take with us. No cooking was allowed after last light, so we'd fill up the flasks before dusk and give ourselves plenty to drink at night when all the lads got into little groups and chatted until late. This is the nearest you ever get to five-star treatment in the SAS.

Peter Rawlings, now the RSM, decided this was the perfect time to convene an extraordinary meeting of the warrant officers' and sergeants' mess, his first opportunity to do so since his promotion in December. At midday on 16 February a quorum of senior NCOs was therefore assembled and the meeting began. Among items on the agenda, all carried without dissent, were a vote of thanks to the retiring RSM; a special thank you to the Christmas party organizers; arrangements for the next mess dinner night; and a discussion about the purchase of a new washing-machine. There was then a motion from the floor that if the president of the mess committee was compromised on the way back to Saudi he should be compelled to eat the minutes. As far as any of us knew, it was the first ever mess meeting to be held behind enemy lines and it perked morale even higher.

The only disquiet in the Regiment concerned R Squadron, which is made up of reservists drawn from Herefordshire, the Midlands and Wales. Having been away for over two months, quite a lot of these bricklayers, plumbers and shopkeepers, many of them self-employed, had decided that they now wanted to go home because they were spending too long away from their jobs. The whole thing was ridiculous – how could a reserve squadron with a wartime role suddenly want to quit a campaign halfway through? It was even more galling when we had full-time lads spread around the world in places like Latin America and Northern Ireland who would have given their right arms to be in the Gulf with us.

The same was true of the lads who arrived with the supply convoy. Most of them were angling to find ways of staying with us rather than go back to Saudi. Among them was 'Piggy' Arnold, who wasn't even in the Army. Piggy had left the Regiment a year or so earlier, yet somehow bluffed his way over to Camp Victor. From there he managed to get to Saudi and then hitch a ride on the convoy into Iraq. It was crazy – he was a civilian, but he stayed with D Squadron until the end.

With good food and plenty of sleep, spirits lifted and pretty soon the banter started. As always, Kiwi got teased about his love for German marching music and Billy because of his support for Newcastle United.

The BBC World Service was our barometer for the war and nightly we gathered around radios to listen to reports from people like Kate Adie and John Simpson. Occasionally we'd also hear Saddam Hussein still spouting his rhetoric. None of us was under any illusion as to what still had to be done. The Iraqis were being hammered from pillar to post, but they were down, not out.

# 19

AFTER FIVE DAYS THE CONVOY PULLED AWAY, COVERING ITS TRACKS SO
completely that it might never have existed. A Squadron was
briefed by Peter Rawlings and moved off first; we followed soon
afterwards.

We were travelling in half squadrons again, with 19 Troop now
teamed with Mobility and SHQ. Our orders were to go back into
the Iron Triangle on bomb damage assessment. This involved
checking out sites that had been blitzed by Allied air attacks and
reporting back on the accuracy and level of destruction. In particular, we had to examine the Iraqi complex that we'd discovered
earlier and destroyed by calling in the American jets.

Driving in daylight, we made good time by brazenly using the
motorways and arrived in the area soon after last light. Now in
extended line, we edged to within 250 metres of the bombed Iraqi
base to our north. The vehicles of Mountain Troop were on the left,
with 20 Troop in the centre and 18 Troop on the right. On the
extreme left of the line, we faced Pegasus outwards to the east, so
that Kiwi could train the double gimpies towards the complex
whilst I faced east with my gimpy to cover that arc, just in case the
Iraqis tried to bump us from that direction.

It was a clear night and the stars were out, creating enough
ambient light for the weapon sights to pick up the outline of the
ruined buildings and debris. It looked deserted but we were too
far away to be absolutely sure.

Now and again there were flashes of light in the distance,

301

followed twenty or thirty seconds later by the inevitable rumble.

'Someone's getting fucked over,' said Billy.

The supply convoy had brought us another spyglass, and Kiwi now stood on the back of the wagon with it, scanning towards the complex. The thermal imager was so powerful it could have picked up a rat moving a mile away.

'There's no life form between us and the site,' he said.

Four vehicles from 20 Troop headed off to do a recce, moving in single file past Pegasus for a short distance before turning south, driving on a bearing to avoid the possibility of a blue-on-blue. Our vehicle had one-in-one tracer fitted to the rear gimpies; if Kiwi had to fire towards the complex the lads from the fire support Troops (18 and 19) would know that 20 Troop were to the east of the red line; on the return leg of the recce, the 20 Troop lads would be able to see the one-in-one and keep to the right of it.

Through my weapon sight I saw that about 100 metres short of the target the rear pair of vehicles, carrying the M19 and .50 cal, came to a halt. The other pair continued slowly towards the complex, with Mad Dog McDonald in charge of one and Bruce Miller commanding the other.

At the edge of the site Bruce's vehicle stopped and Ben Graham and Stu McDonald proceeded cautiously. I watched them through my IWS and got a running commentary from Kiwi with his spyglass.

Twisted metal and blown-up vehicles littered the complex, while every building had collapsed into rubble. Only one wall had been left standing by the air attack and this had the obligatory mug shot of Saddam Hussein in military dress, peering from beneath hooded eyes. More propaganda from the world's biggest bullshit artist.

Ben and McDonald debussed and began edging forward on foot. I could hear a dog start to whinge and bark.

In the same instant a burst of automatic fire erupted from Ben's left. He swung round, pulled his Armalite up and fired on automatic. An Iraqi soldier fell where he stood. Another ran out and Ben fired again. Kiwi reported McDonald down on one knee and struggling to get up, though more or less still firing.

Iraqis began pouring out from an underground complex where they'd probably been sheltering from the original air strike. I could see the tracer rounds zipping back and forth, but with no comms between the vehicles we had no idea what was happening and couldn't do a thing to help. We couldn't keep to the original plan and return fire: we had to wait until all four vehicles were in sight and off to our left.

Without warning, however, Kiwi suddenly opened up directly behind me on the gimpies. It was so unexpected, it fucked my head up completely.

'Stop! Stop! What the fuck are you firing at?' I cried, and a second later the OC came bounding angrily towards the wagon. We'd both forgotten Kiwi had the advantage of superior vision with the spyglass, so even at this distance and in darkness he could make out the difference between the enemy and our lads.

Kiwi reported, 'They're extracting back to Bruce's pinkie . . . reached it now . . . their gimpy's opening up . . .'

We saw their tracer strafing the wildly firing Iraqis. GPMGs still blazing, the vehicle drove back to Bruce Miller's before linking with the other pair of pinkies waiting on the perimeter, then moved off to our left on their back bearing as we let rip.

Kiwi kept up a running commentary until the four vehicles arrived back safely at our position, but as they drove past I could see McDonald slumped over his seat. Seconds later a support vehicle braked to a halt alongside us.

'Mike, we need your medic.'

Billy made his way towards the stricken SSM with his grab bag of medical kit.

Meanwhile the rest of us were hitting the complex with everything we had, as well as calling in the F16s to stomp all over them again.

Looking at the devastation, it was hard to believe the Iraqis had managed to survive the first aerial bombardment. The complex had been wasted, but they had obviously ridden out the storm in an underground bunker. Either that, or they had come afterwards to inspect the damage.

The jets arrived in the early hours of the morning and systematically began rearranging the geography. The night had turned very black and the wind began whipping us, bringing with it a torrential downpour.

Mad Dog was wheezing and complaining that he couldn't breathe. He'd been shot quite badly through the fleshy part of his waist, the round having gone in one side and out the other. Billy made him comfortable and put in a drip before we loaded him onto a wagon and found an LUP position in the desert.

As the hours went by McDonald's breathing became fast and ragged like that of a forty-a-day man who'd just sprinted 100 metres.

'How is he?' I asked.

'He'll live,' said Billy.

'Make fucking sure of it,' Mad Dog coughed.

Ironically, just prior to coming to the Gulf, McDonald had had a big bust-up with Billy over something and now his life rested in the Geordie's hands.

'You're lucky you're such a fat fucker – the bullet went right through your love handles,' teased Billy.

'Shut up and sew,' muttered the patient.

It was a bad night. Rain hammered down, turning the ground to mud, and Mad Dog coughed and hacked. We called in a chopper, but for operational reasons it wouldn't be able to make it until the next day.

At daylight we moved off into a large wadi about 800 metres across and RV'd with the rest of the squadron. Sixteen and 17 Troop were on our left and the other Troops took the far side.

That was when we learned that the chopper wouldn't be coming at all for Mad Dog. It had flown across the border with orders to pick up a Delta patrol and then continue north to cas-evac our man, but the weather had been so terrible, it just managed to get the Delta patrol before turning back to Saudi. As it came in to land in a sandstorm the chopper crashed, killing everyone on board. These were Delta's only casualties of the war, and Mad Dog would have died with them if he'd made the journey.

Another chopper was dispatched and was due to arrive that night. Mad Dog spent most of the day slumped against the side of his pinkie, coughing, spluttering and being typically bad-tempered. His condition was stable, but there was no way we could keep carrying him around the desert in the wagons.

Under cover of darkness a CH47 flew into the wadi, dropped off supplies and then took possession of the patient.

'The cantankerous old fucker is all yours,' yelled Billy, but no-one could hear him over the rotors.

Weeks overdue, they'd finally delivered all the arctic kit from the Regiment's winter warfare stores – gloves, mitts, parkas, bobble hats, face-overs, quilted jackets and trousers. Better late than never. There were also PRMs (patrol radios) and UHF radios, which meant that at long last we had a means of communicating vehicle to vehicle. These should have been with us from the start.

The chopper rose, the rotors kicking up a storm of dust and stones. I lay on top of the equipment to stop it being blown around. Poor old Mad Dog, I thought; the stubborn old bastard would have wanted to see it through to the end. A brilliant soldier and an aggressive fighter, he was going to be missed.

Packing all the kit away, we moved towards MSR2. Our new orders were to ambush the road, attacking convoys at night and laying up during the day. The 'stop, watch and shoot' mission gave us the freedom to hit anything that moved on the motorway, then to drift back into the obscurity of the wilderness.

By first light three days later, we'd reached a large wadi north of the motorway. The cam nets were unfurled and we set up the stag position on a shingle hill that overlooked the bashas. Mountain Troop were in the middle, and for some reason some of the Mobility lads decided to put two vehicles together under the same cam net, only about 10 metres from our position.

We had just been briefed that, in future, if the A10s wanted to talk to us, they would drop low and wiggle their wings. On this particular morning an A10 had been buzzing around for what seemed like hours. Kiwi poked his head outside the cam net.

'Do you think he wants to talk to us?' he said.

'I don't know. When I get up on the stag position I'll check it out,' I said, glancing across the valley. The jet was obviously checking us out, but then appeared to drop out of sight.

I didn't take much more notice; I was too busy getting ready to go on stag. In the distance, however, I could hear the A10 wandering about the sky, making grunting noises as it fired its cannon. What it was aiming at was anybody's guess.

Beside me, Kiwi was tucking into a sachet of peaches with chocolate sauce, part of the new, boil-in-the-bag rations. This particular delicacy looked and tasted like shit; either Kiwi had the world's sweetest tooth or his taste buds had given up the ghost.

'Hey, Kiwi, give us your lamb stew and you can have my fucking peaches,' said Billy.

I left them negotiating and started tabbing up the hill towards the stag position.

I just about heard the explosion – maybe for a nanosecond – before it blew me off my feet. *BOOOOM!*

I found myself lying face down on the shingle. Rolling over and looking back down the hill, I saw the lads from 18 Troop scurrying from under the cam nets like ants from a nest.

'What the fuck was that?' I heard Billy shout.

Down to the right, Kev Phillips was on the ground, holding his ankle and yelling. I got to my feet and grabbed hold of my TACBE.

Up on the stag position, Ted Butterton had had a bird's-eye view of events. He opened up before I did: 'Stop! Stop! Stop! Brit Special Forces!'

Above us the A10 circled like a huge vulture. The stupid fucker of a pilot had mistaken us for a mobile Scud convoy and launched a Sidewinder.

'What are your co-ordinates?' a Yank voice drawled.

'You just fired at us; those are the fucking co-ordinates!' I screamed.

'Repeat that. Repeat that.'

Ted let loose: 'Listen you fucking moron – you're shooting at British Special Forces!'

'Oh my God, oh my God!' said the pilot, shitting himself. 'Is everyone OK?'

By now, all six lads from the adjoining 18 Troop pinkies had managed to get out. Billy and Kiwi were across with them, seeing if anyone had been injured. A smoking, 10-foot-wide hole had been blasted into the shingle, with the remnants of the rocket buried deep inside.

Unbelievably, our only casualty from the 'friendly fire' was Kev, who'd had a stone slice through his ankle. Billy got his medical bag and went to help him.

'Are you OK?' I asked Kiwi.

'I dropped my peaches,' he said.

The fact that no-one died was due to luck more than anything else. The Sidewinder will always go for the centre of the largest mass and the two Land Rovers provided the perfect target. But it was so late in the day, the wagons cast a long shadow, and this confused the missile just enough for it to miss by a few metres. I had no doubt that if the attack had been at midday instead of late afternoon, six lads from Mobility Troop would certainly have been killed.

The other reason they survived was because they were dossing and brewing up between the wagons. The debris and metal fragments sprayed upwards, ripping through the pinkies, but not reaching the occupants.

Even so, the whole incident should never have happened. Our co-ordinates were regularly passed back to RHQ and then passed on to pilots and crew. This tosser should have known our location.

Billy patched up Kev's ankle and, although it slowed him down, he didn't need cas-evaccing. Kev had been a brilliant runner, and if he hadn't joined the Army he would probably have been a top-class athlete.

From then on it became an SOP to drape Union Jacks over the wagons as our business card every time we established an LUP. We also got straight onto the TACBE the moment we heard an aircraft approaching, to make doubly sure we announced our presence.

Invariably the message back would be: 'Yeah, roger that, Brits, we got you visual. You take care down there, y'all!'

We moved off that night, shaken not stirred, towards the motorway. The ambushes were simplicity itself, just a matter of driving to a point where the road would become barely visible – a dark strip against the grey of the desert – then getting in position and waiting for enemy convoys and supply lorries.

We used the linear ambush technique, with a killer group forming an extended line facing the motorway, 20 Troop in the centre, 18 on the left and 19 on the right. One vehicle from the left and right flanks would drive about 150 metres west and east, to act as look-outs. As soon as something was spotted coming down the motorway, the message would be relayed: 'Three vehicles towards the centre from the west.'

'Roger that, three vehicles towards the centre, out.'

When the Iraqi vehicles reached a certain point, the ambush erupted from the centre with 66s, M19s, .50s and gimpies letting loose.

Disappointingly, there was actually very little traffic on the MSR after a while – the A10s and our presence made sure of that – and often it was a case of sitting in the gloom for hour after hour, staring at an empty road.

One particular night, the lightning and thunder was like something I'd only ever seen in a Hammer House of Horror movie. Forked and jagged, it cracked from the sky and lit up our cammed-up faces and beards. Rain pissed down, creating pools of water between our legs as we sat, watched and waited.

At least the cold didn't bother us any more. The arctic clothing was doing the business, although some of the lads had become so attached to the big Arab coats they were reluctant to stop wearing them.

Near first light, we drove off belting out the Doors song, *Riders on the Storm*. It seemed appropriate as we tore across the desert with rain lashing our faces and lightning hitting the distant rocks.

It had been weeks since an Iraqi aircraft had dared take off, but the bullshitter from Baghdad was still insisting that they were winning the war. Along with the A10 bombing raids, our nightly ambushes had effectively cut off the supply lines from Jordan and the number of Scud launches had dwindled to almost nothing.

Now the big question seemed to be when the Allied ground forces would pile across the border into Iraq. It could happen any day.

The other half of the squadron was operating outside the Iron Triangle, towards MSR1 to the east. Boat Troop had been bolstered by the arrival of two lads from B Squadron, Tony and Bob, who were in a smaller Land Rover (a dinkie) with no armaments apart from their own M203 Armalites. Because the dinkie lacked firepower, it was travelling between 16 and 17 Troop. On one particular night, 16 Troop had crossed the MSR from the north and the dinkie followed it over the six-lane motorway. At that precise moment, a large fast-moving truck froze it in its headlights for an instant like a startled rabbit before darkness returned. Tony and Bob hit the gas and managed to get across, just as the 4-tonner unloaded Iraqi troops who started firing into the shadows.

Sixteen Troop managed to cross back over the MSR and hook up with 17 Troop before they moved east a further 2 clicks. Meanwhile the Iraqis were still having a gun battle, lasting over an hour, firing at nothing. Eventually, probably convinced they'd wiped out a battalion, they continued on their way – only to be ambushed by their original 'shadows' a few clicks down the road.

Having created enough mayhem on MSR2, we headed north to MSR3. As we neared the motorway, one of the lead vehicles noticed some JCB-type earthmovers which were being used to resurface a section of the road. Looking east, there appeared to be a vehicle heading away from us. I stood on top of the spare tyre on the bonnet and tried to recognize what it might be. It was moving slowly and kicking up a lot of dust.

'What do you think?' asked Kiwi. 'No civvy vehicle is gonna risk being out.'

'Yeah, but what would a military rig be doing out in daylight?'

We moved after it, heading straight down the MSR3 at top speed, trying to catch up. A few clicks later we watched the vehicle head off on a smaller track.

'It's a mobile Scud launcher,' said Ted, looking through the binos.

Newlands said, 'And it's scurrying back to base.'

We followed at a discreet distance and eventually discovered a large military complex. As the Scud launcher disappeared inside, another vehicle appeared to be leaving; the occupants spied us and quickly returned to base. We were about 2 clicks away, on slightly higher ground, and could watch the Iraqi movements through binos while standing on the bonnets. I couldn't make out the weaponry, but the complex had a number of buildings painted in a creamy grey colour to blend in with the desert.

Now we faced a Mexican stand-off: the Iraqis knew we were watching them and vice versa, yet not a shot was being fired. To break the deadlock, we got on the net, gave the location and scrambled the jets.

Ted Butterton got on the net as they roared overhead an hour or two later. 'Hello US Air, this is Highlight Delta Forty-one. We have some trade for you.' He gave the eastings and northings to our new pal, 'Viper', who told us: 'Sit tight and watch the world ignite.'

The base took a fearsome pounding and explosions shook the desert floor.

'Death from above,' said Mad Mac as we turned and made our way off.

Next morning, the new SSM, Russ Nelson, who'd taken over from Stu McDonald, got us together and announced there were to be no more random targets; we were strictly back on Scud watch in the Iron Triangle until further notice.

We moved off in the late morning. It was a beautiful day – the best so far, with a warm sun and only a slight breeze. Des had been listening to his little radio again, and according to the World Service the ground war was imminent. When that happened we knew RHQ would pull us out.

We RV'd with the rest of the squadron in a long narrow wadi and used this as our base for night raids across the plains. It was now early March; the weather had become warmer and we even had a chance to take off our shirts for a few hours and catch some rays. Listening to the radio, I caught the sports results and discovered Wales had lost to England in the Five Nations Championship and Man United had taken a beating. I was gutted, but it made me feel closer to home.

It was good to walk about freely amongst the other Troops, and a big source of conversation was whether we'd be needed in the ground war. Most of us agreed that Sad Man had to be taken out and that perhaps we'd get a crack at the job, along with Delta. Washington would surely want his balls on a stick.

A few days after St David's Day, on about 3 March, I was rapping with the suntan gang of 16 Troop when Mad Mac called me over.

'Hey, Mike, just heard – A Squadron are moving south towards the border. We're out of here, boyo!'

That night we went out on another ambush patrol – a fairly fruitless exercise because nothing now dared move on the roads day or night. When we arrived back in the wadi the next morning, Ted Butterton gathered us together and said, 'Prepare to move. We're out of here at 0800 hours.'

I looked at Kiwi and Billy. 'Well, that's it, boys.'

'Old pointy tits got us through,' said Billy, slapping the picture of Madonna on Pegasus.

It was a good feeling, with big smiles all round. After packing our kit in the wagons we shared a last brew, using the precious chocolate sachets that we'd been jealously protecting in our bergens. The sun was up as we pulled out of the wadi and began the long journey south towards the Saudi border.

All five Troops formed one long squadron snake, with Union Jacks fluttering from the radio masts. Passing through a tunnel under the MSR1 we left the Iron Triangle behind us.

The Americans insisted on escorting us out and we had A10s above us doing victory rolls.

'It's sort of like having a faithful puppy that's fucked up and now it's rolling around trying to please,' I said.

Kiwi said, 'Yeah, well let's hope they don't do any more whoopsies on us.'

Nearing the border, we began covering the same ground that we'd crashed over in the dead of night, risking life and limb. I realized how lucky we were that none of us had been killed; it seemed impossible that we could have travelled all this way over such grim terrain without being shot to fuck or falling off one of the large features I was now looking at.

Passing the area of our first resupp site, I saw where the empty drums, ammunition boxes and gas bottles had been destroyed by my incendiary charge. What had triggered the anti-tamper release switch prematurely – animals or humans? Should I stop and look? As with the Patagonian who was missing his brother, I decided it was a question that would remain unanswered; I just prayed that it was animals, not kids and women who had stumbled on our rubbish tip.

We drove all day, and at about 4 p.m. crossed the border near another Crusader fort, on the Saudi side. What a fantastic feeling. My mind went back to the Falklands when the Paras walked proudly into Port Stanley and raised the British flag. Now another war was out of the way – how many more would I see, I wondered?

A Jolly Green Giant had landed near the fort, and as we got nearer, I could make out about two-dozen figures standing nearby. General Schwarzkopf and the OC had flown in to greet us, along with a posse of reporters and cameramen. Stormin' Norman came over and shook us each by the hand and patted us on the back.

He looked smaller than I'd imagined him, but had a booming voice. 'You've done Britain and the SAS proud, boys – and I'm mighty proud of you, too.'

The television cameras captured his every utterance for the American news.

After a tough drive, my face felt raw from the wind and sun. I desperately needed a shave and my hair was knotted in tufts like a New Age traveller's. It felt as if it was full of Barry Island beach. Carl Newlands looked like the wild man of Borneo, his two eyes peering out of a beard. Kiwi had chosen the Fu Man Chu look, with a weird droopy moustache, while Billy looked like an extra from *Shaft*.

All of us were exhausted but in high spirits. Mounting up, we drove hard to hit the motorway by 1800 hours. As darkness fell, we stopped briefly to take the hessian covers off the headlights – then I remembered we didn't have any bulbs in Pegasus so we took advantage of the column of light from the other pinkies.

As we drove along the dual carriageway a Saudi police car pulled up alongside our beat-to-shit pinkie, which still bristled with armaments. He started pointing at where our lights should have been.

I gave him a look that said, 'Is this the face that gives a fuck?' After all, what was he going to do – write me a ticket?

After being in the desert for more than six weeks, it felt bizarre to suddenly be back in civilization, surrounded by lights, cars, shops and hotels. Families were strolling through the streets and eating at outdoor cafés. There was a queue outside a cinema.

At the American camp, the news of our endeavours in the desert had obviously spread because as we drove through the main gate one of the military policemen looked up and said, 'Hey, it's the Desert Rats!'

Everybody seemed to know about us, and as we parked the

311

vehicles quite a crowd had gathered. The Yanks put a guard on the pinkies and the support weapons. We were given tents large enough to sleep twenty men in each, and instead of the British army camp beds the Americans had installed de-luxe models they called cots.

'We're having them on the pinkie when we leave,' I said.

'Exactly what I was thinking,' said Billy.

The showers were in a nearby tent. Kiwi and Billy started getting their filthy kit off.

Ray Scott came in and said, 'What the fuck are you doing?'

'I'm going to take a shower.'

'Fuck that, let's get a beer,' he said. 'This is an American camp; they'll have the dog's bollocks here.'

We headed down to the PX, the American version of our NAAFI, and burst through the door like tramps who'd just found a fiver on the footpath. Glancing up at the mirror, I caught sight of my face and didn't recognize it. I looked like some kind of feral animal in a shemag and cam cream. You don't realize how dirty you are until you get back into a clean, sterile environment. We were filthy, with straggly beards, mud-caked coats and body webbing that had clung to our unwashed skin for more than a month.

A group of Delta looked up from the tables and couldn't believe what they saw. They were all dressed in their starched DPM fatigues, looking spick and span, and we were like something the dog dug up in the yard.

My old mate Derek Summers went and got Ray and me a couple of cold Budweisers. The rest of the Delta lads slowly made their excuses and left. I couldn't blame them, we smelled awful.

The first bottle went down in one, washing away a wall of dust covering my throat. Looking up, I saw that quite a few of the others had found the bar. Some of them still wore the Arab coats and carried their Armalites, Minimis and pistols.

After three bottles of Bud I felt light-headed.

'I'm going to crash,' I told Ray.

The steam rising from the shower tent could be seen in the distance. I was so tired that I undressed before realizing I didn't have a towel. One of the Yank guards went and got me one.

Under the red-hot needles of water, I slowly slid down until I sat on the wooden pallet, cross-legged, and let the water soak through, easing away the bumps and bruises of a thousand potholes. And that's where I stayed. They say you can drown in only an inch of water; well, I fell fast asleep in the shower.

The next day, our pinkies were loaded on board the Hercs and we flew down to Riyadh. Stu McDonald was waiting for us, limping and having lost weight. I couldn't believe it; he should have been in hospital but old Mad Dog was up and barking like a rejuvenated Rottweiler.

He pulled D Squadron together and briefed us.

'Well done, lads. You did the business and I'm pleased to be able to say that we didn't lose a man.'

Not one for plaudits, Mad Dog then announced that anybody who had ideas of keeping the gold 'escape' coins had better think again.

'For every coin claimed to be lost, you'll be paying the equivalent into the Clock Tower Fund.' The Regiment had established this fund for the widows and families of guys who died; it was also used for ex-members who had fallen on hard times.

Kiwi and Billy looked at me. When our 'escape bergen' had been lost off the front of Pegasus on one of the worst night drives, we'd hatched a plot to say that we'd each put a gold coin inside. That way, we figured we could keep one each as a souvenir of the war.

'What d'ya reckon?'

'Fuck it,' said Billy.

'Yeah, it's not worth the hassle. We'll hand them back.'

Afterwards, we crowded into a hall and the OC arrived, smoking his cigar like a man who'd just had twins.

'Terrific job, lads. Just terrific. I can tell you that the Regiment is being held in very high esteem at the White House and 10 Downing Street. You've conducted yourselves with honour and done yourselves proud.'

A Squadron had also managed to get through without losing a man. Their sergeant major, Bobby McCann, who'd been shot and captured near Medesis Airfield, was returned by the Iraqis after the ceasefire. He'd been interrogated and tortured, but declined to tell them anything. In between beatings, they sent him to an army hospital near Baghdad where the surgeons did a brilliant job fixing his leg.

The Americans were all over the place and we took advantage of their five-star facilities. The cookhouse had to be seen to be believed. It was open twenty-four hours a day, serving steak, bacon, chops, pancakes, scrambled eggs. We'd been eating boil-in-the-bag crap for so long that my stomach suddenly thought it was Christmas. After piling up our plates, we grabbed handfuls of letters from a huge communal bundle. They'd all been sent by schoolchildren and families in America who wanted a pen pal on Desert Storm.

For the single guys among us there was also the opportunity to make the acquaintance of some of the American servicewomen. You know what they say about women in uniform. All of them were fascinated by the pinkies, which seemed to draw a crowd of spectators wherever they were parked. Among them were journalists like Kate Adie from the BBC, who desperately wanted to interview someone from the SAS. We all managed to give her a wide berth.

Meanwhile, we were swapping bits and pieces of kit with the Yanks. They wanted some of our DPM and we wanted everything they had. I still couldn't believe how much kit they had carted from Stateside. There were boxes of goodies like sunglasses, contact lense solutions, sun creams, shampoos, combs, brushes . . . you name it. There was even an entire warehouse full of mineral water in plastic bottles. We'd been drinking rust-brown water poured out of old drums and these guys had been guzzling fresh Evian.

We ripped them off shamelessly, of course. One of the lads had a pair of Northern Ireland gloves, made of leather with thick padding over the knuckles to protect the hands in a riot. The Yank was told this padding was actually a pouch containing an SAS survival kit. He did a swap for an American quilt cover – a prized possession. Afterwards I had visions of him on exercise absolutely starving and opening up his leather gloves to find a thick layer of foam instead of the expected survival rations.

Pegasus had managed to do the entire tour without getting a puncture; the photograph of Madonna was also intact, although she looked a little ragged at the edges by the finish. We dismantled a lot of the ordnance and packed up the ammunition, preparing for the flight to Camp Victor.

Three days after arriving in Riyadh, we lined up to board the Hercs again. Someone looked up and yelled, 'Hey, look – it's Postman Pat!'

Simon Nichols, the SQMS, was walking down to our snake carrying two enormous blue mailbags. I must have had thirty letters from Liz and my parents, as well as the obligatory one-a-war from Liz's sister and several from friends like Dio, Pauline and Rittaz.

As I started reading them, a massive guy in a USAAF flying suit strolled up to us.

'Are you guys from D Squadron?' he said with a thick Southern accent. He was a bear of a man, about 6 feet 5 inches, with dark glasses and a bald head – like George C. Scott playing Patton. There were flying badges all over his uniform and the front was unbuttoned, showing a carpet of chest hair.

'Who wants to know?' I said.

'I'm looking for some guys who nearly got killed by a Sidewinder about a fortnight ago.'

'Fuck, yes,' said Billy. 'That was us.'

'I can't tell you how sorry I am about that,' he said, lowering his head. His massive chest was shaking and I could see tears in his eyes. 'I don't know what happened. I've flown all over the world – I was even in 'Nam – and nothing like this has ever happened to me before.'

We had a chat and it turned out that he'd also been responsible for giving us an escort out of Iraq after insisting that his troop of A10s shadow us home – he'd been the one doing victory rolls above our heads.

'See those guys?' I pointed out 18 Troop. 'They've got a present for you.'

The lads had kept the tail-fin of the missile and now presented it to its rightful owner.

'Sorry it's broken,' said Big Jim Smith.

Clambering on board the Herc, I strung up a hammock and lay there during the entire flight reading my mail. My folks had sent me all the newspaper cuttings from the Welsh rugby season and also all the copies of the *Rhondda Leader* – weeks and weeks of them.

At one point, I rolled out of my hammock to stretch my legs and climbed the ladder into the cockpit. Ray was there chatting with the crew. Being from Air Troop, he knew most of the Special Forces pilots. They'd be doing their training exercises together somewhere warm like Florida, while Mountain Troop was hanging off a rock face in the pissing rain in North Wales.

The aircrew made us a brew and then Ray did the worst thing possible in that claustrophobic space – he took off his boots. It smelled like a dead sheep's innards and I immediately puked into my coffee cup.

Ray was crying with laughter. It's a wonder the pilot didn't pass out. I escaped to my hammock and the sports pages of the *South Wales Echo*.

After we landed at Victor, Ginge Collins, the Troop staff sergeant of 17 Troop, sought me out. His wife had sent him a video of the Wales v. England game in the Five Nations Championship that had been played at Cardiff Arms Park in January.

'We gotta watch this,' he said.

'Yeah, I'm in.'

First we had to park up next to the hangars, secure the weaponry and hand in the stores – which took bloody hours. All the ammunition, explosives and detonators had to be put away, along with the Milan missiles, GPMGs and Armalites. Most of the explosives, detonators and grenades were underslung on a helicopter and dumped in the Arabian Sea. This was a safety precaution because they'd been opened, bumped around and covered in dust and shit.

Having done the admin, Ginge and I went looking for a video recorder. We found one in the SBS hangar.

'Is it all right if I put on a rugby tape, lads?' I asked, as I found them all crowded around the TV. I thought they must have been leering at a blue movie, but they sheepishly moved back to reveal it was an episode of Walt Disney's *Wonderland*.

Although Wales lost the game, after a few beers I didn't give a shit. We all kicked back and celebrated – some more than most. Tim, the medic from Boat Troop who had helped save Taff in the wadi, got totally rat-arsed and woke me up in the middle of the night wanting to shoot the breeze.

'Fuck off, Tim,' I said, going back to sleep.

When I got up the next morning at seven o'clock he was still drinking, and he got sent to bed with a severe bollocking. I guessed the weeks of tension had finally got to him and he needed to let off steam.

It seemed the whole of Stirling Lines, minus G Squadron, were now occupying the hangars and corridors; I even saw the paymaster and the education officer walking about.

On that first day back, we rigged up a satellite TV connection so we could get CNN coverage of the war as well as BBC World Service. B Squadron were still doing their drills, although it was now clear that they wouldn't play a major role.

The post-exercise administration took for ever, with documentation to be filled out and kit handed back, such as the morphine, escape maps and promissory notes. I got back the letters I'd written to Liz and my parents in case I'd died. I didn't open them – I knew the contents were too morose. Instead I burned them.

A and D Squadrons were given a day of R and R, and the first thing I did was to buy a phone card so I could call home and speak to Liz and my folks. I phoned Liz first.

'Hi, it's me.'

'Who's me?' she said.

'Very funny,' I laughed.

'Where are you?'

'In a telephone box in Abu Dhabi.'

She sounded thrilled to hear from me and know I was safe.

Phone calls over, we hit the piss – all day and all night. Next morning I did a bit of shopping, buying presents for the girls.

Back at Victor we prepared ourselves for the return journey. Unlike after the Falklands, this time there was no fanfare or royal welcome. We crept into RAF Lyneham at night, and it was no different from coming back after a normal exercise. There are no heroes in the Regiment.

We reached Hereford in the early hours of the morning and dumped our kit off in the squadron lines. Then I ran all the way home and knocked on the door until Liz got out of bed. We had a big kiss and cuddle over a cup of coffee, trying not to wake the kids.

A few hours later, they woke up ready for school and came into the bedroom to find me home. All four of us were piled on the bed and it was a lovely feeling to be home. Two days later I was playing for the Regiment in the seven-a-side rugby championship at Bristol, which we won. Life goes on.

# 20

SLIPPING BACK INTO FAMILY LIFE DURING A MONTH'S LEAVE, I SPENT AS much time as I could with the girls. Yet it wasn't long before the strains on our marriage began to show again; the happiness and warm embraces of the first few days gave way to petty arguments over stupid little things that niggled both of us.

I still loved Liz and she loved me, but we both probably knew that our relationship was being held together by Rachel, Sarah and the fact that we'd known each other since childhood in the Rhondda valley. We'd come a long way together and neither of us quite knew how to recognize the end of the road, although we both knew it was coming.

When a soldier has done six or seven years in the SAS and reached the rank of corporal, it's quite common for him to be given a new posting, either within the Regiment or outside. I would happily have stayed and gone on to Training Wing teaching demolitions or CRW (counter-revolutionary warfare), but instead I received an external posting.

These are actually few and far between and tended to involve the LURP (long-range patrol) school in Germany or the jungle-warfare school in Brunei. However, I was offered a newly created position with the Intelligence Corps in Northern Ireland.

Although often affectionately called the 'green slime', the Intelligence Corps play a valuable role in operations, especially in Northern Ireland. This posting meant I would be the only SAS guy with the whole unit, and this appealed to me as I'd be given a free rein within a covert agency in the province.

It turned out to be two of the best years I spent in the Army, although Liz, of course, wasn't happy. During my time away, I was only allowed home for one week in every five.

I saw my mates only occasionally. Kiwi came around to the house one day, soon after he'd got back from an exercise in the States. He sat down in the living-room, drank a cup of tea and told me that he'd found God.

Something stopped me from laughing. I could tell from his eyes that he wasn't taking the piss, he'd actually found religion and become a born-again Christian.

'I'm happy for you,' I said, feeling slightly uncomfortable.

'You should think about it, too,' he said, sharing his new-found beliefs.

I shook my head. The last time I'd prayed to God was at Goose Green. When you're close to death, you need something to lean upon; I admired Kiwi for his stance in peace time.

Back in Hereford, after two years, I was now a sergeant in Mountain Troop – something I'd boldly stated was my ambition all those years ago on one of my surfing expeditions with Peter Terret. He, too, had fulfilled his ambition: I'd recently heard on the Rhondda grapevine that he was the manager of a successful mine in South Africa.

Initially, Liz found it hard having me home. It upset her rhythm and routine. Sometimes I felt like a stranger in my own home, but the saving grace was the girls; they were my focal point. Old-fashioned as it might sound, back home in the Rhondda I didn't know many divorced people; certainly there'd never been one in either of our families.

Back on the anti-terrorist team for at least the next five months, I thought I could spend more time with Liz and build some bridges. That hope was short-lived, however, as within weeks I was told that I was going to Latin America.

I broke the news to Liz in the kitchen.

'Oh, how long this time?'

'About four months.'

'What's the difference anyway, you're always going to be away – even when you finish with the Army you'll always work away.'

I hadn't thought about that. She was right, of course, and I didn't blame her for wanting someone who'd be there for her when the kids were sick or she was tired and upset. But what could I do? I couldn't say, 'Sorry, sir, I can't go to Latin America because there's a sports day at the school next week.'

Being in the Regiment is like a huge roller-coaster ride; you don't get off once you've started. And if I did leave – what would I do in civvy street? Maerdy pit had closed and some of the lads had gone north to Yorkshire to work. The images of the coalface came flooding back and I knew I couldn't go underground again.

Latin America was a better bet, I thought. After that I'd come home and truly give my marriage some serious effort. Somehow, I'd get it back on the right track. Definitely . . .

Two members of the Regiment were required for the four-month secondment training a police-cum-army anti-terrorist unit. The job required good Spanish and would mean living in the capital, with our own apartment and Land Rover.

When I got the posting, I arranged to take an advanced colloquial course in Spanish in preparation, slipping away for a half day here and there to attend classes at the camp.

My partner for the posting was John Geddis, a good mucker from way back. He'd been with 2 Para in the Falklands, passed Selection in 1984, but missed out on the Gulf. Built like a brick shit-house, he'd started Jap-slapping late in life, but had achieved his black belt.

He loved himself, no doubt, and kept telling me that if he wasn't in the Regiment he'd be in the movies.

'Hey, Mike, how long have you known me?'

'About fourteen years, why?'

'Do you think I'm better looking now, or what?'

He was also one of those weird guys who don't feel the cold. I could remember him in the Falklands with jungle boots on his feet, a T-shirt on under his Para smock and no gloves, as if it was a summer's day. Just looking at him then had made me shiver.

My first impression of our destination was the noise. A wall of sound rose from the streets, which were jammed with cars driven by men who steered with one hand permanently on the horn. Our apartment was in one of the wealthier suburbs in the north. The southern suburbs were desperately poor and crime-ridden, with thieves on every street corner. Life was cheap and it wasn't the place for the accidental tourist. On the roadside, everything known to man seemed to be on sale, from packets of condoms to car seats. If you stopped to barter, the cars behind would start blowing their horns. It was infectious, and soon everyone joined in, even cars going in the opposite direction.

Although we worked from the British Embassy, the anti-terrorist unit's camp was on the southern outskirts which meant having to drive through the poorer suburbs every day. I'd been briefed that the anti-terrorist unit was very patriotic and nationalistic, with uniforms that were loaded down with badges and braid. The images on the badges tended to be of things like daggers, skulls and lightning flashes, with slogans such as 'Death Before Dishonour'.

The camp had a training depot, and the recruits were beasted severely, but a captain told me, 'They're better off with us than out there,' pointing beyond the walls of the compound.

On the first day, making my way from the recruits' compound to the top of the camp where the unit were based, I saw a number of young lads in PT kit in trenches, crouching down with their hands on their heads.

'How long will they stay like that?' I said to Captain Gonzales, who was our welcoming committee.

'Until they learn to stop fucking up,' he said.

Gonzales was about 5 feet 6 inches of sheer nastiness and I decided to keep on his good side. He wore Para Reg wings on his chest.

'*Paracaidistas?*' I asked him.

'You too?' he said to me and John.

'Yes,' we both replied.

'Ah, Malvinas,' he said meaningfully.

We looked at each other. 'No, we weren't there,' I said.

As we were waiting outside the CO's office with Gonzales, the door suddenly flew open and we were greeted by a captain who was the 2 i/c. He answered to the name of Freddy and spoke perfect English.

The CO sat behind the desk, mulling over photographs of helicopters. He started jabbering in Spanish at nineteen to the dozen and I couldn't understand a word he said. It seemed to be a long lecture on fuck knows what, then there was silence, so I said, '*Sí.*' This seemed to please him.

It turned out that the CO wanted some new helis for his troops and was seeking our opinions. There was a photo of an Agusta among the pile, the same as we used back in Hereford.

'This one,' we told him.

'Ah!' – big smile on his face.

'That is the CO's choice as well,' said Freddy.

After a further burst of indecipherable Spanish we left with

Gonzales, who explained that we were about to become officers in his army and we were to get our ID cards done in the town.

Gonzales did the driving and seemed to enjoy terrifying people wherever he went. Apart from looking like Hitler's batman, he frequently wound down the window and put the fear of God into the peasants as we drove through the south side of town.

Parking looked as though it might be a problem in the congested streets, but Gonzales said, 'We'll just leave it here,' as we pulled up directly outside a building. There must have been at least sixty people waiting to have their photograph taken for different forms of ID cards. We went right to the front of the queue. Gonzales pulled the curtain across and barked at the photographer, 'Finish.' The woman inside was bundled out and our photographs were taken.

'Ready in twenty minutes,' the photographer said.

'Ten,' said Gonzales.

Outside in the bright sunlight there were stalls every 20 yards or so selling sweets, chocolates, pies, pastries, coffee and Coca-Cola. Gonzales bought us a brew that tasted like tar; we drank it and shuffled back inside. Our ID cards were presented; John and I had become captains in a Latin American army.

Part of the training was at the anti-terrorist camp and the rest in the mountains, where we put them through four-man contact drills, LUPing, caching, patrolling, navigation – all our basic, bread-and-butter drills. The setting was extraordinary, in the foothills of the mountains with snow-capped volcanoes towering above us. The sun was shining through the trees and llamas mooched about freely. Behind us the ground fell away to reveal the massive urban sprawl of the capital.

John and I had our own private army up in the mountains. We both coped well with our Spanish, although we found that the quicker we talked to them the quicker they came back – the same as in Morse code – so we kept it steady and they adjusted likewise. If burying your buddies after a battle is the downside of soldiering, then this had to be the upside – teaching Special Forces tactics to a Third World country's army in a location so beautiful it took your breath away.

The shooting range at the top of the camp consisted of about 200 square metres of open space, which looked more like a rubbish tip than a range. The far wall had been dug out from the side of a mountain and rose 30 metres to where slum houses hung perilously close to the edge. Young children dressed in rags would

322

sit with their legs dangling over the edge watching proceedings. Rounds were ricocheting off the rocks and flying all over the place, but these kids didn't seem to care.

One of the best marksmen in my sniper team was a weird-looking guy with a squashed-up face. The others used to make fun of him but he was an excellent shot. Sadly he was captured by border guards during one of the many jungle skirmishes between opposing countries over disrupted territory. The opposing forces hacked off his hands in punishment.

On one particular day, our trainees turned up late for work. When I asked the reason, I was told that overnight there had been a shoot-up in town. Five robbers had attacked a petrol station, but the anti-terrorist unit had been forewarned and set up an ambush. Four of the thieves had been killed on the spot and the fifth captured, interrogated and executed. Justice was swift and brutal in this part of the world.

As I left the camp one afternoon and walked towards the main gate where my Land Rover was parked, I saw a vision of absolute loveliness coming towards me. It was one of those heart-stopping moments; certainly my first since seeing Ursula Andress emerge from the surf in *Doctor No*. She was beautiful, quite tall for a Latin American, with light-brown skin, long black hair and dark eyes. An absolute goddess.

'*Buenas días*,' I gasped.

'*Buenas días*,' she smiled, walking onwards with her hips swaying.

I saw her again the next day at about the same time, and this continued for almost a week. Finally I asked her where she lived and she explained that she lived with her family in the poorer part of the city. We chatted about general things until she said she was running late.

'Where are you going?'

She laughed. 'I work at the camp, of course.'

I presumed she was an English teacher or a secretary. The next day I asked one of the captains about her.

'You mean the whore?'

'*No comprendo*.'

'*Sí. Sí*. A whore.' He poked his finger into his fist.

'Can you show me?'

He took me to a small outbuilding that looked like a Portacabin. About twenty-five guys were lined up outside, queuing to hump her brains out. My illusions were shattered. The Army employed

323

my goddess and gave her accommodation to service the soldiers.

On our weekends off, I'd often drag John out of bed at the crack of dawn and we'd head for the mountains. One of the Brits at the embassy was a keen mountaineer, so we'd drive up into the hills, pick our mountain and start tabbing. It would take most of the day, sometimes two.

The views from the top were stunning; this had to be one of the most beautiful countries in the world. A lot of the mountains were defunct volcanoes with debris and silt still clinging to the sides. After spending ten or twelve hours reaching the summit, the run down was great fun because it was impossible to hurt yourself; the silt would break any fall. Occasionally we'd meet other mountaineers from Britain and the US, who'd forked deep into their savings to be there, but thanks to the British army we were getting paid for it.

This particular part of Latin America is also one of those places where trouble is always lurking not far below the surface. Someone at the Brit Embassy told us that trouble was brewing in the capital because the major American-owned oil company had decided to double petrol prices overnight. For the poor it was a hammer-blow and, not surprisingly, there was a great deal of anger towards Americans.

The youths who regularly hung around the south and central part of the city had always looked menacing, but now they had an excuse. Covering their faces with scarves, they began torching cars with petrol bombs, burning tyres and building barricades in the streets.

Because of the riots and roadblocks, John and I couldn't get from our apartment to the training camp. We tried to run the gauntlet one morning and eventually had to turn back because of the flames and storm of rocks hurled by rioters. We phoned the camp and they told us that for our own safety we should seek sanctuary in the British Embassy. Only the two most senior diplomats knew exactly what we were doing in the country. The rest of the staff assumed we were on a language course.

After a week of rioting we came out of the apartment one morning to find all the windows smashed on the Land Rover, probably because it had a small Union Jack on the side window. After getting it repaired we made sure to keep it garaged for the duration.

During one particular lull in the fighting, John and I thought we'd go out for a couple of beers. The streets were fairly deserted downtown except for the roaming gangs of looters and hoods. We found a bar and settled down for a quiet ale or two.

A few hours later, we emerged to find a gang of seven youths around the Land Rover. I noticed the back window had been smashed and that one of the guys had some rice flails – the sort of thing I remembered seeing Bruce Lee spinning around his body.

I had my own theory about Jap-slapping. It looks good, just like a choreographed dance routine, but put Bruce Lee in a confined space with Mike Tyson and I knew who I'd put my tenner on.

One of these wankers was busy rummaging around inside our vehicle, looking for something to steal. It was mindless vandalism, not political protest.

As we moved towards the wagon they made the first move, and their last. That night there must have been quite a run on steaks and ice-packs in that part of town because my knuckles were certainly sore by the time I'd finished doling out the shiners.

The next day we had the Land Rover fixed and decided to stay indoors until public order had been restored.

Eventually things settled down a little, although as gringos we still had to be careful. The south side of the city was strictly out of bounds; getting robbed was a certainty, but there was also a good chance you'd finish up floating face-down in the faeces-infested river.

On a relatively quiet night, John and I went down to our super-market to stock up. It was on the edge of the red-light district and I noticed a blue Honda cruising up and down – five up, not a problem. They spotted us, again not a problem – it's a fact of life in Latin America; you just have to be aware of things.

Inside the supermarket, two girls, one blonde, the other coloured, were paying for their groceries. We bought our groceries and as we left I noticed that the two women were being hassled by the occupants of the Honda, who were clearly drunk. Two of them had got out and the other three were shouting encouragement from inside the car.

'Are you having any problems?' I asked the women.

'Fuck off, gringo,' spat one of the men.

I ignored him and asked the women if I could give them a lift home. By now the other men were jostling me, believing that I'd somehow robbed them of sex with an American woman. They weren't like the youths we'd seen off a few nights earlier – they were grown men who had some size as well as a gutful of liquor. I tried to calm them down as John opened the Land Rover doors and the women jumped in the back.

Just as the women were telling us that they were both schoolteachers who taught at the local American school, the Honda Civic drove onto the pavement, parallel to our car, effectively blocking our escape. The leader of the gang started banging on my window. I wound it down and asked him what he wanted. He had a whisky bottle in his hand which he pushed into my chest, wanting me to drink. I never touched the stuff and certainly wasn't about to share a bottle of the local gut-rot with him. His breath stank and he had the sort of face you want to slap.

'*Señoritas! Señoritas!*' He leered through the window, licking his lips.

I thought about the baseball bat we kept under the front seat in case of trouble. Because of the angle, there was no way I could get it out. At the same time there were five of them, all big boys, drunk and dangerous.

'Fuck this, let's get out of here,' said John.

I couldn't back out as there was a line of cars behind. There was only one way to go. I put the V8 Land Rover in first gear, slammed my foot on the accelerator, let out the clutch and hit their car side on with enough force to push it clear into the centre of the road. The panels along one side were completely crushed.

As we drove off, the gang leader hurled the bottle of whisky. It shattered the back window and hit one of the girls on the back of the head, opening up a nasty gash. Her blond hair was soon soaked red.

'We've got to find a police station,' I said.

'And then a hospital,' said John, trying to stem the flow of blood.

The Honda began to follow. The police station was behind us, and because of the city's complicated one-way system it was going to take hours to get round, particularly as the streets were still a mess of burned-out cars, with gangs of kids running around carrying guns and Molotov cocktails.

The Land Rover stunk of cheap whisky and the blonde girl was shrieking. It turned out the coloured girl was a local, not American, which explained why she was so calm. She'd have been there, seen it, bought the T-shirt.

The city was flashing past us in a kaleidoscope of colours. I kept trying to lose the Honda – even driving the wrong way down a dual carriageway – but couldn't shake it off. The blonde was screaming and crying into her friend's lap; John surveyed the situation, looking back through the rear-view mirror.

'Shit! What was that?'

'They've got a gun,' he said.

'Get down! Get down!'

A second shot shattered the wing mirror beside me.

'How many guns?' I asked John.

'I can see at least one. Passenger side at the front. The driver is throwing stuff out of the car.'

Four more rounds whizzed past us, thankfully missing their target. I used all my fast-driving training to stay ahead, but he had the extra speed and local knowledge to catch up.

By now it was about ten o'clock at night, with no police around. It seemed to be open season, with looters smashing shop-front windows and torching cars. Our little battle hardly attracted any attention. After fifteen minutes of trying to escape, I realized there was no chance of out-running them. They were right behind us and obviously in no mood to negotiate.

'I've had enough of this,' I said to John.

He looked at me and knew immediately what I was thinking. 'Yeah, so have I, let's do it.'

We stopped on a dual carriageway beside a large park which was crowded with people. The Honda overtook us and cut in, but by then I'd already grabbed the baseball bat and was out of the door.

John was already flying towards the passenger door of the Honda, knocking the occupant backwards. The driver had a blade; this was the fucker that had thrown the bottle. The bat hit him square on the head and he went down.

Furious, and hell-bent on damage, I wasn't in the mood to show mercy. These arse-holes had terrorized us, shot at us, and would probably have raped the two girls if we hadn't been there.

John was inside the car, piling into two of them in the back; a third was starting to crawl away. I pounced on him like a cat from a wall; the bat did the rest.

I pounded the back window, shattering the glass. The car and its occupants were my entire world in that mad moment; I went completely nuts and began smashing the headlights and windows. I even ripped off the bonnet and began tearing up the engine. Knowing that a car was such a luxury in this part of the world, I knew it would hurt their credibility and their wallets.

As I finally stopped swinging, the enormity of the situation began to sink in. We were facing the wrong way on a dual carriageway, with a large crowd starting to form. Five of their compatriots had been beaten senseless, the baseball bat had cracked and split in two and we were about 20 feet from our Land Rover.

'Let's get the fuck out of here,' I said.

'You start up, I'll stay by the door.'

The crowd moved closer, seething with resentment. If one moves, they'll all come, I thought. Holding their stares for as long as possible, I finally leaped behind the wheel. For one fleeting second I thought about Pegasus in the Gulf not starting. Then click, *boom*, the V8 roared. John jumped in, we crossed the central reservation and pulled away, not stopping until we reached the nearest hospital.

The blonde teacher had twelve stitches in the back of her head and, in the mêlée, I'd accidentally hit John's hand and busted all his fingers. Because of the adrenalin, it took him a while to feel the pain.

Although we got a big thank you from the American school for protecting their staff members, we decided not to report the incident to the embassy. For one thing, we didn't know if the police had been informed, or whether some of our attackers had been seriously hurt.

'It was self-defence,' I said. 'They had knives and guns.'

'Yeah, I know,' John shrugged, 'but what if we killed one of them? There was a lot of the red stuff . . .'

'But at least it wasn't ours.'

Neither of us went out again until the riots were over.

Near the end of my four-month stint, the news on CNN was dominated by the civil war in Bosnia. I was due to be replaced, while John stayed on in Latin America for another few months to create some continuity with the change-overs.

About a week before I was due to leave, I rang the squadron office in Hereford to make my weekly report.

'Just reporting in,' I said to the squadron clerk. 'Any news?'

'The head shed are in a meeting right now – some lucky fuckers are off!' he said.

'Where to?'

'You know I can't say that,' he said.

It didn't take me long to put the pieces together. Some of the boys are off to Bosnia, I thought, and I'm stuck here.

The next day, I arranged an appointment to see the ambassador and explained that I had orders to get back to England at once because of Bosnia. This wasn't exactly true, but it worked, and he arranged a ticket for me. I flew back to London within twenty-four hours and, as usual, was met by a driver from the MT section.

328

He laughed as he saw me emerge from the customs hall.

'I know why you're back, Mike, but I took a carload of lads to Lyneham this afternoon.'

'Fuck it!'

I'd missed the boat by just three hours.

At Hereford I went to see the 2 i/c, Peter Davies, and asked him about the chances of going out to Bosnia. A couple of other lads who'd been away on various courses were also trying to link up. The word was good – we'd be on a flight within a week.

I couldn't have asked for anything more. It gave me a chance to see the girls and to get across to the Rhondda for a few days. I arrived back in Hereford for the following weekend and sat tight until the flight left for Bosnia on 8 March.

Just before leaving, I heard some sad news about Geordie Vale. Unbeknownst to me he'd been down at Brecon, working at Derring Lines; he'd developed cancer and had been taken into hospital there and died alone.

I'd lost touch with all my 2 Para mates except Stan the Man. Geordie was too young to have died that way and it saddened me deeply that nobody from the Parachute Regiment, including me, had been with him – and all the time I'd only been an hour up the road.

# 21

I FLEW INTO SPLIT A WEEK BEHIND THE OTHER LADS. AS I STEPPED OFF THE plane into a blast of freezing Adriatic air, Ian saw me grinning.

'Finally, a war in a cold climate and I've actually packed my woolly vest,' I said, slinging my bergen into the back of a Land Rover.

The smile didn't last; as I looked around me, there was barely an airport building that didn't show signs of damage by Serbian artillery.

British HQ was in the Croatian army barracks and my orders were to move off the next day to join the elements of UKSF (United Kingdom Special Forces) at Gornji Vakuf, about 200Ks away to the north-east. I'd been briefed that our objectives were first, to map out the front lines so that the UN would have a clear idea where each ethnic side was located; secondly, we had to report on the situation in the Muslim enclaves that were holding out against the Serbs. Horror stories had been coming back to UNHCR about malnutrition and atrocities in these designated areas, but nobody knew exactly what was happening because no observers had managed to get in or out. Our job was to report the truth.

'How do we get to this Gorny Fuckoff?' said Ian. He'd decided against trying to wrestle with Serbo-Croat.

'They're giving us a driver.'

The Land Rover was painted like a milk bottle, with the UN peace-keeping insignia stencilled on the doors. 'We call them white elephants,' said our wheels man. 'We'll be taking the diamond route – it's 100Ks or so to Livno and then we go across the Raduša mountains towards Prozor. That's the main HQ for the Croats in the area. Then we go up to Gornji Vakuf.'

'Looks a bit bumpy,' I said, studying the map on my lap.

'The engineers have kept the roads open. They're in section strength, seen a bit of action. There's a lot of rogue Muslim elements up in the mountains. One lot are called the Fishhead Gang: they just stop people, tie them up, take their money and rape their women.'

I turned to Ian. 'Fishhead Gang? I didn't know they still made Flash Gordon movies.'

According to the driver, another gang, who claimed to be mujahidin, used to come into the Royal Engineers camp up in the mountains to have a smoke and a drink. One day they turned nasty, held the engineers at gunpoint, took an armoured APC and kidnapped the lieutenant. They found it abandoned miles away, with the rupert tied up in the back.

'Charming,' I said.

'Welcome to Bosnia.'

It must have been quite a feat of engineering to push a route through the mountains and we were humming along the slushy dirt tracks; heavy snowdrifts were still piled up at the roadside, the legacy of a harsh winter. After a couple of hours, I gave the driver guy a break behind the wheel. Within twenty minutes, a Lada full of civvies came round a blind bend at a rapid rate of knots. It hit us head on, spun off the road and tumbled over the edge.

The driver and I grabbed the medic kit and scrambled down the ravine while Ian drove back to the nearest village. The car had fallen more than 30 metres and was a wreck but, unbelievably, the passengers, all Croatians, had survived. We got them out, bandaged them up and helped them back up the road. Despite all this, they still managed to find the wherewithal to scream and swear at us.

Ian arrived with some engineers to pull out their vehicle, along with an MP who took the particulars. As soon as he opened his mouth I knew he was Welsh. Normally, two Taffs in the one place would pause to reminisce about the Grand Slam rugby teams of the Seventies, but the walking wounded were getting nasty. They'd been driving on the wrong side of the road, but insisted we were to blame for the accident.

'You boys had better make tracks,' said the MP. 'I've got your details.'

As we disappeared down the road the driver turned to me and grinned, 'Like I said, welcome to Bosnia.'

Up in the mountains, looking down towards Prozor, it seemed as if nothing was the matter in this beautiful terrain. The sun was shining and the last of the winter snow and slush was beginning to thaw.

As we neared the town, the reality of war-torn former Yugoslavia impinged on the scenery. Croat soldiers were walking about in twos and threes, all carrying G3s. Although most seemed to be wearing the same German army jumpers and cut-off DPM jackets, their boots were all different styles. This was the sign of a put-together army, which was exactly what the Croats were – butchers, bakers, carpenters, schoolteachers – all uniting against the Serbs or the Muslims.

Prozor was the Croat HQ in this part of the world and, apart from the sight of so many soldiers, it could have been any village in any European country. As we climbed the long winding hill out of the town, my eyes were drawn to heaps of rubble where the odd house had been flattened by artillery shells.

At the top of the mountain there was a strange statue known as Tito's Monument, that looked like something Salvador Dali might have sculpted after a night on the piss. Alongside, the Croats had positioned some triple-As and anti-tank weapons and, further up in the woods, a howitzer. Artillery cases and empty boxes littered the ground.

On the outskirts of Gornji Vakuf we bumped into a UKSF patrol. I recognized three of the lads immediately, but there was a new guy with them. He strode across to the Land Rover.

'I'm Raymond Wallis, your boss out here.'

Boss Wallis looked all right. Ian knew him as ex-1 Para and a good guy.

The patrol were coming back from the Croat positions above Gornji Vakuf. Leaving them, we drove into the Muslim enclave. The village looked like the news footage I'd seen of bombed-out Beirut. Not one single house had been left untouched and many had been totally flattened. The mosque stood battle-scarred and pock-marked.

The closer we came to the town centre the more devastated Gornji Vakuf became, yet somehow daily life carried on; kids picked through the rubble of bombed-out buildings, grizzled old men smoked cigarettes in the shade and grandmothers, dressed in black, queued to buy food and to collect water.

The Croats dominated the surrounding ridges and had pounded the Muslims for months, yet they couldn't take the village. The Muslims simply refused to yield, fighting in trenches outside their gardens, from their cellars and kitchen windows. This was their home.

'If the occupants survive,' our driver said, pointing at the demolished house, 'they just go off and move into someone else's house.'

This pattern was being repeated across Bosnia.

Ironically, the Muslims and Croats had once been united in their fight against the Serbs, but now they were bitter enemies. This stemmed from the fate of a Muslim village in the Zavidovići area, which was being defended jointly by Croats and Muslims against the Serb aggressors, until the Croats decided to pull out at short notice, thereby fracturing the fragile alliance. Gornji Vakuf was testament to the fall-out.

As we reached the far end of the village, we neared the front line. Above us, to the left, was the cemetery, and the front line ran along the cemetery wall. A no man's land of about 50 metres separated the Croat and Muslim trenches.

The only way I could fathom it was to imagine that Maerdy and Ferndale were at war back home in the Rhondda valley and the front line was my old grammar school.

HQ for us was an old factory that had been bombed by Croat heavy weapons. In happier times it had made JCB-type vehicles. There was also a company of Coldstream Guards based inside the hangar and we were separated from their sleeping quarters by black hessian sacks that formed makeshift curtains. There were personnel, too, from other units, civvies from the UNHCR and peacekeepers from Malaysia and France – a right jumble.

Over a brew, I caught up on what was happening. Four of the lads were off that night to Maglaj, a Muslim enclave 75 kilometres north of Sarajevo. Entirely surrounded by Serbians, apart from a gap in the line held by the Croats, the town and inhabitants had been continually bombed and starved for eight months.

Maglaj was a special case because all three sides were fighting for the same piece of territory – the Croatians (HVO), Bosnian Muslims (BIH) and the Serbs (VRS). I wasn't told much about the four lads' mission because of OPSEC (operation security); everything was on a need-to-know basis in case of capture. It was always better for you and everyone else if you didn't know too much of the story. The lads' immediate task was to find a way to get into Maglaj, report their findings and to set up a designated LS with transmitters (CADs). This would hopefully clear the way for aid flights to feed the starving population.

Previous attempts to parachute food had failed because they needed better guidance from the ground. The planes were being forced to fly at 14,000 feet because the Serbs had SAM missiles with a range of 12,500 feet; as a result, more than half of the food containers that were being ejected were falling into Serbian hands.

In Maglaj, the mostly Muslim women and children would hear the chutes open and run outside waiting for the food to land. It was dark, and they had tin cans on sticks with candles burning inside. The Serb soldiers blockading the town then tried to pick them off, one by one, firing at the lights. They were killing women and children looking for food. That was the type of war we were involved in.

Mark Clayton, Kiwi, Billy Adams and Pete, a new lad from Air Troop, were going to Maglaj. The rest of us were to stay at Gornji Vakuf and continue mapping out the front lines for the UN. This seemed an enormously difficult task because it involved winning the trust of both sides, Croats and Muslims, while we tried to establish the exact position of the foremost trenches.

That evening, I sat around a table with Raymond Wallis, Ian and Nick Farmer, another Geordie with an indecipherable accent. Poring over the maps, we analysed the best way to proceed.

We'd been tasked to deal with the Croatian commanders, while four other lads, all from A Squadron, negotiated with the Muslims. The idea was to gain permission to go up on the front line and then use the Rockwell Collins GPS (global positioning system) to record the exact location of every trench, heavy weapon and troop HQ. This information would then be given to the UN.

'So how do we get permission from the Croats?' I asked, pouring another brew.

'A guy called Krakowski is the key,' Wallis said. 'He's a former major in the Foreign Legion and runs the brigade HQ at Prozor. The troops love him because he's a professional soldier – most of them are part-timers. If we get him onside, he'll give us the nod.'

'It's a shame these fuckers can't stop fighting themselves,' I said. 'They could join forces against the Serbs.'

'The common enemy,' said Ian.

'Right now we just have to map the lines and report,' said Raymond.

The next morning we had a briefing with the A Squadron gang, and then we set off in Land Rovers to our respective sides – us to the Croats and the others to the Muslims.

Although Raymond could speak French and I had Spanish, neither of us could speak Serbo-Croat. Kiwi would normally have done the interpreting, but he'd been sent to Maglaj. Sue, a young captain in the WRAC, was assigned to us as interpreter. The idea of having a woman on the mission didn't appeal to me and I said as much to Boss Wallis, although I couldn't change the decision. I wasn't sexist, but I worried about her physical fitness in this mountainous terrain.

Krakowski's HQ was in an old warehouse and showroom on the outskirts of Prozor. As we pulled up outside there were soldiers going in and out, wearing all types of uniform. The four of us – Raymond, Nick, Sue and myself – were taken through various corridors until we reached a large door flanked by two bodyguards wearing DPM with the red and white chequered Croatian flag on their arms.

Inside, a grey-haired man of medium height and swarthy complexion sat at a desk with one of his commanders. Krakowski rose, put his cigarette in an overflowing ashtray, and shook each of us by the hand. Sue made the introductions as chairs were found.

Because Krakowski had been a legionnaire, Raymond asked him a question in French. Immediately they clicked. Krakowski had been in the 2nd Rep, a famous parachute battalion in the Legion.

'We're both ex-Paras,' said Raymond, motioning to me.

'Which battalion?' asked Krakowski.

'I was in 2 Para,' I said.

'Ah, the Falklands.' He was smiling.

'Yeah, Goose Green.'

He blew air out of his cheeks and shook his head.

Suddenly we had a rapport going. The airborne brotherhood had worked in our favour, and before long Raymond and Krakowski were chatting like old muckers, discussing foreign armies and different campaigns. After conversing fluently with the Latin Americans for the last four months I found it frustrating not being able to join in.

We explained to Krakowski that we wanted to map the front lines and needed his permission. 'It would be helpful to us if you pulled back until we're finished,' said Raymond. 'We're asking the Muslims to do the same.'

Krakowski thought about this and had a brief conversation with

335

his 2 i/c. Then he picked up the phone and asked to speak to the Thomaslavgrad Brigade, one of the front-line units.

'You've got some people coming to see you,' he said to them. 'I want you to listen to their requests.'

He gave us the grid of a farmhouse which served as the HQ for the Thomaslavgrad Brigade. All the main honchos of the Croat units under Krakowski's command were meeting there that morning, and Krakowski was sending us to see them.

Leaving Prozor, we followed the directions until we reached a muddy track that twisted through the fir trees, finally emerging into a large clearing with a farmhouse in the centre. Smoke billowed from the chimney and there were blazing oil drums dotted outside with bodyguards huddled around them.

The two bouncers at the main door were expecting us. Ian took a packet of cigarettes over to the rest of the bodyguards, who were eyeing us suspiciously. Western cigarettes are like an international currency.

The head shed were inside, sitting around a large open fire. Most of them were older types, captains and majors in their thirties and forties who were big and weather-beaten; everyone seemed to be smoking. Coffee arrived in tiny little cups and was strong enough to keep you awake for a month. It tasted like a cocktail of Bovril and Pernod – absolute shite – but I drank it because I didn't want to offend anyone.

Then a bottle was produced and they began pouring a clear liquid into glasses.

'What is it?' I asked Sue.

'Slivovitz,' she whispered. 'It's the local drink.'

'Like vodka?'

'It's like nothing you've ever tasted.'

Someone proposed a toast. OK, here goes. It felt like I had swallowed a landmine as it exploded in my guts.

When the formalities were over, we explained that we wanted safe passage to the front lines. There was very little discussion; Krakowski's message had done the trick and they offered us guides.

The two lieutenants met us in a village about 2 clicks down the road. One of them carried an SMG (sub-machine-gun) that looked like a relic from the Second World War and the other had a Heckler & Koch G3. Neither went big on small talk.

I still couldn't believe the size of the Croatians; they were huge fuckers and made most of the UN troops look like boy scouts.

They had no idea we were SAS, but I thought they sensed we weren't exactly cartographers from the *AA Guide to Bosnia* because we were operating at the forward edge of the battle area.

We set off into the hills on a seriously hard-core tab, through forests and along ridges. The Croatian guides could really move, but they were 'clean fatigue', weapons only. We carried sat nav, VHF radios and our bergens packed with spare batteries, doss bags, ponchos, clothing and rations in case we kipped out.

I'd had reservations about whether Sue would have the stamina to keep up, but now I had egg all over my face; it turned out she was a fell runner and fitter than a whippet. She also had excellent linguistic skills, and her softer image had helped in the negotiations.

Eventually, through the woods, I could make out the Croatian positions, two or three soldiers in each. This section of the line had sustained various attacks from the Muslims, but they had held their position for over a year.

Looking closer, I could see little huts and even a makeshift bar and café set back from the front line. The trench positions were excellent and well organized. Having been there for so long, the soldiers had turned them into a home from home, with bunk beds, all tidily made, and little windows. I half expected to see net curtains and flower boxes. The only thing I didn't like was the way they left their mortars pointing down into Gornji Vakuf. That's how accidents happen.

The soldiers seemed friendly and quickly produced another bottle of slivovitz. They all fancied Sue, of course, and a few wanted to look at our SA80s because of the good x4 optic sights. Most of them had AKs and the Heckler & Koch G3s – the BMW of rifles. Their weapons were actually better than ours, but I wasn't going to tell them that. We had been given SA80s to blend in with the regular army, much to our displeasure.

I had the Rockwell Collins, which could give our position down to 1 metre on the ground within thirty seconds, using satellites. This was how we mapped the front line, plotting the exact positions of every trench, HQ hut and heavy weapon. Meanwhile, on the other side of the valley, the three or four A Squadron blokes were doing exactly the same with the Bosnian Muslims.

At every new position, a bottle of fiery slivovitz came out. Feeling obliged not to spurn their hospitality, pretty soon I started to feel light-headed.

The Thomaslavgrad unit had been drawn from an area below

the mountains and they operated virtually on a shift system. They'd tab from their village into the mountains, with one shift doing days and another doing nights. Most of the other Croat troops were from further away, near Split. They'd do two weeks at a time and then travel 60 miles back to their villages in coaches for R and R. They looked like football fans going home after a game.

That night, back in Gornji Vakuf, we plotted the TAOR (territorial area of responsibility) for each side and then sent the information back to HQ.

The following morning, Raymond, Sue and I went back to see Krakowski and asked him for permission to visit another section of the front line. This became almost the daily routine and, more often than not, he gave us the nod. The A Squadron boys had similar success with the Muslims on the far side of the valley, and slowly both sides began to trust us.

One particular morning, we met Victor, a Croatian unit leader who must have been about forty years old and had the complexion of someone who'd spent most of his life out of doors. His troops had been shelling Muslim houses down in the valley and we needed them to stop if we were to map the line.

Victor invited us into his bunker, which had a bed, table and chairs. He dragged out the inevitable slivovitz and I handed him a cigarette, leaving the packet on the table.

'We would like you to pull back, Victor, to this position further back off the ridge,' said Raymond, unfurling a map.

'Why should I do that?' he growled.

'Because we want to get down into no man's land.' Raymond nodded towards the valley floor which was covered in fir trees and criss-crossed by muddy tracks.

'We're also getting the Muslims to agree to pull back. Call it a temporary truce.'

Angrily, he spat: 'I don't make deals.'

I said to Sue, 'Tell him the Muslim BIH are with our comrades; tell him they've agreed to pull back. They're even giving us a guide into no man's land.'

I saw Victor's eyes widen. This was a complete bluff, of course, but these men were so proud that neither side was likely to agree unless they felt the other had conceded first. They'd been trying to kill each other for two years and the hatred ran deep.

After much posturing, Victor agreed with a slight nod of his head.

'Will you give us a guide?' asked Raymond.

'Yes, the best guide,' said Victor. 'I will take you.'

The next morning, we drove down the mountain in the Land Rover with Victor and a posse of bodyguards. Meanwhile, on the far side of the valley, another UKSF patrol was being guided into no man's land by the local BIH leader.

Nestled on the valley floor beside a river was a Muslim village that had been mostly abandoned, apart from the houses farther up the mountainside which were occupied by the BIH. It had probably once been an idyllic place but now it bore the scars of two years of fighting; windows, walls and doors were riddled with small-arms fire; clothing and household goods littered the streets and an upturned wheelchair lay in the dirt. The sight of it made me feel sick.

What the fuck happened here? I thought. The village had been ravaged, but by whom? Which side?

The other UKSF lads entered the village at about the same time as we did and a confrontation between Victor and his Muslim counterpart seemed inevitable.

I was surprised when I saw the BIH leader. He'd been a university professor before the war and had a long grey beard that made him look like a kindly grandfather. His band of bodyguards were all young, in their twenties, wearing bandanas and looking like extras from an MTV video shoot.

Greybeard and Victor immediately recognized each other. Victor had been a former pupil and they shook hands warmly. Then they started chatting away, discussing the possibility of coming to an arrangement about the front line. The gist of things was that Greybeard wanted the village back, and Victor kept pointing down the valley to the pine woods that were held by his troops but were overlooked by Muslim positions.

One of the younger Croat soldiers recognized a childhood friend among the Muslims. They had gone to the same school and later worked together as disc jockeys. Suddenly they were hugging and patting each other on the back. There were tears in their eyes. It was crazy. For two years they'd been trying to kill each other.

Ian went back to the Land Rover to get the tension easers – cigarettes – and we let them talk and smoke themselves into an early grave.

'It's fucking unbelievable,' I said, wandering over to the river with Fergie, an ex-Para with A Squadron. 'Why are they fighting each other?'

We went up the hill towards the Muslim positions that the A

Squadron lads had been mapping. These boys had good inter-locking trenches that ran from house to house, enabling them to fall back to another position if one house was taken. The Croats had done some frontal assaults over the months here but had been unable to dislodge their enemy. The Muslims had the right idea, and it was rooted in sound infantry tactics from Gettysburg to Goose Green: if you have the high ground and well-defended positions, you are the kings of the castle. The Argies had strayed from the plot, but these boys hadn't.

By the time I returned a bargain had been struck: teacher and pupil had negotiated for the Croats to pull back off the ridge above the village and the Muslims would retreat from positions over-looking the pine forest to the east.

Our exercise to map the front lines had triggered a genuine dialogue between rival commanders and an agreement that might ease the tension and save lives. The satisfaction I felt was enormous.

Not all of our forays into no man's land were this successful. One Croat leader refused to co-operate in pulling back; somehow the A Squadron lads managed to convince the local Muslim commander to visit the Croat positions in a show of good faith and to help our mission. We picked him up and drove him into the Croatian area. A short man with nervous eyes, he was absolutely terrified and stuck closely to me, but I admired his courage. Muslims had been bombing this area for years and he could see the hatred and disdain on the faces of the Croats. It would have been so easy for one of them to shoot him – there were only three of us and Sue – but I would have defended him. We'd given our word.

We drove to a small village above Prozor that had changed hands a number of times. The Muslims would win it back from the Croatians only to lose it again. It was in a hell of a state, with every house either torched or bullet-ridden.

As light rain fell, we walked through the streets with our small passenger and the local HVO commander. There was no love lost between them. This time the Muslims held and dominated the higher ground, while the Croats had built an intricate system of trenches up to the front line like something from the First World War.

'What's this building?' Sue asked.

'The schoolhouse,' said the Croat leader.

'Christ!' said Ian.

There was so much debris, it was hard to imagine children sitting in classrooms and playing outside. I shook my head and let it pass.

Two shots rang out. The Muslim commander stiffened.

'OK, OK,' I said. 'Stay here.'

Raymond, Sue and I went forward to investigate.

Through my binos I could make out a figure lying prone on the hillside, motionless. He'd been shot from the forward trench by a Croat with a G3. The shooter explained to his leader that the Muslim had been venturing forward into no man's land to take up a sniper position on the hill.

A man lay dead and the rival commanders began arguing. The situation grew tense. Ian and I went forward, working our way up a track in the Land Rover and stopping in dead ground a couple of hundred metres from the top. I knew landmines were scattered like confetti on the ridge.

Getting out, we carefully walked towards the body. I looked up to see Muslim soldiers skylined on the ridge, watching us approach.

'They must have seen the Land Rovers,' Ian said.

'I hope so.'

I stuck my arms out with my SA80 in one hand in a surrender symbol; they acknowledged me with a wave back. Then they started down the hill towards the prone soldier; they wanted to collect their dead mate.

As we reached him, I noticed a collection of dead wood around him. One round had taken away the side of his head, another had driven an airway through his chest.

In the drizzling rain, the Muslims wrapped the body in a poncho and dragged it away.

'Why was he here?' I asked. 'What possessed him . . .'

'He was collecting firewood,' said his friend. 'He wasn't armed.'

Another day, another pointless death in Bosnia.

The Land Rover carrying Nick, Raymond, Sue and the Muslim commander approached across the dead ground. Amazingly, a deal had been struck between the two factions and both sides had agreed to pull back to create a buffer zone and stop the sniping we'd just witnessed.

The Croatian marksman was unrepentant. He claimed the Muslim had come down into no man's land without asking permission. I took an accurate grid with the Rockwell Collins. It was 700 metres between the shooter and the body. The guy had been hit with both rounds; in any soldier's language that's fucking amazing shooting.

What began as a process of a few UKSF guys mapping the front lines for the UN had provided an opportunity for opposing troops to make decisions and reach agreements that would prevent casualties and perhaps pave the way for peace. It was a far cry from the usual cut and thrust, blood and guts activities of the SAS.

Occasionally, it became necessary to split the team when we had to cover a wide area. On one particular day, Sue, Ian and I were walking the lines in the mountains west of Prozor, tabbing across a high feature to meet up with the others 15 kilometres to the north. Our guides had left us, wishing us well; as far as they were concerned there were no more positions between us and our RV.

On the tough hot tab, Ian and I were sweating buckets, but Sue, annoyingly, looked as fresh as a daisy. We climbed for three hours along the front line before reaching the top. As we came down off the steep ridge it was getting dark, and we entered a farming area.

Nearing some buildings, I heard a commotion at the back. As we rounded the corner of a barn, we stumbled upon about thirty or forty Croatian soldiers who were having some kind of meeting. By the looks on their faces, they obviously weren't expecting company.

'Shit! I don't like this,' I muttered to Ian.

I pulled Sue back, wanting her behind me.

These guys hadn't been briefed that we were coming and we had no guide.

The soldiers were eyeing Sue up and down, making leery comments. She stepped forward wearing her UN beret and asked for their leader. There was no response. They didn't take her seriously.

'Ask them again,' I said, making clear the question was coming from me.

There was still no answer, only menace. I wished I had a G3 instead of the SA80; better still a gimpy.

One of the soldiers said something and I could see Sue flinch.

'What did he say?'

'It doesn't matter,' she said.

The same Croat sauntered across and brushed past me. He grinned lecherously and reached out towards Sue.

He grunted in surprise. I had a grip on his wrist like a vice and was close enough to whisper several words in his ear. I doubt whether he understood any of them, but he got the message.

Around us the tension had just doubled, and I knew that there were fingers on triggers. Sue tried again. She told them that I'd been briefed by Krakowski to mark out the front line for the UN. We had permission to be there.

One of them went away with his radio to get confirmation. When he came back, the tension eased slightly, but I wanted out of there pronto. We backed away, eyeballing them. From a safe distance I punched in the grid of the farmhouse, noting that it was some type of HQ.

Ten minutes later, we met up with Raymond and Nick. While we were waiting for a Land Rover pick-up to take us back to Gornji Vakuf, one of the local farmers came out and invited us inside. He'd been in the *Luftwaffe* in the Second World War and had dropped bombs on Birmingham and Coventry.

Once he got talking about Britain there was no stopping him. It turned out he supported Nottingham Forest, and we both admired the manager, Brian Clough. The dreaded slivovitz came out and then some smoked ham, freshly baked bread and cheese; it was probably all the food they had in the house. As I broke bread with my grandfathers' enemies, I thought, What a difference fifty years makes.

A few days earlier, on the front line, I'd come across a couple of Croatians in their seventies who wore Iron Crosses. They'd fought for the Germans in the Second World War, one as a Para and the other in the SS. By rights they should have been watching their children pushing their grandkids on swings or playing chess in the dappled shade, but instead they were on the front line of yet another war.

Gornji Vakuf had not seen a UN patrol on foot for a very long time, certainly not since hostilities between the Croats and Muslims began. The resident battalion, the Coldstream Guards, were a keen unit, but their OC didn't seem interested in leaving the barracks. We figured we might shame him into action if we started patrolling the village, and then they could take over from us.

On our first daily patrol, we got dropped off at the southern end of the village where it was sparsely populated. Placing our blue berets firmly on our heads, Ian, Sue, Nick, Raymond and myself worked together, treating it like a Northern Ireland brick patrol.

Entering the village from the road, we pushed left along streets that were deserted save for a couple of people. Locals eyed us suspiciously from behind boarded-up windows. Many of the windows and doorways were bricked up and they entered their

343

houses via the cellars. They'd dug tunnels and built passageways so they could visit neighbours without venturing into the open.

The streets were narrow and littered with the stone from houses that had taken direct hits. This same debris had been used to brick up windows.

I was shocked by the destruction. I could see where mines had gone off and mortars had hit – most of them fired from the very ridges that we'd been mapping. The scene reminded me again of Beirut, total devastation apart from a few crumbling chimneys and shrapnel-pocked walls.

Slowly the children began leaving the doorways and shuffling closer. Sue was like a magnet for the kids, who were still wary of us and our weapons.

'What are they saying, Sue?'

'They're glad to see us.'

I had chocolate and biscuits on my webbing and I looked at the parents. They nodded and I began dishing them out. The kids were in seventh heaven, laughing and dancing about us.

It doesn't matter where you are, from Belfast to Bosnia, it's always the children who suffer most in war. They might not have a clue what's going on around them, save for the pain and suffering, yet a hatred for the enemy is formed in their young minds which they will carry throughout their lives. Just ask any Catholic kid up on the Falls what he thinks of the Proddies over the wall in the Shankhill.

At the bottom end of the village there was one particular breeze-block wall that a round from a heavy-calibre weapon had gone clean through, and that allowed villagers to peer through to see if the Croatians were on the other side. If the coast looked clear, they'd sprint across a small gap and climb towards their neighbours. This is how you borrowed a cup of sugar in Gornji Vakuf. The resilience of these people amazed me.

There were snipers' slits on the gable ends of the buildings that peered over the wall into no man's land. The ground beyond was littered with debris: burned-out cars, a stinking dead dog, an upturned pram.

When we reached the site of the cemetery the children disappeared. This marked the front line between the factions and, looking up, I could see the Croats' positions just above the headstones.

Continuing down the road, we crossed Edwards' Bridge, named after Lance Corporal Edwards from the Royal Welsh Fusiliers, who'd been shot from the cemetery by the Croats. Looking at the distance, it was another example of the Croats' amazing marksmanship. Then again, they got a lot of practice.

Back at the factory, we had a debrief.

'What do you think?' asked Raymond.

'Well, we didn't get shot,' said Nick, grinning.

Sue added, 'The parents were suspicious, but I can't blame them . . .'

'At least the kids were won over.'

Raymond said, 'OK, we'll go out again tomorrow. We'll start talking with the locals, first the soldiers, then the civvies. We'll show them that the UN cares.'

The next day we visited a local café where a lot of the Muslim fighters congregated out of sight of the Croat weapons. Having Sue on the team gave us an edge because she could cut through the machismo bollocks that male fighters normally adopt, giving each other the 1000-yard stare. She gave us a softer image and made us more approachable.

At first they were wary, but after a while they opened up. Compared to the Croats and Serbs, the Muslim troops were quite small and mostly young lads, yet they all looked battle-hardened and were heavily armed. They were all schooled in the theory of street fighting, because so many of their villages had been under siege from Croats or Serbs.

These guys had been through a rough time. Many were living underground in trenches and defending a wasteland. It was crazy. You only had to turn the corner from the café and you could see the Croat campfires about 250 metres away.

I got chatting to Ivan, one of the main Muslim leaders in Gornji Vakuf. Blond, blue-eyed and wiry, he spoke excellent English.

'Where did you study our language?' I asked.

'I'm Swiss,' he said, smiling wryly.

'So what the fuck are you doing here?'

'I came here three years ago on a holiday to visit my family. Then this happened.'

'Why don't you go home?'

'When I tried to get out, the Croatians wouldn't let me go,' he shrugged. 'So I fight.'

It was so blunt and matter-of-fact, I had no answer.

Ivan said the village folk appreciated our patrols – it gave them security. Just like the Catholics in Northern Ireland in 1969, I thought. I hoped we didn't make a similar mess of it.

The hearts-and-minds campaign continued and we began putting out two patrols every day – one in the morning and one in the evening. I used to arm myself with sweets – the local kids called them *bon-bons* – and it was real Pied Piper stuff. They'd skip along beside me, giggling and trying to reach into my pockets.

Then one morning, the Coldstream Guards followed our lead. Their very first patrol was led by the OC, a major. He'd obviously seen us going through the town and decided, if they can do it, then so can we.

It was good to see the crap hats patrolling – it saved our sweets.

A few days later, we had orders to visit a village near Tracanica in the mountains. It, too, had changed hands three or four times and nobody had been there for months. We were escorting three UN observers, a woman and two men, who wanted to investigate reports of atrocities.

The village was way up in the mountains with sheer cliffs on either side. God only knew how anybody lived there in the first place. The Croats were on one cliff and the Muslims on the other.

Krakowski agreed to give us access through his front line and the A Squadron representative got the local Muslim leader to approve our visit. We were met by the Croatian commander, the biggest fucker I'd ever seen. He was festooned with ammunition and carried a grenade launcher under his arm as if it was a stick of French bread.

It took all morning for the Royal Engineers to clear a path through the mines. As we walked into town, a crystal-clear mountain stream bubbled over rocks alongside us and the sun warmed our backs. Below us, the team from A Squadron were waiting with the local Muslim commander – another symbolic meeting was about to take place.

I noticed a body lying beside the road. It had no head and was a pile of rag and bones that had been decomposing for six or seven months. I couldn't tell if it was male or female.

'I know this man,' the Croat commander said. 'I recognize the clothing.'

The village had a name that sounded like Hell – an apt description. At first glance it looked like something out of Hansel and Gretel – all cobbled stones and white-washed walls. Then, after 10 yards, we came to another body. Again, no head. Then another. Then, as we turned a corner, there were more. One, I could tell by the clothes, was that of a young woman; next to her outstretched

346

hand was a Madonna album. I logged the locations on the Rockwell Collins and moved on.

Items of property were strewn all over the road. Books; an old-fashioned transistor radio, smashed; bottles of shampoo; baby stuff. Bullet holes had ripped through the walls and roofs had been torched. Every now and then, part of a body protruded through the rubble.

Did these people try and run? Did they stay and fight? Did they try and hide? There must have been a hundred dark secrets that this pretty little village held.

It had clearly been ransacked and the people raped and murdered. I didn't know who was responsible. Perhaps it had been taken by Hoss, the Croat extremists, who were known to pillage entire villages and slaughter the occupants. Or maybe it was taken over again by Muslims and mujahidin.

But why cut off their heads?

The UN observers took photographs while I tried to log the bodies. It was futile really; they were all over the place.

In the Falklands I'd seen dead men strewn across battlefields and the devastation of places like Port Stanley. In Iraq I'd seen desert encampments flattened by air raids that no-one could have survived. Yet nothing in my soldiering career had prepared me for this. I sat down and put my head in my hands, my job done.

One of the UNHCR people came over.

'We've found one of the heads . . .' he said, motioning towards a football field at the top of the village.

I walked towards it and then wished I'd stayed away. The head was in the centre of the field; for all I knew I was standing where the world's most grotesque football match had been played.

As a soldier I had witnessed many gruesome things, but this place sickened me to the pit of my stomach. Mick Connor's words at Goose Green came back to me: 'If you pray for rain you've got to deal with the mud.'

The engineer in charge was from Wales; he came and stood beside me, slowly shaking his head.

'I haven't seen anything as bad as this,' he said.

'It's never going to end, you know.'

'What do you mean?' he said.

'There's too much hatred.'

Just a few weeks later he stepped on a mine while clearing a path into another village and was killed.

# 22

MEANWHILE THE SIEGE OF MAGLAJ CONTINUED AND SOME OF THE UKSF lads were trying to get inside the blockaded town to report to the outside world what was happening.

According to local intelligence, the Serbs held seven-eighths of the line around Maglaj, including the checkpoint on the approach road; they also had most of the high ground, from where they were shelling the enclave with heavy guns. The Croats had the remainder – a small piece of the line to the west of the town and north of Novi Seher, a Croatian stronghold.

International media attention was focused on the enclave. Not much was known about it, except that it had a population of about 40,000 and that the main industry was a large paper-pulp factory to the south of the town which employed most of the menfolk; they were also protecting this from the Serbs. UN forces had been trying to get inside for weeks, using conventional routes and means, but had been driven back. There were stories circulating of women and children starving to death, and we'd heard rumours that one European newspaper was offering seventy grand to anyone who could get a reporter and photographer inside. Yet despite all the pressure, the Croatian military command refused to let their 'gap' in the Serbian line be used by the UN, the foreign media or Muslim refugees. Anyone attempting to enter or leave would be shot.

The River Bosnia runs north to south through the area, and one option that was considered was floating down the river by canoe

348

into Maglaj. An LO (liaison officer) heard about an interpreter who'd managed to escape from Maglaj; he went to see the woman, who told him that her husband had also tried to rescue her by canoe. He'd been blown up by the Serbs.

'People have tried to swim, too,' she said, 'but the river's forty metres wide in places and the Serbs have mined every stretch of it.'

Back to the drawing board.

Another option considered was to use a small back road that ran from Zavidovići to Maglaj. Perhaps, using IR headlights and NVGs, a small vehicle could slip through the Serb line without being spotted. This, too, got knocked on the head after a recce of the route: the Serbs had cratered the road and blown the bridges.

They considered free-falling into the town by parachute, but this was against UN regulations, so eventually they settled on trying a night-time helicopter drop. An operation was put together using Norwegian pilots, but on the first night the heli was hammered by machine-guns and almost shot down by a SAM rocket fired by the Serbs. Abandoning the mission, they returned to Tuzla, but volunteered to try again. The following night, Mark Buckler, Kiwi, Billy and Pete clambered aboard one of the Norwegians' Sea Kings. The chopper landed for just long enough for the lads to get out and then came under fire. The tail fin was strafed by rounds but the pilot managed to fly off again.

Once on the ground, the four lads were hammered from all sides, with both the Serbs and Muslims assuming they were the enemy. They scrambled for cover and sat tight till daybreak when they crept down to Maglaj and surrendered to the Muslims.

That same night, operating entirely independently, Tony from G Squadron and Paul from D Squadron succeeded in sneaking through the Croatian line and entering the enclave from the north-west. After months of trying, two patrols had managed to reach Maglaj within hours of each other.

It was several days before they linked up. In the meantime, Muslim commanders took Mark and the lads to a bank building, where they were interrogated. With Kiwi interpreting, Mark explained that they were UN troops who had come to help. They were given a room at the bank, where they set up a comms centre to communicate with Hereford and Gornji Vakuf.

They discovered a town slowly being squeezed to death. 40,000 people were on the verge of starvation, with stocks of food running dangerously low. The Muslim fighters had been under intense pressure for almost eight months, showing remarkable

349

courage. They worked on a shift system, spending two days on the front line, fighting two different armies, before being relieved by the next shift.

With the Coldstream Guards patrolling Gornji Vakuf and most of the front lines having been mapped, our job was over. I was itching to get to Maglaj. The OC gave us the nod and we set off in two Land Rovers – myself, Ian, the boss and Mark.

We aimed to stop off at the ECO factory, the HQ of a large UN force based at Zavidovići, 25Ks to the south of Maglaj. The Light Dragoons and a platoon of engineers were stationed there, along with a few UKSF boys, including my old mate Greg Richards.

We drove north on the main supply route via the Muslim stronghold of Zenica. Out of range of the Croat and Serb artillery, this town had never been bombed. As a result, the minarets of local mosques still dominated the skyline – I still called them 'wailing towers' after my sleepless nights in the Gulf.

Just outside Zenica, as the light faded, the road disappeared without warning.

I slammed on the brakes and Ian, who'd been dozing, hit the dashboard.

'Fucking hell! What is it?'

'Look at that.'

'What happened to the bridge?'

'Good question.'

We got out of the Land Rover and peered over the edge. More than 60 feet below, water swirled and tumbled over rocks. The bridge had been bombed, and if we'd arrived a few minutes later, in total darkness, we would probably have driven straight over the edge and almost certainly have been killed.

The road from Zenica to Zavidovići was dodgy as hell. Two relief workers driving lorries had earlier been ambushed and beaten up by a rebel band of Muslims. Fearing they were going to be shot, the lads had jumped in the river. One of them escaped, but the other was dashed to death on the rocks.

That was the problem with this sort of war. A lot of fuckers were just doing their own thing – looting, burning, raping and killing.

We found the ECO factory by another route. Greg Richards seemed to be running the joint along with Boss Clark and it was great to see Greg again. I hadn't seen him since before our Latin American stint and he always made me laugh. They had Tim Nixon with them, the medic who'd saved Taff Powell in the Gulf, together with an interpreter who was so bald and grossly over-weight there was no other name for him but 'Mr Blobby'.

Only 6 clicks to the east of the factory was the Serb front line, which ran north up towards Maglaj along the high ground. This was where their heavy guns were located, well within range of Maglaj and also Muslim-held Zavidovići.

The UKSF lads here had been doing much the same as we had in Gornji Vakuf. They had LOs with the Croats and Muslims who would provide tip-offs about upcoming brigade meetings of the various factions so that the UN could keep tabs on exactly what was happening.

Meanwhile, Mark Buckler and the lads in Maglaj continued sending situation reports on the tac sat. The UN finally had eyes inside the enclave, and the first priority was to get medical supplies to the embattled Muslims.

At Zavidovići Greg and the lads had made arrangements to be billeted at houses with local families. Raymond and Mark bunked at the ECO factory, while Ian and I stayed with Greg, whose 'land-lady' was a nice old Muslim woman whose husband was off fight-ing at the front line.

Sitting around the kitchen table, we discussed how to get a road open into Maglaj for the relief lorries. We all agreed that the Croatian 'gap' in the ring of steel around Maglaj was still the most realistic route and conversation centred around Novi Seher, a Croatian stronghold just north of Žepče

'What if we arranged a meeting with the local commanders at their HQ?' I suggested. 'You know, tell them we want to map the front line and do a recce at the same time?'

Greg said, 'The commander is a guy called Nico; I've met him.'

'What's he like?'

'Young, smart – he's a good egg.'

'OK, let's ask the LO to do the necessary.'

Greg stayed in Zavidovići while Ian and I drove to Žepče and met the UN's LO. That night we stayed at his house, which had no roof or electricity and was isolated on the edge of town.

'Why don't you stay with the rest of the squadron?' I asked him.

'This way the Croats know where to find me.'

Next morning, on the net, we heard Greg report that Serb rounds were landing in Zavidovići. I could hear them exploding as he spoke. Apparently it was a retaliatory strike because, the previ-ous day, the Muslims had brought several artillery pieces into the town and hidden them inside a shell of a building. Overnight they'd fired at the Serb front lines east of the town, obviously hoping to knock out some of the big guns that were bombarding Maglaj.

It was a daft idea and the Serbs took swift revenge. They didn't give a fuck about civilian casualties and launched an artillery strike directly at Zavidovići. Quite a few shells landed in the village that morning but, miraculously, no-one died.

Our meeting with Nico had been arranged, but first we had to drive back to Zavidovići to pick up Greg. Just before we arrived, the Serbs shelled again. Two rounds rocked the houses, smashing windows and sending plates and crockery flying.

Tim, Greg and Mr Blobby had run outside. Two children, no more than ten years old, wandered about dazed, bleeding and crying. Their grandmother had fallen in the potato field with a huge chunk of shrapnel embedded in her back. Tim went for the woman, Greg for the children. Mr Blobby radioed for an ambulance from the ECO factory.

The kids had lacerations that needed stitching, but their grandmother was seriously wounded and there was no doubt she was dying. Ian and I arrived on the scene just as she was being casevacced; we heard on the radio an hour or so later that she'd died on the way to hospital.

I knew I was supposed to be impartial, but seeing such mindless violence made my blood boil. At least the Muslims had fired at enemy artillery; the Serbs had retaliated by bombing innocent women and kids, not giving a fuck who they killed.

Although their stitches would eventually heal, I knew the children would be scarred for life by the sight of their grandmother dying before their eyes as she picked potatoes for their supper.

That afternoon we drove to the Croatian stronghold of Novi Seher for a meeting at the brigade HQ. The village had to be seen to be believed. All three factions were fighting over it and every house had been hit, some completely flattened and others bullet-scarred inside and out. It reminded me, on a smaller scale, of images I'd seen of Warsaw in the Second World War.

Nico's headquarters was in an old hotel – one of the few buildings that was still intact. Nearby, a group of old women sat on some steps and dried out beans they'd gathered from the fields. Younger women were making soup for the HVO troops who wandered in and out.

'Nico's ready to see us now,' said the LO, emerging from the hotel.

He took us upstairs and ushered us into a room where Nico sat behind a desk. Brigade commanders in the British army are normally over fifty and senile; Nico was much younger, in his thirties. He was big, with long hair down his back and he reminded me of a Hell's Angel.

'You want to go up to the front line?' he said, chewing on a burned match and eyeing Sue.

'Yes,' said Raymond.

'If you want, you can do that.'

'Brilliant.'

'But I wouldn't if I were you.'

'Why not?' I asked him.

'Parts of the road have been mined.'

'Which parts?'

He shrugged. 'Exactly.'

Coffee and slivovitz were poured. Nico relented a little and said that he'd guide us towards the front line, but then we were on our own. Afterwards we'd have to come back and report our findings.

As we left the hotel, I looked at the utter devastation and asked him, 'Why are you fighting?'

He raised his hand and pointed up the hill at a building in Serb-held territory. 'You see that house there?'

'Yeah?'

'That's my fucking house.'

I couldn't argue with that.

Ian and Mark stayed at the brigade HQ while the rest of us pushed through Novi Seher, north towards the front line between the Croatians and the Serbs. In this neck of the woods the main thrust of the Serb offensive was against the Muslims in Maglaj and the Serb versus Croat contest had been relegated to second division. That was how confusing it all was. One of the few certainties was that Maglaj was surrounded and locked up tight.

Towards the high ground, there were various farmhouses where platoons of HVO would sleep, eat and rest before returning to the front line. Landmines had been scattered like confetti, and eventually we stopped the Land Rovers and went forward on foot rather than risk getting a gearbox through the arse.

As we reached the front line, the Serbs could clearly be seen manning positions below us. The Croats were fiercely protecting a piece of ground about 700 or 800 metres long that dominated the surrounding land. The Serbs wanted it badly but had been unable to take it.

As I walked the line, marking positions with the Rockwell Collins, I realized there was little hope of establishing a safe route into Maglaj through the Croatian 'gap'. There was simply too much activity.

I thought about Paul and Tony. This was where they'd managed to sneak through at night into the enclave – a remarkable achievement that took a lot of balls.

Turning back, we arrived at Novi Seher late that afternoon. Nico had a visitor – the local commander of the Hoss. These guys were Murder Incorporated. The regular Croatian soldiers capture a village and then they send in the Hoss to rape and pillage. In the Second World War, the Nazis and the SS thought the Hoss were too barbaric in their interrogation methods, which gave some idea of their table manners.

The Hoss commander was just a kid really, no more than twenty-five. He had a skinhead haircut and a face full of scars. Nico had brought out a bottle of slivovitz and offered Raymond and me a drink. We felt obliged, even though neither of us wanted to drink with the Hoss commander.

This wasn't to say that the Muslims didn't commit atrocities. They had their own outlaws and butchers, many of them drawn from the Afghani mujahidin, yet no other group had the power to strike such terror into people's hearts as the Hoss.

Still no closer to finding a way into Maglaj, we headed back to Zavidovići that evening, none of us realizing how dramatically the political landscape would change within the next twenty-four hours.

It began the next morning when the UN LO observed a Croatian brigade meeting at Novi Seher. Surprisingly, there were Serbian leaders present, and he radioed back to Greg that something big was brewing.

Rather than go to the ECO factory and wait for further word, Greg used his initiative and drove directly to the Serbian checkpoint about three miles south of Maglaj on the MSR. The Serbs seemed to be moving south, pulling away from the enclave.

Greg radioed the ECO factory, asking for the dragoons to be sent up to the checkpoint. The reinforcements duly arrived, bringing their Scimitars and Scorpions, giving the UN a strong presence at the checkpoint. Then Greg pulled a carton of 200 fags from the Land Rover and went to do some 'negotiating'.

The Serbs were still moving south. Tanks and coaches, piled

with soldiers, drove through the checkpoint, firing their weapons into the air. Croatian troops began arriving. The whole scene was bizarre – I thought these guys were supposed to be fighting each other.

The Serbs made it clear that Greg wasn't welcome. They began pointing towards the Land Rover and telling him to fuck off, but he wasn't having any of it.

It emerged that a deal had been struck and the Croatians were replacing the Serbians at the checkpoint. The ordinary Serb soldiers couldn't understand this. They'd been fighting there for months and were suddenly surrendering territory.

The deal was shrouded in mystery. All I could think was that the Serbs had given up on Maglaj, having miscalculated the resilience of the population; now they wanted to get out of the checkpoint area and the only way was to cross Croatian territory, past Žepče and Novi Seher, then north to Serb-held Tešanj. In return for providing safe passage for Serb troops, the Croats took control of the checkpoint.

Whatever the motives, the deal was destined to go down in Bosnian history as having broken the eight-month siege of Maglaj.

Amid the commotion at the checkpoint, Greg spied Nico.

'I've got to get inside Maglaj,' he told him, slipping him the carton of cigarettes.

Nico shook his head. 'The Serbs don't want the UN involved.' He wasn't about to jeopardize the deal.

'But we've already got UN soldiers inside the town – they're friends of mine.'

Nico laughed. 'There are no UN in Maglaj.'

'Yes there are. They're coming to meet me.'

Greg said he'd radioed Mark Buckler at the bank in town and he was coming out. Nico still didn't believe him.

Serb tanks and coaches continued to stream out as Greg, accompanied by Nico, headed off towards Maglaj for an RV with Mark. At one point he spied two T55 Russian tanks hidden inside houses. Only a few inches of the barrel protruded, facing towards Maglaj. This was how the Serbs camouflaged the tanks – they simply drove through the walls of houses and hid inside.

Mark and Greg met on the road to Maglaj and shook each other's hand. The meeting was quite symbolic because the road had been shut for eight months.

When Nico saw Mark, the look on his face said it all: How the fuck did you get in there? He turned to Greg. 'OK, get your boys in there as quickly as you can.'

We'd been listening to Greg's messages on the net from our position in the hills above Novi Seher. Driving like the clappers, we headed back towards the ECO factory and RV'd with Greg and the rest of his patrol.

Already the news was being transmitted that the siege of Maglaj had ended. Within hours the international media, UNHCR and a wagon-load of food were on their way. The road to Maglaj had been officially reopened by Greg Richards, using only bribes and a lot of balls. There was no way of knowing how long the situation would hold. As we drove past the checkpoint we could see that the Croatians were clearly pissed off at UN involvement, but we had to get relief lorries in there pronto.

Under grey skies and in drizzling rain, we drove through the deserted outskirts. Maglaj was a large town, with a well-established hospital and schools. Blocks of flats lined the streets, some of them reduced to rubble by the Serb artillery.

The Muslim soldiers had done well to hold out and groups of them eyed us suspiciously as we drove into town. Although we offered the hope of food and other supplies, many of them thought of us as intruders on their turf.

Billy was waiting outside the bank to meet us. He had a group of kids dancing around him, laughing and smiling.

'At least someone's pleased to see us,' I said, shaking his hand.

'I hope you bought some bon-bons.'

All the windows of the bank had been bricked or boarded up, so inside it was dark and dismal. There was no running water or electricity anywhere in the town. Instead the villagers had been using a handpump in the street to draw water from an underground well.

The Muslim HQ was also in the bank and they'd provided the lads with some bunk beds. Dumping our gear upstairs, Mark Buckler gave us an update on recent events. He said there was to be a relief flight coming in that night and we had to monitor the parachute drop and liaise with the Muslim commander about timings.

Using the tac sat on the flat roof of the bank, we could communicate with Hereford and also with Italy, where many of the Allied aircraft were stationed. These, along with carrier-based jets in the Adriatic, were enforcing the no-fly zone over Bosnia.

Mark and the lads had already deployed CADs (controlled air delivery system) on the landing site and C130s had made several drops during the previous week. We went out that afternoon to check the CADs again, making sure everything was OK for that night's drop.

Muslim fighters milled around the place, cradling their weapons and looking sullen. They didn't like us at all. Huddled in groups of five or six, they stood around doorways and occasionally fired a full magazine into the air, taunting us.

This was where it all fell down for me. We'd been instrumental in opening the road into Maglaj; Mark's patrol and guys like Paul and Tony had risked their lives to get through, and now we had food coming for their starving wives and children. I felt like firing a burst back and saying, 'Is that how you fuckers say thank you?'

For the first time in months, the streets were packed with women and children, who skipped after us, giggling and laughing. This made the menfolk even angrier.

I could understand how the pressure had got to some of them. The night before I arrived, one of the fighters had burst into the bank with an AK47 and threatened to kill Kiwi, Pete and Billy. A big bearded bloke, he was yelling and screaming his head off – after eight months on the front line, he'd finally cracked. Kiwi spoke to him for a long while and convinced him to put down the gun. In a flash the lads were on him, pinning him to the ground. He was hauled off by the Muslim authorities and got a fearsome beating at the local nick. You had to feel sorry for the guy.

Darkness was normally the time to hide in Maglaj, and the streets were deserted as we made our way to the LS that night. We crossed the disused railway line and walked past the empty station, aware that in the dark hills around us there were Serb snipers with itchy trigger fingers, looking for a target. There were no lights burning in Maglaj.

Sitting in the rain on a small roundabout, we waited for the C130. Sporadic bursts of gunfire could be heard from up on the front line. Two or three rounds from a heavy-calibre weapon cracked above our heads. We were in a European town, sitting on a round-about next to some football fields. It was totally bizarre.

We didn't hear the C130 above us, but the whistle and crack of the parachutes was unmistakable. The townsfolk, hiding in the darkness, descended on the vital supplies.

Afterwards I went with Mark Buckler to check out the hospital, which had the same sickly stale smell that I remembered from the infirmary at Port Stanley. We used subdued torches to find our way down into the operating theatre, below ground, where candles acted as the lighting. The medical cabinets were bare except for two small bottles of aspirin.

The resident doctor was probably about forty-five years old, but looked closer to ninety. He and his nurse had both witnessed the full horror of the war and had performed countless operations without anaesthetic, on a table lit by candles and lanterns.

Looking at the table, I wondered how many men, women and children had suffered there, biting on a leather strap and probably drunk on slivovitz as bones were put back into place and shrapnel was dug out of their bodies.

Mark told them that medical supplies were on their way, and the doctor thanked us in broken English. It was nice to meet a person of integrity who was genuinely thankful; it didn't happen often. The mayoress of Maglaj, who ruled with an iron hand, had already demanded a say in dishing out the expected supplies – her friends first, of course. The lads discovered that the cellar of her house was crammed with food and medical supplies; throughout the siege she'd been looking after her family and council friends while people outside were starving.

That's Bosnia, I thought, fucked up from start to finish.

The relief convoy arrived the next day, escorted by Scimitars. Women and children lined the streets, cheering and waving as the lorries drove into town. Larry Hollingsworth, a white-bearded UN Father Christmas, began dishing out supplies. He had food for the hungry, vaccines for the children and medical supplies for the hospital.

Kiwi and I wandered down to the schoolhouse, which was to become the base for British soldiers. The classroom walls were decorated with various paintings from the Second World War, many depicting young children with weapons defending Yugoslavia against the Nazi invaders. One showed a group of kids carrying their wounded friend on a stretcher.

Another generation raised amid bloodshed, I thought: it never seems to end. The truth of this was hammered home to me a few days later when a woman invited Kiwi and me to her house. She could speak English and lived with her father, daughters and grandchildren. The house still had thick drapes over the windows and was very dark inside. She poured us tea and we gave her powdered milk from our rations.

She's the reason we're here, I thought to myself. It's for people like her who've suffered enough. This woman had lost sons fighting up on the front line around Maglaj, as well as a daughter and a granddaughter killed by Serbian artillery. Her hatred of the Serbs was all-consuming.

'The Muslims will never give up,' she told us. 'If we lose a dozen Muslim men in battle tomorrow, a dozen Muslim babies will also be born tomorrow.'

# 23

FIVE DAYS AFTER ARRIVING IN MAGLAJ WE WERE SENT BACK TO GORNJI
Vakuf to continue our original task of mapping the front lines. I
came off patrol one day and was told the senior officer wanted to
see me.

'You've got a BG (bodyguarding) task,' he said.

'Who is it?'

'I can't tell you that. Let's call him Mr Mills. He's a British dig-
nitary; he arrives in two days and I want you to pick a couple of
lads and prepare a team. I'll brief you when I have more details.'

'Yes, sir.'

'And Mike – I wouldn't want to be in your fucking shoes if this
one gets away from us.'

The Regiment has always run BG courses and is universally
recognized as being the finest training ground in the world; even
the Royal Protection Group is trained at Stirling Lines, on a course
that covers everything from CQB using a variety of weapons, to
driver training, first aid and signals and covert comms procedures.

The first priority was to pick a team. One of them had to be a
medic and I chose Fergie, an excellent lad from A Squadron who'd
been working alongside me in the hills above Prozor.

The other member of the team was Roger, an officer who'd not
long finished the BG course. You'd never have taken him for a
rupert; he was one of the lads.

The major called me in again the next day.

'Got your team?'

'Yes, sir. I'd have preferred three guys, but I know we're strapped for manpower. The two I've got are both experienced.'

'Good – because the BG subject is the prime minister, John Major.'

Shit, I thought, the big cheese!

'He'll be flying into Gornji Vakuf at 0900 hours the day after tomorrow, with the defence secretary, Malcolm Rifkind. You're to liaise with his Special Branch team and go over the itinerary and the route.' He handed me copies. 'The prime minister is arriving by helicopter to inspect various British army bases and UN projects. He'll also be visiting Sarajevo and meeting the Bosnian president . . .'

I raised my eyebrows. Sarajevo was like an amusement arcade for snipers.

'Is the visit going to be publicized?' I asked.

'He's a politician – it's going to be a fucking media circus.'

The major saw my concern.

'You take everything you need and you stick to him like fucking glue.'

I sat down with Fergie and Roger in the hangar. The vehicles had already arrived – a convoy of gleaming white Range Rovers. Fergie had been busy checking the medical packs in each vehicle.

'They'll do,' he said.

'What about the drivers?' I asked.

'They're being assigned tomorrow.'

'I want you and Roger to brief them. They'll have to know exactly what to do if we hit a landmine or come under attack. Also what action to take for accidents, illegal VCPs (vehicle checkpoints) or breakdowns. If anyone looks nervous or not up to it, get rid of them. They'll be briefed again on the day and given a map of the route. Roger, I want you to look after Rifkind at Gornji Vakuf. When we get to Sarajevo, you're with me; we'll leave Rifkind to the police.'

'What about me?' Fergie said.

'I'm with the principal and you shadow me. You're the eyes in the back of my head. Make sure all the drivers know about those medical packs.'

He nodded. I knew that Fergie would be carrying his own pack for the prime minister.

'Who's checking the comms?'

Roger said, 'I'll do it.'

'They have to be perfect. No faults, no fuck-ups.' Comms were even more vital than weapons in a BG operation.

A full set of plans was drawn up to cover every eventuality, from the principal popping a button on his shirt to being fired at with an automatic weapon. These were drills we'd practised time and again.

Ideally I would have liked a bigger team, but there weren't many of us and we were spread all over Bosnia. I had to make do with Fergie and Roger in the Gornji Vakuf area and then get some extra help in Sarajevo.

The next day, I drove into Gornji Vakuf and met with the commander and intelligence sections, trying to iron out any potential problems. It was going to be a big convoy. The commander of the British forces would be in Major's vehicle, along with Rifkind and the driver. I'd be in the 'backing' vehicle, directly behind, with Fergie. Roger would be in the 'fronting' vehicle. The rest of the convoy consisted of all manner of hangers-on from the CO's batman to the UN's cat. I couldn't give a toss about them – my principal was the prime minister.

That night, Fergie, Roger and I went through the orders, making sure everything was covered.

'It's a shame we don't have the MP5Ks,' I said. These were excellent machine pistols: sixty rounds on full automatic with two magazines and only 12 inches long. Perfect for BG work.

'We've got to make do with the SA80 for long range and our pistols for anything closer. There shouldn't be crowd problems but you never know.'

Roger said, 'What happens if there is?'

'If the crowd is big, you close in with my team around the premier. The police will go with Rifkind.'

One by one, we covered the actions-on, the 'what ifs' – vehicle breakdown, medical emergency, RTA (road traffic accident), VCP (vehicle checkpoint), IVCP (illegal vehicle checkpoint), contacts on route, contacts on arrival . . . there were hundreds of possibilities.

'Make sure every one of the drivers has a written set of our SOPs,' I said, wrapping up the briefing.

The following morning, 14 March 1994, three of the prime minister's BG team arrived in Gornji Vakuf an hour before his flight. Surprisingly, they were unarmed, which I thought was strange considering they were entering a war zone. Also they didn't have radios – a big oversight. How did they expect to communicate with each other?

From the outset, I'd assumed that Major's own team would form the inner cordon around him and that my team would supply the outer cordon. Instead his team leader now handed responsibility to me.

'It's your show,' he said, 'tell us what you want.'

'For the moment, you can split your team between the prime minister and the defence secretary. In Sarajevo I want you all to stay with Rifkind.'

He nodded in agreement.

Shortly before 0850, the Wessex touched down in the car park. The rotors had barely stopped spinning when John Major stepped onto the concrete and shook my hand.

'Welcome to Bosnia, Mr Prime Minister.'

'Thank you.'

'I'm Mike Curtis and I'm looking after your personal security. Will you be wearing body armour, sir?'

'I'd prefer not to,' he said. 'I wore it the last time I was here, but now there's a ceasefire. I want to portray that sense of growing peace.'

I wasn't happy about this, but I understood his reasons. Malcolm Rifkind made the same decision.

The whole shebang of ruperts from HQ were waiting to meet them, along with a media circus who trailed Major everywhere. He toured the base, meeting various UNHCR people, talking to troops and administrators. Shadowing his every step, I wondered how he could possibly take in so much information. He looked so ordinary. Michael Heseltine had an aura about him and so did Maggie Thatcher, but Major looked like my next door neighbour.

Through an earpiece and a pressel switch for transmitting that nestled in the palm of my hand, I knew exactly the state of play outside. Fergie and Roger kept up a running commentary and got the vehicles sorted.

As the prime minister prepared to leave the building I gave the, 'Standby, standby.'

The lads knew to be ready. As we strode into the sunshine, Fergie signalled the driver to start the engine. A dozen paces and Major slid into the back seat of the car, along with Rifkind. The most senior British officer took the front. We stayed at the door, shielding the windows, until everyone was inside.

Roger darted for the front car while Fergie and I got into the backing vehicle. We were mobile.

It's always a dodgy time when the principal is on his way from a building to his car because for those few seconds he's out in the open. This is when an assassin would be most likely to strike.

Our next destination was a checkpoint on the outskirts of Gornji Vakuf. There were journalists and camera crews everywhere, scrambling to get the best viewpoints and yelling questions at the PM.

Mr Major inspected the troops and the OC of the Coldstream Guards told him about the town patrols that his men had been doing. I smiled. Until a handful of SAS blokes had shown them it was possible, this rupert hadn't set foot in the war-torn village.

The checkpoint had once been a regular Croatian shooting gallery, where they took pot-shots from their positions across the valley. However, because of the absurd rules of engagement adopted by the UN in Bosnia, we couldn't actually return fire unless the incoming rounds had hit us or were near to hitting us. A Brit commander solved the problem when he was fired on by retaliating with about 100 rounds from a Warrior cannon. The Croats had been quiet ever since.

From Gornji Vakuf we drove straight down the Bugoijne Road, passing through Croat and Muslim communities *en route* to another British army base where the Duke of Wellington Regiment was stationed. I knew this area well and had grown used to the destruction, but I could see how it shocked Mr Major, coming straight from London.

Flying by helicopter, the prime minister visited a handful of army bases in central Bosnia. At every camp the troops were on parade, the RSMs were desperately trying to put on their best show for the main man, and the COs were soaking up the kudos. Fair dos to Major, he was very pleasant, speaking to most people and shaking their hands.

At the last British base at Vitez, we boarded the helicopter for Sarajevo. I had a gnawing fear in the pit of my stomach. So far I'd been able to control the situation, but the main Muslim stronghold was likely to present far greater problems.

During the flight, Major asked me how long I'd been in Bosnia. Whether or not he knew I was SAS was anyone's guess. He seemed a nice guy and was quite talkative, but no-one got a word out of Malcolm Rifkind, who looked like a train-spotter.

I got chatting to Major's press secretary, who seemed to be managing the whole show.

'How do you get to be a press secretary?' Fergie asked me.

'Fucked if I know, but I don't think it will help coming from Para Reg.'

Landing at Sarajevo, Roger got off the chopper first, followed by myself, Major, Rifkind and Fergie. We were on the tarmac and a huge crowd was waiting. Cameras were flashing and journalists of all nationalities jockeyed for position.

Waiting to greet the prime minister was Lieutenant General Mike Rose, the ex-CO of the SAS and now the commander of land forces in Bosnia. A charismatic, confident man, Rose had become quite a celebrity since arriving in Bosnia. The media loved him, although he'd put a lot of noses out of joint among the various factions because he wouldn't pander to any particular side's requirements – especially the Serbs.

The scrum of journalists, photographers and well-wishers closed around us and I was hanging on to the prime minister with my arm around his waist, pushing a path through the throng.

'Come on, come on, come on,' I told myself. Too many people, much too close. I didn't like it one bit.

The convoy of Range Rovers was waiting. I got the door and shielded Major with my body as he entered. Roger covered Rifkind at the opposite door. Rose got in front and my team piled into the backing car. We screamed away from the airport through Sarajevo.

We drove at breakneck speed through the war-torn capital in blazing sunshine. When we stopped at the Bosnian parliament building a throng of people screamed at the PM as if he was Elvis reincarnated. Mr Major received a presidential salute from a Bosnian guard of honour all done out in their Sunday best, and then disappeared inside for a meeting with the Bosnian head of state, Izerbegović. Rose and Rifkind accompanied him.

As the large oak-panelled doors closed behind them, I stayed outside.

I kept in touch with Fergie and Roger on the radio. They were waiting outside at the vehicles, where the world's media had caught up from the airport. Swelled by well-wishers and spectators, the crowd had grown into hundreds.

An hour later, as the doors opened, I gave the, 'Standby, standby!' again.

'Standby, standby,' echoed back, as Fergie and Roger acknowledged my message.

Stepping out again into the sunshine, the PM hesitated on the steps. The car door rested open and waiting.

Don't fucking stay here, John, I thought. My eyes scanned the crowd and the windows beyond.

'I want to go and meet these people,' said Major.

'I don't think it's a good idea, Mr Prime Minister.'

'I'd like to.' He was adamant.

Major marched straight across the road and began shaking people's hands. On his left side he had a woman interpreter who was telling him what people were saying to him. Mainly it was, 'Thank you for coming.' He kept reaching out for another hand, and then another, asking, 'How are you? What's your job?'

The mob grew more desperate to reach him and suddenly I got scared. One shot from a pistol and the prime minister would be dead. The SA80 was slung across my back, no good in these circumstances anyway because of the proximity of the crowd, so I had one hand on my pistol, eyeballing the throng. I had my arm around Major's waist. I kept looking at the faces – that's how I'd know, from the menace or the madness in their eyes.

Major was like a saviour to these people, young and old, all trying to touch him, all smiling. One of them wasn't. He was so close I could almost smell his breath – all bad teeth and hostility. He raised his arm with a closed fist. With one arm around the prime minister, I pushed him back into the throng.

Come on, John, let's go man!

I could just make out Fergie's voice: 'We gotta get out of here, Mike.'

'Yeah, I know. I know. Standby, standby!'

Finally we were clear. Fergie fell into his usual place and Roger was at the vehicles. I was drenched with sweat.

On the way to the vehicle, the prime minister seemed totally at ease. Then his press secretary told him we were running late for a meeting with Lynda Chalker, the Minister for Overseas Development; this seemed to worry him more than the security nightmare he'd just caused.

As the convoy sped through the city streets, my troubles were far from over. The next appointment, at a water-purification plant, was smack bang in the middle of an area known as 'Sniper Alley'.

# 24

EVEN BEFORE THE CONVOY HAD STOPPED MOVING I WAS OUT AND running. I shielded the windows of Major's car until the last possible moment before opening the doors. I couldn't believe the stupidity of bringing the prime minister to Sniper Alley.

On either side of the street there were buildings four or five storeys high, rising to eight storeys further down the street. Windows were bricked up or shot away and the walls were pock-marked with bullet holes. The flats had been abandoned long ago and had become a favoured hiding place for snipers.

Having run the red lights, we arrived at the water-purification plant ahead of the media, although some had second-guessed the destination. I put my body between the crowd and the PM.

Lynda Chalker greeted Major at the top, flanked by some of her aides.

'Get through the door, Roger,' I said.

He acknowledged. It wasn't safe to dither on the steps with the PM in direct line with the flats.

'Let's get inside, sir.'

Mrs Chalker looked agitated as she followed us through.

'You're a little late, John.'

'Yes, we got caught in traffic,' he replied.

I quickly gave the lads a comms check. Out of the corner of my eye I saw the PM trying to appear interested in Lynda Chalker's water-purification efforts.

General Rose wandered across to me. 'You look like one of the

Bulky Brothers,' he joked.

Just then Fergie opened up on the net. 'We got a load of journalists outside. They want to interview the prime minister.'

I looked at my watch and spoke to the press secretary. He said there was time for one interview.

'Any of them British?' I asked Fergie.

'Kate Adie's here.'

I hadn't seen Kate since the Gulf War, when we'd been on our way back to UAE from Saudi.

'I'm coming out.'

A throng of photographers and cameramen jostled for position. I recognized Kate; she was wearing tight jeans and a sports jacket, looking incredibly cool despite the heat. I grabbed her by the hand. 'Come on, Kate, you can have a chat with the man.'

The French and Italian reporters went mad, swearing and cursing at me. She got five minutes and then we had to leave; Major still had to visit another British camp across town and then catch a flight out of Sarajevo. The airport was under Serb control and closed at 1800 hours.

The convoy sped back into the heart of Sarajevo and then out again to the dividing line where the Serbian and Muslim fighters were being kept apart by UN peacekeepers, among them a large contingent of British soldiers.

Major chatted to the troops and seemed genuinely interested in their work. Part of no man's land consisted of a substantial bridge scattered with debris that was being patrolled by Ukrainian peacekeepers. On one side the Serbs looked down from high-rise blocks of flats and on the other side were the Muslim positions.

'Can I get a closer look?' said the prime minister, looking towards no man's land.

'I advise against . . .'

Before I could finish, General Rose cut in, 'Yes, of course.'

I didn't like it one bit. This had been the scene of fierce fighting and tensions remained high. Only recently the Serbs had been firing in the area.

As we walked towards the bridge, I kept eyeing the high-rise flats, thinking how crazy we were – someone could so easily take out the PM.

As we walked onto the bridge, we came across a UN APC parked on the side. I looked in first, then John Major looked inside; then he looked at me and started laughing. The soldiers inside were sound asleep.

'Who are these people?' he asked.

'Ukrainians,' I said.

As we walked further along the bridge, we grew even more isolated and vulnerable. I glanced at my watch: 1740. We had twenty minutes to make the airport.

Looking right and left along the deserted, shell-torn streets, the prime minister turned to General Rose and said, 'How can we get the Serbs to stop firing?'

'We've got to put pressure on the Russians.'

'How can we put pressure on the Russians?'

Mr Rifkind said, 'We'd have to put pressure on the Americans to put pressure on the Russians.'

John Major looked at his secretary of defence and said, 'Malcolm, next week I want you to go to the White House.'

I felt I was witnessing history in the making. It was impressive to watch a prime minister thinking on his feet, something this particular one wasn't supposedly renowned for doing.

In a mad dash, we managed to make the airport before the nightly curfew. The Serbs, dressed in black uniforms, didn't allow us through immediately. They wanted to know the names of everyone in the entire convoy. One guard began writing them down, including John Major's.

We were eventually waved through to find the C130 waiting, along with a large crowd of dignitaries and well-wishers.

'Mike, thank you for looking after me today,' said John Major as we took him across the tarmac towards the waiting Herc. 'I felt very secure.' Then he grinned, 'I take it you don't want a signed photograph?'

I grinned back and shook my head.

Major laughed. 'Better give you something.'

He reached into the inside pocket of his jacket and presented me with his pen, complete with 10 Downing Street crest.

'Thank you, Mr Prime Minister. Have a good journey home.'

As the aircraft screamed down the runway and lifted off, my CO, Lieutenant Colonel Wyn Griffiths, wandered across. I had a lot of time for this guy; ex-Welsh Guards, he supported the rugby team and was the only CO I'd ever seen on the piss downtown in Hereford. 'Good work, Taff,' he said. 'Let's have a drink later.'

Moments later, on board another C130, we were flying towards the British HQ in Split. That evening we gathered in the crowded REME toms' bar – Wyn Griffiths, Fergie, Roger and me – squeezing into a corner amid the smoke and noise.

None of the REME lads seemed to recognize the CO. One young squaddie even leaned over and said, 'Oi, mate, give us a fag.' The colonel happily obliged, saying nothing. He was that sort of bloke.

We were now getting ready to pull out of Bosnia because of commitments in other parts of the world, but other lads from the Regiment would take over and continue the work.

During the last few days before we left, the supposedly 'safe' Muslim haven of Gorazde came under intense Serbian fire. It was a similar situation to Maglaj, with Serb forces totally surrounding the town and slowly squeezing it to death. Thousands of civilians, many of them women and children, were trapped inside.

A composite six-man SAS team was dispatched, including Fergie, Scouse McVey, Jim Smith and Boss Clark. The aim was to get into the enclave and report to the outside world what was happening.

So much disinformation is spread and so many lies are told in wartime that it's often difficult to find the truth. In this case, the Serbians denied shelling Gorazde and claimed that the Muslims were using artillery against their own people, with the intention of increasing international condemnation and perhaps prompting the UN to launch air strikes against Serb targets.

Gorazde lay in a valley beside the Drina River and was linked to Sarajevo by a main road. The initial plan was to drive through the Serbian lines in two Land Rovers. Steve asked for a cammed-up vehicle but the request was turned down: they were UN peace-keepers and would have to drive the 'white elephants'.

The lads managed to get through and set up their HQ in a bank. Their OP was in a large hotel further down the street, where they could use powerful binos from the rooftop and watch Serb troop movements in the surrounding hills. These were reported back to UNHCR using the tac sat.

Regularly, they also drove out to where the Muslims had dug front-line and fall-back trenches around Gorazde. Sometimes one of these would be overrun by the Serbs and the fighters would simply fall back to another position.

One particular unit, known as the Chetniks, frightened the Muslims more than any other. They had a fearsome reputation and were rumoured to have committed many atrocities. Decked out in old DPM, the Chetniks took their name from the anti-communist Chetnik units of the Second World War. You could recognize them by the bandanas they wore around their heads.

The assault on Gorazde intensified, with the Serbs shelling day and night. They appeared determined to capture the enclave as quickly as possible, regardless of international opinion and outrage.

At one point, Scouse McVey and Big Jim Smith were in the Muslim trenches when the Chetniks came storming down the hill towards them. They were taking a barrage of incomers – mortars, grenades and AK rounds. Muslim soldiers were falling all around them. Scouse and Jim had no choice but to pull back, fighting each step of the way alongside the Muslims, until they reached the reserve positions.

They held off the first attack, but it was clearly only a matter of hours before the Chetniks overran the Muslim defences and stormed Gorazde. The lads made it back to the hotel and asked for an air strike.

The jets were scrambled and arrived in the nick of time. From the roof of the hotel, one of the lads kept up a running commentary on the net, giving directions to the jets. His voice was eventually heard on national news bulletins around the world.

The air strikes stopped the Serbs in their tracks. After so many months of having it their own way, they didn't expect them.

About four days later, some of the lads went out in the vehicles to check on the Serb positions and to recce possible escape routes. There seemed to be little chance of driving out; tabbing was still a possibility, but that would mean leaving behind the vehicles and some of the heavier OP kit.

Investigating further, they drove up towards a plateau where the ground flattened out before rising again. Suddenly, over the top of the ridge, came the Serbs with their Russian tanks in an extended line. It was like something out of the film *Zulu*, only the tanks were far more lethal than spears and stones.

The Chetnik unit started piling down towards the enclave, covering the flat ground quickly in tanks and APCs. They opened fire on the Land Rovers, despite the UN colours. They knew damn well who they were attacking.

Scouse and Jim went one way and Clarky and Fergie went the other.

Scouse took a track in sight of Serb positions that skirted around a heavily wooded area. Meanwhile, in the other 'white elephant', Boss Clark got hit through the arm and young Fergie, who was driving, took a round in the head. The Land Rover speared off the road. Under intense fire, the Muslims came out of their trenches and helped drag the foreign soldiers to cover. Clarky got on the net and

371

sent a contact report: Fergie was in a really bad way.

Scouse and Jim picked up the message and had to make a quick decision. By now Fergie and the boss were 4 clicks away, but to reach them by Land Rover meant driving down into Gorazde and back up again, leaving themselves exposed. The enclave itself was under intense fire. Instead they decided to tab like fuck through the wooded area.

There were always Serb renegades and snipers in the woods, but most of their soldiers wouldn't enter the trees because they feared what the Muslims had waiting for them. I didn't blame them. I'd grown to admire the Muslims' backs-to-the-wall spirit, particularly when it came to the close-quarter stuff.

Scouse and Jim had several contacts on the way, but eventually reached the others. The Muslims had arranged a vehicle for Fergie, which got him back to Gorazde. The lads then returned across the ridges and through the trees to pick up the Land Rover.

With the Serbs again threatening to overrun the enclave, they called another air strike and a British Harrier came screaming down. It didn't drop its bombs on the first approach, but banked on its side and came back for another run. Big mistake. The Serbian Chetniks opened up from the ridge and the Harrier started spouting flames. The British pilot ejected and, luckily for him, he fell towards Gorazde. The boys went out and rescued him, bringing him back to the bank.

The Serbs had clearly realized that the FAC (forward air controller) must be situated in the highest point of Gorazde, so the tanks and artillery now put their heavy weapons in the direct-fire role and started hitting the hotel.

As the shells exploded around them, the lads called in a helicopter to cas-evac Fergie. The heli pilot did bloody well to get through all the shit the Serbs were throwing at Gorazde, and it was just as well he made it: as they lifted Fergie on board, his hands were moving and his eyes were open, but that was all. Meanwhile, Clarky was having an operation on his arm to remove the bullet and repair the shattered bones – he couldn't be airlifted because the operation was still in progress.

That night, the Muslims came into the bank and forced Scouse and the lads into the hotel basement under armed guard. Despite the fact that the SAS had saved Gorazde by calling in air strikes, the Muslims had decided that having UN prisoners might be a useful bargaining tool. Yet more of the madness and convoluted logic of Bosnia.

Surprisingly, they let the lads keep their weapons – just in case the Serbs overran the town. By now the Harrier pilot was with them and had armed himself with Fergie's SA80.

A local Muslim who'd been helping them as an interpreter slipped into the basement that night and told them that the guards outside were leaving their posts for five to ten minutes. This was their chance to escape. From the hotel, they crept through the streets of Gorazde to the hospital. Clarky had just come out of the anaesthetic and still had a metal frame attached to pins sticking out of his right arm at his elbow and shoulder. They slung an SA80 over his neck and slipped outside.

The problem they now faced wasn't getting out of Gorazde, but finding a way through the Serbian lines. They tabbed up into the mountains, with Clarky spewing up all the way. Knowing they were vastly outnumbered, they crept past Chetnik campfires and OPs, crossing terrain that would have been hard-core in daylight, let alone darkness. Ten clicks outside Gorazde, they managed to call in a chopper which airlifted them to the relative safety of Sarajevo.

The escape typified the SAS and Scouse McVey was awarded the Military Cross for his actions. He'd taken charge when Clarky was wounded and managed to get the lads out safely. I was chuffed to see a good mate honoured.

The interpreter who helped them escape wasn't so lucky. He was imprisoned in Gorazde and got a hammering from the Muslims. Eventually transferred to Sarajevo, he was recognized by one of our lads and reunited with his family, who were also in the city. Later, Scouse and Jim Smith sponsored his trip to Britain and he came to Hereford where the Squadron thanked him for having risked his life to get the boys to safety.

Meanwhile, others of us had to fly back to the UK on a very sad mission. Soon after reaching the hospital in Sarajevo, Fergie had died of his wounds.

On the day that Fergie was buried, the sun was shining. We were gathered at the pretty graveyard not far from Stirling Lines where the Regiment buries its dead.

On two headstones, beneath the Regimental crest, I saw the names of Vince Phillips and Bob Consiglio and, on a commemorative plaque, that of Legs Lane – casualties of the Bravo Two Zero mission. We'd buried them after the Gulf war.

The lads who'd been with Fergie at Gorazde carried his coffin draped with the Union Jack. Many had tears in their eyes. I looked down and gave Fergie a final salute, wondering how many more mates I was going to lose. Having a flashback to the day we reburied Stevie Illingsworth at Aldershot graveyard, I realized it had been years since I'd been back there. I made up my mind to visit his grave the next day and pay my respects.

Afterwards, in the sergeants' mess, I met Fergie's brothers and his father. I told them how he and I had bodyguarded the prime minister. They said that Mr Major had sent the family a letter, expressing his sorrow and saying how well Fergie had looked after him in Sarajevo. It was nice of him to remember.

As it grew late and the family departed, just the lads remained. We continued drinking, getting absolutely hammered, because that's all you can do. It's what Fergie would have wanted.

The SAS had proved a point in Bosnia. We'd shown that we could operate in a UN theatre and play a valuable role as mediators and peacekeepers. At the outset, I'd heard there weren't many senior people in the UN who thought we could do it. After all, the reputation of the SAS had been forged in combat. Now, however, there was a realization that besides all the various jobs we did internationally, meeting and communicating with heads of state and dignitaries in Third World countries, we also had the maturity and experience to negotiate with leaders and politicians in a war zone, particularly if they were military men. It's often easier for two soldiers to talk on equal terms than for a soldier to be confronted by politicians, diplomats and old officers from a different era.

Bosnia was a crazy war that had no true winners, yet the Regiment had emerged with its reputation enhanced. It had carved itself a niche in the UN's history and perhaps created an additional role for itself in the future.

# 25

THEY GAVE US THREE WEEKS OFF AFTER RETURNING FROM BOSNIA AND I took Liz to the Canaries for a holiday. We left the girls with my parents, so it was just the two of us; the sunshine, warm nights and romantic dinners would hopefully rescue our marriage. It had teetered on the brink for so many years now that there wasn't much left that either of us could say; we simply had to be with each other and hope that whatever spark still remained between us would flicker and reignite.

I felt the holiday went well and things were looking more hopeful. Needless to say, as soon as we got back and I had settled into home life, it was time to say goodbye again: the whole squadron was going to Latin America for a jungle exercise. Liz and the girls drove me to the block and there were big hugs at the gate.

We arrived in-country in the early hours of Tuesday morning and took an internal flight down to an army camp in a village near the border. After sorting out our kit, we choppered into a jungle camp the next day and started tabbing straight away.

Each Troop had a different entry point and had to babysit a group of eight local soldiers. The squadron's last jungle trip had been to Malaya just before the Gulf war in 1990, so the idea was to practise our SOPs, sharpen our skills and pass on some of our knowledge.

Rain absolutely teemed down, leaking into every pore and crease. The ground turned to mud beneath our feet and bergens rubbed the skin raw through wet shirts. As usual, Barry Taylor

375

went down and needed his liquid fix through the arm like some crazed junkie.

On about the third day, we tabbed over a large feature and stumbled upon a small village perched on top of a hill in the middle of nowhere. It had been hacked out of the jungle and consisted of about eight long huts and a schoolhouse made of wood and vines. The view was spectacular, with the jungle stretching out beneath us like a green carpet and a river snaking through the trees.

Chickens and pigs foraged in the open or wandered in and out of the huts. The women were cooking and washing, while their elders sat in the shade. Barefoot children with huge smiles peered out of the schoolhouse. They wore immaculate school uniforms with white shirts and dark trousers for the boys and white blouses and blue skirts for the girls. The teacher told us he came from a nearby village and had to walk 25 kilometres back to his home at the end of each school week.

After marking the clearing on the map as an ideal LS, Mark Clayton, the troop sergeant, and I wandered over to say hello to the village head man. Acting as interpreter, I explained that we were moving through the area and would be working in the valley below.

He nodded in agreement and then asked, 'Do you have a doctor?'

'Yes.'

'What's wrong?' asked Mark.

'He says his daughter is sick and so is her baby.'

'Ask him to show us.'

Doctor Billy was summoned and we were taken to one of the long huts. Inside we found a baby girl who was about a month old and a mother who couldn't have been more than fifteen. The baby was in rag order, with diarrhoea and severe dehydration. She hadn't fed from the breast in nearly three days and was clearly dying. Wrapped in an old towel, with her eyes half closed, she looked no bigger than a bag of sugar.

'They both need cas-evaccing, Mike,' said Billy. 'I think the mum's bleeding internally and the baby needs fluids badly.'

'Let's call in a chopper,' said Mark.

An hour or so later, a Gazelle from the army camp skimmed over the trees and came down on the LS. The villagers were flabbergasted; to them, it must have looked like a huge mechanical monster carving up the air. The entire population turned out and

376

the school kids were given time off class.

The young mother began crying and was absolutely terrified. She'd never ridden in a car before, let alone in a helicopter, but unless she got on board she risked losing her own life and, almost certainly, her baby's.

Finally we coaxed her on board and got them both to the hospital at the army camp. The baby weighed only 3 or 4 pounds and was given little chance, but somehow pulled through. Meanwhile, the doctors patched up the girl and within a few weeks they were both ready to go home.

As the chopper landed at the village, the head man was overjoyed to see his daughter and granddaughter again. As if on cue, the baby began screaming her head off – just like babies are supposed to. I had to smile. He arranged a big scoff for us to say thank you – a wonderful gesture, but I couldn't help feeling guilty, knowing that they'd be offering us more than they could probably spare.

As I watched the preparations, I began to wish even more that we'd made our excuses and left. The women collected armfuls of yucca plants, then sat around chewing on its stems and leaves and spitting out the juices into a bucket. This went on all morning, then they waited for the juice and spit to ferment.

That evening we were called across to toast the health of mother and child. The bucket was now full of a yellowy, pusy, stringy cocktail of saliva and yucca juice and pulp. Tuberculosis was rife in this part of the world, and I exchanged worried glances with the rest of the patrol. But we couldn't offend these people; to a man, we all took a big swig of their delicacy, and to tell the truth it didn't taste half as bad as Kiwi's peaches in chocolate sauce.

After three weeks in-theatre we set off on a tracking exercise upriver from one of the camps. For three days the rain hammered down. There's nothing worse than being in the jungle when it rains incessantly, and this was the dirtiest jungle I'd ever seen. It crawled with leeches, ants, snakes and mosquitoes.

One morning I was stood to, soaked to the skin, when I opened my bergen to find it seething with termites. It was hideous, all my gear was moving. At other times, the ground would be black with ants and thousands died with every footstep. They crawled inside my clothing and through my hair. At night, in my hammock, the ants would eat their way through the mosquito net and crawl down my neck and into my ears. In the torchlight, I could see the unstoppable tide pouring through.

377

After about a week of this, a longboat came downriver with supplies. Ian, Kiwi and I went to pick them up and there was a letter waiting for me – the only mail for the whole Troop. I saw it was from Liz and noticed the date stamp: it had been posted the same day that I left Hereford.

'Aren't you gonna read it?' asked Kiwi and Ian.

'Nah, I'm saving it for tonight,' I said, tucking it into my waterproof notebook. 'It'll be my one little luxury in this shit-hole.'

Six hours later, stood down and lying in my hammock, I put my head torch on and opened the letter. I was thousands of miles from home, soaking wet, covered in fucking ants. It couldn't be any worse than this.

I was wrong.

'This is the last letter I'll be writing to you,' Liz said. 'The girls will still be writing to you, but there will be no more mail from me . . .'

My marriage was over. I was three weeks into a seven-week jungle exercise. Why the fuck hadn't she waited until I got home? I knew that hundreds of guys had been in the same position, but it didn't make it any easier. And even though in my heart of hearts I'd known it was coming, the jolt was devastating. A romance that had begun in a school playground in Wales had died deep in the Latin American jungle.

What do you do? What do you say? Nothing – there's nothing I could have done.

My emotions ran the whole spectrum. Sometimes I was angry or pissed off, then I'd feel sorry for myself, then I'd tell myself I could patch things up again, but each time I read the letter, I knew that it was really over.

I always tended to keep things to myself and I didn't share the news with any of the lads. My routines slipped a little, but it didn't affect my soldiering.

On the first day of the final exercise I woke at stand to and felt like shit. As I pulled on my wet kit, my head was throbbing and I was shivering. By the time we started tabbing to the top of a ridge, I was vomiting and had diarrhoea. We had to locate a drug-cartel encampment where they were manufacturing cocaine from coca leaves, and we were doing a grid search of the ground.

I pushed on, tabbing for hours until it became late afternoon. Suddenly I was face down in the mud, shivering and shaking.

Barry Taylor came across to me as Billy Adams was putting in the first drip.

378

'Imitation is the sincerest form of flattery, Mike,' he grinned. 'I suppose you'll be smoking next!'

Billy didn't mess about; they got two drips into me and I started feeling a bit better. The cold was unbelievable. We were in a steaming jungle yet I couldn't get warm.

The exercise was in the middle of nowhere, beyond the reach of choppers, so I had no alternative but to keep tabbing. By nightfall, I thought I was dying. The shivers and pains were hideous and I didn't sleep. Next morning I hauled myself to my feet and started tabbing again.

This went on for three days and nights. The days weren't too bad because we were moving, but at night I got unbelievably cold. By the end of the operation, I'd lost touch with reality and was hallucinating.

Away from the jungle, my condition seemed to improve, but I still had no idea what I was suffering from. All I could think about was flying home to an estranged wife and a ruined marriage.

My key still fitted in the lock. She heard me come in and met me at the door.

'You can see the girls but then I want you to leave.'

'But I've only just got home.'

'This isn't your home any more, Mike. You don't live here any more.'

'So you basically want me to collect my bags and fuck off?'

She nodded.

I stayed with Kiwi for the first few days, still feeling like shit. On the Friday I moved into the sergeants' mess. There was a mess photograph being taken that afternoon and then I planned to take the girls to Wales.

As I dressed for the photo my head was thumping and I was sweating buckets. I couldn't do up my top button because I was shaking so much. One minute I was freezing and the next I was burning up. Somehow I managed to get through the session and went to pick up the girls.

On the drive to Rhondda I could hardly breathe. I went straight to bed when I got to my parents' and for the next two days I gave my mother hell. She was frantic with worry as I hallucinated and cried out in a fever.

Eventually, my dad called Kiwi and asked him to bring Liz down in the car to pick up the girls. Downstairs I could hear Liz arguing with my mam. I'd said nothing about the separation.

My dad drove me back to Hereford in his car, booking me straight into the hospital. I wanted to be close to the camp because I knew the doctors were experienced in treating tropical diseases.

They came back with the results of my blood tests and gave the diagnosis that deep down I was already expecting: malaria. 'Although there are vaccines, malaria never entirely disappears,' the doctor said. 'It comes back periodically when the body has least resistance because of tiredness and exhaustion. And I'm sorry to tell you this, but the strain that you have contracted will probably kill you one day.'

I didn't bat an eyelid; I simply didn't care. I'd lost 2 stones in weight by this stage and felt weaker than a kitten.

I spent two weeks in hospital and came out to find some of the lads on standby to go back to Bosnia in the event of a hostage situation. There were fears of UN soldiers being taken as bargaining tools or being used as human shields to deter air attacks. As a result, a few of us would begin refreshers on FIBUA (fighting in built-up areas) and hostage-evacuation drills with helicopters. Not wanting to miss out, I went against doctor's orders and got myself back into the fray straight away.

'It's got to be better than the sergeants' mess,' I told myself, and declared myself fully fit.

As I packed my kit, Scouse McVey shouted across, 'Fuck me, Mike, what time you got to be back in the cemetery?' He was right, I was thinner than a rake.

'Why didn't you come visit me in hospital, Scouse?' I yelled back.

'Couldn't find any flowers.'

There's no sympathy in the Regiment, and none expected, just stacks of piss-taking. That's what it's all about, army life, and having lost Liz, I needed to feel as if I belonged somewhere.

First on the agenda was a series of heli-dunking drills off the Cornish coast. The insertion exercise involved the chopper coming in low, about 30 metres above the sea to avoid radar detection, and dropping us 150 metres from the beach. Two Geminis (inflatable boats) had been dropped minutes earlier, manned by 17 (Boat) Troop, whose task was to pick us up and take us ashore. At least that was the plan.

It was a horrible grey morning, with rain teeming down. The chopper skimmed over the water, and as the tailgate opened I could see the whitecaps. Looking out the back, I tried to recognize the shoreline. I remembered surfing these same beaches with Peter

Terret as a teenager. The chopper banked to one side and headed out to sea, beyond the crashing waves.

Each of us wore a 'dry bag' – a wetsuit with a hood that completely covered the body, apart from our hands and face. Our weapons and webbing had been stripped down and put into a zip-lock waterproof bag. Fins were strapped to the front of our legs with paracord and we had a large diver's knife on our wrists.

'Red on.'

'Green on.'

'Go!'

I ran, jumped, and hit the water 30 feet below us, shooting beneath the waves. After the initial shock of the cold, I kicked for the surface. The Gemini was about 50 metres away.

Slipping on my fins, I rolled onto my back and started kicking towards the boat, clutching my waterproof bag to my chest. So far so good. The gang converged – myself, Greg Richards, Billy Adams, Little Glen Unwin, Nick Farmer and Barry Taylor. Baz wasn't a strong swimmer and hadn't been looking forward to the day.

The coxswain of the Gemini was Willy.

'You OK, Mike?' he shouted.

'Yeah, fine,' I said, breathing hard.

The swell was horrendous and Willy fought with the motor to keep the boat upright. 'It's gonna flip!' he yelled.

We leaned on the front, trying to keep it down.

'It's no use, Mike, you'll have to fin to the beach. This is gonna go.'

Rolling onto my back, I began finning like fuck towards the shore. The other lads did the same. Although quite a good swimmer, I was only five days out of hospital and still weak. As the swell lifted me up, I could see the beach and it didn't seem to be getting any closer. A rip tide was running, going out fast.

Shit! We're going nowhere, I thought. Around me, lads were fighting hard just to stay still. Looking over my shoulder, I saw figures on the sand. I recognized Ray's bald head. They were shouting to us, but I couldn't make out the words.

Everyone had a Mae West and a lot of the lads began pulling the toggles and inflating them. I put off pulling mine – I didn't want to walk up the beach with a big orange balloon around my neck. Instead I'd leave it till the last moment.

Little Glen, probably the smallest man in the squadron, was in distress right next to me. He could hardly breathe, so I grabbed hold of him.

'C'mon, let's fin in together,' I said.

But instead of helping him, my body weight was pulling him under the water. I was using him like a flotation device, fucking him even more, so I pushed him away.

I spied Greg in disarray – he'd lost one of his fins and had to bin the other. Now he was trying to front crawl to the beach, fighting against the rip tide.

I was shouting as best I could to the lads on the beach, but nobody could hear. The Geminis were still capsized and useless; the blades of the Chinook thumped the air in the distance.

Waves were crashing down on top of me, I was taking too much water into my mouth and I was feeling nauseous and light-headed. The moment had come. I reached for the toggle and pulled. Fuck all happened. It didn't inflate. I pulled again. Nothing.

Now very weak, I couldn't see anyone around me. The waves were pinning me under for longer periods and I was drowning. I was fucked and on my own.

A voice in my head was screaming, 'Don't give up!' But I had nothing left to give. Each wave bashed me down and I took huge gulps of water. I came up, spluttering, and got hit again and again.

This is it, I thought, after all the battles I've been through, it's all going to end off a fucking beach in Cornwall. I should have stayed home and recuperated properly.

Just then a gigantic wave hit me; water filled my mouth and nose. As I fought for the surface my fin touched the bottom; it gave me confidence. I put in one last effort, kicking my legs as hard as I could.

I put my hand over my face to stop the water going into my mouth and just kept finning and finning and finning. I stole 5 yards, then 10, then 15. Another wave hit me and I could actually touch the bottom – neck deep. I tried to stand but the rip kicked my feet away. I finned again, putting in one last effort and reached waist-deep water. *Whoosh*, the tide took me straight back out again.

I could see Ray Scott running down the beach. I kicked again and again – back to waist-deep, I tried to stand and wade. Ray reached me, grabbing hold of my hair as I went under and pulling me out. I collapsed, my chest heaving, and looked at the angry churning surf.

Around me, exhausted bodies and equipment were strewn

382

along the beach like a shipwreck. The Geminis had lost their motors and were in rag order. Billy Adams was still trying to wade ashore. I took off my fins, yelled to Ray, and a few of us ran into the surf, dragging him onto the beach.

Then I lay on the sand, honking up sea water.

The exercise had been horrendous and very nearly a terrible tragedy. Yet there was no chance to dwell on it. The Chinook landed on the beachhead and we clambered on board and were taken back to camp. After a brew and some scoff, we went straight out for more.

That afternoon the Bosnia standby gang was dropped into the sea again and had to fin to a Gemini. Then we climbed a swaying, 25-metre metal caving ladder, through the down draught from the rotors, into the Chinook hovering above. I was still bollocksed from the morning, but managed to get up and inside.

I barely had time to think about how close I'd come to checking out. It never seems so bad when you're tucking into a second helping of scoff and sipping on a brew. Rather than dwell on my mortality, I decided I'd concentrate on getting my strength back. Army food isn't the most nutritious in the world but at least there's plenty of it.

The C130 took off at 1800 hours and flew to co-ordinates in the North Sea off the east coast of Scotland. Over the next few days we had a number of day and night parachute jumps into the sea, where Geminis picked us up and ferried us to the para-ship RV.

Parachuting into the sea is a lot different from parachuting onto land. For a start, you get a soft landing. But two of the things you have to remember are to turn into the wind, or the chute will go over the top of you in the water, then 20 metres from impact release your harness straps – otherwise, the chute will get loaded with water and drag you under.

Only a year earlier, a lad from the Artillery had gone into water in daylight with the chute still attached to him. The safety boat, a Gemini, went to pick him up. They pulled him out of the water and started rolling him onto the boat, but the wind inflated his chute and took him off again. Chasing after him, they pulled him into the boat again, but before they could hit the box on his chest and release the chute, it inflated again and took him away. The poor bastard drowned.

In the final exercise, the Geminis went off the tailgate from 800 feet. Moments later we got the 'Red on – Green on' and followed them down. I jumped in a 'dry bag' with a steerable square-rig canopy. My bergen, with dry webbing and split-down weapons, was inside a waterproof container that dangled below me.

Falling, I could make out the Gemini on its parachute beneath me and to my left the grey hull of the ship against the black sea. It was 2000 hours and was growing dark. I flew over the large frigate, steering away from it. I could make out the sailors on deck, probably pissing themselves laughing at the crazy fuckers in the air.

There was just enough light to see the Gemini landing – I was losing altitude and coming down between it and the ship. Remembering to land with the wind in my face and the chute behind, I hit the junction box on my chest 20 metres above the waves and held on to the shoulder harness until I hit the water. Then I let go and kicked away from the chute.

Looking up, I saw the other lads coming down around me. Then the swell took me down and I couldn't see anybody. I knew the Gemini was somewhere to my left and the ship . . . Oh fuck! I spun around to see the huge mass of the frigate bearing down on me. It sliced through the water just metres to my right.

The swell of the ship carried me up and I could make out the other lads. Taking out my knife, I cut the paracord holding my fins and slipped them onto my feet. Finning towards the Gemini, I kept losing sight of it in the swell, but at least there were no waves.

The Geminis were rigged up and ready to go. The first task was to get their chutes off and pump them fully, using the oxygen tanks inside. Then we headed towards the ship about 200 metres away. Mission accomplished.

Although I managed to get through the fortnight, I shouldn't really have been there. My body hadn't fully recovered, and I could easily have died or put someone else's life in jeopardy. In any event, we weren't needed in Bosnia and we stayed in Hereford on standby.

Divorce is a fact of life in the Regiment; a lot of guys split up, but I always felt it was different with me and Liz because we'd been together since we were kids. As I was to discover, however, there's no such thing as a quick, painless end to a marriage. It doesn't happen overnight; everything has to be signed and sealed. You're in it for months and sometimes years before the knot is actually severed and you can get on with your life.

I bought a little terraced house so the girls could come and stay, but it wasn't the same. Hereford is such a small town that I'd often go out and see Liz in a pub or a restaurant. It was bizarre that the girl I'd known since I was sixteen years old would be standing a few yards away, having a drink with her friends, yet we didn't talk to each other.

I found life in the Regiment very strange without Liz. The first six months were the worst. Things weren't the same and a part of me began looking for a way out. I just wasn't driven on with the same enthusiasm that I'd felt back in 1986; I was still doing everything to the best of my ability, but I felt that I was going through the motions.

In the course of my service there was little that I hadn't done, but one glaring gap was obvious in my record. In 1983 I'd done my Junior Brecon to become a lance corporal, but I had never undertaken my Senior Brecon, which was normally done two years later. By 1985 I knew that I was going to pass SAS Selection, so it didn't seem important.

Now, ten years later, a new ruling had come down from RHQ that any potential troop sergeant must have completed a Senior Brecon course.

In the sergeants' mess after a rugby game, I approached the colonel of the regiment, Wyn Griffiths. 'Hey, Boss, can I have a word?'

'Of course, Taff.'

'What the fuck am I doing Senior Brecon for?'

'Because you want to be a troop boss, Mike,' he said.

He was right, of course. If anything was going to rekindle my passion for the SAS, it was the opportunity to lead Mountain Troop. The price I had to pay was eight weeks of getting fucked about and run ragged in the mountains of Wales.

So be it, I thought.

Scouse McVey pissed himself laughing when he heard the news. He'd done his course whilst in Para Reg; I was thirty-seven years old and was going to be doing Senior Brecon with guys who were ten years younger.

The first two weeks nearly killed me. Then I found myself getting into it, enjoying the team spirit and camaraderie that reminded me of my days in Para Reg. Lads from all over the infantry had been pulled together for the course – corporals who would then get made up to platoon sergeant within their own units.

However, one of the things that dismayed me about the new

385

infantry teaching was the fall from favour of two weapons that had won the Falklands conflict for us – the 66mm anti-tank rocket launcher and the GPMG. The 66mm is a fire-and-forget weapon that weighs a little more than 2 pounds, yet the Army had relegated it to war stocks. None of the lads on the course had ever fired one. My favourite, the gimpy, had been replaced by the LSW, a heavy-barrelled version of the SA80 with a tripod. The replacement weapon simply wasn't as good. If it ain't broke, I kept asking myself, then why the fuck fix it?

I didn't expect or get any favours from the instructors on Senior Brecon. Remembering the lessons I learned at Depot Para, I shadowed the DS on tabs, staying right at the front. My chest and legs were burning but the pain felt good.

Ironically, some of the courses would cite examples from the Gulf War and the Falklands and I'd seen active service in both of them. The colour-sergeant running our particular platoon hadn't even been in the Army when I was fighting at Goose Green.

There were over a hundred lads on the course and I realized that all eyes were on me: I was from the SAS and had seen combat in theatres around the world. For my own sake and for the reputation of the Regiment, I had to live up to their expectations.

Despite being eleven years older than anyone else on the course, I achieved the only distinction. The colonel in charge was chuffed to fuck; he phoned up Hereford and said he wanted me to be an instructor for a year.

Nearing the end of Senior Brecon, I went Troop rock climbing near Bristol with some of the lads. We stopped at a petrol station on the way, just this side of the Severn Bridge, and I recognized a familiar face.

Bob Powell had been my platoon sergeant at Depot Para, my colour-sergeant in the battalion and my sergeant-major in B Company. More than anyone else, it was Bob who had convinced me to join the SAS. It was something he'd always wanted to do himself, but his wife wouldn't put up with the time away.

Although a little greyer and carrying a few extra pounds, Bob seemed fine. He'd ended up as a major in the Paras before resigning his commission and becoming a civvy. Now he was selling insurance.

'How's your wife?' I asked.

He looked down. 'We're getting divorced.'

'I'm sorry.'

'How's Liz?'

'We split up a few months back.'

We both looked at each other, unable to find the words. Bob had probably been the hardest man in the Parachute Regiment – and that's saying something – but now he looked sad and vulnerable. We shook each other's hand.

'I'll give you my number,' he said.

'Sure. Great.'

He scribbled it on a scrap of paper. 'Make sure you call me.'

'I will.'

'We can talk about old times.'

Old times, I thought. Bob had been my mentor and hero, but civilian life can sometimes shrink a man. Is that what would happen to me, I wondered?

I sat down with Kiwi and talked it over. He'd left Mountain Troop and was now a DS on training wing; his Christian views on life had shut some doors within the Regiment that normally would have been open for someone of his intelligence and ability. Along with Greg, Kiwi probably knew me better than anyone in the Regiment, and he had also remained friends with Liz. I explained that the challenges weren't there for me any more and I felt as if I was coasting. 'Maybe it's time for me to leave?'

'Why don't you give it six months and then decide?'

That Christmas was my first without the girls, who stayed in Hereford with Liz. I spent it at my parents' house but found little to celebrate. The divorce proceedings had started and lawyers had their faces in the trough; once they got going any chance of an amicable split evaporated into thin air.

In January, I did a Born Leaders' course with Scouse McVey in Norway for potential staff sergeants of their troop. It was good to be soldiering again and I started feeling better.

Getting back to Hereford, we heard about trouble brewing in Algiers. Well-armed and organized opposition groups were clashing with troops loyal to the government, creating a volcanic mixture of guerrillas, guns and greed. Hundreds of people had died in the fighting over recent months.

As the situation in the capital grew unbearable, twenty lads from D Squadron were briefed at RHQ. Our mission was to escort families of workers at the British Embassy safely out of the country and back to Britain.

A C130 was fuelled and waiting at RAF Lyneham to take half of D Squadron and a couple of lads from RHQ to a FMB (forward mounting base) in Gibraltar. From there we flew onwards and landed in Algiers. Taking up positions around the plane, we acted as a quick-reaction force on the tarmac. In case of attack, we had .50 cals, GPMGs, sniper weapons and Milan. Meanwhile, the lads from RHQ took a waiting Transit van from the airport to the embassy.

The wives and children were obviously glad to see us. We bundled them on board and took off for Gibraltar. After so many flights, I'd become accustomed to the roar of the engines and smell of oil and aviation fuel. Sitting opposite me were Scouse McVey and John Geddis. Both had been at Goose Green and their careers mirrored mine in many ways. Scouse had been through two Selections with me but missed the Gulf War. He more than made up for it at Gorazde. Glancing up, he grinned at me, and I grinned back. It was one of those strange moments; we both knew that we'd never do another mission together. It was my last one.

Geordie Cochrane, the RSM, tried to talk me out of leaving. 'I know what you're going through,' he said, 'but remember it's a shark's pool out there.'

That's often the soldier's perception of civilian life. They see older guys in their fifties struggling to hold on to their desk jobs as the young bucks come through. People get stabbed in the back, trampled and left behind. It's not always the case, of course, but that's how it looks to someone in the services.

After seventeen years in the Army, I made the decision – it was just a case of telling the colonel. Having lost my partner in life, I didn't want to stay in Hereford any longer; it held too many painful memories.

That weekend, a close friend of mine from the Welsh Guards was getting married. As I left the reception early to get a taxi home, I spotted a scuffle going on further down the road. A pal from G Squadron shouted, 'Mike, it's Greg; he's in trouble.'

Greg Richards was pinned down on the deck, getting filled in by some civvies. One guy was holding him down by the throat, and the others were delivering a fearsome kicking. I ran to help, punching my way into the fray until Greg could get to his feet; then, between us, we dispatched the fuckers, and that was that. Or so I thought. It turned out that the whole incident had been recorded on closed-circuit TV cameras, and the one pinning Greg down was an off-duty MoD policeman trying to stop the fight.

The following week I had to front up before the colonel.

Throughout my entire army career I'd never been in trouble – this was my first time in front of a CO.

'I don't want to lose you, Mike, you're one of the best NCOs we've got in the Regiment, but I have to be seen to be disciplining you. So what I'm going to do is send you away to Bosnia for twelve months with the Light Infantry.'

'No you're not,' I said softly. 'I'm leaving.'

'Don't be silly! Once you've been RTU'd for a year, you can do Endurance again and come back.'

I didn't blame him, he was only doing his job. He'd suggested the Light Infantry because I was 'permanent cadre' SAS – and had no unit to go back to. That was one of the flaws in the system – your shadow rank and previous unit were wiped off the slate and you become SAS through and through.

It wasn't the thought of doing Selection again that bothered me – I'd only have to do the hills. After sitting in brigade meetings with the HVO in Bosnia and keeping the prime minister safe in 'Sniper Alley', how could I be happy being an ordinary squaddie again? Taff Evans had a saying about leaving the SAS – one minute you're a fighting cockerel and the next minute you're a feather duster. That's how it felt.

The CO gave me a few days to reconsider, but I'd made up my mind. I'd take my chances in the shark's pool. I threw my money on the table and bought myself early retirement – three years before my contract was up. Then I packed my things, walked over to the block and looked at all the pictures on the walls in D Squadron's interest room.

Some of the images were very famous, but I kept being drawn back to the painting of Yugoslav children carrying the wounded in the Second World War, which Kiwi and I had helped liberate from the walls of the schoolhouse in Maglaj.

Without looking back, I walked out of the gates of Stirling Lines. After seventeen years of service to my country, I had a tenner in my pocket, £1,500 in the bank and no idea what I was going to do with the rest of my life.

Most of the lads who leave the Regiment go on the 'circuit', which involves working for the major London-based security companies on contracts in Africa, South America and the Middle East.

When I got to my terraced house I made a cup of tea and sat down. The phone rang. It was Jim, an old boy who'd left the Regiment years earlier.

'Mike, I hear you're out? I just might have work for you . . .'

The next day I was on the train to London. My 'boss' was a wealthy Arab businessman who was terrified of everyone and I was to look after him; as it turned out, although he thought quite highly of me, I couldn't help thinking that I was a glorified servant.

London can be a desperately lonely place. Early one morning, after working all night for the Arab, I was walking through Hyde Park. The sun was shining at the beginning of a beautiful day and at that moment the Life Guards rode by on their horses. Seeing the pride in their eyes and the purpose on their faces, I suddenly wondered if I'd thrown it all away.

'What the fuck have you done?' I asked myself, with tears in my eyes. But I had made the right decision. I simply had to find a new role – something that would let me do what I do best: soldiering. It didn't take me long. Within a month, a job came up running the security at different oil rigs in South America.

What a fucked-up country! Apart from the drug cartels and everyday gangsters, there were bands of guerrillas wandering about, pissed off at the big conglomerates who they claim are raping their country's mineral wealth. Maybe they are – it wasn't for me to say. I found myself working alongside one of the original SAS gypsies from Sussex Mountain, Ginge Easterby, an old mate of Mad Dog McDonald's and a good lad.

We operated solo at rig sites high up in the mountains, each with a force of about twenty-five paramilitary police at our disposal. Our job was to make sure the local workers and Texan foremen were safe from guerrilla attacks. The threat of ambush was very real and in one contact I lost three police lads.

During another attack, Ginge was coming in to land when the chopper carrying him was shot out of the sky and crash-landed. He leaped out, but the pilot was strapped into his seat and unable to get out. Under heavy fire, Ginge went back to the LS and extracted him. In the Regiment such bravery would probably have won him a Military Cross, but instead he got a couple of beers from the pilot.

This was the world where I now operated. It wasn't about kudos or Queen and country; I did a job and got well paid – end of story.

Although I've travelled the world many times over, I'm still a Rhondda boy at heart. I don't believe I've done anything special; I'm the same as everyone else, driven by personal challenges to achieve my aims and goals.

It's true what they say: 'You can take the boy out of the valley, but you can't take the valley out of the boy'. Nowadays I try not to make plans for the future, but I'll probably only spend a year or two in South America and then return home. I'd like to do a rugby-coaching course and then try to put back into the valley what the valley has given me. At the same time, my parents aren't getting any younger and I'd like to be there to look after them.

Ferndale and Maerdy haven't changed dramatically since the days when I ran around the streets and hills with Steve Evans. The mines have gone, of course, grassed over but not forgotten. There's even a rugby pitch on one of them. The black filthy river beside Maerdy pit has now turned crystal clear and the trout have returned. The banks are landscaped and the sheep have white woollen coats again. Pauline and Dio still live in the same house, as do Rittaz and Libby.

There aren't many jobs for youngsters any more. Nowadays, they find themselves on the dole and some of them turn to drugs and crime, when they should be working to put money in their arse pocket. Maerdy and Ferndale always had a strong sense of community and hard work, but when the Tories closed the pits they took away the heart and soul of the area. What hope is there for the next generation?

On one of my visits home I visited my old school, Ferndale Grammar. John Elwyn Jones had long ago retired and I was shocked to discover there wasn't a rugby team any more. School sports have been relegated to the weekends and the teachers' unions had decided that no sports master could turn out on a Saturday without pay, not even for love of the game.

Yes, it's a different place from the one I left, but the valley is still where I want to live and die. All those years ago, when I finally had the courage to tell Liz that I'd signed up for the Paras, I told her that I wanted to see the world, and then we'd come back to the Rhondda.

'It'll change our lives, I promise.'

I was right.

# GLOSSARY

| | |
|---|---|
| 2 i/c | second-in-command |
| 66 | lightweight, throwaway anti-tank rocket |
| Agusta | type of helicopter |
| APC | armoured personnel carrier |
| basha | shelter |
| BDA | bomb damage assessment |
| bears | observation aircraft |
| beasting | army slang for a beating or bollocking |
| bergen | pack carried by British forces on active service |
| BG | bodyguard |
| BIH | Bosnian Muslims |
| blue-on-blue | friendly fire |
| BMP | wheeled armour |
| C130 | Hercules transport aircraft |
| C4 | American plastic explosive (contained inside claymores) |
| CAD | controlled air delivery system |
| claymore | anti-personnel mine used for area protection |
| CO | commanding officer |
| crows | new boys |
| CRW | counter-revolutionary wing |
| CTR | close target recce |
| Delta Force | US equivalent of 22 SAS Regiment |
| dems | demolitions |
| DF | direction find |

| | |
|---|---|
| DOP | drop off point |
| DPM | disrupted pattern material (camouflage) |
| DS | directing staff (instructor) |
| ERA | explosive reactive armour |
| ERV | emergency rendezvous points |
| FAC | forward air controller |
| FARP | forward air refuelling point |
| FIBUA | fighting in built-up areas |
| FMB | forward mounting base |
| FNS | rifle of Belgian manufacture |
| FOB | forward operating base |
| FOO | forward observation officer |
| fresh | fresh foods |
| FRV | final rendezvous |
| gollock | machete |
| GPMG | general purpose machine-gun |
| GPS | global positioning system |
| green slime | Intelligence Corps |
| Head Shed | nickname for anyone in authority. From Malaya days, this is what any form of leadership in the Regiment has been called, after the term for the start of the river course |
| hexamine | solid fuel |
| HME | home-made explosives |
| HVO | Croatians |
| IR | infrared |
| Iso prep | isolation preparation |
| IV | intravenous drip |
| IVCP | illegal vehicle checkpoint |
| IWS | individual weapon sights |
| laager | an armoured vehicle LUP |
| LO | liaison officer |
| loc stat | location status |
| LS | landing site |
| LSV | light strike vehicle |
| LTM | laser target marker |
| LUP | lying-up position |
| LURP | long-range patrol |
| M57 | claymore clacker (firing device) |
| MIA | missing in action |
| MID | mentioned in dispatches |
| MOE | method of entry |

| | |
|---|---|
| MP | military policeman |
| MSI | military ski instructor |
| MSR | main supply route |
| NBC kit | nuclear, biological, chemical (warfare) kit |
| ND | negligent discharge |
| net | comms network |
| NVG | night viewing goggles |
| OC | officer commanding |
| OP | observation post |
| OPSEC | operational security |
| OTR | on the run |
| pad | married soldier |
| pads | married quarters |
| papa sierra | platoon sergeant |
| PE | plastic explosive |
| pinkie | 110, a long-wheel-base Land Rover |
| PJI | parachute jump instructor |
| PNG | passive night goggles |
| PRM | patrol radio |
| PT | physical training |
| PTI | physical training instructor |
| QM | quartermaster |
| RCT | Royal Corps of Transport |
| REME | Royal Electrical and Mechanical Engineers |
| remf | rear echelon motherfucker |
| remount | training exercise |
| RHQ | regimental headquarters |
| RMP | regimental military police |
| RSM | regimental sergeant major |
| RTA | road traffic accident |
| RTU | return to unit |
| rupert | nickname for officer – not always derogatory |
| RV | rendezvous |
| sangar | protected trench |
| sat nav | satellite navigation |
| SBS | Special Boat Squadron |
| scaleys | signallers |
| SF | sustained fire |
| SHQ | squadron headquarters |
| sit rep | situation report |
| SMG | sub-machine-gun |
| SOP | standard operating procedure |

| | |
|---|---|
| SQMS | squadron quartermaster sergeant |
| SSM | squadron sergeant-major |
| stag | sentry or sentry duty |
| stand to | prepare to defend against attack |
| syrette | automatic one-time injector |
| tab | tactical advance to battle |
| tac sat | satellite communications |
| TACBE | radio/distress beacon |
| TAOR | territorial area of responsibility |
| TLZ | tactical landing zone |
| tom | private soldier |
| Triple A | anti-aircraft artillery |
| UKSF | United Kingdom Special Forces |
| UNHCR | United Nations High Commission for Refugees |
| VCP | vehicle checkpoint |
| VRS | Serbs |
| Willie Pete | white phos grenades |
| WPS | water pumping stations |